W9-DIM-078

The Tyranny of Elegance

❧

The Tyranny of Elegance

CONSUMER COSMOPOLITANISM
IN THE ERA OF GOETHE

Daniel L. Purdy

The Johns Hopkins University Press

Baltimore and London

For Ruth and Noah

© 1998 The Johns Hopkins University Press
All rights reserved. Published 1998
Printed in the United States of America on acid-free paper
9 8 7 6 5 4 3 2 1

The Johns Hopkins University Press
2715 North Charles Street
Baltimore, Maryland 21218-4363
www.press.jhu.edu

All illustrations in this book are from the Lippenheidische Kostümsammlung, Berlin.

Library of Congress Cataloging-in-Publication Data
will be found at the end of this book.

A catalog record for this book is available from the British Library.

ISBN 0-8018-5874-7

Contents

CONTENTS
⚜

6

Paranoid Geography and the European Dispersion of Fashion

7

The Veil of Masculinity: Clothing and Identity via Goethe's
Die Leiden des jungen Werthers

8

Civilian Uniforms as a Cure for Luxury

9

The Uniform's Tactical Control: Execution over Performance

10

Signification as Discipline: The Demotion of
Ostentation and the Hard-Working Suit

Notes

Bibliography

Index

Illustrations appear following page 90.

Acknowledgements

Like many first books, this one has been a long time in coming. Along the way I have received suggestions and encouragement from many friends and colleagues. Ruth Mendum has seen every side of this project. I am most grateful for her love and insight. Katharine Gerstenberger and John Heins, old friends from graduate school, have shared with me the anxiety of writing. Peter Hohendahl was unwaivering in his support when it mattered the most. Biddy Martin, Isabell Hull, and Sander Gilman have provided invaluable comments. Andreas Huyssen and Dorothea von Mücke read chapters at crucial junctures; their advice has been kind and critical in the same breath. I am most fortunate to have them as colleagues. A great thanks is due to David Levin, a most generouus colleague, as well as to Michael Levine, Adam Bresnick, Nelson Moe, and James Schamus; without the loyal comradery and friendly criticism of our writing group I would never have managed to finish. Jennifer Weisberg helped bring a historical perspective to the work. Michelle Mattson lent moral support. Ulrich Schönherr instilled confidence. Mary Mcleod provided a wealth of suggestions. Bettina Brandt has helped me regain the wider world after writing for too long; her wit and kindness have inspired me. Wolfgang Walter, Ali and Henning Lobb-Rabe, Ose and Ferdinand Jensen, and Grete Peters, all have provided shelter and comfort during lonely trips to the archives. My grandmothers Vera Purdy and Eva Walther, my parents Gregory and Doris Purdy, my sister Tamara Purdy, and my mother-in-law Ann Mendum have all given me great encouragement.

Financial support has been forthcoming at every stage. The German Academic Exchange Service has been most generous with its research grants and its administrators have had a discreet, nurturing touch. Columbia University's Council for Research in the Humanities and the Social Sciences has provided summer support. The Lipperheidische Kostümsammlung in Berlin was an invaluable resource. For its permission to reprint the images within this book, I am most thankful. Andrew Glickman kindly stepped in to take many of these photographs just as I was at my wit's end. Linda Tripp

ACKNOWLEDGMENTS

at Johns Hopkins University Press has been helpful and understanding from the start. And a very special thanks goes to the Ruth Mendum Post-doctoral Spousal Stipend, without which none of this would have come to pass.

Introduction

LONG BEFORE industrialization, there developed in the Central European principalities we now call Germany a vibrant and complex consumer culture that from its earliest stages exhibited many of the features we associate with mass consumer culture. Removed from the centers of industry, Germans were forced to rely on journals, travelogues, letters, and novels to experience the fashions and luxuries visible on London streets and in Paris salons. With participation in fashionable society predicated almost exclusively upon reading about distant events, commodities appeared to the German reader with a particularly luminous aura because they were accessible only indirectly.

The goal of this book is to demonstrate how German writers and consumers, on the edge of the European market system, developed a discourse predicated simultaneously on disciplinary and aesthetic modes of perception. The eighteenth-century German example is particularly instructive for understanding contemporary consumer culture because it allows us to isolate the influence of representation and reading in the formation of consumer desire. The German consumer's dependence on printed media, as opposed to more direct forms of participation in fashionable society, is analogous to the contemporary consumer's reliance on television and film to participate in the trends created by elite tastemakers living in distant capitals. In both contexts, fashion is enjoyed in the absence of physical proximity to the sources that generate the newest trends.

By foregrounding the discursive character of consumption, this study insists that fashion and luxury consumption is not a secondary manifestation of capitalism, a material surplus of industrial production. I argue against the dominant sociological tradition—extending from Bernard Mandeville through Karl Marx, Georg Simmel, and Thorstein Veblen, up to Roland Barthes and the early works of Jean Baudrillard—that treats decorative con-

sumer goods as status symbols that reflect the relative position of their owners in the class hierarchy. By thus linking consumer culture with class identity as constructed within industrial capitalism, this status-oriented model
rules out the possibility that dress culture is itself constitutive of modern
identities, that it is does not reflect a more fundamental power relationship.
The following chapters seek to show that commodities, and clothes in
particular, function as instruments of power, even as they signal social allegiances. Removed from the tumultuous life of London and Paris, the
journals, novels, and letters that constituted eighteenth-century German
consumer culture isolated the semiotic and disciplinary operations of clothes
and commodities on the provincial German *Bildungsbürgertum* (middle-class
intelligentsia).

In the long run, eighteenth-century strategies of representing consumer
goods and fashion trends provided nineteenth-century industrial society
with a nuanced code for interpreting the objects of domestic life. Earlier discussions of fashion made their way into the common sense of urban classes,
so that by the time industrialization made mass marketing possible, the literate German public already had a frame of reference for organizing their
consumer desires. Although the actual designs for products changed over
time, nineteenth-century consumers carried over from the previous century
the aesthetic and moral standards for evaluating commodities and their
pleasures. These discursive practices were legitimated for the nineteenth-
century bourgeois consumer by the classical literature of Goethe and the
Romantics.

It has long been noted that the nineteenth-century German bourgeoisie
found its cultural identity and legitimation in classical literature. The manner in which these texts celebrate the artist's aesthetic vision of reality provided a language for nineteenth-century consumerism. The experience of
reading thus remained a fundamental step in the formation of consumer
desire, for in the process of educating themselves in classical aesthetics,
bourgeois readers developed a model whereby they could interpret surrounding objects in terms of their aesthetic vision—which in the consumer
marketplace translated into an evaluation of a commodity's position within
the individual consumer's lifestyle. Literary discourse of the late eighteenth
century taught its adherents to judge objects in terms of their relation to
the individual's emotional and aesthetic identity.

English historians have called into question the claim that middle-class fashion and luxury came into existence only after a phase of frugal, cost-conscious industrialization. They have in a sense revived one of the discarded maxims of eighteenth-century economic theory, namely, that luxury spurs manufacturing. In his history of European industrial growth, David Landes noted that the English industrial revolution was facilitated by "a consumption pattern favourable to the growth of manufacturers." Neil McKendrick's groundbreaking study on eighteenth-century England insisted that a rise in personal demand for goods was the key to England's industrial development; subsequent research has only reiterated and expanded upon his claim that late-eighteenth-century England witnessed the first mass consumer society. Coming in the wake of McKendrick's research, French historians have similarly shown that Paris's long-standing position as the center of taste was not just a result of aristocratic consumption. Daniel Roche and Cissie Fairchilds both employed probate records to demonstrate that the pleasures of buying niceties were not confined to the elite.[1]

While English and French historians might argue about the causal relation between consumer demand and manufacturing, there would seem to be little reason for German historians of the eighteenth century to worry about which came first. Aside from Roman Sandgruber's researches on Austria, very little recent scholarship has been done on fashion-driven consumption in the German principalities.[2] The vast scholarship on German manufacturing in the eighteenth century has focused primarily on the history of production; the strongest evidence for an eighteenth-century German consumer culture has come from outside the field of economic history: costume history and ethnography.[3] German ethnography (*Volkskünde*), as it moved beyond its traditional concern for peasant culture, examined the history of daily life in a manner reminiscent of the anthropological tendency in American cultural studies.[4]

One nineteenth-century cultural critic did recognize the preceding century as a turning point in the aesthetic character of dress culture. The post-Hegelian idealist Friedrich Vischer argued that fashion acquired the characteristically modern quality of self-conscious transitoriness in the eighteenth century:

One can say that fashion, regardless of how brightly it has burned in the present century, reached its innermost essence in the previous century. The degree of self-reflection, so characteristic of fashion's physiognomy, is modern and a fruit of the pointed reflection with which the intellectual currents of the eighteenth century whetted and sharpened [human] consciousness.[5]

The great sociological studies of the late nineteenth and early twentieth centuries, however—which were the source for so much critical theory about modern society—considered their own period of industrialization and mass marketing the origin of consumer culture.[6] Eduard Fuchs's books on fashion have collected a vast array of important material, and Georg Simmel's essays on fashion are probably the most sophisticated and elegant treatments of the topic. Yet, neither writer seriously considered the proposition that a consumer culture existed prior to the second half of the nineteenth century.[7]

The only sociological study in prewar Germany that did not equate consumption with mass industrialization was Werner Sombart's *Liebe, Luxus, und Kapitalismus*.[8] Unlike most of his colleagues, Sombart did not treat consumer culture as an effect produced by capitalist industry to sustain itself, after having first developed such heavy industries as steel and pharmaceuticals. Rather, he maintained that luxury consumption by the princely courts had been, from the earliest stages, instrumental in the formation of trading and manufacturing enterprises that were organized financially as modern capitalist ventures. Sombart argued that the court's tremendous demand for luxury goods generated an industry that had not existed before the Renaissance. The important and unique aspect of Sombart's thesis is the importance he assigned to consumer demand in the development of capitalism. Most sociologists and historians, Karl Marx and Max Weber most notably, insisted that the Industrial Revolution and the rise of capitalist forms of finance were brought about by changes in the organization of production. Along with technological innovation, new techniques for managing labor and resources were considered quite literally the "motor" of modern industrial society. Sombart argued against this presumption by maintaining that the desire to consume certain types of goods gave rise to the industries required to produce them. In reestablishing the link between luxury consumption and development of manufacturing in seventeenth- and eighteenth-century Europe, Sombart pointed out that he was merely reiterating arguments that had been made in the period:

The question of whether and by what means luxury could promote capital-ism occupied economists of the seventeenth and eighteenth centuries, prac-titioners as well as theoreticians, most intensely. It was in a certain sense the central question around which all other questions were grouped. . . . Back then, one did not speak of capitalism, per se; rather, one referred to indus-try or manufacturing or wealth or whatever. However, all were in agreement on one point, that luxury brought about those economic forms that were just then developing, namely capitalism. Thus, all friends of economic "progress" were advocates of luxury.[9]

Sombart did more than uncover a tradition of political economy over-shadowed by nineteenth-century economics: his theory conceptualized consumer desire as historically contingent, as something that developed out of specific conditions and that was not inherent in human nature. The rise in princely courts, Sombart argued, introduced a new psychological desire for luxury. The political centralization of power allowed new forms of subjectivity, new feelings and yearnings, to develop among the handful of persons empowered to enjoy them. Changes in the drives and motiva-tions that organized subjectivity were for him fundamental forces in the history of European economic development.[10]

My argument in favor of an eighteenth-century German consumer cul-ture does not follow Sombart's path, from the first stirrings of desire to the first formulations of capitalist industries. As the case of eighteenth-century Germany should make clear, the impact of consumer desire on economic activity is far from obvious. However, like Sombart, I seek to make a case for the importance of luxury consumption and fashion-driven desire in the formation of modern society. While an interest in fashion goods did lead to German industrial development, the eighteenth-century discourse on con-sumption had profound effects on the organization of public life. Rather than discuss the origins of capitalism, as Sombart did, I move my histori-cal argument along a line that stretches from a literary culture in which the imaginary relationship between text and reader predominated to a public sphere in which the individual operated bodily, politically, and economi-cally within a network of social relations.[11] And whereas Sombart stressed his opposition to Max Weber's "Protestant ethic" by concentrating on the luxurious pleasures of the court, I look at how a bourgeois consumer culture developed outside, or even in opposition to, the rituals of monarchs and princes.

Most German social critics writing on consumption, from Eduard Fuchs to Walter Benjamin, accepted that England and France were the forerunners of a development that reached Germany (and the United States) in the middle of the nineteenth century.[12] Their understanding of German social developments depended on an implicit comparison with France and England. With the French and English examples presupposing the simultaneous emergence of an industrial and a consumer society, it seemed ludicrous at the end of the nineteenth century to argue that Germany had, in the previous century, already developed a meaningful consumer culture when it had only just developed an industrial economy. How could one speak of a consumer culture in a region that did not have the prerequisite capitalist class structure and its concomitant relations of production? How could one posit a superstructure for which there is no determinate base? One needed hardly be a Marxist to presume that modern consumer practices required the existence of an industrial class.

While these objections persuaded sociologists writing at the beginning of the twentieth century, the absence of the industrial conditions that produced a consumer society in England and, later, in France should not allow the contemporary cultural historian to ignore the vast discussion of fashion and luxury consumption in eighteenth-century Germany. Given that the *representation* of material goods in their absence plays such an important role in late-twentieth-century consumer culture, it should come as no surprise that eighteenth-century German readers could engage in lengthy discussions and fantasies about products and styles they could never own. This is not to say that German consumer culture was entirely based on the simulation of real products through textual and imagistic representations; however, a considerable proportion of what counted as material reality in London and Paris passed as a literary reconstruction among the German *Bildungsbürgertum*.

German journalists and manufacturers assumed that an increased desire for fashionable commodities would result in an increased demand for these products. While desire (a psychological and cultural condition) and demand (an economic activity, or its potential) are certainly related, they are not identical, nor does one necessarily follow the other. For Friedrich Bertuch, the publisher of Germany's most successful fashion journal, and his generation of economists, the distinction was far less obvious. Indeed, the difference between an object and its representation was equally obscure for many readers of Bertuch's *Journal des Luxus und der Moden*.

This study focuses on the cultural impact of the eighteenth-century German discussion of European fashion and luxury, connecting the emerging discourse on consumption with larger changes in the German reading public. While further investigation is required to calculate the economic impact of fashion culture in Germany, ample evidence exists that bourgeois views on the social functions of clothing altered the manner in which people presented themselves in public. The *Journal des Luxus und der Moden* served as a vehicle for this transformation, which redefined the very nature of the human body and its relation to personal identity and public occupations. These changes in personal appearance, which swept through European society at the end of the eighteenth century, were not mere alterations in style; the new clothes, decorations, and appliances shown in the *Journal des Luxus und der Moden* were more than replacements for worn-out objects. These products represented a fundamental shift in the epistemology of the subject and the body. They introduced, on the level of ordinary social interactions, the kinds of disciplinary interests Michel Foucault has described. However, they did so by relying on the promise of pleasure and comfort than on the threat of physical punishment or confinement. The coercions of eighteenth-century bourgeois dress culture were very different from the punishments meted out in prisons, schools, and barracks, yet both were working toward similar goals. Within these cultural and discursive arenas, which were only tangentially connected to the marketplace, eighteenth-century German writing about fashionable consumption exercised an important influence on the practices of everyday life, in which "desires" spoke as sartorial and material performances of personal identity.

The Tyranny of Elegance

❧

CHAPTER ONE

Fashion Journals and the Education of Enlightened Consumers

In NOVEMBER 1785, Friedrich Justin Bertuch, a young editor at the *Teutscher Merkur*, a leading German literary journal, announced an entirely new enterprise dedicated to the promotion and critique of new fashion and luxury goods.[1] Filled with boastful self-confidence, the novice publisher began with a rhetorical question: Why, given the tremendous interest in new reading materials and the concomitant expansion of industry within the German principalities, had no one thought to print a journal solely concerned with *Mode und Luxus*? Surely, he reasoned, with so many gifted authors in Germany, someone would have ventured to write directly about the new commodities being produced by Europe's burgeoning manufacturing industries.

The German Enlightenment had produced a class of readers interested in novels, histories, philosophical treatises, scientific manuals, and reports from distant travelers, but Bertuch was aware that the German principalities lagged behind the industrial production of England and France. While eager to cast German aristocratic and upper-class bourgeois society in the light of recent European fashion trends, his *Mode Journal* acknowledged that German cities displayed less luxury than other European capitals. Bertuch explained the absence of luxury according to the precepts of eighteenth-century cameralist thought:

> London, Vienna, Paris, etc., All these cities are as famous for their luxury and fashion inventions as they are for a thousand other wonderful things. They would be just as incapable as we are of sustaining their immense luxury and opulence at the level they do if they did not have what we lack: a large population and a lively circulation of money.[2]

The root problem was, according to Bertuch, a relative weakness in industrial production—a point that the French historian Francois Dreyfus reiterated in his analysis of the eighteenth-century economies of the German states:

> Germany around 1790 still had an almost purely agrarian character. The agricultural yields were low, qualitatively mediocre, and highly uncertain. The industrial sector remained very limited. The first efforts at development were confined only to Brandenburg, Saxony, and the northern Rhineland. German production at this time reached only a low level. It amounted to a quarter of Britain's production and barely a third of France's.[3]

Arguing in what might today seem a backward and almost contradictory logic, Bertuch maintained that the underdeveloped state of the German principalities was the very reason for publishing a fashion journal. He expected that his *Mode Journal* would, by instilling in consumers new desires for luxury goods, directly assist in the development of German-based manufacturing. Out of desire would come higher consumer demand, which would in turn produce a number of economic benefits. Implicit in Bertuch's thinking was the assumption that consumer desire was independent of either the ability to purchase commodities or the existence of a domestic market. Written texts, he assumed, were sufficient to inspire a personal inclination for consumer goods, even if those products were not yet widely available in Central Europe. Popular, widespread reading of literary and journalistic writing about fashionable society and its consumer goods was, for Bertuch, a viable mechanism for generating "home demand." Once the reading public had been "educated" to want products, they would find a way to purchase them, preferably at low cost from regional manufacturers.

In tracing the contours and implications of Bertuch's project, I hope to show that eighteenth-century German consumer culture began within the readerly imagination and that an elaborate and self-critical discourse on consumption existed in Germany well before any portion of that diverse Central European region approached industrialization on the scale of England or France. The one link in Bertuch's argument that, at this point, cannot be demonstrated is his presumption that desire, an imaginary urge inspired by reading, would translate into demand, an economically quantifiable activity.

Without question, Bertuch believed his journal would have far-reaching economic consequences. Only after German speakers had learned to want the material things of an elegant life, he reasoned, would domestic manufacturers be assured of a market for their products. Reading fashion journals, and other tasteful texts, was the avenue toward a consumer *Bildung*, which would in turn propagate commerce. In the long run, Bertuch hoped to reproduce in Germany the industrial developments that were unfolding in England at the end of the century. Written for consumers, the journal would also have a salutary influence on manufacturers, Bertuch insisted, for they too could benefit from the journal's fashion information.

> It is the well-known plan and purpose of this journal to make Germany more aware of its own industriousness; to awaken in our rulers, the great, and the wealthy, a warm patriotic support for [this industry]; to give our artists and craftsmen greater trust in their ability to lend taste and artistry to their work while making them familiar with the inventions and beautiful forms of foreigners; and, above all, to protect our purses from being sacked by foreigners.[4]

Educating producers was not Bertuch's primary interest, however; his articles were always directed at the individual user. Only through a revolution in German consumer practices would manufacturing receive the necessary impetus for growth on the scale of England or France.

Bertuch seems to have been correct in linking low manufacturing output with the absence of demand from individual consumers. His diagnosis of German development has been supported by Roman Sandgruber's research on eighteenth-century Austrian consumption. Sandgruber's conclusions about the Austrian textile industry confirmed Bertuch's assertion that weak consumer demand hindered economic development in Central Europe at the end of the eighteenth century. Both Austria and Prussia had, through state subsidies, developed significant textile manufacturers, in part to provide a steady, domestic supply of uniforms for their armies. Over the course of the century, the productivity of textile manufacturers had advanced beyond the demands of consumers:

> One cannot ignore that prices had been reduced by advances in productivity to such an extent that they would have allowed a mass market, and yet, on the other hand, that the burning problem for all early factories was the absence of a corresponding market.[5]

Austrian textile producers were, according to Sandgruber, in a position to expand their production significantly; however, they lacked the market demand to support such expansion. Given the uncertainties of distributing products and the imperfect lines of communication between Central European marketplaces, it comes as no surprise that demand did not "automatically" respond to lowered prices and that other, noneconomic means of informing potential consumers were necessary to expand the market in manufactured goods. Wilhelm Treue made a similar diagnosis for the textile industry around Berlin. Large-scale textile producers were by 1800 responsible for employing 20 percent of all skilled workers. The demand that enabled large-scale producers to organize themselves as industrial enterprises was, however, provided primarily by the military and the court. A wider market of middle-class consumers had not yet developed in Berlin/Brandenburg.[6]

Within a few years of its appearance, the *Mode Journal* had become an important voice in the cultural life of the Bildungsbürgertum and had begun to exercise an influence on the traditionally Francophile aristocracy. In the years before the French Revolution, the fashion monthly distinguished itself by extending and elaborating upon the discussion of fashion and consumption that had emerged in the Enlightenment critiques of absolutism.[7] The *Mode Journal* redefined the terms of the earlier attacks on courtly luxury by producing its own fashion aesthetic, one that encouraged members of the bourgeoisie to see themselves as "rational and pragmatic" consumers. Its wide readership, its preeminence in Germany as a tastemaker, allowed Friedrich Bertuch to postulate that his journal would have a broad impact on society.

According to this new, critical, bourgeois consumer ethic, the relative backwardness of Germany only heightened the moral imperative that consumer goods should not foster wasteful displays of wealth but, instead, should enhance the mental and physical capabilities of the consumer. Clothes should protect the body while allowing greater physical movement. Household appliances should simplify burdensome household tasks. Decorations should sooth and ease the mind, rather than distract its attention from important tasks. New products should provide technical aids in understanding the natural environment and facilitate meaningful intellectual exchange. They should allow the individual to perform more tasks with greater efficiency. Consumer goods, should support the general well-being while advancing the standing of their owners. Ideally, they would assist in the production of wealth and knowledge, producing in the person and the household the same structural transformation that Bertuch imagined a strong consumer market would generate in domestic manufacturing.

Bertuch's larger economic plans depended upon convincing tradition-bound Germans to alter their motives for making purchases. The hope was that, if readers began buying commodities because they were in fashion, then they would be likely to buy more goods more often. The *Mode Journal* presented readers with a range of products they had never seen before, and it provided them with new reasons for wanting to acquire them.[8] At the same time, the journal hoped to shift attention from imported goods already available in German markets to domestically produced goods not yet in existence.

> Our journal, and all our future works about luxury and fashion, shall please and educate our readers, not only through the interesting tableaus we will from time to time deliver but also through the general overview they will receive. Readers will be taught to better evaluate and employ this tremendous ebb and flow. They will thereby hold on to hundreds and thousands of *Livres* that otherwise would leave Germany to buy fashion dolls and useless models.[9]

The purchasing of expensive clothes and household adornments had certainly been customary for provincial Germans before the publication of the *Mode Journal*; however, the occasions that warranted such expenditures were infrequent, and the goods were usually manufactured by local guild artisans committed to their decorative traditions. A wealthy burgher or farmer might have taken the opportunity of his daughter's wedding to spend lavishly. Baptisms, engagements, funerals, and religious holidays also were occasions for the purchase of fancy clothes and the presentation of elaborate feasts. The *Mode Journal*, however, sought to move these affluent farmers and burghers beyond their local calendar of consumption.[10]

For the academics and administrators of the Bildungsbürgertum, who were already somewhat removed from rural tradition, the *Mode Journal* offered the opportunity to mark their distinction from agrarian society as well as to display their allegiance to the progressive liberalism associated with many of the *Mode Journal*'s English fashions. By keeping readers informed of changes in foreign styles, the journal dramatically increased the moments in people's lifetimes when they might feel compelled to buy new clothes or redecorate their living quarters. In a sense, the journal sought to alter the temporal rhythm of German consumer habits, a point Georg Lichtenberg acknowledged when, in 1793, he made a pun about a girl barely "twelve fashions old" (Ein Mädchen, kaum zwölf *Moden* alt).[11]

Bertuch initially proposed three different publications devoted to the continually expanding domain of consumer culture. A monthly pamphlet would keep Germans apprised of the newest foreign styles; an annual pocket-sized *Kalender* would summarize the year's developments in broad terms; and an *Annalen* would be concerned with the comparative history of luxury. These three journals were quickly consolidated into a single entity, *Das Journal des Luxus und der Moden*. Known to virtually all literate Germans simply as the *Mode Journal*, Bertuch's monthly review of contemporary taste and consumer innovations quickly became widely successful. Although scorned by most Enlightenment thinkers as well as by the Weimar literary elite, the *Mode Journal* became a fixture in the many provincial courts throughout Germany.[12] It also served as a valuable resource for Germany's administrative bourgeoisie, who aspired to move in elite circles but lacked the necessary training in elegance. The late Enlightenment philosopher Christian Garve described the awkwardness of the newly elevated burgher as a failure in education:

> Commonly, the affluent burgher learns the etiquette and luxury of the refined world in stages, according to how much his increasing wealth allows him to buy or his accumulated connections allow him to observe. Likewise, he equips himself and his household in stages. However, the traces of his first condition, where he began, almost always remain. The old and the modern, the base and the refined are mixed together far more in his case than with someone who was born and raised in an opulent and fashionable household.[13]

Shut out of the aristocratic travel circuit between European courts, the German Bildungsbürgertum counted on the journal's precise descriptions and colored prints for knowledge of what passed as elegant in London and Paris. Even the relatively small merchant classes in Frankfurt, Leipzig, Hamburg, and the Baltic trading centers were eager to subscribe, even though

they already enjoyed direct business contacts with foreign capitals.[14] The
Mode Journal had declared itself an organ of domestic industrial development, and the prospect of participating within a coherent German consumer culture appealed directly to the interests and inclinations of merchant
traders. German enthusiasm for fashion journals was so intense that it
quickly became a necessity for any public person. Adolph von Knigge
warned German men of the ridicule that accompanied anyone unfamiliar
their contents: "How embarrassed is the man who does not read many journals or the newest fashion publications, when he finds himself in the company of 'aesthetic' gentlemen and ladies."[15] More than Knigge's own *Über
den Umgang mit Menschen*, which was the most famous German book on
manners, the *Mode Journal* and its smaller German competitors defined how
respectable individuals were to act and dress within the public sphere.

For forty-one years, through articles that provided both precise descriptions of tailoring and moral critiques of luxury, the journal's monthly issues
instructed Germans on French and English trends. Most important to its
success were the three or four hand-colored lithographs, depicting clothes
and furnishings, that accompanied each issue. A 1792 letter to the editor remarked that many young "Mode-Puppen" hardly even read the articles; they
simply imitated the prints.[16] The vividness and detail of these images account for the journal's early success and its continued ability to fend off the
many competing publications appearing in its wake.

Monthly reports from Paris and London reported the fabrics, colors, decorative touches, and sewing techniques required to reproduce the clothes at
home.[17] Analytical articles organized consumption as a field of knowledge
and a means of regulating the body, combining historical ethnography with
medical proscriptions. An article might outline the manner in which a given
practice, such as the use of cosmetics, had developed in Europe, while emphasizing the health risks of facial creams mixed with lead or quicksilver. The
warnings were never so sweeping as to forbid the use of cosmetics; rather,
the journal inevitably recommended certain powders as acceptable, provided they were applied properly.[18] Critical discussions were generally directed against one particular fashion and in favor of another.

The range of informative and evaluative articles typical of the *Mode Journal*'s first decades is illustrated by the February 1787 issue's table of contents:

1. Musical dice game
2. Historical remarks concerning the application of cosmetics
3. Safe makeup and coloring for actors
4. On children's dress
5. French fashion
6. Furniture—an elegant worktable for ladies and a corner cabinet
7. Letters to the editor

Attached to every issue was an *Intelligenzblatt*, or advertising supplement, listing expensive products manufactured with early industrial techniques: jewelry, clocks, eyeglasses, telescopes, musical instruments, books.

From the start, the journal's articles, its advertisements, and the market for consumer goods were cautiously interconnected. In his own factory, the Landes-Industrie Comptoir, Bertuch sought to reproduce the goods that the journal presented to the public. English products, in particular, were imitated in Bertuch's Weimar enterprise. Just how profitable this venture was remains unclear, for while he alludes in a letter to the duke of Weimar to having employed many local carpenters, glaziers, and tin and leather artisans in reproducing English wares, he seems later to have abandoned the manufacturing business once his publishing house expanded.[19]

The journal proceeded cautiously with the manufacturing side of Bertuch's business. Readers were simply informed that they could write to the editors for further information on how to acquire the products depicted. Bertuch made no secret of his desire to foster German manufacturing, so it is unlikely that he feared or was embarrassed by repercussions from England. However, it does seem that other German manufacturers were initially hesitant to advertise their products in the journal out of fear that they would have to provide detailed blueprints and manufacturing specifications. During the first year of publication, Bertuch was obliged to print disclaimers, assuring German craftsmen that their goods could be safely advertised in his pages. The potential conflict between attracting other advertisers and imitating foreign goods might have persuaded Bertuch to abandon manufacturing once his publishing industry flourished.

At almost the same time that Bertuch was preparing to organize consumption into a field of knowledge and economic activity, the first fashion journals appeared in England and France.[20] We know that Bertuch hurried his publication date to prevent the Parisian *Cabinet des Modes*, which had also just appeared in 1785, from developing a readership among Germans.[21] The competition between the *Mode Journal* and the *Cabinet des Modes* continued through the first years. Contemporaries noted similarities between the two journals, and Bertuch was compelled to rebut charges that he copied the Parisian journal.[22] But while he may have drawn "inspiration" from the *Cabinet des Modes*, the *Mode Journal* differed significantly from the Parisian publication in that Bertuch provided extensive commentary on each fashion, whereas the *Cabinet* reported new styles uncritically.[23]

After the obvious success of the *Mode Journal*, fashion publications appeared throughout northern Germany and Saxony.[24] The first German competitor to establish a wide readership was *Die Zeitung für die elegante Welt*, which appeared three times a week beginning in 1801.[25] In England, *The Lady's Magazine* began in 1771 to include color prints of contemporary dresses.[26] On the whole, the English magazine did not concentrate on style and consumption, comments on Parisian fashion constituting only a small part of each issue. German fashion journals, on the other hand, focused during the last decades of the century exclusively on fashion and luxury, abandoning this focus only with the emergence of *Die Zeitung für die elegante Welt*, which sought to integrate literature and fashion within a broad Romantic aesthetic.[27]

The two Italian journals that also appeared around the time of the first publication of the *Mode Journal*—the *Giornale delle Dame e delle Mode di Francia* (1786) and the *Giornale delle Mode* (1788)—had only an indirect influence in Germany.[28] While Bertuch promised in his preface to the first edition of the *Mode Journal* to keep German readers abreast of Italian fashions, very little mention was ever made of contemporary Italian fashion in later issues. However, because the *Giornale delle Mode* appeared on a list Bertuch composed of leading European fashion journals, we can assume he had at least a passing knowledge of the Italian fashion scene.[29] Sandgruber claimed that the first Viennese journal devoted exclusively to fashion appeared in 1816 (*Wiener Modezeitung*, renamed in 1817 *Wiener Zeitschrift für Kunst, Literatur und Mode*); however, it seems unlikely that there were no earlier Viennese fashion publications.[30]

Prints were first provided by Bertuch's partner, the Weimar artist Georg Melchior Kraus. Daniel Chodowiecki, the renowned illustrator of bourgeois life in Berlin, had been approached by Bertuch, but he turned down the opportunity, claiming that he was too old to keep up with "new vanities."[31] Just how important the prints were to the early success of the journal is demonstrated by the fact that Kraus and Bertuch took equal shares of the journal's profit during the first years. Kraus would produce the master for each print, and then teams of colorists would paint in the figures. In all likelihood, Bertuch relied on his wife's artificial flower factory for the expertise and labor required to color six thousand to eight thousand prints a month. Fifty young women from the lower *Mittelstand* (middle class) worked on the first floor of Bertuch's house on the Ilm, the largest and most elegant private building in Weimar.[32] Goethe's future common-law wife, Christine Vulpius, was among them. Similar assembly line processes were used in England by the publishers of the *Lady's Magazine*. These prints were intended "to stimulate demand, to spread new fashions, to encourage imitation of the 'taste-makers.'"[33]

Judging by the *Mode Journal*'s addresses to its readers, men were almost as eager as women to read about foreign fashion. And while the journal occasionally alluded to fashion as a feminine activity, it did so far less than the sentimental *Wochenschriften* (weeklies), which were directly aimed at female readers. Not until the first decades of the nineteenth century did fashion journals address men as if they were not regular readers. Unlike later fashion publications, the *Mode Journal* did not make overt appeals to male heads of households to "tolerate" feminine fashion.[34] Even if the majority of articles and prints in the *Mode Journal* were dedicated to female dress, it was always assumed that male readers would want to be kept abreast of the newest trends. Unquestionably, a significant number of the inventions, mechanical devices, and articles of furniture featured in the journal were intended to appeal to a male readership.

This relative evenhandedness can be detected in other, smaller publications, such as the *Hamburger Journal für Mode und Eleganz*, wherein a great percentage of the prints displayed male and female figures together. The ideal audience for the first German journals included both sexes. In the 1780s, no firm gender ideology separated masculinity from fashion culture. While the English *Ladies Magazine* did imply a female audience, the Parisian *Cabinet des Modes* "wanted to reach 'the two sexes who always and everywhere have sought to adorn themselves in order to please each other.' . . . In the last analysis, the target was 'good society.'"[35] Bertuch's journal held a sim-

ilar gender-balanced editorial position; however, unlike the Parisian journal, it appealed to both sexes more out of an ideological commitment to
universal Enlightenment reform than an adherence to old-fashioned gal-
lantry.

Without question, the creation and exploitation of a bourgeois fashion
culture in Germany was profitable. Christoph Wieland noted in 1802, with
some contempt, that fashion journals were among the most lucrative ventures in publishing:

> You can no longer earn a living from journals. The *Zeitung für die elegante
> Welt* and the *Mode Journal* are virtually the only ones that have a high cir-
> culation, because they are based on the public's vanity, frivolity, and lust for
> anecdotes. What man of feeling and honor would want to live from the vices
> and follies of his age?[36]

Bertuch did live well. The wealthiest entrepreneur in Weimar, he served
as Duke Karl August's treasurer from 1785 until 1796. During the first year
of its publication, the *Mode Journal* attracted 1,488 subscriptions and
brought Bertuch and Kraus a profit of 1,154 Reichsthaler. (A yearly subscription was a rather expensive four Reichsthaler.) Three years later, the
journal had 1,765 paying subscriptions, which provided 1,875 Reichsthaler
in profit.[37] The short-lived *Mode Kalender*, which Bertuch abandoned after
three years, was also extremely well received, selling 2,893 copies in 1787.[38]

These figures can be contrasted with Wieland's *Teutscher Merkur*, which
did not sell more than a thousand copies, and G. J. Goschen's 1789 edition
of the *Historischer Kalender für Damen*, which had seven thousand sub-
scribers.[39] The actual number of readers for these publications would have
been much higher than the subscriptions; the figure Goschen proposed—
that each volume sold was circulated to between ten and twenty readers—
is still accepted, although some estimates are lower.[40] As letters printed in
the journal demonstrate, the multiplier effect was particularly relevant for
the expensive *Mode Journal*: one correspondent revealed that her town
shared a subscription among sixteen families.[41] A letter from a small-town
burgomaster recounted how the leading townswomen would gather with
his wife whenever the new *Mode Journal* arrived by mail. He intimated that
on rainy days even husbands joined the reading circle.

The *Mode Journal* brought domestic readers monthly accounts of all that
was available abroad, presenting London as a consumer utopia, where the
material distinctions of rank and wealth were superseded by an abundance

of goods. The sheer volume of goods available at low prices gave German visitors the impression that class distinctions were less important in England. The monopoly that the Central European nobility maintained over luxury goods and everyday conveniences was, it seemed, overwhelmed in London by the flood of new products. The journal's London correspondent wrote in 1803: "I have often wondered how in England the class of people who are not really poor, but who cannot be counted as well-to-do, can keep up with ladies' costumes which in Germany only the highest ranks wear, and even then only the richest among them."[42]

In 1758 the first German fashion journal, a short-lived venture, had declared England the center of men's fashion.[43] Germans first learned about English designs through the importation of furniture and household appliances.[44] In northern German cities such as Hanover, Hamburg, and Altona, which had close connections to the English court or the London trade, it was common to find an English influence in the interiors of bourgeois households. The term *simplicity and solidity* was eventually extended to all English goods, so that clothes were ascribed with the same virtues as cupboards:

> The tasteful simplicity and solidity that England has given all its factory wares is, for us Germans, so exceptionally worthwhile and attractive that the words "English" and "product of England" have an irresistible magical allure for us and have become virtual synonyms for perfection and beauty in craftsmanship.[45]

By the end of the century, *Mode Journal*'s readers had become acquainted with a wide assortment of English products. Their enthusiasm for the understated simplicity of Wedgwood china and loose-fitting chemise dresses was so strong that the *Mode Journal* warned that the fervor for English fashion threatened to sweep aside France's long-standing preeminence in fashion.

Bertuch himself played an ambivalent role in the German swing toward English commodities. Although he clearly favored almost everything produced there, he warned that the English "invasion" of German markets threatened to replace one foreign dependence with another, for while shopkeepers' conveniences displaced noble luxuries, German manufacturers were not in a position to compete with either: "We do not have to fear only France's magical power. England and the perfected craftsmanship of its factories will inevitably become as dangerous for us if we are not more careful about guarding ourselves against this trap."[46] This economic concern did not deflect consumer interest, but it did lead the *Mode Journal* occasionally to take a cautious, worried tone as it praised all things English. Bertuch sought to use the example of English commodities and their manufacturers as a model for restructuring local industry; thus, the journal's discussion of English goods took on a prescriptive, rather than a proscriptive, tone. The following letter to the editor summarizes the journal's overall position:

> You have warned us often in your journal about the dangers of "Anglomania," and you have predicted that our wealthy, luxurious, and indolent classes will transfer their thirst for fashion from France to England and, thereby, drown themselves in their own hot thirst. In part, your prophecy seems already to have been fulfilled.[47]

The reader's reference to the journal's "prophecy" points to its twofold function of criticizing fashions while encouraging their adoption simply by informing the public of their existence. As we shall see, this ambiguous role laid Bertuch open to the charge of hypocrisy. Many contemporaries felt that the journal's very existence encouraged precisely the practices it claimed to objurgate.

While the German Bildungsbürgertum developed a zeal for an English lifestyle, Paris continued to function as the acknowledged center of aristocratic elegance. Its prominence in setting the tone for good taste was perhaps diminished, but certainly not eliminated, by England's emergence. Many English garments became fashionable throughout Europe only after they had first been adopted in Paris. The predominance of French names for English articles of dress (*robe à l'anglaise* and redingote) illustrates the importance of French approval in guiding Continental good taste.[48] For much of the century, the French court's baroque and rococo manners had advised the aesthetic decisions of German aristocrats, who would otherwise have remained isolated within their regional decorative traditions. By praising England, the *Mode Journal* was simply seeking to redefine the German emulation of foreign civilization. The newfound preference for England was in many ways an attempt to escape the French standard:

> In our day, it is often bemoaned, and with reason, that we Germans are slavish imitators of the French in clothes, manners, and mores and that not only are we daily losing any visible originality or distinctiveness but these imitators are introducing a form of luxury among us that is equally dangerous to our morality, our finances, and our ability to act.[49]

As far as the German reading market was concerned, Bertuch recognized Parisian journals as his primary competitors. His "bewilderment" that no German publisher had undertaken a fashion journal was quite false, for he acknowledged in his 1785 announcement that the recent appearance in Paris of the *Cabinet des Modes* had spurred his own journalistic efforts. While Bertuch clearly favored England in matters of taste, he understood that the monthly reports from Paris established his journal's legitimacy as a harbinger of coming trends. Bertuch criticized French designs, he disparaged their decorative character, yet he always included regular accounts of Parisian developments. Indeed, the *Mode Journal* relied on the supposed difference between French and English fashions to generate excitement among readers, a difference that was in many ways a product of the fashion world's own internal discourse. This is not to say that the eighteenth-century contest between England and France was not serious in military, economic, and political terms; however, the French-English debate was also a distinction that gave a sense of urgency and importance to differences in dress and interior decor. One dressed in either a French or an English manner; it was unacceptable to mix the two design traditions. The *Mode Journal* invested much of its identity in maintaining this national distinction. Its mission of educating the German public in matters of taste centered in large part on explaining, and thereby preserving, the subtle, and sometimes obvious, differences in the garments and goods produced in the two nations:[50]

> England and France are today the two countries that set the tone in clothing, and in men's clothing, England does so even in France. We Germans have always been imitators of foreign fashions; however, we rarely adopt them in a pure form. Instead, we usually mix them with an element of our own invention. This produces a kind of hybrid that is neither English, French, nor German; rather, it is a complete crossbreed [*Zwitter*]. The peculiar tastelessness of such practices is obvious. It has the unpleasant result that when a person dressed in this way travels to a large city, he becomes a figure of ridicule because he has a little of everything, but nothing whole, and thereby unmistakably betrays his ignorance.[51]

Historically, the isolation of upper-class Germans from the fashion centers of Europe was remedied by the grand tour. While only the wealthy could afford to send their sons on trips to the leading courts of Europe, their journeys had a formative influence on those who never left their homes. A gentleman just returned from a long sojourn abroad could be expected to set the tone within the society of his home.

As the flow of information and people across Europe increased, these fashionable travelers were viewed as an imperfect source of information, for they were often the ones who introduced a mixture of diverse styles. Writing at the end of his life, while living among German communities in Riga, St. Petersburg, and Moscow, J. M. R. Lenz confirmed Bertuch's assessment of the stylistic confusion among Germans who copied foreign fashion:

> Dangerous divisions soon developed. One half of the German salons had seen nothing besides England; the other had studied life in Paris. Both camps did battle for their own standard of taste. The one sect introduced among us a type of Anglomania; the other dressed only according to Parisian measure. In the end, the reconciliation of both parties produced the real heresy, whose adherents, like centaurs, set one sort of head on another sort of body without considering whether they fit together. This is how things now stand.[52]

The great advantage of the *Mode Journal* was that it was more reliable than human memory, that it provided regular accounts of foreign styles, and that it formulated a consistent national code of style. The journal's wider information was arranged according to Bertuch's understanding of national differences in dress. Thus, the reader received a much simpler and less contradictory impression of how the residents of Paris and London appeared in public.

By describing fashion culture as a struggle between France and England, the *Mode Journal* placed German society in a simultaneously marginal and privileged position. Removed from the centers of taste, Germans were forced to rely on mediated representations of beauty and consumption. However, this forced isolation had the indirect, but nevertheless important, effect of providing German readers with the opportunity to reflect critically upon foreign trends, and the *Mode Journal* took full advantage of this reflective potential. Only after some time had passed, and a few second thoughts had set in, did foreign styles make their appearance in German households, a lag that allowed the *Mode Journal* to claim a unique vantage point in the European fashion scene. This position required some delicate maneuvering, for at no point did the journal wish to appear out of fashion or even opposed to it.

Bertuch's persistent use of the term *German* to describe the economy of the many principalities of Central Europe implied the existence of a coherent market, one in which goods, materials, and labor could move unencumbered by political boundaries. Clearly, no such unified system existed in the eighteenth century. German principalities competed against one another as well as against France, England, and Italy. Excise taxes on imported goods were applied at many borders within the Holy Roman Empire. Berlin's textile industry was in large part supported by the strict imposition of excise taxes on imported cloth. Given Prussia's high demand for military uniforms, a large number of textile manufacturers established themselves within its boundaries. Other German states sponsored domestic industries through similar forms of taxation. Porcelain manufacturers, for example, were established in German principalities to supply, without import restrictions, the high demand for china of the princely residences.

In 1819, Friedrich List, the spokesperson for the General German Trade and Manufacture Association, complained that a merchant traveling from Hamburg to Austria had to cross ten countries, pay customs ten times, and learn ten codes of law.[53] Before Napoleon simplified the European map, the situation had been even more complex, so it is not surprising that types of industry and their levels of production varied significantly across the German-speaking regions of Europe.

Added to these legal restraints were technical obstacles. Trade was largely confined to river routes because the network of roads was either in poor condition or incomplete.[54] Bertuch's term *German* had an ideological rather than a descriptive function. His notion of the "German nation of consumers and producers" reflected onto Central Europe the coherence and unity Bertuch perceived in England and France.

Despite logistical delays in eighteenth-century communication, by the end of the century bourgeois fashion was becoming an international phenomenon, comparable to the network of courts that had set decorative tastes during the Renaissance and baroque eras. In the *Mode Journal*'s pages, Germany, France, and England existed as imaginary sites of production and consumption, which in their relation to one another replicated an idealized international marketplace. Germany played the cautious consumer, while France and England acted as competing manufacturers engaged in aggressive advertising campaigns.

Through the *Mode Journal*'s first decades, this triad was the central organizing principle of its fashion reporting. Only occasionally was a dissenting voice heard in its articles and then only from its foreign correspondents, who sometimes sought to demonstrate the lines of influence between the two competing sites of fashion. For example, the English correspondent noted that London and Paris were as likely as any other society to prefer the foreign over the domestic: "I must confess that here one yearns for the newest French fashions as much as Parisians crave the latest English styles."[55] The Parisian correspondent also underlined the two-way relationship between fashion centers yet, in keeping with Bertuch's taste, gave preference to English fashion when he wrote:

> If it is true, as the accusation goes, that our women are as infected with *Anglomania* as the majority of our men are, then I must admit that this fever is not particularly harmful, for it produces fewer ridiculous caricatures as the reverse situations would.[56]

These sentiments were largely overlooked by Bertuch when he wrote the *Mode Journal*'s long fashion commentaries. For him, the struggle between English and French consumer manufacturing continued to define the *Mode Journal*'s presentation of foreign trends. The influences between these two foreign powers were, for Bertuch, ultimately less important than the fact that the two countries represented a significant drain on the balance of trade of small Central and Northern European duchies.

Bertuch's reflections on the international character of fashionable tastes always returned to the question of economic development. In the *Mode Journal*'s first issue, Bertuch claimed to seek a middle ground between Physiocratic complaints (that luxury consumption inevitably created an imbalance of trade with more established foreign manufacturers) and the free market position (which saw consumer demand as a motivation for industry on both a personal and market level). The debate over luxury consumption concerned itself with a great deal more than balance of payments and the circulation of money. There was a host of assumptions about economic value, the body's productive forces, sexuality, historiography, cultural ideology, and the maintenance of social order:

> Luxury, says the devotee of the Physiocratic system, is the pest of all nations! It wastes a pure yield, turning it into unfruitful expenses; hindering repro-

duction; enervating the physical strength of the nation; loosening all feeling for morality and honor; ruining the well-being of families; leaving the state with hordes of beggars.

Luxury, says the financier and technologue, is the richest source for the state, the mightiest lever of industry, and the strongest force behind the circulation of money. It erases all traces of barbaric mores; creates the arts, sciences, trade, and commerce; increases the population and the energies of the state while bringing pleasure and happiness to life.[57]

His journal, Bertuch argued, would in the long run help realign the imbalance of trade by fostering home demand for the products of domestic industries. "It is at least a primary goal of our journal to encourage and lift German industry, to take away the prejudice among our great classes that only foreign products are attractive."[58]

While there is no indication when Bertuch first read Adam Smith's *The Wealth of Nations*, it did not take long for the journal to align itself with a free market position.[59] The *Mode Journal*'s criticisms of luxury always insisted that limitations on consumer behavior should be imposed by civil society and the market rather than by the state. As long as an individual's purchases did not exceed his or her financial means, there could be no objection to ostentatious luxury. Bertuch never denied the Physiocratic complaints about the evils of excessive consumption, but he described them as side effects in a liberal economy. Debt spending and bankruptcy were brought on by intemperate personalities. Devastation of family fortunes had to be addressed on the level of personal discipline and moral education.

When the late-Enlightenment moralist Carl Friedrich Bahrdt argued that financial security for the middle classes required abstinence from unnecessary purchases, Bertuch acknowledged the hazards of living beyond one's means but argued that such habits required individualized "treatment."[60] "In his opinions concerning the harmfulness of *abusing luxury*, Doctor Bahrdt seems to agree with our position completely. . . . He is in error only with regard to the *causes* that foster such abuse."[61] A critically informed public, Bertuch insisted, was less likely to fall into insurmountable debt. Societal restrictions in the form of taxes or sumptuary laws, Bertuch insisted repeatedly, were themselves "excessive" and (more important) a hindrance to trade. Writing under a pseudonym as an "enlightened" reader, Bertuch stated that

luxury is a necessity in the sophisticated world and, given the unequal distribution of resources, a benefit to the state; however, its abuse, with which
many a fool and spendthrift has ruined himself, is actually a psychological illness [*Seelenkrankheit*] that cannot be cured by a national costume, nor by
clothing ordinances, nor by any other legislation.[62]

In 1790, Bertuch reprinted an actual reader's letter, with the comment that
the occasional excess does not justify state intervention in consumer behavior:

Vanity, the desire to please, the urge to conquer as well as to imitate are
clearly qualities that, as soon as they transgress their appropriate limits, must
in the eyes of every reasonable man degrade even the most attractive creation; however, they are at the same time the mothers of so many pleasing,
beautiful, useful, and good things that we would be forever impoverished
if these goddesses were to lose their influence on our lives.[63]

The answer to personal wastefulness lay, according to the *Mode Journal*,
in carefully analyzing the value of individual consumer goods. Bertuch developed elaborate criteria for evaluating the specific value of a commodity.
Rather than teach restraint, the journal sought to integrate consumption
with the demands of economically productive labor. It treated clothing and
domestic appliances as instruments that organized the individual, both men-
tally and bodily, within a capitalist economy.

In defending his journal against critics who argued that it should never
have been published at all, Bertuch concentrated primarily on macroeconomic arguments. Throughout his publishing career, Bertuch argued
that the net benefit to the operation of consumer demand within a liberal
economy outweighed the personal tragedies brought on by bankruptcy. The
ripple effect of consumption, its ability to generate employment throughout the economy, meant for Bertuch that the *Mode Journal* could contribute
directly to fostering a German manufacturing industry. In the introduction
to the first issue, he used the example of coffee to show how the consumption of one product increases demand for others. Coffee drinking increased
the production of porcelain cups and metal brewing appliances; it employed
shipbuilders and salespeople and lent support to the sugar industry, which
had a complex economy of its own.[64] It is hardly coincidental that earlier
in the century Bernard Mandeville had used the example of the tea industry

to argue, similarly, that consumer habits had a widespread ripple effect on manufacturing.[65]

Bertuch's position was distinct from older, cameralist arguments in favor of luxury, because he presumed that the *Mode Journal* would dramatically expand the types of manufactured goods considered fashionable and thus worth buying at a premium from specialized manufacturers. Previous economic discussions of elite consumption had presumed that the term *luxury* applied only to the decorative objects found in baroque and rococo palaces. Physiocratic objections would inevitably contrast the labor performed by a handful of highly trained, often foreign, goldsmiths and silversmiths with the potential for employing local workers in factories that produced "more productive" goods. The Physiocrat Johann August Schlettwein contrasted the small workshops of skilled artisans with regional textiles mills and factories that hired large numbers of semiskilled local workers to make the claim that luxury manufacturers failed to increase local employment:

> All these people that luxury employs in gold and silver factories would find work and sufficient merit if they were employed in the manufacture of linen, textiles, or leather or if they worked in iron and steel factories to help satisfy human necessities by producing a hundred different types of indispensable appliances and instruments.[66]

Bertuch's innovation was to help redefine *Luxus* and *Mode* to include precisely those products considered important by Schlettwein. The advertising supplements of the *Mode Journal* were filled with notices from manufacturers of optical devices and measuring instruments, from clock makers and publishers—precisely the type of goods that would appeal to an enlightened readership. While the journal devoted considerable space to the "frivolous" products that Schlettwein derided—hats, shoes, shawls, dresses, and men's jackets—there were many articles on new products of industrial manufacturing, products that had not traditionally belonged to fashion and luxury. At the end of the *Mode Journal*'s first year, Bertuch named some 233 English products available through just a single mail-order catalogue.[67] His intention was not merely to admire the array of goods newly available to the German consumer. Rather, he listed the many wonderful new English products to show how large English imports had become and to provide an inventory of the kinds of merchandise German manufacturers could produce when supported by domestic demand.[68]

Bertuch's optimistic plans were based upon the expectation that, if individuals were made to recognize that the satisfaction of their desires was dependent upon their own labor, such aspirations could be harnessed toward socially productive ends. Bertuch's free-market defense of consumption linked German consumer demand with economic production. Bertuch postulated this link in two ways: first, consumer demand would provide a market for manufactured goods; second, fashionable products would enhance the consumer's physical and mental productivity.

CHAPTER TWO

Reading to Consume
Identificatory Perception and Fashion-Driven Desires

For a large portion of the German Bildungsbürgertum, there was less of a distinction than one might expect between consumption as an act of fantasy, generated by reading, and consumption as a commercial transaction, motivated by emulation and ambition. These two activities, so distinct in the mind of the economist or the formalist literary critic, were blurred by Germans, who could read extensively about consumer culture but who had limited means to engage in it commercially. For readers isolated from central markets, participating in fashionable society meant, first of all, knowing its distinctions.

German consumers became well versed in the nuances of desire. Their yearnings for tasteful objects were never fulfilled as richly as were the desires of the elites living in England and France. Their investment in particular commodities could therefore become particularly intense and laden with a multitude of meanings. The Bildungsbürgertum's reliance on textual mediation and the phenomenology of reading underscored the discursive character of fashion. The eighteenth-century German experienced foreign commodities primarily as textually generated objects and only secondarily as material things. This dependency on representation has parallels in modern consumption. A reliance on media as primary avenues to consumer culture is not confined to societies on the margins of market capitalism. In many ways, eighteenth-century German consumers and their reading-derived fantasies are more typical of the modern consumer than of their contemporary London and Paris elites. Not many people have lived as profligate lords or capricious courtesans, but more than a few have dreamt that they could.

Colin Campbell has argued that modern consumerism developed in the eighteenth century as a form of imaginative hedonism—that a new type of consumer sought out products that could provide pleasurable experiences from self-generated illusions. Consumers were not so much concerned with the satisfaction of material needs as with the enjoyment of the fantasies that arose during their psychic interaction with the material object. Hence, novels in the eighteenth century were prized consumer goods. Campbell linked the fantasies of consumers with a general bourgeois desire for social advancement. The obvious unreality of these fantasies did not vitiate their persuasiveness or their ability to provide pleasure:

> This dynamic interaction between illusion and reality is the key to the understanding of modern consumerism and, indeed, modern hedonism generally. The tension between the two creates longing as a permanent mode, with the concomitant sense of dissatisfaction with "what is" and a yearning for "something better." This is because wish-directed daydreaming turns the future into a perfectly illusioned present.[1]

Campbell used his theory of imaginative pleasure seeking to rebut the claim that fashionable luxury consumption was driven by a status-conscious competition between classes. Instead of acquiring material goods as signs of wealth and power, modern consumers sought products that would respond to their (very subjective) need for illusionary fantasies.

Persuasive as this diagnosis of modern hedonism might be, it does overlook the emulative relation between consumers (as readers of novels) and the texts from which their fantasies arise. The eighteenth-century middle class was decidedly opposed to imitating the aristocracy; however, it was quite active in creating its own culture of sentimental emulation. Novels, histories, and travelogues encouraged readers to imitate characters and scenes. As a means of organizing the minute behavior of individuals, sentimental novels and other genres of imaginative writing were far more pervasive and controlling than the status system of the ancien régime.[2] Sentimental novels served as guides on how to dress, act, speak, feel, and think, instituting an "apparatus of identification" that created and arranged psychic realities unknown and unavailable to the courtly regime.

Furthermore, Campbell's reliance on the term *romanticism* to describe a variety of literary styles that appeared between 1760 and the 1820s led him to underrate the importance of neoclassicism, with its search for eternal laws of aesthetic form. The reaffirmation of Greek and Roman antiquity in the late eighteenth century was far more widespread than Campbell has admitted. Its formalized apprehension of aesthetic objects countered the empathetic union of text and reader encouraged by sentimentalism.

Neoclassicism was but one form of restraint imposed by bourgeois consumers upon themselves. Dress and consumer habits were reorganized decisively by the adoption of bodily regimens derived from military drills and religious sects, such as the Prussian army and the Nonconformist churches of England. The eighteenth century saw the introduction of standardized uniforms in many armies and the formulation of precise parade drilling methods and battle tactics, both of which had a direct impact on male fashion. Regimes for directing and controlling the body within a social arena became instruments for individuals to construct themselves as striking and impressive figures within fashionable society.[3] Like sentimental fantasy, disciplinary regimes instituted an invisible mode of experience, one that constrained the body, unlike the fantasies of sentimentalism, which "liberated" the self from the burdens of ordinary material existence.

Eighteenth-century consumers, at least in Germany, were pulled in many directions. Sentimental fiction encouraged their imaginary identification with idealized fictional characters, thereby fostering a cycle of "hallucinatory" readerly pleasures. Yet middle-class standards of personal restraint were augmented by new mechanisms of self-regulation. A wealth of products and novels appeared in the eighteenth century but so did very specific measures of control. German consumers, as the *Mode Journal* described them, were hybrid figures, contradictory mixtures of utilitarianism and sentimentalism, who alternated between critical detachment and enthusiastic devotion to a fad. These divisions played themselves out in both psychic and material terms, for within the moral and political economy of eighteenth-century German society the passage between the imaginary and the physical was far more fluid than it is today. The relationships produced in readers' minds were potent constructs, which the Enlightenment insisted could restructure social relations.

One of the most striking examples of how German fashion culture produced disjunctures between psychic and material realities, between clothes and feelings, was Goethe's *The Sorrows of Young Werther*. Disparities between sentimental feeling and utilitarian practicality manifested directly on the ex-

terior and interior of Werther's body, most obviously in his careful attention to dress and his staged suicide. But before approaching this paradigmatic and yet radical sentimental novel, I discuss how the *Mode Journal* relied upon and encouraged a way of reading that produced "autonomous,
imaginative, pleasure-seeking hedonism" while seeking to "constitute the
body as a force of production."[4]

On the geopolitical map, these two tendencies—providing illusionary
pleasure while mobilizing the productive body—were combined as an ideological commitment to a bourgeois concept of cosmopolitanism. The
Mode Journal propagated an ideal European market economy, composed of
productive communities enjoying the stylish and comforting fruits of each
other's labor. It sought to shift German readers' identification from their regional communities to a European cosmopolitan society that revolved
around London and Paris, establishing a link between readers and prominent foreign trends through which readers could participate in the fashionable world.[5] Through the mediation of the journal, a reader could establish
a fantastical connection to distant events and enter that amorphous, international institution called fashionable society.

This imaginary relationship was not merely a matter of imitating foreign
trends, for the *Mode Journal*'s cosmopolitan tone also postulated the reader
as a member of the German "nation." Differences in style between German
principalities were subsumed into a European conception of cultural identity, which was itself divided into nations, some of which corresponded to
political entities (France, England), others of which did not (Italy, Germany).[6] Bavarians and Mecklenburgers were evaluated not according to
their local traditions but according to how far they had come in learning
how to dress according to an international culture composed of competing national styles. These two strata of taste—the international and the national—were frequently set in opposition to one another. For example,
when Bertuch sought to distance his journal from from what he defined as
French or English style, he invoked a German nationality that corresponded
not at all to the political map of Central Europe. In any case, both canons
of taste were new to the regionally dispersed Bildungsbürgertum.

The *Mode Journal*'s invocation of national and international allegiances
along with its disavowal of local traditions was typical of the manner in
which the German Bildungsbürgertum constituted itself publicly. The de-

sire to participate in the newest trends motivated liberal aristocrats and elite members of the bourgeoisie to congregate beyond the official palaces and gardens of the absolute state.[7] Rémy Saisselin, in his study of eighteenth-century debates over luxury consumption and aesthetics, explicitly connected the shift in public attention from the court to the city with the acceleration and expansion of fashion culture: "As a result of the power of fashion, court society in the eighteenth century was gradually displaced by a new creation: the beau monde."[8] Likewise, Habermas believed that the bourgeois public sphere emerged at that moment in European history when the French court at Versailles was beginning to lose its position as the exclusive site of important public events.[9] Once salons were established in Paris, away from the king, the hastening cycle of fashion accelerated the emergence of a society apart from the royal court. In England and France, this phenomenon raised the prominence of city life at the expense of the court. In Germany, this same inclination to belong to cosmopolitan society was first manifested as a literary phenomenon. While affluent commoners in London and Paris flocked to salons and meetinghouses to learn about the newest fashions, the German educated elite read about them in fashion journals.

The importance of journals for the eighteenth century cannot be underestimated, particularly in Germany.[10] The small princely courts throughout the German-speaking regions of Central Europe usually excluded commoners, so when a journalistic alternative to the stylistic examples set by these courts was made available, it was quickly adopted. The Bildungsbürgertum's reliance on such journals gives the modern historian the opportunity to examine the processes whereby modern consumer habits and desires came into existence.[11] The *Mode Journal*'s stylistic layout, when interpreted alongside the journal's conflicting ideological aspirations, provides a window on how an educated German-speaking elite, scattered across Northern Europe, participated in the eighteenth-century consumer revolution.[12] The *Mode Journal* gave Germans the opportunity to experience vicariously the English boom in consumption that had long fascinated the few Germans able to tour the British Isles.[13] While visiting London in 1770, the Göttingen professor Georg Lichtenberg was stunned by the variety of goods for sale:

Things you could never buy in other countries, as well as things you would get for free anywhere else, are on sale here. Every manner of thing is available at all hours of the day in every street, packaged in every possible form: dressed up, tied together, by the barrel, wrapped, bound or unbound, made up, marinated, raw, perfumed, covered in silk and wool, with or without sugar. In short, what a person with money cannot buy here, he will not be able to find anywhere else in God's material world.[14]

Sophie von la Roche was impressed by the shopping thoroughfares, particularly their new manner of displaying wares. In 1786, the same year as the *Mode Journal*'s first issue, she wrote:

It is impossible to express how well everything is organised in London. Every article is made more attractive to the eye than in Paris or in any other town. . . . Behind great glass windows absolutely everything one can think is neatly, attractively displayed, and in such abundance of choice as almost to make one greedy.[15]

To describe la Roche's letters as private is perhaps incorrect, for they were published a short time after they had been sent. Addressed to la Roche's two daughters in Germany, la Roche's accounts of England had a pedagogical character intended to provide "Germany's daughters" an edifying knowledge of foreign culture. Readers were encouraged to "see" London through la Roche's eyes. As Michael Maurer put it:

She offered herself as a role model [*Identifikationsfigur*] for bourgeois readers, who were confined to the domestic sphere, but who nevertheless shared the educational aspirations of the author and, therefore, read books to learn something about foreign lands.[16]

The dense urban scene multiplied and intensified the potential for pleasure. Desire for things was closely connected with seeing them laid out behind glass and with seeing the many finely dressed figures passing along the streets. German travelers concluded that the English were more beautifully attired, more graceful, and more desirable in every way than Germans. Lichtenberg thought English women the most beautiful he had ever seen. Playing on the German *Engel* (angel) in recounting England's charms, he wrote: "In my lifetime, I have seen many beautiful women; however, during the last ten days that I have spent in 'Angelland,' I have seen more than in all the rest of my days." Sophie von la Roche maintained, on the other

hand, that there were more beautiful men than women in England: "All observers agree in the statement that England possesses more handsome men
than beautiful women, so that the figures are estimated at five males to three
of our own sex."[17]

But Germans readers no longer had to wait for literate tourists to publish
their impressions from overseas to find out such things. Each issue of the
Mode Journal contained a report from London and Paris, which supplied accounts of the latest foreign developments. The success of these bulletins was
so great that Bertuch eventually produced a journal dedicated solely to that
topic, entitled simply, *London und Paris*.

The *Mode Journal* drew the contempt of Goethe, Schiller, Wieland, and
Herder and the adoration of the German reading public. Herder was ap-
palled by Bertuch's popularization of German neoclassicism. The aesthetic
form that Herder believed embodied the eternal values of grace and beauty
was transformed into the support of transient fads: "Ruinous fashion journal, you undermine domestic prosperity through your constantly changing
decor, just as you induce vanity and damage health, morality, and every
sense of practicality. You destroy authentic Greek taste."[18] Goethe was far
more dialectical, or perhaps diplomatic, in his characterization of Bertuch's
venture. In his *Xenien* he acknowledged the interdependence of the journal's critical appraisal of commodities and its popularization of foreign
styles: "You punish fashion. You condemn luxury. And yet you foster both,
always looking for acclaim."[19] For indeed, Bertuch did not simply celebrate
luxury, he surveyed new products with a a moral and pragmatic eye, which
was a subtler and more effective means of winning the support of the
Enlightenment's reading public. Even when it came to the neoclassical distinction between high art and low mimetic forms of entertainment, to
which luxury and fashion belonged, Goethe maintained a sense of irony. In
an unpublished "Journal der Moden," he answered the hypothetical question, How can the fashion journal finally stop writing about transient fads
and begin to discuss truth and beauty in their organic wholeness? by urging that ideal art be turned into a fad:

The Editor:

We should at least once
write about matters of consequence

and not, as always, pick a quarrel
about bonnets and shawls and hats;

Why not mention what the human spirit
develops out of itself
and not what chance and happenstance
confusingly pastes together;

We want a knowledge that strives for the whole
and an art based upon fundamentals
not how one lives from day to day
with foreign elements.

But how do we set it up?
We have been scheming ourselves to death

The Colleague answers:

By Zeus! What could be more comfortable
We'll just make it the fashion.[20]

The dialogue purports to resolve the opposition between fashion and
high art, yet it intends to illustrate the absurdity of such a reconciliation.
The poem aims to show the impossibility of transforming a self-sufficient
artwork into a passing decoration; however, this conclusion would have
been obvious only to those undaunted in their contempt for fashion, for
throughout the Napoleonic era, the *Mode Journal*, like the rest of Europe,
displayed an intense appreciation of Greek dress, vases, furniture, architecture, and virtually ever other form of interior decoration.

Goethe warned that the mechanical manufacture of ancient forms would
bring about the demise of such art. He held autonomous art to be the only
means of resisting the spiritual degradation brought on by the spread of reproductions: "One recognizes that the only antidote to luxury . . . is true art
and an authentic feeling for art, both of which are threatened by accelerated
mechanical production, sophisticated craftsmen and factory technology."[21]

Writing around 1800, Goethe pointed to the increased manufacture of
decorative artworks and their widespread acceptance by the public.
Bertuch's *Mode Journal* and its aspirations for German economic development were clearly the object of his concern:

We have seen how in the last twenty years a new, enthusiastic segment of the public has gone in for the plastic arts—in speaking, writing, and buying. Clever factory owners and entrepreneurs have taken artists onto their payrolls. With their ingenious mechanical reproductions, which are more likely to gratify than educate collectors, they have misdirected and bankrupted the public's budding inclinations, simply by providing them illusionary gratifications.[22]

For Goethe, the threat to aesthetic knowledge posed by reproductions of art came not only from the practices of manufacturers and publishers like Bertuch but also from the public desire for artistic reproductions. Both Goethe's and Herder's disquiet arose from the "interested" (in Kant's sense) pleasure of the public's perception of art.[23] While Goethe allowed that the "genius" artist would seek to express his sense of beauty in even the most ordinary objects of existence, the average consumer wanted to possess reproductions of classical Greek artworks merely to provide himself a temporary satisfaction. The consumer was not interested in providing himself with an eternally valid representation of beauty; the point of fashionable acquisitions was enjoyment of a momentary pleasure, not personal edification. This qualitative distinction was more important to Goethe than any financial or moral argument against the high cost of luxury consumption:

> Luxury, according to my conception of it, does not consist simply of a rich man who owns many things; rather he must possess things whose form he must first alter, to give himself a moment of pleasure and, thereby, to gain respect in the eyes of others.[24]

Status within bourgeois society did not depend on the object as fetish but rather on its display for personal gratification. This definition fit with Bertuch's insistence that the fashion commodity harmonize with the physical needs of the consumer.

Goethe's delineation of art as distinct from popular consumer tastes was quickly incorporated into the German fashion discourse by *Die Zeitung für die elegante Welt*. In its inaugural issue in 1801, this competitor to the *Mode Journal* made direct reference to the antagonist relationship between art and fashion. (Bertuch largely ignored the neoclassical critique of fashionable emulation of art.) The editors of *Die Zeitung* explained that fashion lacked the formal order of true art and thus would always depart from the standards of eternal beauty.[25] Fashion culture, because of its constant introduction of new styles, was portrayed as inferior to art, yet the editors hoped to combine the two by bringing the finest examples of both to the public's attention. *Die Zeitung* insisted, in an argument not at all alien to Goethe's position, that the true artist sought beauty in even the smallest details; thus it was possible for even the humblest artifacts of daily life to become aesthetic objects when redesigned according to artistic principles. Out of this momentary convergence between art and domestic decor, *Die Zeitung* sought to explain its editorial mission. Over time, however, *Die Zeitung* proved to be more a salon journal, dedicated to literary culture, than to the newest developments in stylish dress and decor.

Behind Goethe's criticism of the consumer's interested desire to gain satisfaction from the objectified artwork was a long-standing eighteenth-century discussion about the manner in which books were read by the expanding class of nonacademic readers.[26] The years during which Bertuch's journal first appeared—and found a wide readership—were the same in which Goethe was distancing himself definitively from the literary interests of the public. The sensational reception of his *Sorrows of Young Werther* (1774) had led many excitable young men to imitate the protagonist's dress, speech, poetic style, and mannerism and had focused much attention on the author's personal life.

Goethe clearly benefited from the literary reputation that *Werther*'s reception had helped established. Taken into the congenial Weimar court of Duke Karl August in 1786, Goethe was a few months shy of fleeing his burdensome administrative post for a two-year sojourn in Italy, a trip that would prove to be a watershed in his literary career as well as the start of a neoclassical literary movement. Goethe's encounters with Karl Phillip Moritz in Rome, his correspondence with Herder back in Weimar, and the transformation that Italy wrought on him (as on so many German intellectuals) removed him even further from the aesthetic proclivities that had made his *Werther* a literary (and fashion) sensation. For Goethe personally, and for most German literary scholars, *Werther*'s reception became the paradigmatic case that demonstrated how identificatory reading can "distort" the literary value of a novel.

Georg Jäger considered the novel's popularity a crisis for the literary culture of eighteenth-century Germany.[27] Having successfully moved beyond the sentimental urgings of the reading public, Goethe passed through a learning process that allowed him—and all literary scholarship after him—to draw a sharp distinction between true art and popular taste. Goethe was portrayed as the theoretical trailblazer for German literature:

> The high value the novel had as an object of identification meant that its aesthetic distance could readily be suspended. The false reception taught Goethe "that authors and the public are separated by an enormous gulf." For the longest time, literary historians have one-sidedly taken up with the author, his classical viewpoint, and his alienated social position.[28]

Critics of the *Mode Journal*, and the fashion culture it helped produce, presumed that the average bourgeois reader comprehended popular writing in much the same identificatory manner with which readers had enthusiastically adopted and imitated Goethe's novel.[29] In one of those puzzling gestures in which fashion culture concedes everything to its harshest critics and then continues on its way, Bertuch himself acknowledged how much his journal's success was dependent on an empathetic readership:

> The largest proportion of the reading public, or at least those who consider fashionable literature to be their daily bread and butter, are and will remain in a state of childhood. They never read in order to educate themselves; rather, they seek merely to replace their wet nurses, who no longer tell them fairy tales to harness their imaginations or to lull the needs of their heart to sleep. As a result, their favorite literature will always revolve around the wondrous or the sentimental. From time to time, they will experience this or that mood swing, but they will seldom abandon their one track.[30]

The enjoyment of books and journals, according to the model, meant that readers assumed the position of a character within the work. For the identificatory reader, the highest praise for a book was that it brought the fictional reality "to life," so that the reader could see it "before his eyes." This mode of reading was particularly common among the readers of sentimental novels, but it was also the intention of much eighteenth-century travel literature to transport readers into a foreign realm so that they might feel they had visited the place themselves. The implication identificatory reading had for eighteenth-century fashion culture was made most explicit by Friederike Brion's comment (as reported by Goethe): "I very much like to read novels; . . . the people in them are so pretty, you want to look like them."[31]

Aesthetic claims about the autonomy of art developed in Germany as a
reaction to the reading public's failure to distinguish between the text as a
literary construction and the world of nature and society it depicted.[32] "One
of the greatest obstacles to a poem's effect occurs when the reader searches
therein for roles to distribute to himself and others. . . . He tries to imitate
the experiences at the expense of his reason and morality."[33] Thus Jakob Lenz
hit directly upon the fashionable function of identificatory reading: it provided bourgeois readers with roles to adopt as their own personality, complete with costume, manners, speeches, and thoughts. While classicist theorists worried that identificatory reading turned literature into nothing more
than a vehicle for the emotional gratification of the reader who empathized
with the trials and travails of the protagonist, they were also shocked by the
conformity that popular tastes produced. A best-selling sentimental novel,
such as Goethe's *Werther*, quickly became a caricature of itself when it was
adopted as a lifestyle by a sizable portion of respectable society.[34] All claims
that one's feeling were authentically one's own were mocked by the spectacle of dozens of young men professing the same feelings at once. The obvious ability of novels to shape the personalities of readers was a shock wave
to the belief in the autonomy of intimate feelings. Rather than reconsider
the sanctity of the self, neoclassicism redefined individual authenticity to include the renunciation of empathetic entertainment. While the discourse on
sentimental literature (along with pietism and other forms of inward writing) might have proposed a previously unknown emotional and moral dimension to the individual subject, neoclassicism sought to establish a capacity for the individual to critically reflect upon, and restrain, that emotional
capacity.

The *Mode Journal*'s success was associated with the spread of the reading
of sentimental fiction and adventurous travelogues, which replaced religious
treatises as the most important mode of textual mediation between Germans confined to their own locality and the broader outside world. Just as
novels and travel literature presented the reader with imaginary spaces filled
with desirable people and objects, so the *Mode Journal* created a distant fantasy world wherein everyone appeared and acted according to the finest
standards of good taste. In *Dichtung und Wahrheit*, Goethe described the
spectatorial involvement of Germans in European affairs as an explicitly
imaginary relation:

In peacetime, there is for most people no more cheerful reading than those public journals that bring us hasty news of the latest world events. They provide the orderly and comfortably situated citizen an innocent opportunity to engage in that kind of partisanship that, in all our narrowness, we can never get rid of—nor should. Every secure person creates for himself an arbitrary personal interest, just as in a bet in which winning or losing does not really matter. As in theater, he thereby participates through his imagination in foreign successes and misfortunes.[35]

The promise of bringing a distant and desirable locale into close proximity through textual mediation was an important ingredient in almost every cosmopolitan journal. Roland Barthes noted that it was almost a rule that twentieth-century fashion magazines invoke an imaginary "elsewhere," which was the site of pure elegance: "Travel is the great locus of Fashion: . . . The geography of fashion marks two 'elsewheres'; a utopian 'elsewhere,' represented by everything that is exotic . . . and a real 'elsewhere,' which Fashion borrows from outside itself."[36] The *Mode Journal* provided two exotic elsewheres, London and Paris, and one real elsewhere, "the productive household." Its articles presented the two foreign capitals as realities into which readers could project themselves, so that they might indulge in the material pleasures the text was creating for them.

Modern scholars have documented the rise of reading in the eighteenth century, both in Germany and throughout the rest of Europe.[37] The spread of fashion culture was closely associated with the remarkable dissemination of reading practices in Germany. Educated individuals, isolated in provincial towns far from the fashion centers of Europe, participated indirectly in fashionable society through the reading of journals, a new print media that allowed an imaginary, even hallucinatory, involvement with distant scenes. Not only did the descriptions and colored images allow readers an imaginary entrance into London or Paris society, the act of reading was itself considered a luxury, and novels were viewed as extravagances more dangerous to the social order than the importation of French gold braid. Novels introduced an ability to conceive and experience concepts fictionally; they brought distant objects before the mind's eye, allowing readers to enjoy them through the readerly imagination—a new mode of perception to many eighteenth-century Germans. J. J. Engel claimed that this ability to generate imaginative sensations was the entire point of fiction:

The gift of making the absent present by deceiving oneself so thoroughly that figments of the imagination appear as reality, to associate alien and often unconnected ideas together, and to be moved by everything that has a possible connection to the inclinations of the human heart, in other words fantasy, the capacity for fiction, sentimental wit—these all make an author.[38]

For many eighteenth-century readers, who were just being introduced to fiction after a steady diet of religious treatises, the novel's capacity to generate fantasies made it highly desirable. The Physiocrat August Schlettwein argued that the threat of luxury lay in the simultaneous stimulation of sensual and imaginative pleasure, and he drew a direct correlation between degree of luxury and level of stimulation. "The characteristic of luxury is its ability to stimulate both the senses and the imagination. The more they are stimulated for the sake of pleasure, the greater the luxury."[39] In other words, the danger in luxury lay in the intimate enjoyment granted the individual by the experience of "possessing" a valued object. These pleasures were limitless. "The desires for sensual pleasures and the products of fantastical imagination have no limit. Without restraint, they simply grow."[40] If any single commodity followed Schlettwein's characterization of how luxury created an escalating cycle of sensual desire and gratification, it was the sentimental novel, with its rhetorical appeals for the reader to empathize with the protagonist's emotional state. Once engaged by the fictional character's plight, the sympathetic reader was set off on a series of ever-increasing emotional highs and lows, which continued well after the novel had been read to its conclusion.

Moralists as well as literary critics who defended the sentimental novel agreed that the experience of the novel's fictional reality activated within the reader an emotional capacity previously unknown and that this new imaginative faculty was the ultimate point and pleasure of reading sentimental fiction. Engel valued the way in which empathetic reading gave individuals a new faculty to associate within their minds images and ideas that had no connection with one another in the extraliterary materiality of their ordinary world:

It is not enough if we feel that our fantasy has been elevated and been made one painting richer by the author's lively descriptions; it is not enough if we keep up with his rapid wit so that we recognize the relationships between the ideas he presents; it is not enough if our most intimate empathy is drawn so violently to his sentiments, so that we are compelled to sympathize with his emotions. Our capacity for fantasy is now livelier, all our wits are now quicker, our whole heart is now softer. Our soul has been moved not just this one time; in future it will also have gained greater capabilities, more drive, more tension.[41]

The angry responses of religious leaders and pedagogues to the surge in reading, particularly among young women, took on an almost hysterical tone.[42] Their fearful pronouncements revealed their own imaginative capacity to join seemingly disparate objects. In her discussion of the German pedagogical campaign against masturbation, I. V. Hull demonstrated how eighteenth-century educators associated luxury consumption, imagination, and sexual desire with one another, so that they almost became interchangeable causal agents. Hull described the frustration of Enlightenment reformers powerless to prevent the spread of any one of these pleasures:

> The imagination was dangerous because it epitomized self-centered desire, immoderation, unreality, passion, and greed; in short, it was associated with the extremes of qualities purposely set loose by Enlightenment reforms [and instigated] the ineluctable slide from material improvement and expanded consumer desire, through imagination, to moral and social ruin.[43]

Since Elizabeth Blochmann's 1966 study of women's education in eighteenth-century Germany, historians have noted that the reading of novels and fashion journals was perceived by academic critics as a luxurious extravagance blamed for a cycle of desire within the reader's imagination. Blochmann noted the layered metaphors of consumption that pervaded pedagogical writing about the reading habits of women, particularly servants: "By 1789 fine literature was perceived as serving merely as stimulant for fantasy and the powers of imagination; it was characterized as a 'hot spice of the soul,' which is naturally preferable to the simple domestic fare."[44] Reading was doubly compared to consumer culture, in the sense that reading a novel was like eating foreign foods away from home. The spicy dish was consumed both as food and as foreign commodity, for imported spices were still valued wares in the eighteenth-century consumer market.

Other terms used in the campaign against widespread reading—*Lesewut* (reading madness), *Leseseuche* (reading plague), *Lesesucht* (reading addiction), *Bücherfreude* (ecstasy in books)—emphasized the cycle of desire unleashed by the experience of previously unknown pleasures. Something akin

to addiction, obsession, frenzy, and ecstasy, popular reading was characterized as a pest sweeping through society.[45] Justus Möser wrote of the "the
insatiable appetite for reading material in all social classes."[46] Novels, travelogues, and journals allowed sensations that could not be repressed by
censorship or clerical approbation alone. The act of reading, it was argued,
restructured the psychological development of the young and impression-
able. Once readers were engaged by a text, external authorities had little
opportunity to intervene; only the narrator was granted such influence. The
very personal joys of reading were akin to the imaginary pleasures of the
new bourgeois consumption, with its focus on bodily comfort rather than
on ostentatious spectacle.[47]

If reading fiction could provide the hallucinatory sense of moving through
a distant utopia, consumer goods, when contextualized by fashion journals,
could do the same. The potent combination of an image and a text elevated
the art of consumption to the level aesthetic experience. Illustrated novels
depicting the genteel habits of foreign upper-class society were largely held
responsible for the formation of consumer desire among Germans who previously had had a limited conception of material culture. Johann Gottlieb
Fichte derided reading practices wherein one novel was immediately replaced by another, thereby shifting the imaginary faculty from one locale to
another in a manner that replicated and reinforced the rhythmic tastes of
fashionable judgment:

> Reading took the place of other amusements, which in the last half of the
> century had become unfashionable. From time to time, this new luxury re-
> quired new fashionable wares, for it is impossible to reread what one already
> knows or for that matter the books that some predecessor has read, just as
> it is unacceptable to wear the same dress twice in high society or to dress like
> one's grandparents.[48]

Fichte's complaint concerned the supposed superficial manner in which
readers passed through texts without searching for complex or hidden
meanings through repeated reading. Such a reader glided over the surface
of the text, relying on the succession of impressions produced by the narrative rather than reflecting on the significance of the fictional representation. The point of reading became to enjoy a succession of emotional scenes.

Like Fichte, Janice Radaway, in her study of twentieth-century romance
readers, saw a parallel between the gratification of reading empathetically

and the illusionary pleasure promised by commodities. Both forms of satisfaction were considered temporary: they were both predicated upon entering into an imaginary state, and likewise, both often led to an accelerated process of reading and purchasing. Although Radaway assumed a kinder and more empathetic tone than Fichte, she made much the same argument as the German Enlightenment critics of popular sentimental novel reading:

> It must always be remembered that the good feelings this woman derives from reading romantic fiction are not experienced in the course of her habitual existence in the world of actual social relations but in the separate, free realm of the imaginary. The happiness she permits herself is not only secondhand experience but temporary, as well. By resting satisfied with this form of vicarious pleasure, the romance reader may do nothing to transform her situation, which itself gave rise to the need to seek out such pleasure in the first place. Consumption of one temporary satisfying romance will lead in that case to the need and desire for another. The vicarious pleasure offered by romantic fiction finally may be satisfying enough to forestall the need for more substantial change in the reader's life. At the same time, its very ephemerality may guarantee a perpetual desire to repeat the experience. Consumption, in short, might result only in future consumption.[49]

The narrative serves to connect moments of empathy and does not become itself the object of the reader's reflection. The Russian formalist distinction between story (as causally organized events) and plot (as the literary presentation of events) is not recognized. The literary text is taken as the direct recapitulation of real historical events.

J. A. Bergk represented the fears of established authorities when he equated increased reading with wider effects that directly threatened the interests of the state. It disrupted the state's ability to contain luxury consumption so as to ensure a favorable balance of payments, maintain the citizenry's obedience to judicial authority, and exploit the populace as an economic resource:

> Never has there been more being read in Germany than now. Yet the greatest part of readers devour the most miserable and tasteless novels with such heated appetites that they ruin heart and head. By reading such contentless products, one grows accustomed to an idleness that can later be eradicated only with the greatest effort. . . . The consequences of such tasteless and empty-headed reading are senseless extravagance, an insurmountable shyness in the face of any intellectual challenge, a limitless tendency toward

luxury, the suppression of one's moral conscience, world-weariness, and an early death.[50]

Enlightenment critics of consumer culture associated the public's rising fascination for the newest fashion with the identificatory habits of Germany's expanding market of book buyers. The particularly disturbing quality of the new style of reading was the tendency for readers to follow one book immediately with another, so that their empathetic identification (and the accompanying emotions) would spring from one object to the next. The expanding market in romances and other nonscholarly genres brought about a new relationship between desire and its gratification. The increased availability of emotionally gripping books and journals restructured the time frame within which individual reader's desires were developed, satisfied, and then replaced.

Fichte and others equated the new accelerated reading habits of the nonacademic laity with the cyclical movement of fashion. They saw a similarity between the process whereby one fad replaced another and the new empathetic mode of extensive reading, wherein a popular book would completely monopolize the uncritical reader's attention for a brief period and then be cast aside for a new book, which would similarly dominate the reader's opinions and thoughts, until it too was replaced. The similarity between reading fiction and participating in fashion culture was accentuated by the identificatory model of reading, wherein readers described their experience of a particularly moving passage as a succession of visual perceptions.

When Ernst Brandes, in his 1808 diatribe against contemporary German society, mapped out the relation between the eighteenth century's rise in reading and the expansion of cyclical fashions, he took for granted that readers tended to understand texts by visualizing them. The Enlightenment's pedagogical methods, which taught children to read a wide variety of modern books rather than a few canonical works, were one cause, he stated, for the increasing tendency of the Bildungsbürgertum to consume the latest fashion trend the moment it appeared. The problem with allowing young people to read extensively was that such practices "present children with a large number of visual images [*Anschauungen*] in a the shortest possible time frame, very much in the manner of a magical lantern."[51] By reading novel after novel, identificatory readers could produce a series of intense visual illuminations, which lasted only as long as the book was unfinished. Once done, the reader would move on to the next novel or journal for a new encounter.

For Brandes, these reading habits undermined the transmission of traditional values because, instead of relying on repetitious storytelling and the close study of Scripture, the modern, sentimental reader moved quickly from one experience to the next without a sense of devotion to any one. In describing the "tremendous apathy toward everything," typical of the "rising cosmopolitanism," Brandes blamed the many pictures presented young readers:

> The young were not accustomed to devoting themselves to anything, whether a person or an idea. Dancing before them were thousands of bright pictures, which left no trace. This revolution in education and instruction lasted up until the beginnings of this century.[52]

Once learned, the urge for new visual sensations spilled over into fields of debate previously unconnected to fashion. Most important for the antimodern Brandes, fashion-driven desire provoked an interest in political change:

> The main harm was of a moral character. The inconsequential desires [*Begierde*] for diversions filled head and heart with distressing sensual objects, begetting thereby a rush after change and newness in many other, far more important areas.[53]

Johann August Schlettwein, like Brandes, believed that the short-lived pleasures of luxury consumption and sentimental reading manifested themselves as flickering images, whose disappearance compelled the individual to replicate the act of consumption (or reading) that generated them. The whole point of consuming books and fashion goods was maintaining the serial production of fantastical images. "The purpose, spirit, and sense of all opulence [*Üppigkeit*] is merely to stimulate the senses and the imagination with shapes, colors, and appearances, momentary impressions and a succession of variations on these impressions."[54]

By the early nineteenth century, the separation of critically reflective reading from identificatory modes of reading was, by and large, accepted in Germany as a stable distinction. It marked class differences to some extent, but most certainly it drew a line between intellectuals and ordinary readers.

Identificatory reading became the norm for bourgeois society, because the act of sympathetic perception found strong reinforcement in other, nonliterary, phases of private life. The capacity to empathize with another was for many the basis of their intimate friendships as well as of their entire moral outlook.

Adam Smith, in his *Theory of Moral Sentiment*, argued that the ability to empathize with the suffering and joys of others was the basis for all moral conduct as well as a sign of neostoical masculine honor:

> Our sensibility to the feelings of others, so far from being inconsistent with the manhood of self-command, is the very principle upon which that manhood is founded. The very same principle or instinct that in the misfortune of our neighbor prompts us to compassionate his sorrow, in our own misfortune prompts us to restrain the abject and miserable lamentations of our own sorrow. . . . The propriety of our own sentiments and feelings seems to be exactly in proportion to the vivacity and force with which we enter into and conceive his sentiments and feelings.[55]

The German educator of bourgeois manners, Adolph von Knigge, provided an empathetic version of the Golden Rule when summarizing the ethical rules of his moral handbook *Über den Umgang mit Menschen*:

> An enormous amount of these instructions are grasped by the old rule: think of yourself in the position of someone else and ask yourself, How would you like it, under the same circumstances, if someone required this of you or if someone acted thusly against you, or expected something else from you—this service, this expenditure, this boring labor, this explanation?[56]

Empathy, or sympathy, became an intellectual exercise, a strategy for understanding other persons. It served as a technique for knowing what lay behind the surface of another person's appearance and, thereby, also a means of establishing a social relationship. Empathy functioned as a means of joining bourgeois society together. The capacity to identify with another, whether in a book or in person, was a precondition for membership in the dispersed network of worldly individuals. Empathy was also the mechanisms by which the cosmopolitan world communicated. To empathize with others and to allow others similar access to oneself was a necessary condition for the continual operation of bourgeois society. Accessibility, an openness toward others, was a key means for individuals outside the court and removed from traditional communities to establish an understanding with one another. Sentimentalism presumed a universal moral psychology, a strategy for social engagement, interaction, communication, which could be mediated through texts, images, or the physical presence of a person.

This method of interacting was distinctly different from the procedures of bonding typical of the higher aristocracy. Courtiers throughout Europe recognized one another by established rank distinctions and coded performances. Sociability between two aristocrats depended on a rhetoric of pleasing and respecting each other. Sentimental affection was decidedly not an element of courtly sociability. Agrarian communities were not as concerned with identifying unfamiliar persons as courtiers or the bourgeoisie; they traveled far less, so the question of recognition was more easily answered—and rarely asked.

Next to novels, fashion journals were held responsible for the accelerated dispersion of luxury consumption. They provided style news more quickly than the importers of fashionable goods. Like sentimental fiction, they also seemed to circumvent the corporate barriers that had hampered the Bildungsbürgertum in imitating aristocratic luxury.[57] Unlike novels, magazines could be read in fits and starts. They were not organized along a narrative sequence. The reader of a journal was allowed greater freedom by the medium to jump from image to image, from one article to the next, depending on his imaginative interests. Bertuch saw his journal as a far more influential form of "fashionable reading" than even sentimental novels. He described the widespread popularity of journals and newspapers as a revolution in both the history of reading and the history of fashion:

> Now a new, universal fashion literature, one more powerful than any of its predecessors, has really spread not only across Germany but across all of Europe, drawing all ranks and classes of society and driving out almost every other kind of literature. This is the reading of newspapers and political pamphlets. Without question, this is the most widespread fashion literature that has ever existed, and we are therefore obliged to comment upon it our annals of fashion.[58]

Journals changed the internal organization of fashionable society by providing new avenues for individuals to join an arena that previously had been open only to well-traveled aristocrats. The rules that governed inclusion within the realm of taste and pleasure were rewritten. Access to a prominent European court, either personally or through an intermediary, was no longer a condition determining one's ability to appear fashionably. Johann Heinrich Merck noted the unhappiness of courtiers in congratulating Bertuch on the journal's first year: "There has been a violent buzz in our little hive. The courtiers are jealous that developments that they usually keep to themselves are now being blabbed all over the place, with such speed and, of all things, in German."[59] Not only did journals claim to penetrate class distinctions, they shifted the focus of fashion onto the new, numerically larger, class of readers in the Bildungsbürgertum. Brandes held the *Mode Journal* directly responsible for the reorientation of personal style in Germany: "The *Mode Journal* has spread like the most poisonous epidemic, worse still than the example set by the ruling classes, which do not disseminate their plague into the smaller towns and the countryside with quite the same speed."[60] While a reactionary like Brandes saw the spread of cosmopolitan tastes through reading as a threat to social order, the *Mode Journal* equated it with progress and enlightenment. "The richer and more refined an enlightened a nation is, the more comfortable, beautiful, tasteful, and abundant are its fashions."[61]

Mary Ann Doane, in her summary of how film studies have linked cinematic perception and consumer desire, delineated three instances in which cinema reinforced a consumerist desire. First, the film displayed the female to the audience as a commodity, and the female spectator was encouraged to buy or at least to desire this image of what she might become. Second, the film reinforced the commodity relation through the product tie-in, mediating between the spectator and the object and thus lending the aura of its own fictionality to the commodity, while encouraging the spectator to approximate the cinematic image. Third, the film reinforced a mode of perception that was itself conducive to consumer desire.[62]

All three of these instances occurred within eighteenth-century sentimental reading, albeit in a far more limited way than in Hollywood films. The *Mode Journal* and its counterparts provided both male and female readers with images of how they might look. First, the anonymous quality of the journal's articles and reproductions—as opposed to older costume prints, which depicted the aristocracy—encouraged readers to imagine themselves within the pages of the magazine. Second, travelogues and novels, even more than fashion journals, tied specific commodities to a larger narrative context. The widespread emulation of Werther's blue and yellow suit, as well as Lotte's white chemise, was the most famous example in German literature of a commodity tie-in—unintended but, nevertheless, effective. Finally, sentimental fiction, travelogues, and fashion journals encouraged an identificatory mode of perception, which reinforced the desire to read one novel after the other as well as to wear one new dress after another. These three connections between literature and consumption were only beginning to emerge in eighteenth-century Germany, but they were by no means routine. More often than not, they operated only on the level of representation and desire. However, the furious debate that identificatory reading and consumer desire provoked in the eighteenth century proves that certain members of the reading public saw them as real threats to traditional society, while others accepted them as new-found pleasures.

Twentieth-century critiques of the identificatory reading of novels (and watching of films) often do not reveal the historical character of their arguments, nor do they admit the long life that the object of their scorn has had. While Charles Eckert's essay "The Carole Lombard in Macy's Window" correctly noted the importance of film in fostering consumption, he described consumerism as having been orchestrated by manufacturers in search of new markets. The realization that the demand for personal items could also provide profit coincided with the expansion of the Hollywood film industry. In Eckert's historical summary, the two trends—mass consumption of fashion goods and mass audience for American films—emerged because Depression-era capitalists were forced to form new strategies for selling their products: "We have an economy suddenly aware of the importance of the consumer and of the dominant role of women in the purchasing of most consumer items."[63] Eckert assumed that industrial manufacturers had not considered personal consumer demand an important market before the crisis of the 1930s. Within this historiography, the consumer market was tapped only after the first wave of heavy industries, such as steel mills, chemical plants, and railroads, had been built.

The attraction of this schematic history of capitalism lay in the morality of work that it lent to the development of industries. Capitalism first concentrated on securing a base for further production, and only after an industrial base had been established did manufacturers turn to the luxurious trifles of the personal consumer market.[64] Railroads may have been a prerequisite to the formation of mass markets, but that did not mean that eighteenth- and nineteenth-century manufacturers were uninterested in binding the fiction-inspired desires of individuals with their own products. Film theory tends not to consider how identification as a phenomenon came into existence before the invention of cinematic technology.[65] Because film operates within mass culture, film studies suggest that the dynamics of audience identification occurred only with the industrialization of society and the formation of a mass consumer market. Doane cautiously proposed such a link between mass culture and the desire of audiences to overcome the distance between themselves and the things—commodities, artworks, persons—by citing Benjamin's essay on "The Work of Art in the Age of Mechanical Reproduction."[66]

Judith Mayne stated the connection more directly:

> The emergence of motion pictures occurred at the same time as the development of the modern culture of consumption (e.g., where economic organization is focused more on markets for consumption than on sites for production), and in particular at the same time as the birth of modern advertising.[67]

Mayne, like Doane, was presumably relying upon the sociology of the Frankfurt School in assuming that consumer society developed only after the formation of mass markets. In light of the researches on English luxury consumption in the eighteenth century and the presence of an extensive readerly culture of consumption in the nonindustrialized corners of Germany, the "coincidence" of cinema and consumerism should be reevaluated as one phase in a larger history of consumption. The phenomenology of identification needs to be understood within a longer-ranging investigation of media technologies (book production, lithographs, photography, cinema), modes of aesthetic perception, distribution networks for media and commodities, and the production of consumer goods. As Doane noted, these forces are often inseparable, as in the case of certain commodities (books and films) that advertise new modes of perception, which in turn generate previously unfamiliar desires.

However, the interdependence of technology and perception does mean that one was impossible without the other. In our scholarly urge to be dialectical, we should not overlook how a field such as literature can have a semiautonomous history. The eighteenth-century empathetic reception of literature, especially in Germany, is an example of an aesthetic phenomenon employed by film yet predating industrialization or mass culture. Indeed, the sentimental fantasy of eliminating distances by collapsing into a fictional diegesis was reinforced both by the solitary nature of novel reading and by the geographical isolation of many German readers. Rather than seeing identification as an aesthetic experience that came into being only within mass culture, cinema, by projecting the images generated from reading onto a screen external to the subject, reinvented and reinvigorated an older mode of aesthetic perception.

To some extent, film studies have taken up the question of how the literary imagination overlaps with the experience of watching films. As Mayne pointed out, Radaway's analysis of contemporary romance readers raised issues that "have equal relevance to film studies."[68] This line of scholarship could be expanded to include a longer tradition of theoretical reflection upon the way in which "entertainment" represents its fictional world and thereby encourages certain modes of aesthetic perception.

The hermetic universality of psychoanalytic film theory claims to take into account the many historical factors that have brought the object of its analysis into existence, yet its concentration on the cinematic experience lends uniqueness to its categories, for it is understood that the psychoanalytic claims of film theory are confined to a particular, but always undefined, "modern" audience. What this historical bracketing precludes is the possibility that debates about visual identification could have existed before the invention of cinema. Because critical film theories tend to presume the interdependence of industrial capitalism with cinematic technology and mass markets, they also tend to rule out the possibility that eighteenth-century debates over fashion culture in a fragmented, decentralized, nonindustrial, thoroughly agrarian portion of Europe share remarkable similarities with debates in advanced industrial societies, with mass-market consumption and pervasive communications networks, about an aesthetic form unknown to the eighteenth century. Yet, the eighteenth-century debate over the proliferation of fashion writing and the new-found pleasures provided by imitating novels is an example of how a "barely modern" discourse can echo far beyond the boundaries of its own age.

Likewise, German literary criticism of the eighteenth century would benefit from adopting the seriousness with which film studies have approached
even the most "popular" Hollywood films. Even the most critical film analysis has accepted its object as "an anthropological fact," as Christian Metz put
it.[69] Yet, for many academic critics, the aesthetic value of sentimental literature, which unironically urges the reader to sympathize with its characters,
was settled in the eighteenth century by Weimar classicism and Kant's
Critique of Aesthetic Judgment. The unfortunate effect of literary scholarship's
preference for "autonomous works of art" has been the continued inability
to treat "Trivialliteratur" as anything other than a social historical phenomenon, to be catalogued and counted but not interpreted.

Goethe's rejection of sentimentalism and the later formulation of a neoclassical aesthetics of artistic autonomy by a number of Germany's most
prominent writers formed a lesson that educated German scholars took to
heart. German scholarship, having overcome the embarrassing adolescence
that *Werther* and other sentimental novels represented, has not again evoked
tumultuous desires through "naive" reading practices. In 1967, Helmut
Kreuzer argued against the dichotomy of art and kitsch, struggling against
eighteenth-century aesthetic theories as if they were the reigning orthodoxy
of German literary scholarship, which of course they were.[70] Instead of dismissing art that operated through identificatory modes of understanding,
German literary scholarship might broaden the terms of its field by reen-
gaging with texts and decorative objects that rely on consumers to fantasize
with them rather than to reason about them.

Of course, such engagement would not require the abandonment of all
method and reflection. By easing the tension between autonomous art and
the culture industry, literary criticism could uncover previously overlooked
similarities between texts, thereby demonstrating how nonliterary discourses often employ strategies already familiar to fiction. Nancy Armstrong
and Leonard Tennenhouse alluded to the potential for further investigation
raised by Michel Foucault's historical reaches, while acknowledging that he
too overlooked the "popular" effects of literature.

> Foucault's theory of discourse . . . depends on fiction. Whenever words
> begin to produce an object that is not already there, they behave like little
> fictions, especially when they presume to describe nothing but the object

itself. Foucault concentrates on the fictional dimension of nonfictional genres that multiplied during the late seventeenth and eighteenth centuries—
memoirs, medical treatises, social-scientific writing, educational pamphlets,
and personal confessions—to support his hypothesis that such intellectual
activity actually called into being the recesses of self and the regions of private experience that authors presumed to be discovering. He identifies the
properties and powers we associate with modern fiction in a wide array of
cultural materials, but he does not consider, in turn, the historical impact of
fiction. Here, as in his Eurocentricity, Foucault remains true to philosophical and historical tradition.[71]

This study follows Armstrong and Tennenhouse's suggestion, demonstrating how the fictional quality of material culture came into existence.
Domestic spaces were often arranged, conceptualized, and constructed in a
manner implying the operation of authorial intent, which sought to guide
outsider's perception of the owner—of his physical being and his moral
character. Weimar classicism taught that the principles inherent in domestic decor were secondary to the aesthetic categories of the poetic author, yet
fashion discourse constructed meaning in much the same manner that literature depicted fictional reality.

The resemblance between fashion culture and literature arises from the
fact that both are "practices that . . . form the objects of which they speak."[72]
The diegesis of fiction—that imaginary world of text and film that enthusiastic readers and moviegoers so eagerly accept as valid—has much the
same illusionary status as "being in fashion." Such transient experiences as
reading, viewing, and wearing the newest style construct a fictional truth
through terms of discourse; they absorb impulses from other fields of life,
but they sustain their legitimacy, that is, their grip over an audience,
through their own "presentation." Logically, they engage in circular argu-
mentation: poems define themselves in relation to the poetic tradition, a
fashion is fashionable because it is in fashion, a movie seems real because it
presents photographic images of an event. My goal is not to compare the
several fields by setting "Iphegenia auf Taurus" on an equal footing with a
Wedgwood vase but rather to isolate the discourse of fashion as an entity
worth evaluating in its own right while treating its relation to ancillary cultural fields, such as literature and the plastic arts, as secondary. By focusing
on consumer culture in the eighteenth century, I hope to momentarily neu-

tralize the hierarchy of aesthetic values introduced by neoclassical aesthetics, so that fashion objects become visible in their own terms. The "discursive" (in Foucault's sense), or fictional character, of fashion writing presents serious problems in evaluating the various eighteenth-century pronouncements on the increase of fashion consumption. There remains no clear way to link the very real "imaginary" consumption of eighteenth-century Germans with a method of measuring in material or economic terms the growth of a consumer market in Germany. Here again, the distinction between desire and demand is evident.

A long-time reader of Bertuch's *Mode Journal* would eventually have recognized the circular logic of fashion discourse—that the strongest argument in favor of a particular fashion is the assertion that it is fashionable. Using as his example late-1950s magazines, Barthes pointed out that all fashion writing served one goal: the further diffusion of its own style. "Every description of a garment serves a specific purpose, which is to manifest, or better still, to *transmit* Fashion: any clothing that is noted coincides with the being of Fashion."[73] Barthes's argument can be extended beyond descriptions of clothing: all discussions of fashionable consumption, whether in the particular (a certain new "look") or in general (as a social phenomenon), encouraged the spread of fashion. Put simply, the more fashions were discussed in public, the more important they became. Christian Flittner made this argument in 1833, when he stated that "fashion triumphs as fashion over innocence and modesty, and often with an inconceivable speed."[74] Flittner's point was that practical, financial, or moral arguments had little impact on the spread of certain styles. What mattered most was the sheer fact of an object's acceptance as "stylish."

Barthes dismissed this paradoxical position as a distortion propagated by fashion journalists and editors. However, if we consider consumer culture as a phenomenon that operates within media-dependent institutions such as the publishing industry and the bourgeois public sphere, then we can treat the apparently circular logic of fashion producing fashion as a direct manifestation of modern communication systems. To be "in fashion" implies participation in the networks of communication that pervade and, to some extent, define bourgeois society. The *Mode Journal*'s lengthy and elaborate discussions of English and French consumer goods were, according to this line of reasoning, indications of the Bildungsbürgertum's increasing participation in an international media network. The fact that the journal was so successful suggests that fashion and luxury consumption played a formative role in cultural identity.

Bertuch claimed that the German consumer market existed but was invisible and that German industries were poised to generate goods for that market once his journal called this subterranean desire into view. The current historical understanding of German industrialization does not bear out this claim. There is little doubt that the *Mode Journal* generated public discussion of consumer goods and modern fashion, but the financial and industrial capacity of the German Bildungsbürgertum could not meet consumers' expectations. However, this conclusion by no means vitiates the importance Bertuch's publication had in forming such important cultural institutions as the public sphere. That the *Mode Journal* had a far greater impact in generating desire among readers than in creating financial transactions by consumers does not reduce its historical significance, for it is a common feature of modern fashion writing to inspire the public imagination without taking responsibility for economic consequences.

CHAPTER THREE

The Ever-Expanding Domain
of Mode und Luxus

*M*ode and *Luxus*, the two German words most commonly used in reference to fashion, covered a variety of cultural practices, including the wearing of new and stylish clothes. Because the twentieth-century meaning of
fashion tends to focus on dress, it does not do justice to the eighteenth-
century meaning of the German terms. Often paired, each word had slightly
different references and moral connotations. *Mode* referred to a cycle of
styles and innovative products, whereas *Luxus* pointed to the value of objects as displays of wealth, rank, and status. When used in tandem, as in the
title of Bertuch's journal, Mode und Luxus described a variety of techniques
for adorning the body, beginning with clothing, makeup, and jewelry but
also including furniture, porcelain, silver and glassware, interior design, as
well as riding coaches, uniforms, architecture, garden design, and a host of
mechanical devices.

For much of the eighteenth century, furnishings were not considered vital
to the bodily functioning of their owner. Only at the end of the Enlightenment were household components, everything from beds to building facades,
evaluated in terms of the physical comforts and needs of the individual. Before the eighteenth century's invocation of the "natural" body, Mode and
Luxus referred primarily to the material objects that represented the family genealogy, noble rank, and courtly status of their owner. A pillar of the
ancien régime, Luxus was also perceived as a threat to the established order
if it was taken up by the lower classes. Latin writers like Seneca and Cicero
objected to Luxus in the strongest terms, seeing it as a threat to the Roman
military and a challenge to social hierarchy.[1] A soldier accustomed to sensual pleasures would be far less willing to die in combat; the mere promise

of luxury reduced his effectiveness as a fighter. Christopher Berry suggested that

> [until] the eighteenth century . . . the Roman response to "luxury" [had] attained paradigmatic status in discussions of virtue and corruption. For the Romans, and beyond, luxury was a political question because it signified the presence of a potentially disruptive power of human desire, a power that must be policed.[2]

Like their predecessors, eighteenth-century German Physiocrats argued that widespread Luxus challenged the feudally derived class system, which still dominated German society at midcentury. Johann Süßmilch reiterated the Roman concern in 1761:

> The word "Luxus" I understand to mean that splendor, opulence, and extravagance antithetical to any sense of order. It confuses everything and mixes the distinguished classes with the lowest of the bourgeoisie, who are themselves born of vain pride. "Luxus" never comes to a standstill; rather, it is constantly progressing, allowing everyone to indulge in the arrogance of appearing to be greater than he is, so that eventually all things will be the same, and we will be unable to differentiate one from the other.[3]

Not only did Roman moralists inform later commentaries on Luxus, the eventual collapse of the Roman Empire was taken as evidence of how destructive it could be to a citizenry's fortitude. The early Enlightenment aesthetic theorist Johann Gottsched wrote:

> Splendor is that vice called Luxus. It is an arrogance, a wasteful extravagance of one's energies to rise above one's rank by outdoing one's peers. As in "The splendor of this place is excessive and unheard of." "Private houses here are on a scale of splendor beyond the means even of ruling princes." "Splendor and opulence drive a court, a country, an entire people into the ground." "Self-indulgence and splendor had gotten the upper hand in Rome, just as the barbarians invaded and ruined it."[4]

Ancient tradition advocated state regulation in the form of sumptuary laws and clothing ordinances. This Roman approach, with its combination of moral commentary and legal restrictions, persisted in Germany far longer than in England or France. Laws limiting gold and silver thread, fur collars, foreign fabrics, and sexually provocative designs persisted into the first half of the eighteenth century. When Berry suggested that the Roman tradition had died out in the eighteenth century, he clearly had only England in mind, for the critique of luxury as derived from Latin stoicism continued to have a central place in Enlightenment portrayals of the absolute court. Not until the importation of free market theory at the end of the century did German commentaries on consumption move away from the Roman legacy. Bertuch's *Mode Journal*, with its call for industrial and technological progress supported by fashion-conscious consumers, clearly belonged to the English line of thinking that supplanted Roman concerns over luxury.

In the late eighteenth-century, Luxus was often associated with the politically motivated, dynastic finery of the ancien régime, whereas Mode covered whatever design style or manner was currently favored in the circles of cultural opinion making outside the court.[5] "Society," the somewhat amorphous institution brought into being in the eighteenth century, was defined in large part by its provision of the most up-to-date judgments of taste. The transitory nature of these opinions, their tendency to move from one object to the next, meant that over a relatively short period of time the word *Mode* had acquired a broad range of possible referents. More and more things enjoyed the adoration of public opinion. In its search for tasteful objects, society roamed beyond the French court, which was increasingly confined to the rituals and forms of its own aesthetic and architectural traditions. By the end of the century, almost any social practice could fall under the domain of Mode, as long as it was deemed fashionable by that rather undefined collection of individuals who made such judgments.

In his *Grammatisch-kritisches Wörterbuch*, published in 1775, Johann Adelung associated the breadth of possible referents with the term's transitoriness: "Mode: an imported form of behavior in social life, morals, customs; and in the narrower sense, the variable manner of clothing and everything related to its decoration."[6] Adelung clearly equated *Mode* with *modern* and contrasted the two terms against classical or traditional styles. *Modern* he defined as "that which accords with the newest morals, the newest taste, the newest fashion, in contrast to the antique or the outdated." By providing a negative example of what was not modern, Adelung ran the risk that his definition would soon be outdated. The advent of neoclassical styles of dress following the French Revolution demonstrated that the antique could also be modern.[7] Despite Adelung's understanding of modernity as not classical, his definition made it clear that, in the age of sentimentalism, fashion was equated with being modern. Mode was already distinct from the luxurious displays of the court and their visual defense of the status quo. The equation of Mode with modern marked a fundamental shift in the relationship between dress and society.

Following Adelung's lead, Jacob and Wilhelm Grimm defined *Mode* as "the contemporary manner and custom in general, also the altering taste in how to dress oneself."[8] The Grimms provided its etymology within German. *Mode* first appeared as a distinct term in the beginning of the seventeenth century. Previously, it had been used in the phrase "a la Mode," which referred to the French manner of dress adopted by the aristocracy. When it began to be employed as a German noun, *Mode* had very much the same meaning as *Tracht* and referred strictly to the clothes one wore.[9] Over time, the term grew to include more than manner of dress, as the Grimm brothers noted:

> Mode expands its meaning to also include the momentary taste in behavior and social events [including] typical and conventional manner in dress, furniture, coaches, rooms, buildings, manufactured wares, writing and speaking style, compliments, ceremonies, show, hospitality, and everything else related to sociability.[10]

The late Enlightenment philosopher Christian Garve, an admirer of Immanuel Kant, recognized the difficulty of providing limitations in the field of fashionable objects. Mode, he said, operated in three areas—natural beauty, art, and necessity—and combined the forms of thought that Kant sought to distinguish in his three critiques of reason. Less concerned than Kant with maintaining epistemological boundaries, Garve suggested that fashionable opinion was composed of several types of knowledge, so that it borrowed the concepts, standards, and terminology of other disciplines (medicine, art history, religion, economics). Garve set the tone for nineteenth-century arguments that stressed fashion's lack of artistic autonomy when he described Mode as "the omnipresent opinion about the beautiful and the respectable with regard to small things . . . which do not accord with and cannot be regulated by the application of the rules of taste or purposefulness"[11] These impure judgments (in the philosophical sense) were, furthermore, combined with imaginary desires to produce a realm of social life whose boundaries were undefined and frequently shifting.

The realm of Mode has no definite boundaries. After things have been judged to be of greater or lesser importance; after their degree of tastefulness has been fixed by natural talents or through education and art; after they have been looked at in terms of their usefulness and practicality or according to their convenience; after they have been seen as novelties or innovations; after all these evaluations, objects without firm guidelines are left to the rule of Mode.[12]

Because fashion objects were not rigorously tied to the rational order of other, more systematic, discourses, they had a unique ability to mediate between them. Their ambiguous allegiances to different ideologies, different orders of knowledge, different regimes of power allowed them to fantastically conjoin different modes of intelligibility without abandoning their own unpredictability.[13] Because it had few first principles, Mode was free to acquire knowledge rejected by other discourses. Certain sciences received a second chance to establish themselves in Mode's unstable ground after they had been dismissed by academics. Fashion opinion served as a catchall for propositions, theories, and facts that had lost their footing and as an antechamber for theories not yet established.

Both Garve and Bertuch saw consumer culture as continually adapting to developments in other fields. Fashionable opinion, with its tendency to create cliques and fads, was part of the ebb and flow of public life. It popularized new ideas and products far more effectively than the educational tracts of the Enlightenment. Both writers pointed to social reforms that had come about because of their having been accepted as modern and as in keeping with a sophisticated lifestyle.[14]

But Bertuch was not content to have his journal be simply a source of information about new products. He also envisioned a scholarly side to the *Mode Journal*, as a transcript of German cultural history. To legitimate Mode and Luxus as fields of knowledge that the more accepted, scholarly disciplines would acknowledge, Bertuch sought, somewhat more rigorously than Garve, to define and limit fashion as a social phenomenon. He often referred to the *Mode Journal* as an archive of fashion history, in which the minute details of social life were recorded. To secure this archive as a site of scholarship, Bertuch felt compelled to prescribe the boundaries of what counted as fashionable and what did not.[15] The obvious implication was that his journal would function as an arbiter of taste and not just as a record keeper of social life. Bertuch never really escaped this paradox, for the journal clearly served as the source of many Germans' understanding of taste merely by recording what others considered stylish and modern. Throughout his editorial career, he continued to insist on the validity of his early claim to academic detachment: "We are the history writers of luxury, not its priests; as such, we know precisely the rights and boundaries that a historian has and will not cross them in any of our works."[16]

Organizing the diverse practices and objects of upper-class consumption became more difficult as these conventions and commodities became separated from the formalized rituals of courtly celebrations. The loss of legitimacy suffered by courtly etiquette in the latter half of the eighteenth century was brought on, in part, by the emergence of a functionalized revision of the court's tendency to symbolically represent monarchical authority by luxuriously displaying the king's body. In a limited sense, the journal adapted the courtly principle that all decorations, ceremonies, installations, celebrations, and earthly activities reflected the magnificence of the king. Bertuch set the parameters of his journalistic enterprise by defining Mode and Luxus as those objects that enhanced bodily comfort, pleasure, and appearance. By making universal claims about the importance of comfort and sociability in all human interactions, the *Mode Journal* applied to the household of every bourgeois consumer the logic that all things must revolve around the body.[17] What distinguished this effort was the journal's reconceptualization of what the body did and the recognition that the journal was concerned with the bodies of many individuals, rather than the body of a single monarch.

The importance of the body as a conceptual anchor for the many objects, beliefs, and social rituals that composed the fashionable consumer culture was apparent on Bertuch's title page:

> The objects of our journal are (1) female and male clothing, (2) cosmetics, (3) jewelry, (4) ornaments, (5) furniture, (6) all sorts of tableware and cutlery, (7) riding equipment, (8) architectural and interior decor, (9) gardens and country houses.

As the types of objects on Bertuch's list were counted off, they moved outward from the body, the distance marking the degree of intimacy between the owner and the object. The list revealed the shifting focus of bourgeois fashion judgment: rather than approaching the individual from afar (as in the ceremonial spaces of princes), it sized up the overall figure from a close distance (as if from across a private room), then moved in to examine details, then backed away to consider the person's overall relation to his or her domestic environment. Not only did the list suggest the manner in which individuals examine each other, it also suggested a sequence in which the individual might construct his or her persona, not unlike a person dressing a doll.[18]

First the body was clothed, then the face was decorated, then material things that referred to the figure were placed in proximity to the body. As the focus moved away, objects were introduced that related it to others. Furniture, tableware, and carriages shared the common goal of enabling public intercourse. The first half of the list approached parts of the body, the second half situated the body within an arena. These latter items were less intimate, less likely to bear the personal mark of their owner, not as tailored to his or her physical form. The last two categories stood at the greatest remove from the body: they did not respond to its organic fluidity, to its emotions, health, age, or education. They were also least likely to be replaced and most readily treated as backdrops, inflexible signifiers of the class or aesthetic tradition to which the owner belonged, imprecise references to personal particulars.

Yet the fact that an object (such as the facade of a building) was not in direct contact with the body did not mean that the person's intimate needs were ignored. Each circle of objects arrayed around the body was joined to every other circle by the principle that their design was based upon their role in the individual's mental and physical life. The integration of clothes with bodily functions became the model for designing other types of goods. Just as clothes were supposed to satisfy the wants of the person who wore them (as opposed to clothes representing a social class), so should every object in a household be designed to answer to the requirements of the inhabitants. Bertuch spelled out this sequential logic during the journal's first year of publication. "Clothing determines the furniture in a room, the table settings, the manners, riding gear, servants, and the rest. Everything must be in accord, otherwise it is pointless."[19] Two years later, he extended the design principle to include architecture. Even at the furthest remove, objects needed to respond to their owner's needs. "A house should by rights always fit the needs and conditions of the owner's lifestyle as closely as a coat fits his body. At the very least, I expect this from him when he builds a new one."[20]

While the centering of objects on their owner was hardly unique to eighteenth-century consumer aesthetics, the distinctive feature of the *Mode Journal*'s organizing fashion through the body was that this system served to regulate consumption. Seneca provided a similar list, describing the stages a person passed through as they grew more enamored of luxury:

> Where prosperity has spread luxury over a wide area of society, people start by paying attention to their personal turnout. The next thing that engages people's energies is furniture. Then pains are devoted to the houses themselves, so as to have them running out over broad expanses of territory, to have walls glowing with marble shipped from overseas and the ceilings picked out in gold, to have the floors shining with a lustre matching the panels overhead. Splendor then moves on to the table.[21]

While Seneca expostulated against bodily luxury as a source of moral and practical dissipation, Bertuch understood consumption as means of enhancing an individual's intellectual and physical endowments. For Seneca, the consuming body was the site of unrestrained desire, whereas Bertuch argued the opposite: that the comfortably dressed body surrounded by useful furnishings was the source of fruitful invention. Body and objects conditioned the other's ability to perform useful tasks, their interaction integrating the consumer and the domestic environment into a larger economy of production. The *Mode Journal* helped to transmit into bourgeois households the tactics developed in factories, workhouses, schools, and the parade ground, presenting the German reading public with products that could mobilize the individual's productive talents.

While the body of the consumer was central to the journal's interest in fashion innovation, this did not mean that the journal's readers made their living through physical work. Most of them were merchants, university-trained administrators, or the independently wealthy. The journal focused on bodily comfort and ease as preconditions for intellectual thought and domestic happiness. Masculine products were intended to facilitate administrative work or business transactions. Household gadgets were expected to simplify housework and make it more attractive. The health of consumers, in particular pregnant women, was a distinct concern. The products displayed in the *Mode Journal* supposedly eased the burdens of running a household, facilitated scientific experiments, enhanced sociability, and facilitated personal relations. The conjunction of intellectual work and bodily requirements, which the *Mode Journal* so assiduously pursued, was most obvious in an article on furniture:

> A chair should (1) stand firmly and securely, (2) not be heavy, yet be stable and long-lasting, given that it will be moved many times and often with some force, and (3) be comfortable. According to this theory, an ordinary chair is most perfect when its body, i.e., the seat and its four legs, form as closely as possible a cube, whereby the surface of the seat is no larger than the basis of the four legs. The backrest should never rise above the shoulder blades.[22]

The passage concluded by noting that established French styles were far inferior to English innovations. "Just how thoroughly the medallion chair, which was recently in fashion and which we received from France and not England, sins against these rules is obvious to anyone with eyes."[23]

The journal analyzed with equal rigor a host of other furniture pieces and, in every case, displayed a similar concern for surrounding the bourgeois consumer with objects of ease. A balloon-shaped oven, a wine cooler, a standing clock, a Chinese spittoon, an English foot warmer, a portable washing machine, a travel pillow, a shaving table with mirror, a corner cabinet, and an adjustable writing table were the typical products the journal encouraged readers to buy. The practical value of a writing surface that could be raised and lowered was explained in much the same terms as the need for a comfortable chair:

> For businessmen, who are often obliged to write for long stretches, it is both comfortable and healthy to alter one's bodily position and to be able to work at a desk in both a standing and seated posture. A writing table needs to be constructed to allow both.[24]

The travel pillow allowed the new cosmopolitan German to relax on long journeys through Europe. It was specifically warranted, the journal argued, by the heightened mobility of modern relations. Advances in travel and communication produced new stresses, which made it necessary to find new ways of soothing the body:

> Given the great mobility of our contemporary world, and the increasing necessity of travel brought on by new avenues of business, our own restless tendencies, as well as the closer connections among European nations, our sleeping roll is for those who travel frequently, day or night. It is a thoroughly comfortable and essential piece of travel equipment.[25]

As for the washing machine, the *Mode Journal* quoted directly from its English inventor, a certain Mr. Beetham, who explained the utility of his device in terms familiar to any reader of advertisements:

> The advantages of my washing machine are to be found (1) in its very simple construction, because of which the machine's parts cannot be disturbed or ruined; (2) in the ease of its use, for even a girl of fourteen can operate the machine without difficulty; (3) in the great savings that the machine allows, for one person can wash as much as ten laundresses and with only a quarter of the fire and soap usually required; (4) in the preservation of all pieces washed therein, for the machine's operation is far smoother and generally superior to the usual method of washing by hand . . . and (5) in that the wash is far cleaner, whiter, and more evenly washed than in the usual manner.[26]

The *Mode Journal*'s products were the instruments, and in many cases the symbols, of a new bourgeois asceticism, which enlisted as well as cleansed the body, as both the object and the instrument of its economically oriented discipline. Bertuch's plea for utilitarian consumption was a typical experiment of the Enlightenment, for in advocating "the comfort and ease of the consumer" the *Mode Journal* sought to supplant the ceremonial conventions of ruling institutions as well as to reform the traditional practices of the middle-class household. Bertuch's dissatisfaction with the everyday norms of corporate (*ständische*) society never led him over to the Rousseauean extremes of Sturm und Drang writers.[27] Far from urging an escape from or upheaval of civilization, the *Mode Journal* saw the individual as embedded within a society whose vices could be transformed into virtues. It treated the person as a material resource, as a dormant potential, which could be molded and made to respond to external requirements. Hence, its goal was to rationalize social conditioning rather than elude it.

The journal's editorial aim was to regulate the flow of information about luxury consumption and to occasionally join the public discussion when it could no longer ensure the economically productive coordination of fashion and the body. These strategic interventions inevitably expanded the journal's domain. As fashionable opinion created new objects, the journal responded with a critical evaluation, which had the paradoxical effect of dispersing information on an activity it sought to discourage. The journal responded to this dilemma by continually introducing new fashions to replace those considered dangerous, a strategy distinctly different from the censure employed by religious and pedagogical authorities.[28]

The collecting of fashion news was frequently at odds with its larger plan of incorporating clothing design into a network of productive uses. As an editor, Bertuch had to grapple with the contradiction of criticizing fashion while simultaneously distributing information about it, a tension that is obvious when one reads an entire issue of the *Mode Journal*. The various articles often did not espouse a single coherent position, the most obvious contradictions being between reports sent in from foreign capitals and the judgmental articles by Bertuch himself—between articles purporting to merely inform readers of the newest styles and those that evaluated them. This divergence in editorial interest is perhaps best illustrated by a report from *Mode Journal*'s Parisian reporter:

> You ask me what one considers here in the capital to be the most comfortable, elegant, and practical negligé for a new mother. You realize, of course, that it is now fashionable to wear sensible clothes. Our moody goddess has issued this new stamp for her products. This was certainly not the least fortuitous of her ideas, and one can only hope that her new business venture has a prosperous future. Since our own fashion ladies consider it necessary to approach nature a little more, perhaps even to become mothers and nurturers of children, guardians of domestic order (at least in appearance), and agreeable companions to their husbands, they have begun to decorate themselves, for the sake of their husbands and others, with a new order—elegance and inventive frugality.[29]

The correspondent's dismissal of practical clothing for women, however, was at odds with the *Mode Journal*'s stance on the question of motherhood and the relation of clothes to women's bodily changes during pregnancy.

Justus Möser had pointed out in the 1740s how high fashion would occasionally invoke practicality to explain why a particular fashion had fallen out of favor, citing the demise of daggers and wide sleeves as examples of such a false concern for utility.[30] Puffy sleeves and swords might have been a nuisance to wear, but they were abandoned only because they were outdated, Möser claimed, not because they got in anyone's way. An adherent of the rococo, the youthful Möser elaborated his defense of fashion into a moral axiom: "A person is not virtuous because it fulfills his duties but rather because it is fashionable."[31] This position was associated in Germany with the French moralists of the seventeenth century and was utterly untenable within the *Aufklärung*. (In his later writing, particularly the essays that drew Goethe's admiration, Möser appeared to defend a traditional notion of bourgeois honor and virtue.) The suspicion that "improvements" in fashionable dress were really nothing more than transitory trends always lurked behind even the most optimistic fashion writing of the German Enlightenment. No matter how comfortable or practical popular clothing had become, a significant proportion of the German Bildungsbürgertum looked askance at transitory cosmopolitan styles, preferring instead rural garb or uniforms of state service.

Given the caution with which portions of the middle class adopted new fashions, it was not surprising that the *Mode Journal* augmented the celebratory reports from abroad with longer articles defining the relative virtues of each national style. These pieces sought to contextualize the monthly reports within an ideological framework. The familiar terms of national difference appeared in countless descriptions of garments. This early piece on men's jackets is but one example:

> The French have shown themselves incapable of imitating the rational garb of the English without going to extremes. The Englishman wears his gillet as it was meant to be worn, as a comfortable camisole, made of soft, finely woven wool or cotton or thick silk, with small white, silver-plated buttons. He does not wish to dress fancily but, rather, neatly and comfortably. The Frenchman decorates his with needlework of gold, silk, and precious stones, thereby losing the use and comfort of the gillet.[32]

Clothes and household objects provided, according to Bertuch, the distinct markings of a national tradition. The journal's efforts at explaining style to Germans were repeatedly legitimated by an interest in national character. A complete understanding of French clothes or English furniture would bring, Bertuch maintained, a recognition of the spiritual content of the people who produced it. The first public announcement of the *Mode Journal*, published in Wieland's *Teutscher Merkur*, alleged a correspondence between consumer luxuries and civilization:

> As a matter of fact, a nation does not characterize itself more noticeably and distinctly than in the form of luxury it maintains and the spirit of its fashions. An accurate history of the fashions worn by only some of the peoples who lived a few hundred years ago would be a highly interesting contribution to a future philosophical history of the human spirit.[33]

Despite his pronouncements, it was a long way from Bertuch's historical claims to the *Mode Journal*'s bulletins on recent trends in dress, which were devoid of moral and philosophical judgments. They focused so com-pletely on details that all framings fell away. Foreign reports provided ma-terial descriptions and nothing more; all external influences on taste were erased. In part, this decontextualization depended on the judgment of the correspondent; the French correspondent noted that, since his last report, "nothing new has appeared in our fashion universe worth mentioning, for if some housemaid wears a ribbon or a feather brush on her left or right side is irrelevant; it does not constitute a new fashion."[34] However, the erasure of all background information about particular styles was also an effect of literary style: foreign reports described local scenes in the passive voice.

As this excerpt from the *Zeitung für die elegante Welt* demonstrates, ob-jects were described as either in fashion or as having disappeared: "The long, round headgear in the antique style are still maintaining themselves and are becoming a major trend. . . . They generally come in two colors."[35] For an accessory to be fashionable, it had to be visible. When it dropped below the surface, there was no concern over what accounted for its disappearance. Thus, in 1786 the *Mode Journal* could announce without any further expla-nation: "Medallions have, in Paris, all disappeared from the breasts of women."[36] Causation and motivation were irrelevant when reporting for-eign tastes. German readers received nothing more than a description; de-tailed information, such as who wore the items and on what occasion, was considered unimportant and would no doubt have been confusing to an au-dience only passingly familiar with Parisian society.

Reliance on the passive voice was not a peculiarity of the German lan-guage; it reflected an ambiguous understanding of what fashion was and how it operated. Even in the late eighteenth century, the formation of fash-ionable opinion was seen as something that happened on its own, without any one person or class responsible. Germans might complain that the French created the new styles that Germans aped, but it was understood that the process whereby certain styles were adopted and then later dis-carded was a mysterious social phenomenon. The normal chain of cause and effect was not considered relevant. By the end of the century, alterations in styles were no longer tied to the dynastic successions of French kings. Fur-thermore, the theory that the lower classes always emulated the elites had obviously failed to account for how bourgeois and revolutionary fashions had replaced aristocratic styles. By concentrating on the movement of objects in and out of the public eye, German journals foregrounded fashionableness as a quality in its own right, as something divorced from the individuals who practiced style.

The foreign reports that appeared in every issue of the *Mode Journal* resolved the mystery of fashion change by simply accepting it as inevitable, implying a worldly detachment from social history. Their concentration on fashion objects as "the only thing worth mentioning" conveyed an aesthetic insularity that has characterized fashion writing throughout the modern era. The *Mode Journal*'s monthly descriptions of the scene in Paris and London were forerunners of an interest in fashion for its own sake. Initially, political events, such as the French Revolution, appeared in Parisian reports as an unfortunate interruption in the fabrication of new styles, but soon the Parisian correspondent found sartorial innovations in the politically motivated garb of the sansculottes. Even the guillotine was treated as a fashion object; shortly after the Revolution, the *Mode Journal* published an article claiming that the guillotine was actually a reinvention of an execution device employed in Germany as early as the fifteenth century. The French adaptation was taken, with some irony, as proof of the cyclical nature of fashion development.

> It would be unjust if we did not want to dedicate an article to the newly fashionable revolutionary instrument, the most holy guillotine [*Notre très sainte Guillotine*], as she was recently described by a Parisian sansculotte; for, like our hats, bonnets, and shoe buckles, she must bow down before fashion's scepter, thereby demonstrating the unusual but generally acknowledged rule that fashion never lets anything completely disappear. Rather, fashion's cycles, be they short or long—sometimes taking centuries—give a new birth to all things, even the decapitation machine.[37]

Serious-minded critics have, since the eighteenth century, fumed at the calculated superficiality of fashion reporting. The *Mode Journal* was itself divided over how far it should go in tying fashion to external demand. While the foreign reports described clothes simply in terms of their appearance, the *Mode Journal* dedicated the majority of its space to long, critical articles on the practical, political, and medical merits of the objects mentioned by its correspondents. The journal's pragmatic reflections were set against its own glossy reiteration of foreign trends. This tension appealed to German readers. Bertuch juxtaposed German fascination with Europe's two great capitals with its own Enlightenment tradition of debate and critical appraisal.

The detached style of the foreign reports was already an established tradition in the eighteenth century. Richard Sennett, discussing the careful tone used by Addison and Steele in *The Spectator* and *The Tatler*, two earlier English periodicals that had a wide readership among German Enlightenment intellectuals, pointed out that the society tales that Addison and Steel printed were written with a deliberate generality, allowing diverse readers to meet on common ground.[38] Their accounts of recent events in London alluded to information that might have been known to the cognoscente, but they did not provide direct references. German fashion reports went even farther in filtering out allusions to particular individuals; by describing only the external appearance of public figures, German correspondents eliminated many links between dress and historical particulars, such as personal identity, class, and rank. Only gender, one of the few background facts retained in these reports, was presumed to serve a defining function in dress.

Modern fashion magazines were obvious heirs to these detached eighteenth-century fashion reports. In *The Fashion System*, his definitive study in structuralist semiotics, Roland Barthes noted the tendency for magazines to write about fashion as a simple observed fact. Although he concentrated his analysis on French magazines published between 1958 and 1959, Barthes's categories echo back to the eighteenth century. Statements such as "Women will shorten skirts, adopt pastel checks, and wear two-toned pumps" pointed up the self-referential character of fashion writing.[39] By predicting what women would wear, the magazine in effect declared what they must wear if they were to be in fashion. Barthes argued further that matter-of-fact descriptions of fashion held up the unfashionable as the fashionable's implicit opposite. When an article reported what women were wearing or would be wearing, it effectively banished every other style. Like a good politician, fashion writing never mentioned its opponent by name; rather, it alluded only obliquely to the existence of the unfashionable. This rhetorical strategy created a separation between styles remarked upon and those passed over in silence. Clothes that appeared in the pages of the magazine were implicitly good, whereas those that did not appear were bad, inferior, or tasteless.[40]

Barthes's analysis revealed the sociological assumptions embedded in writing that purported to objectively report on fashion. By withdrawing from the world of historical persons and economic or political forces, fashion writing created "an autarchic universe, where ensembles choose their jackets themselves and nightgowns their length."[41] Barthes implied, but never explicitly stated, that this language distorted the actual historical relations of power and causation. When fashion writing constituted itself as its own force, it did so in order to obfuscate the real source of its existence, namely, the elite group of editors and designers who decided what to sell to consumers. Barthes argued that the rhetorical strategy of fashion writing produced an "exact inversion of reality and its image."[42]

Barthes's point was that much fashion writing turned everything said about itself into a sign of itself. For example, if a social historian were to argue that red jackets were first worn by Parisian plumbers to signal their hatred of classical Greek architecture, even such an academic hypothesis would be used in fashion writing as proof that red jackets were fashionable. Any explanation for fashion was likely to become proof of fashionableness. Similarly, if black evening gowns were reported to have been reintroduced to the fashion world by Karl Lagerfeld in his new Chanel collection, that statement when written in a magazine would become immediately a justification for the stylishness of black evening gowns. It would explain nothing, because the fashion system incorporated into its own rhetoric any explanation of the boundary between itself and the outside world.

In criticizing the apparent self-indulgence of fashion writing, Barthes operated within a model of commodity fetishism inherited from Marx. In *Capital*, Marx argued that the appearance of commodities as magical entities with alluring qualities was due to a misunderstanding of the economic relations that underlay their production. The commodity, according to Marx, seemed to have special value because it was the product of labor. By itself, a dress might exude its own attraction; however, behind that dress were layers of unseen work. Barthes dismissed the seemingly autonomous quality of fashion writing as a distortion of the actual—and by implication, determinate—forces that created the image or text that the consumer absorbed from the magazine's page. These hidden forces were editors and designers in the service of capitalist producers eager to sell more goods. Fashion, according to this line of critique, was a ruse.

To Barthes's credit, he did not push this line of analysis very aggressively, though others writing in the early 1960s did. In their eagerness to expose the ideological veil that fashion was said to represent, these more conventional Marxists, such as W. H. Haug, passed quickly over the nuances of

fashion writing.[43] They sought to explain fashion as merely a secondary effect of capitalist economic relations. Jean Baudrillard provided the most am-
bitious synthesis of semiotic theory and Marxist economic determinism, but
for all the attention Baudrillard gave to the commodity's construction as a
sign, he never allowed for the possibility that consumer culture was anything but a ruse, covering up distant and obscure relations of power.[44] The
lower and middle classes were allowed to indulge in pleasurable consumption, while the ruling elite retained mastery over the relations of economic
production:

> It must be asked whether certain classes are not consecrated to finding their
> salvation in objects, consecrated to a social destiny of consumption and
> thus assigned to a slave morality (enjoyment, immorality, irresponsibility)
> as opposed to a master morality (responsibility and power). Such are the
> heirs of the servile, subaltern classes, or of the courtesans dedicated to *para-*
> *phernalia*.[45]

The trouble with ideological critiques of consumer culture is their false
claim to uniqueness. When Baudrillard denounced luxury consumption as
a deceptive system of status, he failed to recognize that this argument was
itself a basic principle of modern bourgeois consumption. Since at least the
eighteenth century, materialist philosophers have seen through the emptiness of luxury, and Baudrillard inadvertently drew attention to this tradition of commentary by comparing modern consumers with courtesans. Like
Enlightenment opponents of the absolute court, Marxian cultural critics
of consumption have repeatedly asserted the inherent value of economic
production over the illusions of power represented by expensive pleasure-
giving commodities. In doing so, these radicals have inadvertently given the
cycle of fashion a great push, for modern taste has always preferred to synthesize form with practical application. Attacks on luxury that invoke the
forces of production have been a regular feature of the fashion cycle. The
somber colors of late-eighteenth-century bourgeois dress were a rebuke to
the ostentatious brilliance of aristocratic costume. Likewise, the nineteenth-
century dandy's black suit made a "heroic" moral stand against both mass-
produced culture and the late-nineteenth-century alliance between capitalist industry and the old nobility.

Many of the most important fashion statements have claimed to see
through the false veneer of culture. The Hollywood mobster's severe flashi-

ness, the dandy's black suit, and the diaphanous empire gown were extreme and graphic embodiments of a modern aesthetic of consumption that renounced socially significant decoration in order to highlight the individual as the source of value—aesthetic, economic, reproductive, or otherwise. Modern good taste has always played off a showy, glitzy alternative, which it repeatedly has shown to be nothing more than a wasteful and meaningless display of color and material. Critics of consumer culture such as Baudrillard, who insisted that the availability of commodities was nothing more than a distraction from the relations of power, failed to recognize how their critique reiterated the very aesthetic and moral arguments of the ruling classes.[46] The success of the *Mode Journal* was but one example of how an economic critique of luxury could be transformed into an affirmative regime of productive consumption.

The insistence that fashion objects integrated themselves within a design scheme centered upon the body had the effect of continually expanding fashion discourse's influence over material objects as well as over popular opinion concerning health. Because of its tendency to orchestrate the design of material objects and public opinion with the perceived demands of the body, the *Mode Journal* found itself engaged in a series of debates over medical treatment. After only a few years of publication, Bertuch felt that the medicalization of fashion allowed for—and even demanded—the regulation of medical fashions. As an authority on fashionable judgment, the *Mode Journal* defended its conception of health against other claims to medical knowledge that surfaced within a society increasingly concerned with health. In October 1789, an article warned that the public was increasingly susceptible to quackery now that self-diagnosis and the maintenance of a personal *Gesundheitssystem* (health system) had become an aspect of proper *ton*. The author listed twenty-eight recent medical treatments deemed false.[47] A satirical piece in June of that year ridiculed alchemy, physiognomy, magnetism, and exorcism, proposing instead the science of phonognomy and the analysis of pronunciation and voice tone as a means of ascertaining inner character.[48] In an earlier issue, medicinal liqueurs were described as "the surest enemy of human life."[49]

Bertuch declared that his journal would regularly appraise "the newest and most widely circulating fashion articles for health, beauty, longevity, and the like."[50] At stake was the journal's ability to organize the discussions and opinions of fashionable society. While Bertuch's interest was in the fashionable application of medical knowledge, the rise in popular theories that had failed scientifically forced a redefinition of the scope and aim of Mode. Fashion was not confined to objects that met with aesthetic approval; it included a variety of unrelated concepts and theories that shared two primary characteristics: popularity within an elite cultural class and a tangential interest in the preservation and enhancement of the body. The competition among medical theories within fashionable society was due to a variety of factors. The *Mode Journal* complained about an increase in medicinal products on the consumer market:

> Surely there have never been more fashion doctors and charlatans than now. Never has it been easier to bring the most inane products onto the market, now that everyone speaks about medicine; and at some dinner parties more medical information is exchanged than at many dissertation defenses.[51]

Bertuch recognized that having one's own favorite medical theory was a result not only of fashion discourse's fixation on the body but also of the heightened self-consciousness and sense of personal responsibility that the Enlightenment sought to instill in individuals. The fashion for medical diagnosis grew out of the general dispersion of medical knowledge among the reading public:

> Everyone seems today to be have been born a doctor; it has become the fashion for each person to make a precise system of various states of health with which to evaluate oneself and others—patients as well as doctors. Previously, a person hardly thought about his body until it began to cause him pain. At which point, one gave it over to the healer the way a watch is given to a clock maker, who tries his best to improve the condition without it ever occurring to the owner to discuss with him or to reflect upon his method. Now, one takes the responsibility upon oneself, and the consequence is that one is never sure whether one is healthy or sick. Now, one trusts oneself far more than the doctor, who is always suspected of pedantry, self-interest, or some other craftsmanlike error. In this manner, then, medical enlightenment has made it unbelievably difficult for the doctor to practice his profession and for the sick to recover their health.[52]

He was aware of the tenuous nature of medical diagnosis. The spread of scientific jargon and disreputable cures was not the only explanation for the faddish concern for personal health. The body itself was an unstable entity;

its conditions, needs, and requirements, not to speak of its desires, were by no means unchanging. By coupling fashionable judgment with the body, the eighteenth century did not succeed in placing a boundary on fashion discourse's ability to generate an ever-increasing spiral of luxuries. The vague art of diagnosis was as likely to be swayed by public opinion as state policy had been subject to an absolute prince's obligation to always appear magnificently regal. Unlike princes, bourgeois consumers were not susceptible to the flattery of mistresses and courtiers, but they were particularly sensitive to the vagaries of their own bodies. The variety of medical products and explanations escalated within bourgeois fashion, as consumers acquired a greater awareness of their own personal comfort and as the jargon of medical practice pervaded society.

The Roman equation of luxury with decadence provided a time-tested explanation for why German bourgeois readers became interested in medicinal fashions at the end of the eighteenth century. Bertuch recognized that the period's enthusiasm for a host of superstitious sciences could easily have been explained under the terms of the Roman critique:

> With the increase in luxury and the refinement of enjoyment, it was inevitable that a certain sensitivity and sickness, which forces us to think more often about our bodily condition, to formulate concepts of health, sickness, and cure . . . would gain the upper hand.[53]

Bertuch maintained that the fashion for medicine could be contained by his journal's critical evaluation of new products and theories. Public education, he seemed to imply, could correct the unintended side effects of public acquisition of medical knowledge. However, Bertuch's ironic, modernist tone suggested a willingness to accept that fashionable, cosmopolitan individuals had become more sensitive to their bodies. His prose acknowledged that the body had become the site of endless concern and critical examination and that, in binding consumption to the body, modern fashion writing had opened up new terrain.

The *Mode Journal's* outcry against popular pseudosciences reproduced the larger debate over the emergence of bourgeois fashion itself. Bertuch's denunciations of magnetism, for example, took on the same tone and rhetoric as the diatribes of conservatives outraged by the spread of cosmopolitan tastes throughout the middle classes. The vituperative prose of Physiocrats like August Schlettwein and traditionalists like Ernst Brandes reappeared in Bertuch's own writings about magnetism. In a sense, Bertuch was playing out within the pages of his journal the scandal that his publication had generated among an older academic readership. Bertuch seemed to borrow the panicked arguments of Enlightenment *Gelehrte* in characterizing the threat to public well-being posed by the belief in the curative powers of magnetic treatment.

How directly medical debates were used to expand the domain of fashion is demonstrated by the *Mode Journal*'s extensive articles criticizing the popular enthusiasm for magnetism. When Bertuch followed through on his plan to warn against the dangers of quackery, it became clear that the boundaries between health cures and other fashions were very ambiguous. Magnetism operated on the public imagination as potently as other consumer fads:

> Every person who wants to can use [magnetism} for whatever purposes he wishes. It provides him with a new system, new means, and new purposes. It conforms to everything; and . . . as the horde of writings it has produced show, nothing has received on so many forms and such content.[54]

The threat posed by magnetism, its ability to mislead the public into accepting false cures for real illness, justified the journal's intervention:

> At first glance, the subject [of Mesmerism] does not seem to belong in a journal about luxury and fashion. However, upon closer examination, sufficient reasons do present themselves. For we have determined that animal magnetism should be viewed as both a fashionable cure and a curative extravagance. It belongs in the great realm of fashion (whose borders have not been determined by any geographer) and thus does belong in this journal.[55]

Bertuch, an unquestionably shrewd manipulator of public opinion, drew a distinction between his publication and the writings of Mesmer and his followers, thus making magnetism a scapegoat for Bertuch's own controversial reception by the scholarly elite of the Enlightenment. However, more was at stake than the short-term politics of scholarly debate. By exposing the threat of pseudoscientific medical theories and by insisting that the *Mode Journal* was called upon to police public opinion concerning medicine, Bertuch highlighted the broader regulatory function of his publication within the public sphere:

The spirit of a nation has, as is well known, as many and often as baroque and insane fashions as the body, and they change as often as the body's. Who does not know that magic and spiritualism [*Geisterbann*] is now one of those intellectual fashions [*Geistes-Moden*]. Like influenza, it has infected not only Germany but almost all of Europe, the so-called grand (but by no means enlightened) world, to such an extent that even among the serving classes it has become part of the *bon-ton* to practice a little witchcraft and exorcism.[56]

The problem of how the enlightened public should respond to the sudden appearance of fashionable illnesses and their dubious cures spoke directly to the larger question of how society should deal with the spread of fashion-driven consumer culture in Germany. Bertuch as well as many other commentators characterized the spread of fashion throughout the German reading public as an epidemic. The Physiocrat Johann August Schlettwein noted the tendency for fashion to reproduce its own discourse: "The whole point of luxury is to find more shimmer and glare to enjoy and to spread sensual pleasure as widely as possible."[57] Transmitted from one person to another by invisible means, cosmopolitan opinions seemed to ignore the established boundaries of the Central European public life, yet these new judgments of taste were far less substantial than actual plagues. They affected the look and feel of the body's ordinary existence without changing its organic functioning. So if fashion was a epidemic, it was a plague that infected hypochondriacs. The pseudoscientific ailments and cures postulated by magnetism and its ilk were a potent representation as well as a real-life example of how the spread of cosmopolitan fashion sensibilities altered society. When Bertuch promised to provide the public with accurate knowledge about magnetism—"a real Proteus that took on a thousand different forms and was everything to everyone"[58]—he was asserting in microcosm the *Mode Journal*'s larger goal of containing the elusive movement of fashion within public life.

While the *Mode Journal* could claim that the established goal of all adornment was the enhanced comfort and productivity of the body, the terms of this formula were easily relativized, given that they were defined only in relation to one another. Despite the regulatory control exerted by the *Mode Journal*, consumer goods were a hybrid produced by competing discourses and institutional relations. The supposition that Mode covered objects and practices that were neither fully practical nor purely aesthetic allowed it a vast arena for playful transformations of both terms. The same protean quality that Bertuch derided in magnetism he celebrated in textile manufacturing, and he used a similar rhetoric of transformation to describe the prolific generation of feminine fashion:

> This field has simply no boundaries, just as the art [of feminine taste and fashion] has no rules. And if the million forms that have taken root were ever exhausted, then taste and industry would create a million more, or perhaps would look to the past to plagiarize the fashions of our ancestors in order to bring them back into circulation under a new visage.[59]

As to commodities and the demand they hoped to inspire, Bertuch insisted that repressive controls were pointless and economically counterproductive. In the marketplace, he advocated a nonrepressive policy, one starkly at odds with the restrictions he sought to impose on faulty medical sciences. In the following chapters I elaborate on how this difference amounted to a dual strategy that was typical of bourgeois regulation of consumption: to foster the expansion of fashion culture on the level of macroeconomics while insisting that consumers self-regulate their own productive capacities.

CHAPTER FOUR

The Queen of Fashion
An Allegory of Conformity

Fashion—a despot whom the wise ridicule and obey.

Ambrose Bierce, *The Devil's Dictionary*

THE ABILITY of fashion journals, advertisements, and the opinions of a few tastemakers to draw a vast majority of the public to follow its examples has always been viewed with suspicion and resentment by intellectuals trained in the tradition of Enlightenment critique. The success with which the small pressures of vanity and conformity nudge even the dowdiest into performing for the approval of their peers has, in the twentieth century, been characterized as a threat to individual autonomy, comparable to the most egregious political regimes. During World War II, Quentin Bell described the ability of tasteful opinion to direct human behavior as a morally ambivalent and awesome force:

> Fashion for those who live within its empire is a force of tremendous and incalculable power. Fierce and at times ruthless in its operation, it governs our behaviour, informs our sexual appetites, colours our erotic imagination, makes possible but also distorts our conception of history, and determines our aesthetic valuations.[1]

To a postwar British reader, the analogy Bell drew between fashion and totalitarianism would have been unmistakable. Bell provided a more readily understood version of the same critique put forward by Frankfurt School philosophers Theodor Adorno and Max Horkheimer, namely, that the differences between the way capitalism organized popular culture and Nazi Germany mobilized its *Volk* were not as great as Western liberals liked to believe. Adorno's critique of the culture industry has been defined by the parallels drawn both implicitly or directly between the conformity produced by free market mechanisms and fascism's midcentury success in perpetuating its racist ideology:

> Under the private culture monopoly, it is a fact that tyranny leaves the body free and directs its attack at the soul. The ruler no longer says: You must think as I do or die. He says: You are free not to think as I do; your life, your property, everything shall remain yours, but from this day on you are powerless, economically and therefore spiritually—to be "self-employed."[2]

Adorno argued that, like fashion-driven societies, authoritarian regimes subtly employed the threat of ostracism as a means of inducing specific modes of behavior. In recent years, this equation between fascism and advertising, so prevalent in leftist criticism, has waned, not because Adorno's characterization of the culture industry has been proven wrong but because the conditions that produced capitalist advertising have been accepted as unavoidable.

The French philosopher Gilles Lipovetsky took the regulatory role of popular dress culture for granted:

> Fashion is an original system for social regulation and social pressure. Its changes are constraining by nature: they carry with them the obligation that they be adopted and assimilated; they impose themselves with varying degrees of rigor on a specific social milieu. Such is the "despotism" of fashion, so frequently denounced over the centuries. It is a very special form of despotism, since it has no significant sanctions except perhaps for the laughter, scorn, or criticism of one's contemporaries.[3]

Lipovetsky's assessment of the subtle means by which fashionable opinion shapes social behavior is not substantially different from Bell's or Adorno's. What distinguishes him from his midcentury German and British colleagues are the moral connotations he attached to this conformity. For Lipovetsky, the "tyranny of fashion" was an inevitable aspect of how democratic societies formulate consensus. The dominance of a single standard of taste, its emergence within the competitive arena of public discourse, deserved only disdain from those who disagreed with the reigning fad. At bottom, Lipovetsky saw fashion as just one of many media employed by competing classes to affirm their identities. The association between fashion and tyranny has a long history, in which the connotations of *tyranny* have varied significantly. On occasion, the tyranny of opinion was considered a liberating force; at other times, submission to fashion was treated with an ironic detachment, which heightened the aesthetic pleasures of dress.

Eighteenth- and nineteenth-century fashion writers invoked fashion as a queen with vast control over her subjects. Social theory needs to recognize the ambivalent lineages of such tropes and to demonstrate the social assumptions implicit in even the most common statements on social behavior. A trope can also contain within it a philosophical problem, for the invocation of metaphor is itself an attempt to solve through indirect language a concern that cannot be resolved in more direct language. In fashion writing, the figure of a fashion tyrant was sometimes intended to make light of complaints about conformity and to mock those who were out of style. Other times, as in the case of Bell, it was employed as a warning about the potential loss of individual freedom.

My goal here is twofold. In line with the intellectual tradition that critiques the application of force upon persons, the history of this rhetorical figure helps us to understand the many deployments of fashion as a force. In reversing the relationship between the rhetorical figure and what it represents, I hope also to revive some of the playful and ironic meanings that "tyranny of fashion" had before the rise of fascism. If fashion is famous for anything, it is for reviving old garments and assigning them new importance. A similar cyclical process can be found in the metadiscourse about fashion: the same tropes keep reappearing with new gravity, all claiming to have the final word on the social significance of fashionable culture.

The midcentury association of fashion with the coercive manipulation of authoritarian regimes and monopoly capitalism was but one such last word. Fashionable conformity is not merely a form of oppression; on a societal level, it can help establish solidarity. In erotic relations, the male masochist's acceptance of a female dominatrix is but one side of a duplicitous dialectic of mastery and enslavement. Both cases—fashionable conformity and fetishistic submission—are predicated upon a contractual relationship between the participants. Sociologists have noted that fashion serves to differentiate groups, while maintaining internal coherence.

In the eighteenth century, the organization of behavior without coercive force was a still a novelty, a strange phenomenon, which was explained through rhetorical tropes rather than sociological theories. One of the most distinctive features of bourgeois consumer culture in its first formulations was the ubiquitous Queen Mode, an allegorical figure with Latin and Hebraic forebears who was invoked to explain how fashionable society produced conformity while constantly changing its standards of elegance.[4] In every kind of eighteenth-century writing on the subject, fashion was described as a mysteriously powerful feminine monarch or deity whose ever-changing edicts concerning the design and organization of daily life demanded absolute obedience. Regardless of literary genre or ideological leaning, fashion discourse employed this personification to represent the penetration of fashionable opinion into virtually every facet of bourgeois life. Proponents of free market capitalism, defenders of courtly ceremony, Enlightenment reformers, and religious reactionaries all relied upon this allegory to explain the willingness of large and diverse populations to emulate each other.[5] Indeed, the trope's pervasiveness seemed to confirm the magical powers ascribed to it. Queen Mode appeared so often in fashion texts that a reader could not doubt her powers, at least as a rhetorical structure.

The trope of fashion not only was a means for the eighteenth century to represent the new modes of power invisibly at work in bourgeois society, it was also a figuration of visually provoked desire. Fashionable opinion's control over society was equated with the image of a woman appearing in a succession of garments. Within the terms of eighteenth-century discourse, Queen Mode's inconstancy in appearance kept her subjects fascinated. The allegory's pervasiveness must surely have lain in its ability to align desire and submission. Its ambivalent references meant that at times it represented the exercise of power over the individual, while in other contexts the capricious queen signified the stimulation of desire for precisely that force that kept the individual in its grip. In the courtly version of the trope, Queen Mode controlled by issuing commands. These terms were realigned in the bourgeois fashion world. Within the domesticated spaces of the salon, the figure's power was equated with the ability to produce desire:

> Women renew themselves, so to speak, every day, in order to give us a new motive to pay them homage. Through pure inconstancy, they wish to bind us more securely, and they know quite well that if one wishes to pursue the hearts of men, one must learn to perform somersaults.[6]

This passage described the effects of a socially dispersed discursive movement, even though it ascribed a causality to "women." Desire was produced, given a direction, and maintained by the rapid replacement of sanctioned styles. The passage not only described the production of heterosexual male desire but also presented an allegory of the relationship between subjectivity and fashion discourse. For if "woman" was the allegorical representation of fashion as a disciplining discourse, then the "us" corresponded to an autonomous subjectivity that resisted becoming entangled in the web of fashion signification. The pursuit (*Verfolgung*) involved a struggle over the subject's detachment from mechanisms of social regulation. The paradoxical formulation ("Through pure inconstancy, they wish to bind us more securely") alluded to the subtlety of modern fashion's regulation.

By constantly introducing new styles of dress, fashionable discourse enhanced its ability to penetrate the recesses of private subjectivity. With an increase in publicly sanctioned clothing forms, the chances that a style would address the inner character of the individual were enhanced. This allegorical reading was possible only when the Queen Mode figure was read into the text's generalization about women. Such an interpretation is justified because of the manner in which eighteenth-century fashion discourse tried to "naturalize" its discursive character onto the body. Fashion as a media-produced cultural phenomenon was read off women's bodies as if it were produced by them, rather than imposed on them, a deliberate strategy for naturalizing fashion through the body.

We have seen how the late eighteenth century integrated clothes within an ideology of the natural body and its social functions: clothes were interpreted as reflections of personal character or as instruments for the laboring body. This interpretation foregrounded the body while overlooking the effects produced by fashion discourse. Thus, the above passage refers to women's "inconstancy" rather than to the cyclical movement of fashionable opinion. By the end of the century, clothes had lost their older, courtly function of representing rank and were integrated into a symbolic relationship with the body. The increasing tendency to see clothes as organic elements in the construction of an individual meant that the properties ascribed to the Queen Mode allegory were slowly naturalized within the female body.

While bourgeois society in the eighteenth century was willing to employ an allegory to explain its behavior, by the turn of the nineteenth century this trope had lost its rhetorical identity and was increasingly understood as an ideal type or a psychological profile of the fashionable woman.[7] Nineteenth-century accounts of fashion subjected the playful and omnipotent figure to psychological as well as medical and economic analyses. The rococo goddess became the spoiled daughter of the bourgeoisie, her absolute powers redefined as feminine narcissicism. Queen Mode was reduced to a mere fashion queen, and her demands were integrated into the bourgeois family's domestic supervision. An overweening insistence on maintaining appearances and a blind pursuit of tasteful company were treated as passing phases in every girl's maturation. They were given legitimacy within the family's economic calculus by the claim that fancy dresses and balls were a prerequisite for a successful marriage.

With the transformation of the trope from a figure in rhetoric to a case study in psychology came a redefinition of power. Whereas the allegorical figure was said in the eighteenth century to control both men and women through a mysterious command structure, the later psychological figure operated within a heterosexual dynamic of desire. The magic of belonging to elite society was superseded by the magic of female desirability. However, this transition came slowly and in some sense was never completed, for the figure of fashion in its most ambivalent and influential incarnation always combined the production of desire with the issuing of commands.

Like the disciplinary force that Michel Foucault described, the social consensus on taste operated as a mode of power that organized bodies.[8] However, it did so with a visual arrangement different from the panopticon prison described in *Discipline and Punish*. The tyranny of fashion was similar to Jeremy Bentham's model prison because it too exercised force upon the individual through an omnipresent system of surveillance. However, unlike the prison, with its central watchtower, fashionable society's surveillance allowed no position to be the stable center from which force emanated. While fashionable society elevated some individuals as the acknowledged leaders of elegance, their position was highly unstable. Indeed, one could say it was destined to collapse as the cycle of taste moved past their particular form of dress.

These fashion leaders differed from the supervisory agents of Foucault's panopticon model because they exercised their influence not by retreating behind the architectural screen of the prison's watchtower but by openly displaying their submission to the rules of elegance. Trendsetters achieved and maintained their role-giving rank only by continually performing before a public. Their acceptance as models for fashionable society depended upon their ability to synthesize or create a persona that other members of the fashionable world would accept. They were in a sense open to the evaluation of those who deferred to them as role models. The prison model Foucault described relied upon the asymmetrical visual relationship between prisoners and the central tower, which stood as an imposing image before them.

In eighteenth-century fashion culture, there were two moments of asymmetrical observation and two separate lines of force. First, trendsetters submitted their appearance to the judgment of the public. Second, the public responded by imitating their mythic roles. The guardians of taste preserved their privileged position only by more assiduously presenting themselves to the judgment of those who in the end followed their example. The tenuousness of fashion arose from the ebb and flow of this relationship, which played itself out repeatedly as styles were communicated through different strata of society. The two sites of this movement were held in relation to each other by a host of small pressures—fear of ostracism, desire for approval and status, and so on—as well as by the relations of political economy. The distinctive quality of fashion, as opposed to the court ceremony, was its ongoing, everyday mediation between vast social structures and small personal compulsions.

At first glance, fashion and discipline seemed unrelated, even antagonistic, practices, which bent toward each other when considered from a second-order perspective that ignored the intentions avowed by each. Fashion presented itself as all lightness and play, beauty without the ponderousness of critical reflection. Discipline claimed to know only tactical mobilization of resources. Like fashion, it refused to evaluate its own ends, nor did it allow speculation about the unintended, secondary effects of its operation. The logistics of manipulating bodies and other inert resources gave discipline a supposed purity of purpose, an unthinking willingness to execute without regard for the implications of its actions. Similarly, fashion performances might have seemed to ignore the practical preconditions and financial woes that preceded and followed absolute devotion to passing beauty. Each practice gained immeasurably in its purported disregard for what lay beyond its narrowly drawn horizons. In the immediate present of the observer, the beauty of fashion enhanced its obliviousness, and discipline was more effective precisely because of its thoughtlessness. Both led a short-term existence; their strengths arose from their ability to dominate the split second. Their transitoriness was also due to the fact that their primary material was the active body. Unlike art or architecture, fashion and discipline could not establish themselves as monuments, even if through some ironic disavowal. They both operated in an immediacy that could not be preserved, reconstructed, or reexperienced.

All discourses have terms that suggest their own operation. They are tropes that are invoked whenever the discourse needs to explain itself to itself. These concepts are more than just the circular logic of rationalization, such as saying that a garment is in style because it is all the rage or that an action must be executed because it has been ordered. The allegorical figure of Queen Mode introduced the question of power implicit within fashionable standards of taste, without equating them to the disciplinary regimes of state institutions. Only when the trope was stripped of its oxymoronic quality could the aesthetic movements of fashion be treated as instances of power manipulating bodies toward productive ends. Such an interpretation of fashion would miss the pleasure that obedience to its whims brings.

The classic setting for observing the fashions of others while displaying one's own was the brightly lit baroque opera house. In the usual fashion scenario, the audience was more concerned with observing itself than the performance onstage. As long as each participant in fashion remained both an agent and an object of observation, the opera house with its criss-crossing lines of sight was a much more appropriate model for conceptualizing the fashionable gaze than Jeremy Bentham's one-sided panopticon. Foucault also made this point: "The Panopticon is a machine for dissociating the see/being seen dyad."[9] As a latticework of individuals situated within an enclosed space and engaged in simultaneous surveillance and display, the opera house described a system in which no position remained outside observation because each position actively engaged in observation. Privileged locations with the theater's arc, such as the central box of the monarch, provided an expansive view of other audience members and ensured that the monarch was visible to all.[10]

The requirement that the monarch have the best position from which to view the activities within the theater was almost indistinguishable from the expectation that the monarch be placed in the best position to be viewed by the audience and the performers. The king synthesized the functions usually divided between the audience and the actors, projecting his power by drawing all eyes toward him. The monarch's presence, however, did not overrule the participation of other members of the audience in the exchange of observation. Unwilling or unable to completely isolate himself from the noble class, the king did not remove himself from view. The effects of his gaze reflected back onto his own body, subjecting him to the same regime that the courtly system imposed on its weakest members. The distribution of spectators throughout the theater spread out the regulatory apparatus, granting each member the privilege of observing, while requiring, in exchange, submission to observation.

Even in the modern age, when the political economy that baroque spectacle reinforced has disappeared and clothes have taken on a utilitarian and subdued air, fashion culture operates through this predisciplinary mode. Yet at the same time, modern dress culture seeks continually to remove itself from the lines of sight and the pressures to participate competitively within the arena of self-display. Nineteenth-century dress culture instituted a more asymmetrical relation of observation and performance, predicated upon a biological notion of sexual character. The nineteenth-century assertion that fashion was a strictly feminine sphere of activity was not the final confirmation of the Queen Mode figure. Rather, it amounted to the domestication of what had previously been considered a large-scale societal force. What seemed a mystery in the eighteenth century had become a parlor trick once bourgeois society had instituted itself as the arbiter of public life. Only after the authority of the bourgeois male was established within the nuclear family could male dressers retreat from an evenhanded network of observation without also abandoning the social dimension of dress culture. Even at the height of its rigid delineation of gender identity, male dressers were still subject to fashionable observation. The dark, understated appearance of the respectable male never escaped the critical evaluation of his peers. Male culture simply refused to acknowledge that its own competitive displays were fashion driven, at which point the Enlightenment's terms for fashion culture as a whole became symbols of its nineteenth-century bifurcation. In the eighteenth century, as civil society was still tearing itself away from the court, the tyranny trope encompassed the overall operation of fashionable society.

To be sure, a number of people have always existed outside the fashion community. They do not belong to a counterculture, nor do they conform to respectable norms. Like the peasant cultures celebrated in the nineteenth century, they dress themselves in a simple manner appropriate to their needs. This ruse lasts only as long as their style of dress stays out of the cycle

of fashion. With the expansion of communication between previously isolated individuals and groups, fewer and fewer styles of dress can claim to be
innocent of prideful performance.

While the tyranny trope continues to appear in twentieth-century writing about fashion, its recent use is tainted by the misogynist devaluation
that Queen Mode suffered when the nineteenth century demoted fashion
to a secondary effect of gender, that is, a sign of feminine inconstancy.[11]
Most nineteenth- and twentieth-century references to fashion tyranny have
occurred in an abbreviated form, suggesting that the figure is so familiar
as to not require elaboration.[12] In the eighteenth century, however, long,
apostrophic poems outlining the many facets of Queen Mode's sovereignty
were a common feature in popular journals. The *Deutsches Museum* ran a six-
teen-stanza poem in 1776 listing the many fields in which fashion reigned.
The opening stanza began "Friend, no mortal can ever be free / We are all
bound by fashion's tyranny."[13] The *Mode Journal* regularly included lyrical
addresses to fashion as an omnipotent being. Some poems complained, others glorified her qualities, yet they all described her as half deity, half monarch,
who subjected humanity to her ever-changing rule:

O mightiest Fairy! Goddess of Fashion
Demon, Devil or Sorceress!
How we all stream to your altar
Where you are enthroned with submission
Presiding over human will
Sometimes with strength, other times with cunning
And every fancy you excuse as mere folly
For you are nothing but folly itself.[14]

Despite the allegory's obvious allusion to absolutist monarchy, the rule
of fashion was not directly equated with the ceremonies of courtly politics.
The similarity posited by the metaphor actually precluded the two terms
from becoming synonymous. As a monarchy, fashion constituted its own
kingdom, a cultural space distinct from existing institutions. The Queen
Mode allegory drew a parallel in the literal sense of the word, suggesting
both a similarity and a difference between the court and fashion. The two
institutions were alike, yet they never converged.

This epistemological point became increasingly important as the Queen
Mode trope was employed by bourgeois fashion culture to describe its own
inner workings. When writers at the end of the century referred to the ab-

solute commands of fashion, they did so ironically and with the full knowledge that this rule was very different from monarchical law. The antimonarchical connotation of the Queen Mode allegory was already evident by the middle of the century. Astute observers, like Lord Chesterfield, described French fashion as removed from the court at Versailles. The rules governing polite Parisian society were enforced far more thoroughly than monarchical edicts. "Fashion is more tyrannical at Paris than in any other place in the world; it governs even more absolutely than their King, which is saying a great deal. The least revolt against it is punished by proscription."[15]

The trope was widely employed to depict the eighteenth century's emerging sense that cultural life could and should exist apart from state control. When public taste and courtly rules came into direct conflict, the fashion queen was easily elevated to divine heights:

> Thank goodness for the Goddess of Fashion, who in the face of the throne's earnestness has been able to triumph over the tyranny of courtly etiquette. Our Ladies can now, just like the Gentlemen, follow their inclinations by going to court in modern, light-weight, tasteful costumes.[16]

The loosening of court ceremony was an explicit example of how the bourgeois code of civility overcame the older aristocratic standard of respect. Its suggestiveness gave the trope an application beyond the sophisticated world of Parisian salons. A moral weekly, *Daphne*, published in Königsberg, a Prussian trading city on the far shores of the Baltic Sea, invoked the allegory to describe fashion culture among its merchant class. With an ironic tone of submission, a young author, whose gender remains undetermined, acknowledges a personal devotion to the dictates of Queen Mode:

> Fashion is tyrant, whose scepter I kiss with pleasure, because she relishes constant change. Through our obedience, she provides a livelihood for thousands. She unifies entire peoples, while distinguishing them, too. She expels the disobedient by making them seem ridiculous. Her rule is not as monarchical as one imagines. She is satisfied with a modest degree of obedience and gladly grants exceptions and exemptions to her rules.[17]

By acknowledging the authority of Queen Mode, the writer in effect avowed his or her desire to participate in polite society. Chesterfield and this anonymous author invoked Queen Mode in the same year (1750) to describe two very different social arenas. The Prussian played down the monarchical association implied by the allegory, whereas Chesterfield heightened them. In both cases, fashion was described as an authority operating apart from the state.

The monarchical character of fashion referred not only to its autonomy but also to the mysterious process whereby fashionable opinion produced conformity. The trope was frequently used to draw attention to the vexing question of how and why large populations willingly allowed themselves to be regulated according to fashionable opinion.[18] What new and unusual powers did fashion exercise over the populace? How did it manage to re-define bodily appearance when state ordinances had failed? Fashion culture seemed to defy rational political economy. Almost without exception, eigh-teenth-century accounts employ this trope to explain the pervasiveness of fashion-conscious behavior, the mysterious tendency for individuals to transform their appearance in unison. The tyranny metaphor is an intuitive understanding of why fashion statements were at all important in public life. Why did the *Mode Journal*'s descriptions inspire emulation? What motivated individuals regularly to adopt new styles of dress? Why were slight varia-tions in product designs perceived as significant enough to warrant new purchases? The nineteenth-century professor of aesthetics Friedrich Theodor Vischer phrased the question as, Who speaks the rules of fashion?

> We are familiar with the language of fashion journals: "one wears it like this," "such and such is permitted," "this and that is no longer acceptable!"—Who is this "one"? Who does the permitting? Who refuses to accept? Where does all this wisdom come from? On what authority? They sound as if they em-bodied the categorical imperative.[19]

The allegorical figure of fashion was the best answer to Vischer's ques-tions. As a poetic conceit, Queen Mode held the position of the speaking subject who authorized the shifting standards of fashionability. As a poetic conceit, the allegory suggested that, indeed, an actual institution or person was responsible for fashion's volatility. The irony that inevitably accompa-nied eighteenth-century references to fashionable tyranny reinforced the implicit understanding that the allegory of fashion was an imaginary con-struction invoked to authorize the behavior, opinions, and attire of those who claimed themselves to be merely following fashion. The allegorical Queen allowed all actual speakers and persons to eschew responsibility for their stylishness, thereby allowing them to portray themselves as autonomous and rational individuals compelled by necessity to enter into the irrational and even archaic obligations of social life.

This discursive maneuver replicated a certain liberal model of constitutional monarchy, wherein independent bourgeois landowners swore fealty to a monarch whose authority guaranteed a democratic social contract. Given that the later half of the eighteenth century viewed England as the source of progressive designs, it was easy to draw a parallel, as the German Enlightenment philosopher Christian Garve did, between fashionable society and English constitutional monarchy. Queen Mode gave every new turn of taste the sanction of inevitability. She provided a rationale for even the most free-thinking rationalist to participate in fashionable society's materialist drama of inclusion and expulsion. Ambrose Bierce's definition of fashion as "a despot whom the wise ridicule and obey" was very much in this Enlightenment tradition—tolerating, and thereby secretly enjoying, the irrational character of society, a gesture impossible when Adorno and Horkheimer wrote *The Dialectic of Enlightenment*.[20]

The social contract implied by the Queen Mode figure was, in the eighteenth century, deemed progressive. The allegory did not, for example, sanction the preservation of feudal ranks, nor did it suggest that fashionable behavior was motivated by vertical class competition based on emulation and differentiation through the display of consumer goods. The subtle distinctions that marked class differences, according to the emulation model of conspicuous consumption, did not appear in the Queen Mode trope. The requirement to obey fashionable opinion was presented by the allegory as a universal condition, the trope implying that all people were obliged to follow the example of fashion regardless of their position. "High and low, beautiful and ugly, smart and dumb, all are tied to her triumphal parade."[21] This universalism reflected fashion discourse's superficial claim that it was concerned only with taste and beauty and, thus, was blind to class distinction. In the eighteenth century, the fashion world's downplaying of rank belonged to an overall strategy opposed to the older, feudal, representational dress codes. Whereas the older system of consumption, developed within absolutism, insisted on the preservation of class privileges, eighteenth-century fashion discourse insisted on a single standard of good taste. All who participated in the European network of fashion, either by traveling to urban centers or by reading about them, were organized into a single culture.

Queen Mode's edicts pervaded geographical space, even into the German provinces: "Even here [in Breslau] where the piety of the Goodman and the Goodwife still means something, Fashion has asserted her rule and dominates despotically over every critic and skeptic."[22] While to modern readers the allegory suggests a restoration of monarchical law, it actually functioned in the eighteenth century as a representation of cosmopolitan culture. Garve linked the absolute rule of fashion with the code of honor that dominated European aristocratic culture in the early modern period:

> The lawbook of fashion, like the code of honor, is a universal law for all of Europe: and if it is to be improved, then it must be amended in every land. The reforms that one undertakes in one country will not last as long as the others stick by the old system.[23]

The hierarchical model of a ruler issuing edicts did little to explain the motivation of individuals engaging in fashionable behavior. The allegory suggested, paradoxically, that individuals willingly obeyed arbitrary and capricious rules, thereby curiously diverging from the usual resistance shown to state regulation. To account for this unusual situation, fashion critics presumed that Queen Mode enforced her standards through mechanisms unavailable to the state. It was frequently pointed out that failure to abide by tasteful standards meant nothing more than the exclusion from the beau monde, yet members of that society felt that such banishment was a powerful inducement to go along with prevailing opinion.[24] Critics often marveled at the absence of physical coercion in fashionable society, referring to the "nothingness" of Queen Mode's powers, while recognizing that lack of violence was precisely what made fashionable judgment so effective. The *Mode Journal*'s 1819 translation of Jacques Necker's 1798 *Melanges* is an example of this common formulation:

> Fashion's rule of force is of a very peculiar nature. The ordinances she dispenses are promulgated without a single sound, and yet they are heard by the entire world and acknowledged with greater trepidation than any law written down and publicized to the sounds of trumpets. Fashion is a monarch without a royal guard, without a throne, or a palace, and yet she is always referred to as if she were a visible power. This is because everyone is conscious that fashion asserts her law through belief in her, and that skeptics who dare to contradict her judgments are subject to the most frightening punishment imaginable, namely to be considered ridiculous in the opinion of others.

Through this strange apparatus [*Obergewalt*], fashion is held in reverence, even though she changes her tastes and opinions almost every minute. She is a universally acknowledged monarch, despite the fact that it has become fashionable to mock her continuously.[25]

Through its regular use of the Queen Mode figure, fashion discourse continually asserted that social phenomena could be explained only through a causal model of power. If a large population behaved in the same manner, then there must be some force guiding it. Power was presumed to always be in operation, and it was understood as an agent acting upon an object. The diffusion of a single code of behavior across Europe and the successful coordination of minute shifts within that code suggested to eighteenth-century observers the operation of a power. While unable to name specifics, the Queen Mode figure did suggest the existence of a complex web of material and discursive interactions that constituted fashionable society. The rhetorical elision of two modes of causation—one involving a subject and predicate, the other being more diffuse—can be illustrated through Georg Brandes's description of a modern fashion regime:

> No single important voice rules here. The self-made constitution, more oligarchical than aristocratic in nature, refuses to acknowledge one. Only the expressed decisions of this whole [*Gesammtheit*], which subsumes all persons and virtually every object, can express the sanction that governs all souls. The magical word, *society*, has an effect on all participants unlike anything else. Society's statements have the force of an oracle.[26]

Brandes's sociological account of fashion fell back into metaphor even as it denied the grammatical logic of subject and predicate. A succession of tropes overtook his attempt to dispense with agency. The text moved from "no single important voice" to denote the absence of any single cause for fashion, shifted to the "magic word, *society*," and ended with "an oracle," a divinity not unlike Queen Mode. With its use of voice as a metaphor for causation, Brandes's passage suggests that fashion was itself a rhetorical operation—a discourse structured by metaphor and evolving over time in much the same way as ordinary speech (*parole*).

Even the most serious references to the allegory of fashion were made in an ironic mode, so one must be careful in translating the rhetorical figure into a sociolinguistic theory of behavior. The goddess was fashion discourse's witty accounting for its ongoing reorganization of daily life. It accounted for the discourse and thus served the discourse. Queen Mode provided a clever escape from the probing of more serious disciplines. Allusions to the allegory often contradicted one another so blatantly that they only heightened the enigma associated with fashion.

For example, Necker's characterization of Mode suggests that the eighteenth century used the allegory both as a structural account of fashion change in general and as a legitimation of individual styles. The allegory was mocked on an ontological level as a mere fiction as well as on a superficial level as the source of outlandish clothes, and both arguments were generally invoked in criticizing fashionable culture, thereby entangling themselves in contradiction. Queen Mode could not simultaneously not exist and also be the scapegoat for silly-looking clothes. Critiques of fashion might refuse to employ a rhetorical explanation for a social phenomenon, but their denunciations were eventually aimed at some responsible agent. The French nation was a handy scapegoat, as were fashion journals and the aristocracy. Yet even the most provincial critics could recognize that these agents were themselves subject to fashion judgment. The French, the aristocracy, and the journals, despite their pivotal role in relaying the newest good taste to Germany, did not control the formation of fashionable opinion. Once these agents could not be held entirely responsible, the allegory of fashion was again invoked as a catchall explanation. This critical method became so familiar that Necker considered fashion critiques themselves fashionable.

Adam Smith's rhetorical phrase, the invisible hand of the market, had an explanatory function similar to the Queen Mode allegory. The invisible hand served as a fiction to support Smith's assertion that wealth was distributed evenly and fairly by the operation of individual agents within the marketplace. He invoked the trope to explain how the many self-interested actions of individuals worked together to produce a positive result that no individual agent would have desired nor could have achieved. This fair distribution occurred because wealth tends to trickle down to the poor; thus, the rich "are led by an invisible hand to make nearly the same distribution of the necessaries of life which would have been made had the earth been divided into equal portions among all its inhabitants."[27] Like the ontological proof of God's existence, the persuasiveness of the allegories of a fashion tyrant and an invisible hand rests on the deduction of causal agent to explain the appearance of coherence within a system. Two features of these eighteenth-century tropes distinguish them from theological argument: first, their existence was posited only on a discursive level, as rhetorical figures; second, both were deduced from a perceived social order, rather than a natural one. While Smith tended to slip into theological language (he used *providence* as an occasional synonym for *invisible hand*), eighteenth-century suggestions that fashion culture operated according to a divine plan were always ironic.

Modern economic theory claims that the invisible hand trope is nothing more than an allegorical substitute for a genetic theory of economic behavior. Rudi Keller wrote that the trope

> explains what looks to be the product of someone's intentional design, as not being brought about by anyone's intentions. It is a kind of genetic explanation. It explains a phenomenon . . . by explaining how it came into existence or could have come into existence. It is especially useful in the explanation of social institutions such as money, language, taste, ghettos, etc.: that is to say, sociocultural structures which might easily give rise to the idea . . . that they were created intentionally by . . . an inventor, god, or central committee.[28]

The *Mode Journal* described the formation of good taste in just these genetic terms—as a set of constantly shifting conventions whose observance defines membership within a community:

> Fashions are a convention about which people silently reach an agreement without knowing why. It is strange that here [in Paris] the newest fashions are invented and introduced by the greatest fops. The reasonable person submits to these fashions only somewhat later, and does so only so as not to appear ridiculous or to seem misanthropic.[29]

However, like the invisible hand, Queen Mode provided a convenient shorthand that, through its ironic tone, protected fashion discourse from the sobering effects of sociological explanation. That Smith's trope was easily incorporated into the fashion allegory should not be surprising, given that both described power as an invisible operation:

> Your influence, great Goddess, induces a universal striving among mortals, it sets nations in motion, creates new speculations to satisfy your needs, and fosters a thousand individual talents and energies. . . . You bring about new discoveries, thereby enriching the fields of science and our knowledge in general.[30]

Clothes Make the Man,
by Christian Rode

Midcentury *Robe de Cour,* by Georg Probst

Man's full dress in violet satin with gold trim. *Journal des Luxus und der Moden,* 1786

A member of the French court wearing a round hat and riding boots in the English manner. *Journal des Luxus und der Moden,* 1787

English lady in full dress of dark green satin with a train of white crepe.
Journal des Luxus und der Moden, 1787

Two female busts: *left*, Caraco dress and *bonnet demi megligé*; *right*, green English dress and *bonnet à l'Espagnol*. *Journal des Luxus und der Moden*, 1787

Masculine *Negligé* and a hat à *l'androsmane*. *Journal des Luxus und der Moden*, 1786

Two horsemen dressed in the French *(right)* an in the German *(left)* style. *Journal des Luxus un der Moden*, 1786

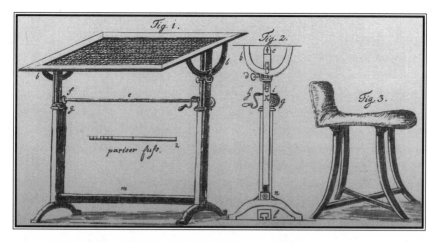

Adjustable writing table with accompanying chair. *Journal des Luxus und der Moden,* 1786

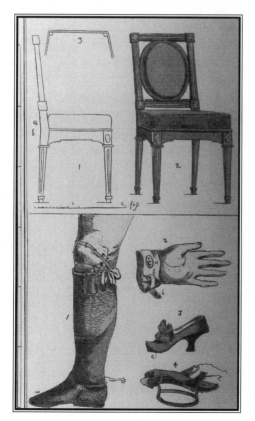

A Parisian half-foot measurement and several English articles: mahagony chair, hunting boot, man's glove, lady's shoe, mud waders. *Journal des Luxus und der Moden,* 1786

Modern and practical children's clothes.
Journal des Luxus und der Moden, 1787

Two feminine busts. *Journal des
Luxus und der Moden,* 1786

Young German woman in morning
dress. *Journal des Luxus und der
Moden,* 1794

A young Parisian woman wearing a *habit à la paysanne*. *Journal des Luxus und der Moden*, 1790

An elegant Parisian wearing the newest style. *Journal des Luxus und der Moden*, 1791

An elegant German. *Journal des Luxus und der Moden*, 1789

Fashions at either end of the eighteenth century compared.
Journal des Luxus und der Moden, 1801

Pianist and flutist. The woman wears a white chemise made of Battist with lace trim and the man is in dark blue frack with a white vest and tafetta leggings. *Hamburger Journal für Mode und Eleganz,* 1801

Walking couple seen from behind.
*Hamburger Journal für Mode und
Eleganz,* 1801

Waltzing pair. *Hamburger Journal
für Mode und Eleganz,* 1802

Woman in blue chemise
and man in brown frack.
*Hamburger Journal für
Mode und Eleganz,* 1802

Accompanied on
the violin. *Ham-
burger Journal
für Mode und
Eleganz,* 1802

Prussian officer, 1st Regiment Dragooners, ca. 1770, by Adolf Menzel, 1851

Prussian noncommissioned officer, 1st Regiment Dragooners, ca. 1770,
by Adolf Menzel, 1851

Frederick II, by Franz Skarbina, 1881

Nürnberg *Trachten* 1680 *(left to right)*: *above*—town councilor, upper-class bride, upper-class bridegroom, typical bride, bride wearing a raincoat, unmarried woman in summer dress; *middle*—scribe, town piper, magistrate, wedding speaker, master fool, coachman; *bottom*—maid carrying presents, country maid, groom (servant), milk maid, farmer's wife, farmer.

Nürnbergischer Rathsherr — Kron Braut vom Geschlecht — Nürnbergischer Geistlicher — Marcks Vorstcher oder Vo...

Gemeine Frau auf Hochzeiten — Nürnbergerin in Regen Tuch — Eine Magd die zur Hochzeit dient — Spruch-Sprecher

Nürnberg *Trachten* 1700 *(left to right)*: *above* — councilor, upper-class bride, minister, merchant; *below* — middle-class wedding guest, woman in raincoat, maid at wedding, wedding speaker

The Legacy of Medieval and Early Modern Sumptuary Laws

THE SOCIAL CONTROL of dress and luxury consumption in Germany, as in the rest of Europe, has varied tremendously since the late Middle Ages. A variety of mechanisms were employed to regulate who would be allowed to enjoy the expensive fineries of their age. Over time, a number of agents felt themselves empowered or obliged to make these decisions. Even the kinds of pleasure allowed varied over the centuries, depending on how personal satisfaction was weighed by each society, each class, each person. Tastes responded, often unpredictably, to these incentives and prohibitions. Adjustments in the mechanism employed to regulate consumers were often matched by shifts in the definition of luxury and its political connotations. Added to these pressures were changes in the availability of resources, improvements in manufacturing technologies, and the expanded distribution of goods and information, developments that provided material possibilities around which new types of desires could develop.

In surveying historical efforts to guide and curtail the consumption of luxury goods, we must distinguish between the changing positions of supervision and subject. Sometimes the supervision and admonishment of consumers was carried out by undefined and amorphous institutions, such as public opinion or "good taste." At other times, specific government officials were empowered by municipal or state governments to monitor the dress and domestic life of citizens. It is not always possible to specify precisely who was responsible for "forcing" individuals to wear certain clothes or cook certain foods. In may cases, the surest sign that social pressures on consumers had changed was the appearance in descriptions of ordinary life of new types of goods or designs.

At first, medieval cities exercised authority over their residents through codes specifying who was allowed to wear what. As princes coalesced their authority over feudal territories, specifically urban codes were augmented by layers of state and imperial legislation, which allowed the central government to extend its rule into the day-to-day affairs of its subjects. In a dramatic shift in strategy, governments stopped prescribing the details of domestic life and instead began to use incentives for achieving its macroeconomic goals. In Germany, this redirection of policy occurred in the eighteenth century; in France and England, its origins were apparent at the beginning of the seventeenth century. The English historian, David Landes stated that sumptuary laws were "dead letters" by the end of the sixteenth century in England (James I repealed the last such ordinance in 1604).[1] France instituted a clothing ordinance for the last time in 1708.[2] The French court abandoned sumptuary regulations just as it became the standard-bearer for European aristocratic elegance and no longer had to fear the importation of foreign luxury products.[3]

By the late eighteenth century, the problem of regulating personal consumption was left to the public sphere's amorphous network of individual property owners, professional associations, clubs, families, and journals. Later, as advertising became more sophisticated, manufacturers sought to counter bourgeois society's pressure on its members to subordinate luxury to work. Direct government regulation of consumption came to an end with the demise of sumptuary laws and clothing ordinances, a legal tradition extending into antiquity. This rather remarkable shift in the policy of eighteenth-century German principalities was explained as the end of the state's obligation to secure the common welfare (the avowed aim of a cameralist political economy) and as the liberation of the individual to pursue his or her own happiness in the marketplace.

When Friedrich Bertuch's *Mode Journal* appeared in 1786, sumptuary laws were already widely perceived an ineffective means of regulating the practices of local populations. The increasing mobility of middle-class Germans—particularly young males, who during their early careers traveled between universities and government posts—augmented the expanding contact via commercial markets and written communication between German localities and the rest of Europe. Sumptuary laws were not repealed; they withered. Some remained on the books, others went into administrative review, never to be seen again. Overworked and frustrated government officials could not continue updating clothing ordinances, as they had since the late Middle Ages.[4] Society had become too complicated—too many interests weighed on lawmakers for them to effectively balance them within a coherent policy.

The *Mode Journal* promised a more flexible response to undesirable practices, one that did not intrude into personal lives with judicial force. It relied more on a rhetoric that incited emulation among readers than on the language of outraged denunciation common to so many Enlightenment moralists. Rather than advocate the abandonment of old habits, the journal urged the adoption of new ones that offered a superior domestic lifestyle. Only occasionally did it speak against an established practice without also providing a preferred, more stylish alternative. When the *Mode Journal* warned against the high cost of large funerals—a frequent target of sumptuary laws—it merely recommended the institution of voluntary associations of individuals willing to leave tradition behind.[5]

To understand the political economy operating through the *Mode Journal* and its fashion-driven system of clothing regulation, we should consider the premodern measures taken to curtail, or at least direct, luxury consumption in Germany. The mechanisms employed to contain consumption varied over the centuries, as did the goals of government policies. While modern clothing conventions do not rely upon an explicit external authority, their operation is not unlike older police laws that punished excessive ostentation as a legal crime. This similarity between modern and medieval clothing codes does not, however, lie in some universal societal tendency to enforce rank through dress, a claim that was argued for explicitly in Thorstein Veblen's *Theory of the Leisure Class* and tacitly accepted in most other sociological accounts of fashion.[6]

Different systems of regulation use similar mechanisms and applications of force. Practical problems, such as the surveillance of a large population, the preservation of systems of rank, the restriction of innovation, the preservation of tradition, and the prevention of impoverishment and indebtedness, appear in all regulatory systems, though they are not always given equal weight. Personal debt is obviously an entirely different concern in the current economy than it was even fifty years ago, let alone in the seventeenth century. The history of clothing regulation has moved through phases that, until the early nineteenth century, were quite distinct. Yet these shifts occurred within a continuous engagement between consumers and the network of limitations within which they represented themselves through dress. The terms of this engagement changed, but just as fashion culture recycles old styles, each transition involved the reapplication of older forms of control in the context of new social relations.

Central European sumptuary regulation began in the late Middle Ages with the implementation of city ordinances defining the type and amount of clothes individuals could wear or possess. Closely related to these codes were ordinances regulating such festivities as weddings, baptisms, funerals, betrothals, and church holidays. Very little luxury consumption occurred in private, away from communal life. Since celebrations inevitably included the extended family as well as guests from the community, they provided opportunities for conspicuous displays of a family's wealth and generosity. Indeed, prior to the eighteenth century, family festivities were thoroughly intertwined with the local community.[7] Expensive clothes, elaborate meals, parading musicians, performing acrobats, and the distribution of alms were part of any successful wedding. Even the poor were expected to spend ostentatiously, hence the tradition of taking up a collection from guests. City governments in such places as Cologne, Göttingen, Speyer, and Nuremberg regulated these celebrations rigorously. Along with taxation, the enforcement of building codes, the establishment of monetary conventions, marketplace regulation, fire control, and the preservation of public peace, health, and sanitation, the suppression of excessive consumption was a regular component of a medieval civil administration. Municipal codes did not distinguish between petty crimes, immorality, and dress code violations. Seemingly unrelated crimes appeared in the same paragraph of statutes.

Clothing ordinances were written unsystematically, in part because they sought to maintain local traditions by prohibiting forms of dress that diverged from forms of dress understood as the local norm. These laws were enacted in mercantile cities in an attempt to preserve a visual local identity, which according to the prefaces of most clothing ordinances was threatened with extinction. Clothing ordinances were fundamentally conservative, seeking to maintain a tradition without defining it. A 1420 law in the city of Ulm ruled that the silver and gold belts worn by residents should not be different from those from the past, sleeves should be no longer nor wider than women had always worn them, and coats should be lined with silk only in the received manner ("as has been passed along from the past"). Ordinances promulgated in Speyer in 1356 and a hundred years later in Constance also insisted on the preservation of traditional styles.[8] By writing down that which was unacceptable, medieval ordinances sought to preserve a material tradition that existed outside the legal text. Clothing ordinances do not provide information on medieval dress and behavior; they tell us only about those factors that threatened the established culture. They were a reaction against innovation, an attempt by local authorities to stymie change.

Complaints against changing dress styles were usually aimed at the introduction of garments from other localities. To stem the tide of innovation, city councils would forbid tailors to use anything but old patterns for cutting clothes, but such methods were not always effective. In 1596, the Leipzig *Rat* despaired of keeping up with the changes that appeared every few years in "Trachten und der Zeug" (clothing and its adornments).[9] The increased travel and commerce between trading centers, which the decline of the plague made possible, enabled decorative styles to be shared by previously isolated localities. Even a marriage between partners from different cities posed a potential challenge to the sartorial order. Whether a wife was permitted to wear the dress of her hometown once she had moved to her husband's city was a serious legal matter. Town councils would consult with one another to become familiar with the other's laws and customs. Once the exchange of legal information began, the potential for complicated cases only increased. For example, a wife's claim to the right to wear a particular cap might lie outside the jurisdiction of the court in her husband's town, and therefore her claim would be referred to the *Rat* of her hometown. Delays in travel and communication only aggravated the legal complexities.

This conserving character is brought out most clearly by the fact that new ordinances were enacted with every new generation: every twenty to twenty-five years a new set of proclamations were read from pulpits and in marketplaces, announcing a new set of prohibitions.[10] Marc Raeff argued that the frequency with which these laws were promulgated corresponded to the rhythms of oral culture, in which personal memory and recitation were the primary vehicles for transmitting information.[11] Sumptuary laws struggled against forgetfulness regarding the past, the tendency to let old practices disappear when their proponents died. The erosion of old norms allowed for the (re)introduction of styles considered impossible twenty years before.

This dynamic is obvious in the cyclical movement of modern fashion as much as it was reflected in the generational reiteration of sumptuary laws. In premodern society, forgetfulness manifested itself as a repeated attempt to avoid restrictions of luxurious dress. In modern society, forgetfulness allows for the cyclical rediscovery of styles considered ugly twenty years before. Historians who have concluded that sumptuary laws were ineffective simply because they were revised and updated every few years have failed to understand how tenuous the conventions of oral cultures were over time. Repetition played an important stabilizing function in preliterate society, a fact often forgotten by scholars engaged in close comparisons of written legislation. Only when laws were no longer reissued every few decades could one speak of a decline in the sumptuary order of dress. Regular restatements of sumptuary laws also allowed urban authorities to incorporate new groups within the medieval city's tight-knit political structure.

New clothing ordinances were markers of a shifting cultural topography, indicating realignments of status and taste on a level almost undetectable from our historical distance. They suggest generational and social conflicts too poorly documented or too subtle for us to reconstruct. The struggles brought on by local migrations, urban political factions, contiguous neighborhoods, competing professions, tenuous guild hierarchies, and stubborn age differences were sometimes too "insignificant" to be registered in any written form other than the regulation of local customs.

The format of the earliest sumptuary laws treated the urban population as a single unit. Therefore, alterations in the political order of a city required complete revision of the legal text. Each law presented a new code for the entire population. City fathers discriminated only between those who had a right to live within the city walls and those who were obliged to leave before nightfall. In the earliest German city codes, differences in rank were drawn primarily on the basis of residence. A Göttingen law from before 1340 applied to "our citizens and those who live with us."[12] Ordinances set standards that determined the overall appearance of a city, thereby preserving the visual identity of their citizens.[13] Political struggles beyond the city walls, between competing princes or a warring nobility, did not touch the codification of social identity.

When distinctions did appear in the laws, they were drawn without reference to genealogy or noble rank. A 1436 dress ordinance, for example, acknowledged only a gender distinction. Its rules cut across such class boundaries as would have existed in a medieval city: "All women, virgins, maids here in Constance, rich and poor, none excepted" were included in its domain.[14] When class distinctions were acknowledged, as in a 1341 Osnabrück regulation on the size of wedding banquets, the division was drawn on a simple economic basis. Brides with a dowry of more than a hundred marks were allowed more guests at their weddings than those with a smaller dowry. Even here, the municipality's interest was primarily economic rather than hierarchical. The prefaces of many sumptuary laws explicitly stated that their intention was to prevent citizens from accumulating insurmountable debt through ostentatious banquets. As long as families could demonstrate their ability to pay for a large wedding, they were free to do so.[15]

Separation of gender was justified on moral and religious, rather than economic, grounds. A 1356 ordinance in Speyer, the city in which Holy Roman emperors were buried, prohibited women from wearing male overgarments. In Strasbourg in 1493 women were forbidden to wear "Knabenmentel" (knave's coats). The city of Zittau required the servant girls of the town executioner to wear men's hoods, thereby ensuring that no other woman would want to wear them. Men were banned from wearing women's caps and from greasing their hair in the manner of women.[16] A Nuremberg code from the late fourteenth century stipulated that "the native citizen, be he old or young, shall not part his hair; he shall gather his locks as has been done since the old times." Parted hair, according to the code, was reserved for women.[17]

The distinctions between masculine and feminine dress were not based upon any biologically derived notion of identity; rather, they were defined within a heterogeneous collection of traditions and religious teachings, which lasted well into the early modern period.[18] Gottlieb Sigmund Corvinus's 1739 definition of *hermaphrodite* provided a convention for the public display of gender identity. Although Corvinus wrote long after medieval codes had been superseded, the regulation of gender in its outward appearance was fairly consistent throughout the premodern period because it did not touch upon the central axes of political power. Religious and moral arguments invoked by medieval city councils to justify a gendered separation in dress codes were not significantly altered once princely states began to centralize police authority.[19] Corvinus's seemingly pragmatic approach to establishing the identity of individuals born with male and female genital organs reflects a premodern interest in maintaining visible identities, paying only cursory attention to the particulars of the body beneath the clothes. In a lexicon written to introduce female readers to the complexities of gallant social convention, he defined *hybrid*, or *hermaphrodite*, as "someone who has female as well as male genitals. Such a person must select one of the two classes. Once he [sic] has chosen one, he must hold to it and conduct himself accordingly."[20] The hermaphrodite posed little threat to the conventional order of gender appearance and behavior as long as she or he conformed to one dress tradition or the other. Adopting a sexual identity was much like marrying—a choice was implied, but once it had been made, a consistent mode of behavior was mandatory.

The enforcement of clothing ordinances in medieval cities required a network of surveillance and informers commonly associated with modern states. On the streets and in the marketplace, burghers were constantly exposed to the observation of their fellow citizens, who were not above enforcing sumptuary standards themselves. Even as late as the mid-eighteenth century, there were reports of common women in Munich having their gold trimmed bonnets (*Hauben*) torn from their heads while leaving church because they were not entitled to decorate themselves with precious metals.[21] The Nordlingen ordinance of 1467 promised a reward of up to one half of the amount of the fine to anyone reporting a violation.[22] Council members, as well as the *Sittenpolizei*, were responsible for observing the citizenry. Since most premodern luxury consumption occurred in the form of ostentatious displays during family celebrations such as weddings, baptisms, betrothals, and funerals, members of the community were always potential witnesses. Neighborly denunciations surely were often vindictive. Bribery would have also been common. A 1540 Berlin and Cologne ordinance specified that weddings be supervised by a constable, paid by the host, to ensure that no regulations were violated during the celebration.[23] In Osnabrück, the town cook was called in to inspect the ingredients used in preparing a wedding feast.[24] From the buckles on shoes to the fabric of bonnets, municipal laws presumed the existence of an enforcement mechanism that scrutinized every citizen. Nuremberg laws went so far as to mandate that men wear scarves around their necks and to specify the exact width and length of their saddle blankets.[25]

Even if enforcement was impossible, the mere codification of these rules demonstrates a municipal interest in regulating the appearance and practices of its citizenry. The control of "wasteful" consumption was not the only issue; these laws sought to codify the representation of identity, to define an individual, such as a married woman born to Göttingen. Over time, the garments associated with that identity would change, and thus new ordinances would be enacted. Small towns practice a loose form of such regulation to this day.

Legislative control over luxury consumption entered a new phase in the last years of the fifteenth century. Whereas medieval ordinances were broad and had few distinctions, the sumptuary laws promulgated by princes during the sixteenth and seventeenth centuries multiplied the number and degree of distinctions, increasing fantastically the information contained within one law. These distinctions were made comprehensible only because the later laws were organized more systematically than the municipal codes. The transformation usually appeared in the form of complaints about the demise of traditional distinctions. In addition to the usual concerns over "the extremely damaging vice of pomp," the burgomaster and town council of Villigen, for example, felt called upon to preserve the visible differences in rank "which God and all propriety requires, without which also the political harmony and the commonwealth of continued well-being would no longer exist."[26] Municipal authorities were concerned that clothes had been misused in such a manner that people of rank had been misrecognized. Throughout Germany, the prefaces to most sixteenth- and seventeenth-century codes announced their intention to regulate appearances, both in persons and in festivities, according to hierarchy.

Initially, the distinctions were few, but over time they increased dramatically. The 1516 marriage ordinance in Osnabrück, for example, divided the population into distinct groups, marking the beginning of a trend. By 1648, the city's residents were legally divided into four classes of quality, and the ability to afford a luxurious garment or a large wedding was no longer relevant. In 1506, Leipzig divided men into two classes and women into four, with an allowance made for the traditional costume worn by doctors and academics.[27] And while most ordinances arranged clothing privileges into three divisions, the 1660 Strasbourg code organized the populace into six ranks and subdivided the highest two into further groups.[28]

The impetus for these measures came from outside the municipality. Throughout the fifteenth century and again after the Thirty Years' War, princely authorities waged campaigns to organize the minute affairs of social life.[29] The first German law to draw a separation between high- and low-born dress was passed in Saxony in 1482.[30] City records still have a letter dated January 14, 1478, from the Saxon Kurfürst Ernst to the city council, in which he criticized the municipality for failing to control extravagance among its inhabitants and insisted that measures be taken so that the traditional *Stände* would be preserved and visibly recognizable. The *Reichstage* in Lindau (1497), Freiburg (1498), and Augsburg (1500) soon followed suit. Noble distinctions in dress were announced in an imperial police ordinance in 1530 and elaborated upon in the 1548, because "the expense of clothes among knights, nobility, burghers, and farmers has so very much taken the upper hand." The framers complained that money spent on "foreign" (presumably French, Italian, and Burgundian) clothes led to the impoverishment of entire regions and the dissolution of ranks:

> Not only particular persons, but also entire regions, have had their subsistence reduced and devalued because an effusion of money has been sent out of the German nation for gold cloth, velvet, damask, satin, exotic fabrics, expensive birettas, pearls, and gold ounces, which now serve in the making of extravagant clothes. Envy, hatred, and indignation have also been awakened, contrary to all Christian love. These extravagances have been used with such a lack of restraint that no distinction can be recognized between princes and counts, counts and noblemen, noblemen and burghers, burghers and farmers.[31]

While the Holy Roman Empire's clothing regulations provided a model for the legislation, the administrative initiative for regulating consumption remained with the principalities.[32] The introduction of noble distinctions in clothing ordinances marked the beginning of the modern state's interest in centralized economic regulation. By introducing ordinances covering regions outside the authority of medieval cities and by insisting that urban codes reflect a feudal hierarchy of distinction in dress and ostentation, centralized bureaucracies consolidated control over the various legal authorities within the princely territories. The sumptuary laws of the absolutist era superseded the traditions unique to each city.

In absolutist society, clothing functioned as signs of a person's rank within the corporate *Stände*.[33] Each social group was assigned an array of garments and decorations with which to portray themselves before others. In addition, politically influential classes could acquire the specific right to wear garments or accouterments to convey an extra degree of status. Sumptuary laws enforced the correspondence between signifier and signified. Privileges and special distinctions increased as the corporate system of rank developed; feudal law changed and expanded through a patchwork of legislation. Privileges might lapse and be revived or might be replaced by another set of laws. As the number of distinctions increased, so did the number of sartorial privileges. The "police" were obliged to preserve the integrity of an increasing number of signs.

A 1680 illustration of Nuremberg *Trachten* (native costumes) arranged each figure according to rank, the *Rathsherr* (town councillor) at the upper left of a grid, the ordinary farmer at the bottom right. Each figure stood in relation to the others; none was outside the hierarchy. The centrality of ceremonies in establishing rank was brought out by the fact that most of the figures were depicted as they would have been dressed for a wedding. The print included several figures who would have had prominent ceremonial roles in a wedding (the town piper and the master fool). A 1700 illustration concentrated on the costumes worn by guests at a wedding; occupational garb was left out, as if the illustrator wanted to represent only ceremonial costume. These illustrations did not function as fashion plates that viewers might have sought to imitate; rather, they represented splendor. They were visual reminders of the wealth and finery of the Nuremberg elite and did not demonstrate the "newness" of any garment. Fashionableness in the modern sense tended to work against clothing's representational function. New luxuries had the unfortunate effect of confusing the established code, because when they first appeared in public they lacked a clear reference to rank. The correlation between garb and privilege that organized the corporate system was brought out by the text under a print of two gentlemen accompanying a Nuremberg bride, stating that the city had for many years enjoyed the Holy Roman Emperor's favor and that, therefore, the bride wore a crown rich in pearls. Her headdress was both an effect and a sign of the bestowal of imperial honor. The bride's representational function included, therefore, both her family and the city. Through her right to wear a pearl crown (undoubtedly reserved only for the urban elite), the bride became a sign for Nuremberg's wealth and its privileged place within the Holy Roman Empire.

The incremental refinements and reformulations in the clothing ordinances of the sixteenth and seventeenth centuries brought diverse groups under a single authority. Medieval city codes had governed a nonaristocratic populace, for the nobility rarely resided within a city's walls for any length of time. Furthermore, urban authorities never had the legitimacy to regulate aristocratic privilege. Princely codes managed, or at least asserted the right, to regulate the urban populace as well as the lesser nobility. These laws followed a twofold strategy: to defend aristocratic privileges, while the centralizing legal authority guaranteed them. The new absolutist ordinances generally exempted the court nobility and the highest princely servants from the rules applied to the general population. However, they carefully distinguished between royal or ducal prerogatives and those enjoyed by the rest of the court.

At first implicitly and later in direct terms, dress codes drew limits on the nobility's right to compete with the monarch. Certain forms of ostentatious display were reserved strictly for the monarch. For example, in Brandenburg, only members of the Kurfürst family were allowed to wear cloth laced with gold and silver, to decorate their servants with gold chain, and to cover the cushions in their carriages with velvet and silk.[34] The splendor of the royal household set the standard; it also secured the privileges granted each rank, through its jealous preservation of monarchical rights. Because the prince displayed his power through spectacular ceremonies and dress, claimants to social prestige felt compelled to perform variations on the same theme, and yet, because the monarch reserved certain privileges to himself, all other classes were empowered to guard their own rights.

The monarch's spectacular display of wealth was suffused with power. Norbert Elias has shown how Louis XIV's levees functioned as a means for distributing favors and admonishing political rivals.[35] The elaborate choreography involved in dressing the monarch, the order in which aristocrats were allowed to enter his bedchamber, their position around his bed, and their proximity to his clothes and his body all were signs of power and were understood by all others present. Outside the exclusive context of the princely palace, larger spectacles involving clothes and other luxury objects associated with the monarch's body were staged so as to make the strongest possible visual impression upon the gathered audience. Meals were traditionally an occasion for displaying the monarch's abundant wealth. The vast array of food, the expensive tableware, and the important guests were visual testaments to the monarch's power. In these celebrations, monarchical power was shown to overflow the normal bounds of behavior.

The ceremonies of consumption constituted a triangular relationship, wherein the monarch's physical possession of luxury goods signified the more abstract possession of power and legitimacy. Legitimacy was understood within this framework as distinct from power; the luxuries surrounding the monarch joined the two in his person. The seventeenth-century philosopher and cameralist Christian Wolff wrote:

> If the subjects are to recognize the majesty of the king, they must recognize that in him resides the highest force and power. Accordingly, it is necessary that a king and sovereign establish his household, so that one has occasion to recognize his force and power.[36]

Recognition, in the political sense of acknowledging authority, was equated with the sensual, primarily visual, recognition of splendor. Wolff regretted the importance of images, yet he acknowledged their effectiveness in securing popular acceptance:

> The common man, who relies on his senses and can hardly use his reason, may not be able to grasp what the king's majesty is; however, through things that spring into sight and that move the other senses, he receives an indistinct, yet clear concept of his majesty, or force and power.[37]

Jürgen Kruedener argued that, over the course of time, the obligations of ceremonial luxury overruled the traditional privileges of noble rank. Citing a Bavarian source, *Mundus Christiana-bravard-politicus*, Kruedener argued that the mere possession of a noble title did not establish political credibility. Once the princely courts of the absolutist era had established the rituals of ostentation, it became a requirement that all contenders for political power participate:

> Distinguished birth and title did not suffice alone . . . to preserve the greatness of princes, "especially if they sought to achieve greater ends than others": hence the prominence of honorary ornaments, splendor, and magnificence at princely courts. These are the only means for making a prince renowned among foreigners and for creating greater obedience and respect among his subjects.[38]

Daniel Roche noted that a similar process of erosion in France began as the public ceremonial took on a greater role in political life and the neatly divided ranks explicitly defined in sumptuary laws became less important. From the perspective of the court nobility, the pressure to imitate the king overruled any interest in preserving traditional aristocratic costumes.[39]

Recognition and submission to princely authority meant not only a willingness to respect his privileges but also the nobility's participation in courtly ceremonies. Elizabeth I and Louis XIV manipulated the leading nobility by enmeshing them within expensive and time-consuming rituals. As McKendrick, Brewer, and Plumb explained:

> The famous extravagance of Queen Elizabeth's wardrobe fulfilled a very political need. It was the visible external proof of her divinity; it buttressed her political power; and her courtiers were expected to buttress it further with a spectacular display of satellite finery.[40]

The system effectively produced an economy of prestige, which required the leading figures of the land to spend virtually all their resources in a competitive display of luxury. Elias's study of courtly society provided a thorough account of how the cultivation of appearances through etiquette overtook the older feudal system of ranks. A patent of nobility was a prerequisite for participating in elite society; however, without regular participation in the beau monde, no aristocrat would know the proper form to give to his exalted status.[41] Resistance to the court's attractions inevitably resulted in banishment from the mechanisms that established social prestige. The intense concentration on the court—the fact that all decisions filtered through its labyrinthian channels—resulted in a de facto redefinition of social classes. Karin Plodeck argued that the court's administration over resources produced three new groupings: (1) nobility attached to the court, (2) commoners involved with the court, and (3) commoners excluded from the court.[42]

The baroque court was organized in such a manner that the monarch was always situated at its head, almost as a godhead.[43] The fundamental tenet of courtly ritual was that no person was permitted to in any way exceed the king. Elias noted that the French encyclopedists included this rule in their discussion of architecture. The palatial "hotels" of the "grand seigneurs" should be built in a grandiose manner befitting the owners' exalted rank, they wrote; however, these structures must never exhibit the magnificence reserved for the king.[44] The monarch's judicial legitimacy was also established through dramatic public executions, in which the king's anointed representatives overwhelmed and crushed the body of the offending criminal. Michel Foucault recounted how in 1757 the regicide Damiens was put to death in a lengthy ceremony: his flesh was torn off with red-hot pincers, and his wounds were doused with molten lead, boiling oil, burning resin, wax, and sulphur.[45] Eventually, he was drawn and quartered by four horses, and his limbs were burned to ashes, which were then scattered in the air. What seems barbarian and almost unimaginable to modern sensibilities was, Foucault argued, a public drama to secure the authority of the monarch. "The public execution . . . has a juridico-political function. It is a ceremonial by which a momentarily injured sovereignty is reconstituted."[46] Wolff explained the political implications of ceremonial punishments in much the same way:

> Precisely because the punishment, by showing the criminal, is supposed to serve as an example to others so that they may be moved to guard against committing similar crimes and to gain an aversion against them, the spectator must be given an opportunity to vividly imagine not only the disgrace of the crime but also the earnestness with which the authorities punish it. Since they serve such an end, suitable ceremonies must be invented to carry out the prosecution, condemnation, and execution of the sentence.[47]

While judicial punishments have received much critical attention since Foucault's study, there is no question that the greatest energies were devoted to the production of celebratory spectacles. The fantastical fetes at Versailles were highly complex arrangements; a single performance was orchestrated at great expense and required the finest artists. The scale and duration of these events far exceeded the measures taken to kill a single criminal; thus, they provided an apparently limitless opportunity to glorify royal superiority. The 1674 commemoration of Burgundy's submission to France lasted six days. The evening of the first day began with a meal in the Bosquet du Marais. This was followed by an opera performed in the Cour de Marbre, which had been illuminated and decorated with orange trees and flowers. The open-air performance was based on a libretto by Quinault and a musical score by Lully. It was followed with a *souper de medianoche* in the palace and then with a ball, which lasted through the night.

On the second day, a structure made entirely of lace was erected in the Garden des Trianon, wherein "Eglogue de Versailles," an intermedium by

Lully and Quinault, was performed. The subsequent *souper* was taken on a floating island in the Grand Canal. The island was surrounded by twenty-three water streams. On the third evening was a meal in the menagerie, followed by a procession, to music, down the brightly illuminated canal, and concluding with a performance of Molière's "Malade Imaginaire." The fourth night was celebrated with a meal—served on three levels among 160 fruit trees—which included 120 baskets of pastries, 400 dishes of iced dessert, and 1,000 carafes of liquor. Fountains were on display during the meal. In another section of the park was a fete celebrating Amor and Bacchus. Following a torch-lit procession, accompanied by fireworks, the celebrants retired to the Cour de Marbre for a *souper*.

On the fifth night, a production of Racine's "Iphigénie" in the orangerie was followed by a magical illumination of the Grand Canal, arranged by the court painter, Le Brun. Out of the canal's midst arose an obelisk of light; on its peak was a brilliant sun, and at its base was a majestic dragon. Submissive captives paraded before the triumphant king. Suddenly, 1,500 firecrackers exploded, the canal and the surrounding fountains poured forth streams of water, and the dragon spewed fire and smoke from its mouth and nostrils. Then 5,000 rockets shot into the air above the canal, forming a cathedral of light before falling to the earth in a shower of sparkles. The last night was particularly dark and still; at one o'clock A.M. the entire park at Versailles was illuminated. Terraces, lawns, water basins, and canals were filled with small glowing pearls. The fountains flowed quietly, the canal was as still as a mirror. At its far end stood the facade of a magical palace. The entire court stepped onto gondolas accompanied by the figure of Neptune, who led his guests across the water to the palace, where music and dances were performed into the night.[48]

The iconography of the Versailles celebration—its allegorical representation of French dominance and its mythical portrayal of the monarch as Neptune—sent a clear message to the community present. Louis XIV appeared in an earthly guise as a conqueror and in a classical form as the god Neptune. The gardens themselves were an important aspect of the celebration: as stylized constructions of earth, fauna, and water, they represented the monarch's dominion over natural forces.[49] Furthermore, the celebration's movement through the garden would have been seen as a reenactment of France's takeover of Burgundian territory.

These grand festivals differed from executions in that they were reserved for the immediate members of the court. Other aristocrats learned of the festivities through acquaintances, letters, or the *Mercure Galante*, the most important aristocratic periodical in Europe. By limiting participation to a few qualified, or favored, individuals, the court did not necessarily remove itself from the public eye. If carried out successfully, the gala's exclusivity served to heighten the belief that the court embodied the height of political power. And even when the court was not engaged in specific celebrations, it was generating an ongoing festival. Virtually no room or activity was removed from the pageantry. Whatever lay beyond, was nonexistent.[50]

In his famous study of baroque festivals, Richard Alewyn wrote that "the life of the court is a total celebration. Within its confines, there is nothing but celebration; apart from it, there is no ordinary existence, no work, only empty time and boredom."[51] One implication of this inward focus was disregard of financial considerations.[52] Just as important, the court's neglect of all that did not fit its gala atmosphere tended to draw other activities into its orbit. The brilliant example was irresistible; the sight of so much splendor evoked a desire to lessen the distance between oneself and the prince. Just as certain German dukes and electors mimicked the French monarch at Versailles, so did the lesser nobility and upper middle class in Germany seek to emulate their princely masters.

Unlike public executions, the point of exclusive ceremonies was not the production of respect and fear; rather, they sought to compel onlookers to invest themselves in a hierarchical network of daily obligations derived from tradition and adapted by the centralized state.[53] Ambition would certainly lead some to seek higher rank and greater privileges, yet advancement was possible only through the largesse of the king. From the grandest duke on down, the display of monarchical authority was intended to elicit obedience to the status quo. Any shift in the vertical arrangement of power and prestige at Versailles required the sanction of the king. The carefully constructed rituals, the pageants, and the daily routine of etiquette served to display the shifting relative position of each courtier. Where a nobleman stood in a procession, his place in a dance, a noblewoman's relation to the queen—all these trifles were interpreted as signs of where each person stood in relation to the pinnacle of authority. Elias drew a correspondence between ceremonies and political favor:

A shift in the hierarchy that was not reflected in a change of etiquette could not occur. Conversely, the slightest change in people's position in etiquette meant a change in the order of rank at court and within court society. And, for this reason, each individual was hypersensitive to the slightest change in the mechanism, stood watch over the existing order, attended to its finest nuances, unless he happened to be trying to change it to his own advantage. In this way . . . the court mechanism revolved in perpetual motion, fed by the need for prestige and the tensions which, once they were there, it endlessly renewed by its competitive process.[54]

If viewed over an extended period of time, the etiquette of the court was more than a representation of prestige and favor; rather, it amounted to the actual exercise of political power. The court at Versailles, and those of its many Central European imitators, drew economic and political forces into its machinations so thoroughly that one would be hard pressed to find at the highest levels of the state administration a distinction between the exercise of political power and ceremony. All that mattered happened in the king's presence; hence, important decisions could not be decided except in relation to how they positioned a courtier within the king's highly ritualized vicinity.

Kirstiaan Aercke has warned that "it would be fallacious to assume these feasts were merely so many forms of political discourse; they were also, quite simply, festive celebrations, elaborate games, forms of play for a limited number of players."[55] However, it has been difficult for interpreters accustomed to the universalizing claims of modern art not to read these events in terms other than the pleasure they provided participants. Aercke's point seemed to be directed at traditional art historians, whose analysis rests on the details in portraiture—or in this case, gala performances. However, political interpretations do not rely on interpreting every nuance of a theatrical event. If we step back from the festival's events, we might add another dimension to our understanding. In addition to the code of political meanings embedded in court festivals are the formal dynamics of exclusion and inclusion. The question of who participated and in what manner would have been very important to courtiers attending a masque or an opera.

Indeed, one might claim that the actual events of the gala fade as one considers the question of who participated. Members of the court might worry about the semiotics of the performance, but those excluded were more likely to focus on the question of who was permitted to enter the festivities in the first place. The court's control over who had access to the king was a central mechanism for exercising political power. The internal dynamics of the court—the complicated formality of the king's morning routine, for example—extended the overall strategy, which understood the exercise of political power as a matter of maintaining distance between the ruler and his subjects. The many types of spectacle generated around the absolute monarch—from beheadings to birthdays—manipulated the populace's desire to see the king as the wellspring of all social good and their fear before his seemingly unlimited control over their fates once they drew close.

The rise of the princely court as the exclusive site of ostentatious display went hand in hand with the new, stricter regulation of consumption. As many eighteenth-century commentators noted, the representation of rank through luxuries was highly unstable, because it was always possible for low-ranking members of society to acquire the material signs of the elite without possessing the legal authority to own or wear them. This problem was most acute in large cities such as London and Paris, and thus the earliest portrayals of class emulation emerged from these quarters.[56] In Germany, the courts were perhaps small enough to be supervised, but there were so many of them that it was possible for individuals masquerading as nobility to move from one to another, acquiring an income and title along the way. German lore and literature is filled with tales of connivers who deceive a locality into accepting them as nobility on the basis of their refined appearance, dress, and manners.[57] Adolph von Knigge was particularly vituperative in describing such courtiers:

> Wherever there is a rich widow to be married, a pension or office to be had at any court, they are quickly on the scent. They baptise themselves, give themselves titles, recreate themselves as often as they please and as the matter in hand requires. What they cannot pull off as a simple nobleman, they attempt as a marquis or an abbé or an officer.[58]

Sumptuary laws represented the negative formulation of a social system bent on the affirmation of symbolic authority. They sought to prevent transgressions against upper-class privileges. They did not, however, function merely as instruments of repression. By defining what was forbidden, they also clarified what was permissible. The absolutist hierarchical codification of dress distinctions created and maintained the visual proof of differences between classes, something that had not occurred in medieval city codes, which sought to preserve the continuity of tradition against loss of memory and the importation of foreign styles. The spectacle of the court only spurred on the populace's inclination for ostentation, which in turn heightened the state's concern over the indebtedness of the lower classes, particularly after the Thirty Years' War. To justify clamping down on luxury, statutes increasingly invoked the economic dangers of consumption. But while the monarch was legally the richest and most powerful figure, the classes beneath him sought to maintain their own privileges by spending and consuming up to the legal limits of their ranks—and then just a little more. One German court, the Prussian royal household in Berlin, did manage to curtail luxury consumption among its affluent citizens, and the Hohenzollerns, renowned for their frugality, were held up as having eschewed representational ostentation in favor of an ideology of individual worth.[59]

Absolutist codes acknowledged the pressure citizens felt to display their worth in material terms. Even honest, industrious citizens, officials surmised, sought to secure their reputations by spending more than they could afford.[60] Just like courtiers, the lower middle class as well as successful farmers had developed a feeling for the status and importance attributed to persons through wealth. While they could not build houses on the scale of counts, nor dress in the grand style of a French aristocrat, ordinary citizens could spend lavishly enough on specific occasions to impress their neighbors. Like the nobility, they were subject to a system that revolved around the visible representation of wealth and status.[61]

The intervention of the state into their competition did not stifle the terms by which the lower classes interpreted one another's rank; rather, it enhanced their awareness of small details and big spending. By setting strict limits on festive displays, absolutist regulators reasoned that ordinary people would be spared the obligation to spend their way out of neighborly contempt. Stricter enforcement of distinctions, the ordinances claimed, would end the pressure on each class to compete within itself by emulating those above.[62] Yet paradoxically, sumptuary laws reinforced and extended the system that measured individuals by their representative material objects. Just as the rules of etiquette provided a set of coordinates with which courtiers measured their status in relation to others, sumptuary laws became a scale for weighing the relative value of each person, a set of thresholds that allowed minute distinctions and that recorded the slightest acts of symbolic aggression.[63] The efforts to curtail largesse had the effect of setting a standard, a minimum that provided everyone a yardstick for judging the ceremonial enactment of rank.

Police codes defined the scope and scale of family ceremonies with an impressive thoroughness. The Margrave of Brandenburg had by the seventeenth century a very precise notion of how his subjects should celebrate weddings, one that they could just as readily invoke to evaluate the luxuriousness of their neighbors' *Feste*. In an ordinance from the late seventeenth century covering weddings celebrated in Berlin and the adjacent town of Cologne, limits were set on the number of guests, the number of tables, the celebration's duration (the exact time when it was to begin and end), the number of out-of-town guests who might be fed, when they were to arrive and return home, the length of the church service, when a torch might be carried at the head of the bridal procession (in winter only), and the number of times the bride and groom could appear on the *Rathaus* steps. The law also required that all dancing be supervised for immorality.

The bridal soup was not to be given to beggars. (It was noted that sometimes half an ox was wasted this way.) The monetary value of tips to be given to the church organist and other persons running the church ceremony were stipulated; furthermore, these persons were prohibited from joining in the wedding banquet. The number of groomsmen was restricted, as were the gifts given to them. Wedding guests were not to be invited to the bathhouse. Brides were permitted to give a gift of one shirt each to the groom, his father, and his brothers but not to her sisters' husbands or their children. The number of wreaths worn by celebrants was set by law, as was the amount of gold used in putting them together. A police constable was to be paid to be present during the entire celebration, but he was not permitted to remain at the banquet past nine at night. The host was required to negotiate with the constable regarding the number of musicians permitted. The musicians were not allowed to perform in front of the tables where the guests were seated. Children were allowed to sing up to four songs, but they were required to be in school by one in the afternoon. Alms could be given to the poor but only on the night before the wedding. Tips for the cook, kitchen help, dishwasher, and doorman were prescribed. Children were not permitted to enter the house once the wedding guests were inside. And, finally, only local citizens were permitted to dance—out-of-town guests were not.[64] This ordinance was far more detailed than earlier codes. Its complexity was heightened by the distinctions drawn between what was permitted to the various ranks. It did not seek to simply curtail activities considered excessive or dangerous; it set specific levels of acceptable behavior for each class, establishing a grammar of permissible forms of expression.

While the modern notion of police power is limited to public security, in the absolutist period the term included a far broader field of regulation, one that state bureaucracies had taken over from medieval municipalities and had extended. Within this tradition, the regulation of clothes and celebrations was an important responsibility but was by no means the only intervention into daily life. Over the course of the sixteenth and seventeenth centuries, an ever-increasing array of laws were introduced. The state assumed the right to impose all regulations necessary for providing the comforts and necessities of the nation, with the avowed goal the well-being of society. However, the ordinances also had a political aim. Police laws controlled by the local nobility, because they generally fell outside the jurisdiction of traditional courts, enhanced the ability of the princely administration to redefine the inherited feudal structure.[65] In the seventeenth and early-eighteenth centuries, police laws covered virtually every activity not within the local nobility's patrimonial authority. Johann Jacob Möser defined them as "those laws that do not concern judicial matters, contracts, or inheritances . . . but instead are supposed to serve as a legal guide for common life, business, and trade in general."[66] At the beginning of the eighteenth century, police laws were oriented in two directions: the bureaucracy's internal coherence and the external propagation of social order. These two realms were to be harmonized by systematic reforms that sought to align administrative operation with policies encouraging the production of wealth. Both of these reform directions tended to eliminate guild-oriented ordinances on manufacture and consumption inherited from the medieval period. Eighteenth-century *Polizeiwissenschaft* (police science) avowed the need to eliminate the "blind observance" of "idiotic guild customs."[67]

The broad concern for social welfare implicit in police regulation of all public life was radically constricted in the eighteenth century by cameralist theorists such as Joseph von Sonnenfels and Johann Heinrich Gottlob von Justi.[68] Theories suggesting the ability of civil society to regulate itself led centralized authorities to abandon the principal responsibility for preserving the public well-being. Administrative experiences suggested that all dress prescriptions had a potential to be misunderstood and misapplied. These frustrations were coupled with arguments against medieval codes.[69] Instead of regulating the minutiae of social life, police authority was constrained to the modern understanding of maintaining the peace. The Prussian *Allgemeine Landrecht* set public security, not the creation of the common good, as the goal of police power. According to Hans Boldt, "measures required for the preservation of public peace, security, and order, as well as the defense of the public or its single members against immediate danger [was] the office of the police."[70] Adam Smith's free market economic theory was a factor only at the very end of the century; Christian Garve's 1794 translation of *The Wealth of Nations* was the first to catch the attention of German readers.

In liberal legal histories, the eighteenth-century reform period was represented as the last phase in the history of sumptuary legislation. However, the corollary—that the restructuring of police laws eliminated the supervision of clothing—is far from true, for when the German principalities ceased to regulate consumer ostentation, that responsibility was adopted by another, less clearly defined but nevertheless omnipotent, institution: society. Once the management of luxury and dress style was no longer carried out by judicial authority, it was secured—even more effectively—by a fashion discourse that integrated clothing, psychology, and the body within an economy of production. Central to the effectiveness of this new mode of determining consumer behavior was its ideological critique of the court and its understanding of identity. The absolutist presumption that dress and ceremony represented an individual's rank was countered by new systems for determining value through economic and biological labor. The contradiction between symbolic displays of wealth and their economic cost, which had plagued police ordinances of the past, was buried by a discourse that subordinated sartorial representation to the newly "active" physical body and mental spirit. According to the new fashion ideology accompanying this reappraisal of personal appearance, fanciful display was judged to be immoral, unhealthy, unmanly, and aesthetically disharmonious.

Without the demise of police codes, this new system of regulation imposed by the administrative and economic elite upon itself could never have come into being, for its effectiveness depended upon the presumption that all members of society would conform voluntarily to the new code. The regulatory force of fashion operated through a notion of subjectivity that was not derived from social rank. Bourgeois conformity in dress arose from the paradoxical conceit that fashionable individuals acted of their own accord. Even the most self-conscious slave to fashion, such as the dandy, asserted a unique and, according to Baudelaire, heroic individuality because the underlying presumption was that all individuals enter the domain of self-representation freely. The dandy's absolute conformity to the reigning style inevitably enhanced his image. His conformity led others to so strongly associate him with the system that regulated dress and consumption that he was held responsible for its operation. As Beau Brummel noted, the cardinal rule of all good taste is to never stand out.

Even though police laws no longer applied to the domestic practices of daily life, the application of regulatory force upon consumption intensified over time. A sharper and more subtle system developed. Cameralists had often pointed out that police laws were most effective when they motivated citizens to obey rather than when they compelled them through threat of force. However, in the period coterminous with the end of sumptuary legislation, the *Mode Journal* actualized that regulative force that could motivate consumer conformity within a regulatory network.

In his preface to the journal's first issue, Bertuch stated explicitly that the *Mode Journal* provided an effective alternative to police laws. A critically evaluative fashion journal, he argued, could increase consumption while organizing it within specific pedagogical and economic regimes. The moral and economic hazards of luxury were personal ruin and unfavorable balance of trade, but his journal would instruct readers on the manner and degree of luxury appropriate to their occupation ("hand them the proper measuring stick").[71] At the same time, the journal could induce the consumer demand necessary to sustain domestic manufacturing. Bertuch's model of organizing consumption was more wide ranging than sumptuary laws because it brought the individual into a network rather than simply prohibiting certain behaviors. The *Mode Journal* created a fashion culture that coordinated the production of commodities and the rules governing their use and enjoyment.

A series of articles published in the *Mode Journal* described the effectiveness of police laws and other state measures to control consumption. In praising Prussian control of foreign luxury goods, the anonymous female author also implicitly mapped the limitations of economic and criminal disincentives to consume:

> Actually, many Berliners would do more in the way of luxury; some charming foreign fashion ware would certainly tempt the ordinary Berliner for once to not let his left hand know what his right is doing; however, the excise taxes and customs charges applied to everything foreign are out of proportion compared to other countries. The Berliner thinks it over, resignedly turns his desiring eyes from the alluring object, and falls back into formation with his dear old sense of economy. His wife reads in the *Mode Journal* that her sisters along the Danube and the Rhine are wearing French linen and English muslin.—"O dearest husband, I would so very much like a little muslin dress!" "Of course, dear child, but the custom duties!" And Madame continues to wear Silesian linen.[72]

The writer's description of why Berliners consumed fewer imported fashion products began on the level of economic policy. She then portrayed a man giving in to visually provoked desire for a commodity, only to have his frugality restored by a military sense of self-command. The decision against consuming was represented by this obviously masculine subject as the invasion of disorder into a parade formation, a synecdoche for Prussia. In the last scene, desire and command, first evident within the husband, were divided between husband and wife. The disagreement was then concluded by the husband reaffirming his earlier decision by extending it to his wife. What appeared first as an internal dialogue, an exercise of the self upon itself, became an application of patriarchal authority within the family. In the sentimentalized, patronizing language of private life, the husband reiterated official economic policy, halting the diffusion of consumer desire by aligning self and family with state interests. Readers were left with a concluding image, the effect and sign of discipline: the wife wearing a dress of domestically produced Silesian cloth. What lay beyond this conclusion was unexpressed. The limits of the regulatory apparatus had been reached, and readers drew back to the level of outside observers, neighbors perhaps, who after overhearing a short exchange and seeing the public appearance were left to conclude that the financial drain of foreign luxuries was averted.

The passage outlined three fields within which regulation occurred. In each, "normal" existence was disrupted by an unexpected intrusion, which disturbed an established equilibrium. In each instance, a tension between desire for a commodity and resistance to consuming was provoked by the penetration of the object into a preexisting domain of control. First, commodities crossed into Prussian territory as imports. Then one particularly attractive commodity entered the man's field of vision as a product on display and into the household via an illustrated journal. Each entry provoked a response to counter desire—an excise tax, an economic calculation, a patriarchal judgment. Prussian efforts against luxury were portrayed as succeeding within the family, the marketplace, and the national economy because all three were joined through a succession of interconnected regulative decisions.

The text also suggested that the state's ability to project regulatory power was enhanced by its continual mobilization of new enforcing agents. Individuals who practiced consumer restraint were portrayed as continuing the regulatory interest within domains that might otherwise lie beyond the range of state policy. By imposing restraint upon himself, the husband acquired the ability to deny his wife's request. Not only did each stage in the sequence of control presume the previous stage, each application of a regulative principle intersected with some preexisting configuration of local power. By allowing the regulative force to ripple through themselves, objects-turned-agents enhanced their standing. The husband, for example, implicitly affirmed his patriarchal status by enforcing more broadly the economic calculus that he imposed upon himself.

The female reader was not presented as overcoming consumer desire. Whether she adopted the same reflective financial calculation as her husband remained unexplained. She represented the limit to state regulation of consumption. By not portraying her subjective responses, the text implied that the Prussian apparatus curtailing consumption stopped just inside the family sphere. Aside from spurring the self-disciplinary reflections of the household's titular head, the state-derived regulatory system had little ability to organize the subjective manifestations of consumer desire. Yet as long as the family's expenditures depended on the approval of a well-trained male, its interests would be served.

The *Mode Journal* entered into the consumption economy at the point farthest from financial and judicial control. While the passage presented the *Mode Journal* as the vehicle for foreign goods to penetrate the Prussian family, this portrayal was contradicted by the publication, within the very same issue of the journal, of an article praising Prussian parsimony. Furthermore, this author was also identified as female, which, although it did not guarantee that a woman wrote the piece, implied a feminine mode of self-reflection on consumer practices. This writer responded to a visitor's criticism of Berlin's lack of a fashionable society thus:

> Nothing is noticed by foreigners so much as *that we have hardly any luxury and fashion*. But please, my so very surprised sir, what would you say if you heard that precisely this *lack of luxury* is our pride. Allow us to be the only city dwellers who do not wish to appear but prefer instead to simply be. In short, we want nothing of your luxury and your newest fashions.[73]

This passage illustrates how bourgeois fashion at the end of the eighteenth century affirmed the values of production and nonostentation that had earlier in the century been promulgated by cameralism. The clumsy consumer restrictions abandoned by Enlightenment reformers acquired a new life when the Bildungsbürgertum reworked the economic interests of the state into an aesthetic of sartorial understatement.

The apparent contradiction between the *Mode Journal*'s function as an inspiration to consumers and its criticism of ostentation point to the journal's essentially Enlightenment strategy of disseminating fashion information while reflecting upon its moral and practical value. Rather than restricting consumption, the journal fostered it through an analysis of the fashion system. The effect was that the journal deployed an economic rationality in the arena farthest removed from the state's apparatus: the reading public. As the foremost fashion publication in Germany, the *Mode Journal* managed a consumer culture with built-in restraining mechanisms. The attacks on the journal as an invitation to consume were not invalid; however, its articles and images also generated a new kind of self-disciplining consumer, who participated in fashion by insisting on it meeting their practical needs. Sumptuary laws supported a minimum standard of ostentation even as they sought to curtail ostentation. However, each law functioned as a single intervention into consumer culture, an attempt to solve once and for all the pressure on feudal limitations by setting yet another legal limit. The *Mode Journal*, on the other hand, spurred readers to desire new and previously unseen products while simultaneously reflecting upon the moral, medical, and economic value of each. It organized fashionable consumption from within, through the act of consumption itself. The Prussian mode of consumption, with its legacy of administrative discipline, was not at all contrary to the journal's goals, for by the turn of the nineteenth century Berlin's lack of foreign style established its legitimacy within German fashion culture.

Like the older police laws, modern fashion discourse incorporated within itself all activities not already under the control of some other institution. However, unlike the absolutist system of spectacle, fashion did not distinguish between injunctions and ideals. Absolutism presented gradations of luxury from which the individual was enjoined to refrain, whereas bourgeois fashion culture synthesized its negative pronouncements with affirmative goals. To dress and live according to the finest standards of taste was synonymous with the requirement to avoid the unfashionable. Fashion discourse did not so much forbid particular forms of consumption as fabricate the exclusive realm within which all dress and luxury appeared.

CHAPTER SIX

Paranoid Geography and the European Dispersion of Fashion

In 1898, the Viennese architect Alfred Loos spoke of the impossibility of buying in Austria a hat in the style worn at that moment by the British royal family:

> The correct hat is only sold in London. When the hat I bought in London wore out, I tried to find one here with the "correct shape." It was then that I discovered that the English hats sold here do not correspond to those sold in London.[1]

Efforts by the Vienna Hatters Association to create a national style only showed Loos that Austrian haberdashers were in the end uninterested in responding to foreign trends. Loos's dissatisfaction with Austrian hats was prompted by an adherence to the cosmopolitan ideal that all modern men should wear the same style of functionally elegant (English) hat, a desire born of the Enlightenment. This aesthetic presumed that national boundaries, local customs, and practical obstacles were immaterial. The restrained modern style ignored all local claims to beauty; its universality did not acknowledge the constraints of distance and delay.

Loos's complaints were distinctly modern, but they were hardly new. Eighteenth-century Germans were also obsessed with what they believed were the wellsprings of fashions. First, they wanted to know exactly where the new styles came from? Who invented them? Then they asked, How do we stand in relation to the center of fashion? Are we close enough to keep up? Are we being left out? Are we provincial, and does it show? By knowing the origin of fashions, it might be possible to explain why they changed at such a feverish pace. The *Mode Journal*, with its monthly bulletins from Paris and London, soothed this anxiety while feeding it, each issue providing up-to-date information on what was worn abroad.

And yet readers still doubted whether the news was really current. The problem was an old one. Tales about the speed of fashion change were common even before the advent of modern fashion journals. One famous anecdote told of a young Hamburg merchant who, while in London on business, bought the exact suits that the leading English lords wore so that he might impress his colleagues back home. After two weeks in London, he set sail for Germany with a trunkful of the finest English menswear. On the journey home, however, his ship ran into a storm in the North Sea and anchored at an island off Scotland for five days. When he made it back to Hamburg and appeared at the Exchange in his English attire, the fashion news from England had beaten him across the North Sea, and he was laughed out of the place for wearing last week's fad.[2] The story presumed that the listener identified with the unfortunate merchant: no matter how much he tried, he was always a few steps behind the center of fashion— even when he had just been there! To make matters worse, he was mocked for being out of style, not that his colleagues were themselves all wearing the very newest from London. They may well have had no better clothes of their own, and yet they recognized the merchant's lack of *ton*.

The concern over whether one was truly in fashion was entwined with cameralist notions of economic nationalism. The simple in/out opposition of fashion was mapped onto the difference between the German and French economies, thereby grounding a discursive operation in economic relations. Even before Thomasius's *Von der Nachahmung der Franzosen* (1687), the distribution of luxury goods in Europe was characterized as a German dependence on France. The perpetuation of this distinction ensured the belatedness of all fashion trends in the Holy Roman Empire. The economic explanation for this condition was the time it took to import French goods. The Germanic sense of backwardness was produced only when individual travelers (or even more important, the mail) arrived from Paris. The disjuncture in travel time was noted in a letter to the *Mode Journal*:

> The shortest route, by which we receive ladies fashions, runs over Frankfurt and Leipzig. The French merchant packs up the newest fashions in a box, some of which were never worn in Paris, others no one wants to wear anymore. He consigns the whole lot to the barbarians of the North and sends it to the Frankfurt and Leipzig fairs—that already takes time. From there, our merchants bring it to Berlin, but only after another two months have

passed. The French industry always sends us fashions that are already old; we phlegmatic Germans receive them months later, and then take it badly when a foreigner stares at us, thinking he has landed among Vandals, simply because he has traveled more quickly than the goods that make us look like his grandparents.[3]

This concern for having the most recent fashions was not the simple effect of imperfect market distribution; rather, it was an inherent feature of modern fashion discourse. An acute awareness of temporal and spatial distortions in the distribution of information began in the eighteenth century. Merchants relied on a biannual *Messe* (fair) to introduce their new products, whereas journals were able to introduce stylistic innovations to the reading public every month. The rapid circulation of fashion news through the periodicals destroyed the French merchants' exclusive claim to newness. Georg Melchior Kraus wrote in an early issue of the *Mode Journal* that "the Parisian fashion merchants curse and swear at our journal as well as the Parisian one, because we appear every month, while they present new fashions only every six months."[4] Improvements in the distribution of goods were always outpaced by the speed with which information moved through Europe; railroads, telegraphs, and steamships only accentuated the awareness of temporal disjuncture. As Europe "grew smaller," temporal differences in the dissemination of knowledge grew more significant for the fashionable.

The more cosmopolitan a society considered itself, the more disdainful it was of a failure to "keep up." An awareness of distance was an inevitable component of fashion culture's internal mechanism. Not only were classes kept apart, but each class had its own standard of measurement. At Versailles under Louis XIV, this measure could be almost literally paced out in terms of one's distance from the king's body. In the bourgeois culture of the late-eighteenth century, the scale of measurement extended over greater distances. For the nobility around Louis XIV, those shut out of Versailles were simply in oblivion. By the end of the century, the map of inclusion and exclusion had been extended to cover large portions of Europe.

Distance from a source still determined whether a person belonged to fine society; however, faster communication allowed the network of fashionable society to incorporate more geographical space than before. The expansion of fashionable society over regions and populations of Europe previously outside the elite culture of style gave the impression that the new nonaristocratic fashions of bourgeois society were universally accepted as elegant, comfortable, handsome, and practical. However, the increased speed of communication and the corresponding expansion of fashion over larger areas also heightened the network's sensitivity to delay in the transmission of fashion information or its geographical distance from the network's centers. Thus, as fashion culture expanded over larger territories and populations, ever more attention was given to knowing the intimate, everyday details of life at the center of the network. The farther one was from London or Paris, the more important it was to receive accurate information about its cultural life.

The European fashion network was itself an object of fashion knowledge. The "educated consumer" sought to understand the mechanisms of production, distribution, and retail sales, which would in any other business be uninteresting to the nonprofessional. What ordinary citizen would worry about the process whereby refrigerators were designed and distributed? Yet those in fashion rigorously investigated the infrastructure of their society in order to participate in its movements. This fascination presumed a causal chain that could explain the operation of fashion, and thus it sought the "original moment" of style. As the fashion media became more sophisticated, addressing more universal tastes and incorporating more classes, an interest in the source of style became more intense and the gradations between imitation and authenticity more minute.

Germany at the end of the century lay between two market networks. French lines of distribution came up the Rhine; British lines extended from Hamburg down the Elbe and into the Leipzig *Messe.* The two systems propagated, according to the *Mode Journal,* two distinct styles of consumption and decoration:

> One can count on the fact that one portion of Germany is provided with fashion articles that are more tasteful, elegant, solid, and graceful, while the other has wares that are more delicate, dainty, and frivolous as well as being more stiff and overly ornamental.[5]

The ideological connotations arising from the division between English and French were explained in terms of the physical terrain and the flow of rivers, but they were by no means exhausted by these accounts. That geographical factors conditioned the expansion of two competing economies and that these two nations left their distinctive mark on the regions that imported their goods would seem unrelated to the rhetoric of fashion. Culture is, after all, conditioned by physical geography. However, the distinction between German states in the north and south was more than geographical; it was fraught with the religious and political conflicts that permeate German history. Within the context of fashion and consumption, the north/south, English/French division served as the basis for finer ideological distinctions. However, its most remarkable extension was the gendering of these geographical terms.

The distribution of fashion information did coincide with the marketing of commodities, but it also extended beyond the limited sites where English and French luxury goods were sold. Fashion was brought into the hinterlands of the German principalities primarily by written accounts but also by itinerant merchants. Because the condition of being fashionable is a social determination, a judgment formed by consensus, the actual presence of consumer goods was not as important as the belief that one was a participant in the discourse of fashion. The reading of journals satisfied this minimal condition and enabled a fantastical participation in a cosmopolitan culture. The reception of international fashion news varied, of course, subject to the specific social relations of the locality. For all its interest in the international and the distant, fashionable dress and domestic decoration was always practiced in a specific time and place. Well-dressed individuals presented themselves within the existing network of social relations. Thus, a German may have fantasized about Paris or London, but he did so in contrast to, or in denial of, his immediate surroundings. His particular conception of foreign elegance was conditioned not only by his (imperfect) knowledge of foreign habits but also by local relations of power. Commodities might have the aura of having traveled directly from the spring of good taste, but the institutions that formed the social consensus governing good taste mediated the relation between the "original elsewhere" of fashion and its local application. The *Mode Journal* was such an institution, and so were princely residences and burgomasters' sitting rooms.

The myth of an urban center—within which the newest styles developed and spread—organized modern fashion. The invocation of a landscape, a terrain across which fashions were transported, provided a stable background against which appearances could be defined and related to each other. The chaos of consumer culture's multifarious images and objects were comprehended as a stream whose content was never stable but whose contours and directions were defined by the cultural geography of Europe. The map of fashion allowed one to postulate a pattern of diffusion across time. Clothes worn in Prague or Dresden were at the moment of their first entry into society somehow derivative merely because they were not worn in Paris or London:

> Just as there is almost always a single primary residence for European fashion, and one point from which it spreads, in the same manner there is such a point for every state, every province, every city, and every class. In every circle of closely connected people, one finds certain leading people who set the tone, whose choices are communally accepted, or whose prestige moves others to emulate their example.[6]

The movement of fashion across its own mythic landscape was explained in terms of a drive to imitate. The inclination to dress like others, particularly those admired from afar, was theorized during the late Enlightenment as an inevitable, though often undesirable, component of social life. Emulation was one of the mechanisms by which the social contract maintained its cohesion. Christian Garve explained fashionable behavior by referring to a drive to imitate (*Nachshmungstrieb*), which he claimed operated on the national as well as the personal level. This drive joined individuals into groups; it allowed individuals to identify others who were like them or at least useful to them. But in forming groups, the urge to imitate also distinguished dissimilar groups.[7] Garve saw imitation as an operation of the "will" that occurred both unintentionally and through deliberate planning. The first, almost passive, form of imitation developed from social intercourse. "People who have daily contact become increasingly like one another. Each person loses certain qualities while acquiring the characteristics of others."[8] The second form of imitation involved the deliberate copying of others in order to acquire the values perceived to reside in them. This calculated mode of imitation could completely retrain the person to alter his tastes and his sensory perceptions.[9]

Garve constructed his theory of emulation as an explanation for both the disciplined education of civilized individuals and the diffusion of artifacts and practices across Europe. The movement of fashion across space was related to the malleability of the subject. The way emulation restructured personal desires and tastes was distinct from "disciplinary" models of training, such as those used in schools or the military, because fashionable emulation was most effective and attractive when it was "voluntary," which meant that adoption of etiquette and bodily decor had to proceed, or at least appear to proceed, from the inner desires of the person. Garve contrasted this almost artistic mode of emulation from the more typical, mechanical imitation of fashionable individuals. The automatic, unreflective adoption of a style that failed to be integrated into the organic harmony of the person was unfortunate and often repellent. Garve warned of the impoverishment visited upon poorer families that sought to emulate the wealthier classes. In weighing the harms and benefits of fashionable emulation, he isolated two motives: the urge to cut a striking figure before one's peers, which was associated with class competition and division, and sartorial emulation, which was motivated by a desire to conform for the sake of sociability. The latter motive was typical of the businessman who conformed to convention so he might turn his attention to other, more important topics.[10]

Objects of imitation—individuals or nations considered worthy of emulation—were found at every level of society. Certain admired tastemakers could be found in most communities, and they functioned in much the same manner as London and Paris.[11] Each person or institution relayed fashion within a certain sphere of influence. The status of these tastemakers depended in part on their economic, political, and cultural power. Garve, like Bertuch, assumed that countries that set fashion standards did so because of their dominance in other fields. However, their privileged position within fashionable society was also derived from a consensus of that society. Garve suggested that the network of fashion emulation functioned as a social contract or as a language community. In either case, fashionable society existed as a collective institution, distinct and separate from government regimes:

> These subordinated, smaller parties, with their ringleaders, fall under the influence of the larger ones. The whole system of fashion inventors and stylish people in Europe forms a type of larger state that operates from a distance, with invisible and far-removed rulers. Although it has many subdivisions, the influence of the universal lawgivers is unified with the authority of the smaller regents and dynasties.[12]

Garve explicitly refrained from mentioning the aristocracy as tastemakers. Rather, he referred to them simply as innovators, people admired for their ability to formulate new and exciting clothes or products. Garve's careful abstention from naming the aristocracy was typical of late-eighteenth-century fashion discourse. The *Mode Journal*'s reliance on anonymous references to abstract figures, rather than to specific historical persons, was part of a rhetorical strategy that allowed every reader to assume the imaginary position of the fashionable figure in the text. When Garve wrote about tastemakers he presumed the existence of a bourgeois society composed of individuals, rather than a corporate hierarchy (*Stände*).

Garve's description of a secret network of fashion creators distributed throughout European society did little to answer eighteenth-century questions about where fashion came from and how it managed to reshape appearances in far-flung provinces. Garve's model, while emphasizing the consensual formation and distribution of fashions, placed great importance on the individual persons considered instrumental in the process. They could be as well known as the king of France or they could be some anonymous person who had a clever notion at the right time and in the right place. The entry of these unknown innovators into the system of fashion creation and dispersion, Garve noted, made their sartorial invention a European fashion. The character of innovators was less important than their placement within the network:

> The largest and most widespread changes in European fashion often had their origin in the inspiration of a single person, who happened to live in such a location under such circumstances that their example made an impression and was able to awaken imitators in many countries.[13]

For most eighteenth-century dressers, the French court had had this particular function, but as the centers of information grew, more and more lesser-known figures had a potential influence on the movement of style.

The apparent ability of certain localities to influence bourgeois manners and decor throughout Europe fascinated German fashion readers. They speculated, with the encouragement of fashion journals, on the exact circumstances of such fashion inventions. The greatest moment in fashion was the moment of a style's inception, its debut into bourgeois society. It became the imaginary goal of many fashion-conscious Germans to know exactly, in the most intimate detail, how a style came into existence. Who first wore that garment? For what purpose? On what occasion? Who was present at the time? Were they duly impressed? Did they realize what was unfolding before them? What was said and to whom? Was any connection drawn between the garment and the gathering itself? These questions have probably always fascinated the leisured European elite, but in the eighteenth century they became part of the public domain. News of private gatherings in distant cities spread across countries with a speed they had never before had. Tidbits of socially significant gossip reached ears that would previously never have known or cared about foreign goings-on. The secret, inside information and practices of closed societies became part and parcel of European cosmopolitanism.

The sites of these fashion "happenings" were by no means confined to the drawing rooms of nobility. The eighteenth-century German Enlightenment preferred more humble arenas, gatherings that consciously eschewed claims to representational ostentation. They might be family meals or religious gatherings, places overlooked by the courtly culture of luxury, because they included individuals opposed to the grand ceremonies of the nobility. Running through many of the most famous "moments" of bourgeois fashion was a contest over what constituted good taste and who might be included in the society of the truly elegant.

There were two explanations for fashion emulation. One presumed that styles trickled down from an elite culture to a broader mass, explaining the fashion cycle's connection with class conflict. This explanation suggested that the upper classes invented new styles of dress to distinguish themselves from the lower classes, who then imitated the elites in order to acquire prestige. The more the lower classes imitated, the more the elites would innovate. The second explanation argued that diffusion of new styles did not reinforce hierarchy but, rather, undermined it. Garments and instruments were introduced to the public by a small group considered unworthy of status emulation. For example, bourgeois society frequently adopted the work clothes of the lower classes.

Diffusion does, however, often involve notable adjustments in the meaning and social function of objects. Religious garments, for example, have on occasion been worn with a secular intent. In general, the routes and motivations of fashion diffusion have been far more ambiguous than the status-conscious emulation of elites. Diffusion often produces unusual pairings: objects that might once have had antithetical connotations and purposes might be allied in a new context. Thus, one can speak of fashion genealogy, in the Nietzschean sense, in which an earlier culture put an object to a completely different use, and with an antithetical value, than a later culture. Because material objects appear to exist on their own, independent of cultural meanings, they can acquire connotations that perhaps only allude to a previous meaning but that otherwise completely reformulate it.[14] In the late twentieth century, an example of such a radical symbolic refunctioning of clothes can be seen in the wearing of military uniforms by antiwar protesters. More than just an attempt to degrade what the army considered sacred, ragged military fatigues became as much a symbol of the antiwar movement as a polished uniform represented the government's pursuit of the Vietnam War. Redefinitions of clothing became more dramatic when the garments passed between cultures; the *Mode Journal* considered its primary function to counteract the German public's "incorrect" appropriation of foreign dress.

Nonhierarchical emulation involved the imitation of models, which consumers in the eighteenth century discovered in books, theater performances, and journals; today, models are also found in posters, movies, television, compact disk covers, concerts, and other entertainment media. Critics of the trickle-down theory of fashion have pointed to the influence of mass media as proof that class differentiation no longer explains the cyclical change of styles. Charles King wrote in 1963: "Mass communication media rapidly accelerate the spread of fashion awareness and influence mass markets endorsements. The traditional upper-class fashion leader directing the lower levels is largely short-circuited in the communication process."[15] While the first fashion journals in eighteenth-century Europe began the media circumvention of the hierarchical clothing culture, class distinctions were reflected in literacy rates. Furthermore, the new media usually introduced new forms of dress and new methods of interpreting public appearance. The democratization of fashion was both the effect and the content of fashion magazines.

Shifts in the pathways of communication are usually accompanied by redefinitions of the message transmitted, so that publications that appeal to a broad audience tend to reflect the tastes of that audience. The *Mode Journal* provided a new means of integrating luxury consumption and fashion into bourgeois culture as it expanded the base of German consumers. Instead of imitating the examples of the nobility, German readers emulated the figures presented in journals and novels. By broadening the range of models to emulate, eighteenth-century fashion media allowed influences from the lower classes and from ideologically isolated groups to penetrate into respectable society. Twentieth-century media have also created an upward diffusion of fashion innovation, most notably the adoption of African-American culture by the mainstream.[16] In the eighteenth-century German context, such upward diffusion was usually produced by the introduction of a foreign example of lower-class dress. However, the German Enlightenment's admiration of English novels brought a fascination, also, with the rough garb of the English rural gentry.

The trickle-down model presumed that the French king or some other high-ranking French aristocrat could set a European trend in motion merely by appearing at some important event dressed in a new and striking garment. Such a revelatory introduction of a fashion was the imaginary ideal, but with the decline of the French court's prominence in setting trends, it became more difficult for provincials to recognize the moment that a style first appeared. The *Mode Journal*, and the many German publications that followed its example, created imaginary, almost mythical, figures who were deemed responsible for European good taste. A great deal of fashion historiography maintains this mythic manner of thinking. Nineteenth-century dandies, Beau Brummel in particular, are credited with having invented certain looks, as if society as a whole had no role in the formation of a fashion consensus. The dandy was isolated as a hero of modernity because he personified the discursive operation of fashion and provided the illusion of an original agent whose creative accomplishments, in word and dress, were imitated by the less brilliant. Brummel's famous confrontations and bon mots were culled years after their supposed performance, allowing recollection and repetition among storytellers to strengthen their force and *pointe*. Through the figure of the dandy, fashion discourse legitimated itself as the product of genius, while assigning agency to its diffuse and systemic operation. The dandy was to fashion history what the old peasant mother was to Romantic folklorists—a focal point around which concepts and allegorical incidents clustered. Garve's suggestion that a single, well-situated individual could determine the appearance of the European bourgeoisie has been played out in many biographies and histories of the eighteenth and nineteenth centuries, each reinforcing the illusion that there was a single point in time when beauty and elegance, like Athena, emerged fully garbed.

While both aristocratic and bourgeois cultures indulged in the vanity of fashionable mythology, gender and its implied sexuality was a central category of the rhetoric of modern fashion. Sexual practices were perhaps incidental motivations in the courtly mythology of how fashions came into existence—a particular hat or vest was sewn in order to seduce a certain beauty—however, bourgeois fashion culture introduced gender distinctions as an abstract category comparable to national identity. National and gender identity were invoked within bourgeois fashion writing to explain the origin and diffusion of styles across Europe. These categories were also invoked to explain why fashion changed so quickly. The transitoriness of taste was increasingly accounted for by invoking gender characteristics, which were often blended into national differences. The rapid shift in taste, it was argued, could be traced to the psychology of certain individuals, who were responsible for the creation of new styles. The fashion system could therefore be understood as a manifestation of a character that existed simultaneously on the levels of a historical nation, an empirical individual, and a natural sex.

In Germany and elsewhere, bourgeois fashionable society considered London and Paris the primary sites of fashion production. For each location, fashion discourse invented corresponding figures, who served as imaginary agents in the design of new looks: the slim, darkly dressed English lord and the young Parisian coquette. They each moved in a limited but elite society: the circle around the prince of Wales and in the salons of the leading Parisian mistresses. Depending on the historical person, sometimes the prince of Wales was specifically named as the "primary" agent of male fashion innovation; other times, that responsibility was transferred to a close confidant, as happened in the time of Beau Brummel's association with the English heir.

From the start, the prince of Wales and Parisian mistresses figured as points of origin in the *Mode Journal*'s map of Europe. In its first issue, the journal included a list of "Priesterinnen der Venus zu Paris." The Parisian correspondent explained that these women belonged to the fashions of the world, implying that they were both fashions themselves (i.e., objects to be desired and acquired) as well as the source for women's styles. Then, in a manner that the journal quickly abandoned, the article actually gave names and descriptions of these women. For German readers, the article was a scandal (never a bad thing for a new fashion journal). Still, Bertuch, hav-

ing outraged bourgeois morality, never again printed such a rococo celebration of mistresses and prostitutes. He did, however, argue that "the characterization of today's first-class Phryniens in Paris was very much an es-
sential component of our plan, in part because it is precisely these women
who give every new fashion in Paris its being."[17] And, when in the same year,
the prince of Wales was obliged to auction his wardrobe, the event was reported throughout Germany:

> The speculation is fundamentally admirable, for the whole world is stream-
> ing to this famous auction. Our distinguished gentlemen and distinguished
> ladies are outbidding each other mightily to buy and heartily divide his es-
> tate, just as in the time of the early church people tore after the bones of
> saints.[18]

This mythology of fashion's development continued well into the nineteenth and twentieth centuries. Friedrich Vischer described Paris as a witch's
kettle from which all feminine fashions bubbled forth. Half the respectable
women and all of the demimonde participated in the process, which he also
compared to the rituals surrounding the ancient Oracle at Delphi. He ex-
oticized the social life of the bourgeoisie, pointing out the importance of
secret societies and unseen social divisions by claiming that the trend-set-
ting women of Paris composed a mysterious order of priestesses.[19]

In 1906, Eduard Fuchs reiterated the *Mode Journal*'s description: "the
majority of the most successful fashion creations were brought out by the
professional priestesses of Venus. This assertion is true in the main and is
readily proven historically."[20] Fuchs, whose work is strangely bifurcated between Marxist sociological text and erotic images of women, incorporated
the "scandal" of feminine fashion into his lascivious account of bourgeois
society: "For the respectable lady there remains nothing to do but imitate
as closely as possible the accomplishments of the priestesses of Venus."[21]
Gender and national differences augmented distinctions between political
economies. Capitalism was quite simply masculine and English:

> These days, one is asked: Why is it that men's fashion today, as always, re-
> ceives its directives from London, with as much consistency as women's fash-
> ion turns to Paris? The answer is quite simple: the bourgeois spirit has
> uniquely and thoroughly penetrated everything in England, so that it has be-
> come the only true bourgeois culture and because bourgeois culture rests
> upon the rule of the masses, which makes it a masculine culture. Aristocratic
> culture, by way of contrast, is in the final analysis a feminine culture.[22]

Werner Sombart invoked the myth even as he sought to incorporate its personages into a more abstract economy of fashion. He begrudgingly allowed their star quality to find a place in his dialectical sociology: "The efforts of the Parisian coquette and the prince of Wales provide a mediating contribution."[23]

Unquestionably, modern fashion editors and clothing designers have sought, through carefully orchestrated unveilings of their collections, to usurp the privilege previously assigned to these two figures. As the interdependence of media and fashion has grown, the creators of style have become the vehicles for its distribution and commodification. However, the celebration of fashion professionals as the inventors of public opinion does not abandon the principle that fashion is created by some act prior to its finding acceptance with the general public. The design studio and the editorial room have replaced the salon and the club as the place outside the public's gaze where creation occurs. Even Roland Barthes posited such an origin when he insisted that new styles were not the manifestation of popular practice but rather the creation of a few designers and editors.[24]

The diffusion model of fashion emulation was also discussed in the eighteenth century, though it has had few advocates since then. The strength of Garve's long essay was that, even as he noted the tendency of the lower classes to imitate the upper classes, he hypothesized that new styles moved across Europe by a process of diffusion. He likened the introduction of foreign fashions into Germany to the adoption of foreign words, a telling comparison given that the word *Mode* was still marked in the German language as a French introduction. Earlier in the century, Johann Gottsched alluded to the etymology of *Mode* as well as the importation of its products: "Fashion [*Die Mode*] is a French guest on German soil, who has so ingratiated himself that one can well accept him."[25]

Garve carried the linguistic comparison farther. First, he drew a semiotic comparison between the signification of language and the physical gestures and objects of fashion. Second, he argued that fashions, like languages, constituted social groups by their very existence. Like many Enlightenment thinkers, he worried about the origin of languages. However, he also noted that a social consensus underlay all speech communities. Within each speech community, individual actors or speakers were faced with choices as to how to communicate. Likewise, the individual dresser could only make what linguistics calls paradigmatic substitutions. One could wear a yellow vest, or a grey one, or even no vest, but in the end one could not depart from the expectation of eighteenth-century respectable society that a properly attired man wore a vest. Fashionable dressers did not have the option of creating a public persona from nothing.[26] The act of representing oneself through clothes could occur only within the code acknowledged by the community. The advantage of learning many languages, Garve argued, was that one became familiar with more codes of sartorial representation and, therefore, became more facile at communicating and interpreting the appearance of others. This cosmopolitanism led Garve to the rather liberal conclusion that having a wide range of tasteful products available in the marketplace was like knowing many foreign languages. Consumers faced with an assortment of products were not unlike polyglots who, when with equally well-equipped listeners, could choose among several languages to express their thoughts.

Garve gave four reasons for comparing fashion to language. First, he argued that the relation between fashion objects and their referents was arbitrary, not unlike the arbitrary connection between a sound and its meaning. He conceded that gestures, mannerisms, clothes, and decorative objects were more closely connected to their meanings than words were. The symbolic and the functional values of courtesies, such as bowing and holding an umbrella for someone, were related, whereas utterances had no formal relation to the objects they represented. He concluded that because language was more arbitrary, communities of speakers were inherently more conservative about introducing change.[27]

What separates Barthes's theory from Garve's is their almost antithetical understandings of how fashion and language signification were similar yet different. Garve held to the Enlightenment conceit that language was created at some point in history, though his remarks on the topic were skeptical. He used the origin of language as a fiction for the sake of distinguishing fashion from language. The fashionable dresser did not create a language. He merely made choices, whereas the founder of a language actually invented words for things and then convinced society to accept them. Barthes argued the opposite. He did not accept Garve's assumption that the rules of dress and decorum were social contracts. Like Garve, he distinguished between a system in which signs are first created and then forced onto a community and a system in which speakers make choices between different signs, without regard to their origin. However, Barthes insisted that fashion was a created system of signification and that language existed as a social consensus. For Barthes, the arbitrariness of the fashion sign was "tyrannical," because it was imposed annually on the public by an elite circle of designers and editors.[28] Barthes, unlike Garve, did not consider fashion changes to be the product of collective action.[29]

A further difference between Garve and Barthes was their assessment of the "arbitrariness" of linguistic and fashion signs. Barthes corrected Ferdinand de Saussure, stating that the linguistic sign was not arbitrary but, rather, that the relation between the sign and its referent was "unmotivated," a distinction that was more a question of terminology than a critique of Saussure.[30] Garve argued that both linguistic and fashion signs were arbitrary but noted that fashion signs sometimes had an iconic relation to their referents and thus were, at times, motivated. The rules of etiquette sometimes physically performed their symbolic meanings, so that bowing down before a person enacted its meaning, that is, humility. Garve also insisted that fashion products had real use values, a claim that served as the basis for his entire defense of consumer culture as a vehicle for rationalizing everyday practices.

Barthes made no argument about clothes as such; he was only concerned with clothes in writing. Still, Garve did not accept Barthes's assertion that all references to utility in fashion magazines were nothing more than alibis for the fashion system's internal distinctions. As a good member of the Enlightenment, he insisted that writing about the practicality of clothes had a real referent in the use value of each garment. Whereas Barthes maintained that writing about the functions of fashionable clothes generally meant making distinctions of a strictly fashionable variety, Garve argued that fashion garments had important uses in the material world and that, therefore, written references to those practical uses were meaningful. Garve's position did not mean that references to practicality could not also have a normative value in fashion culture's distinctions between style and its absence; he was writing within an epistemological framework that assumed that language was transparent, that words referred directly to their referents. He did not consider "writing about doing" to be a paradox.[31]

The practical and sometimes even iconic connection between fashion items and their meanings allowed for playful adjustments. Hats could come in a wide variety of colors, materials, and shapes because, satirists aside, rarely did fashionable experimentation advance so far that ordinary people would wonder whether that thing on a person's head was really a hat. Herein lay the second similarity between language and fashion convention: both had a basic font of elements, largely unaffected by short-term variations.[32] The grammar and root words of a language were not subject to significant change, Garve argued, and so, too, fashion culture presumed that certain garments, behaviors, and household objects were unlikely to suddenly become unimportant. Hats would always be worn, for example, just as the roots of certain words would always be Germanic.[33]

Garve's comparison between fashion and language ended with a discussion of how both structures changed over time and across cultural contexts. Imported trends in dress and decor had an effect similar to foreign words in a language: both could be evaluated in terms of the purpose they served within their new community; consumer goods were ultimately judged as either instruments of productive labor or nonverbal signs. Likewise, words, especially new ones, were evaluated as to whether they referred to an object previously unknown, refined an existing term by more precisely differentiating between referents, or gave an affected air of meaning by replacing an existing word with a foreign equivalent.[34] The goal of importing either words or fashions was to improve the existing system of expression. Language, like fashion, was functionalized; Garve presumed that both were instruments in the progressive education and material advancement of humanity.

Garve noted that changes in language and in fashion occurred without the application of force. Fashionable swings in public behavior intrigued him because they raised the possibility of altering the practices of large communities without coercion. The transformation of languages over time provided a model of social progress in which the imposition of harsh disciplinary measures was seemingly unnecessary. Garve presumed that language became increasingly more refined and responsive to the personal needs of its speakers and proposed that the market similarly refined commodities. The degree of cultivation that a society attained, Garve argued, was reflected in the subtleties of both language and the practices of daily life. The nuances of grammar and an expansive vocabulary were, like a rich variety of consumer goods, indications of progressive enlightenment carried out through "voluntary" means. If less refined societies chose to imitate more refined societies, then they were engaged in a free process of education. Language diffusion and the transmission of style across Europe operated through the consensus of a community, not the regulatory authority of state institutions. The "educators" of European fashion culture changed traditional society without having to employ disciplinary force; rather, the communicative network needed only to present the examples of foreign style for provincials to change their habits.[35]

Garve suggested that the broad semantic transformations of language and fashion were an example of Enlightenment rationality operating according to its own principle of differentiation. The increasing refinement of vocabulary and grammatical structures was akin to the expanding world of goods available at the end of the eighteenth century. Although there were obvious affinities between Garve's praise of consumer culture and Bertuch's hopes for developing German industry, Garve's equation of popular culture and teleological rationality failed to resonate within the German intellectual culture. Romantic writers did not share Garve's faith that middle-class consumerism was a manifestation of spiritual rationality. Garve's essay, in turn, did not participate in the Romantic tendency to locate popular, collective culture outside the Bildungsbürgertum; its openness toward foreign influences was far removed from the belligerence of E. M. Arndt, who also equated language and dress as markers of identity: "The things most important for the virtue of the German race were the interior and the exterior: *a German language and a German costume.*"[36]

Garve's comparison between the emulation of foreign fashions and the acceptance of foreign words pointed to the importance of travel and the corresponding ideal of "cosmopolitanism." His analogy also unwittingly revealed the potential for both fashion and foreign words to be jarred loose from their original context. Just as foreign words were unwittingly redefined by their adopted language, so too could garments and decorative objects gain new, and unforeseen, connotations when they were absorbed into a society other than the one that first manufactured them. The *Mode Journal*'s efforts to show Germans how to "properly" wear English and French styles could be understood as an attempt to educate them in the correct syntax of foreign dress. Wearing a French wig with English riding boots would, for a cosmopolitan speaker of both languages, be as unfitting as placing

French adjectives in the word order of an English sentence. In the scenario that the *Mode Journal* sought most assiduously to correct, the ignorant German speaker used both English and French words without understanding their meaning or grammatical function in the original language.

Foreign words, like foreign products, were charged with an exotic eroticism as well as with the markings of a higher-class education.[37] Their appearance in everyday speech and material culture disputed any claim that language, dress, or decor were natural features of a culture; foreign fashions and words suggested the penetration of distant forces into the local community. Garve clearly considered such linguistic cross-fertilization as inherent in the formation of any civilization.[38] The more nations interacted through speech and trade, the more societies would learn new and more precise forms of expression as well as more productive means of satisfying personal needs. The flow of goods would even out, Garve reasoned, as nations developed their manufacturing bases. A Europe in which fashions were exchanged in a balanced market would, Garve claimed, eliminate the distortions that were an inevitable by-product of fashion's movement across Europe. A diverse economy would not only reduce the time lag in bringing new styles to Central Europeans but also eliminate the fetishism of foreign fashions, which the communication network encouraged. The *Mode Journal* argued that stylish garments and decorations lost their relation to the body once they were removed from their original context: what might have looked good on the original proponent of a style could look distorted on other people's bodies.[39] Ideally, all people would dress in clothes that expressed their own personalities and would decorate their own bodies in the most gracious way.

The geographical dimension of fashionable emulation manifested throughout eighteenth-century fashion discourse. Fashion journals wrote about products as if there were distinct and absolute standards of style. Good taste existed simply as itself, and every style that diverged from this ideal was inelegant. That there were in fact two major centers of fashion was eventually incorporated into this principle as a reflection of both market competition and sexual difference. Paris and London simulated the free market by creating disparate goods, which were in turn specifically gendered.

This semiotic model was, however, relativized somewhat as it was translated onto the map of Europe. To insist that fashionable people lived only in London or Paris was incompatible with the market's expanding demand for consumer goods. The distribution of products along European trade routes introduced a scale of fashionableness calibrated by distance. This new geographical standard of fashionableness did not, however, result in the abandonment of fashion's absolute rule of good taste—namely, that one was either in style or not. German fashion journals sought to create the illusion for their readers that they were in Paris or London; and yet they always labored under the knowledge that they were still far away.

Nowhere was the sense of distance and the attractions of exploration greater than within the many principalities and geographical regions of the Holy Roman Empire. The *Mode Journal* and its competitors often ran articles on the fashionable society of various smaller German cities. More often than not, they were commentaries on the absence of worldly taste among the residents. Writers liked to draw distinctions between regions based on their adherence to a European standard of taste. About cities on the Baltic coast, one German traveler observed

> I have noticed that one is much more aware of the alterations in fashion here than in south Germany, which is no doubt due to the prevailing trade of Hamburg and Lübeck and the easy communication the sea allows with the two fashion kingdoms.[40]

From the viewpoint of bourgeois fashion, the German provinces were a vast unexplored territory, akin to the non-European tracts of North America, where strange new garments and customs might be discovered, to be marveled over and catalogued. At the very least, these regions provided contradictions to the standards of good taste, as one correspondent to the *Zeitung für die elegante Welt* wrote in 1802: "For the elegant world, Bamberg, with regard to its social tone and public amusements, is a true *terra incognita*." Ironically invoking the pleasures of reading explorers' accounts of their adventures, he predicted that "an accurate description would at the very least provide your readers with some novel stimulation."[41] Clearly, the author and his implied readers did not identify with the colorfully medieval inhabitants of Bamberg; as members of a broader cultural class, their preferences lay abroad. The backwardness of old German cities provided a sensitive point: within the progressive time frame of the Enlightenment bourgeoisie, the garments of rural society represented a past wherein social mobility and its attendant conflicts were suspended.

Readers of German fashion journals distanced themselves from provincial practices not only through their "disbelief" at the quaint manners of small-town residents but also through their eagerness to excuse them by explaining differences in dress as the effect of geopolitics. The awareness of a European map never left the fashionable German. If it was not possible to dress in an English manner, then at least one should understand the economic and political forces that stood in the way of utter stylishness. Such self-knowledge allowed journal readers to know how they failed to be perfectly stylish as well as the reasons why this failure was unavoidable. The small-town inhabitant who wore traditional garb knew neither. The tension between impatient worldliness and local sympathy shows up in many of the *Mode Journal*'s reports on rural German dress, such as the following travelogue:

> Among the many smaller cities that I had opportunity to observe, I found the Saxon and Thuringian towns far more elegant than those along the Rhine, particularly the Hessian. By comparing Sunday parades to church, one becomes most aware of these differences. One can also observe . . . that the fashionable decoration of the beautiful sex becomes more striking and perceptible the nearer the town is to a residence or an academy, or when the beauties are located near a garrison.[42]

Having pointed out the relative differences in fashionableness and having taken account of the political and economic factors that explain the degree to which a region's inhabitants could pursue foreign styles, the author switched into an uncompromising aesthetic tone:

> In small towns . . . one meets . . . the old and the new, not just next to each other in some curious harmony, but often a local beauty will wear the hairstyle of one city, a scarf from another, an apron from a third, and a dress from still another, thereby unifying with smiling innocence and obvious satisfaction fashions of distinctly different characters in one outfit.

The two-step description, combining a sociological explanation with a tolerant but superior criticism of local garb, showed the disparity between fashion judgments, which insisted on an uncompromising standard (one was either elegant or not), and the material forces that hindered one's ability to "keep up." Behind the author's sociological excuse lay an affection for the ignorant dress of the provinces, an embarrassed recognition of "Germanness," which was never left unpunished—hence the author's patronizing acceptance of the mismatched imitations of foreign styles found in small towns. The superior cosmopolitan recognized the tastelessness of rural customs and yet tolerated them as the pleasure that he denied himself.

As an imaginary construction, the map of European fashion allowed cosmopolitan Germans to project themselves into the position of the ideal English lord or Parisian mistress in order to critically evaluate their surroundings. No matter where they were located, taste-conscious individuals were empowered by the knowledge gleaned from journals to assume a paranoid relation to local habits. Every article of clothing, household appliance, decoration, and mannerism could be found wanting in relation to the stylish perfection of life in the distant capitals of Europe. Despite Bertuch's great ambitions, there was no chance that Germans would ever perceive their surroundings as anything but inferior, because the fashion discourse was organized in such a manner that London and Paris were by definition the only sites of pure style. To argue in defense of a local custom, one would have had to dismiss the assumptions underlying cosmopolitanism (the diffusion of taste across the continent) as well as its interpretive practices (judgments based on projective knowledge). Folkloric investigations of peasant costumes (*Tracht*) were conceived as way out of the paranoid tendency to devalue local customs. However, rather than resolving the suspicion that regional and small-town traditions were antiquated, their celebration only heightened these tensions.

The severity of fashionable conformity, the constant anxiety that one had missed a new twist, was tempered by a second, pragmatic as well as narcissistic principle: that clothes and household products should always be harmonious with the activities and personal needs of their owners. Thus, the only space that truly mattered was the one currently occupied by the material thing. Bertuch tried to invoke this second principle to suggest that German manufacturers should produce goods that met local needs. However, he also acknowledged that the most suitable goods were manufactured in England. British manufacturing thus combined two ideals: London was the center of taste as well as the source for the most comfortable and adaptable goods.

The education of German men to dress in the modern English style was a central concern for the *Mode Journal*, as the following passage from 1786 makes clear:

I wish to borrow only one example from the dress of men and to concentrate on authentic English fashion, not just because of its predominance but
because its comfort and simple elegance has earned it that place. It has
greater permanence and is thus less subject to change. Someone dressed in
an English suit can certainly, in whatever country he may travel, not fall out
of fashion. He dresses like an Englishman! they will say by way of praise,
not mockery.[43]

English masculine style had the paradoxical ability to be in fashion while
standing aloof from fashion. However much the standards of good taste
might change, English suits were always acceptable (a standard that nineteenth-century bourgeois society would formalize in evening attire). The sartorial goal of modern male dress was to move between social strata without
conforming conspicuously to their particular expectations. The dark elegance
of late-eighteenth-century male dress was associated with a particular national
identity as well as a specific city, yet this fashion claimed to transcend precisely
those types of boundary. The glory of English goods, according to Bertuch,
was that they allowed themselves to be integrated into local conditions. Like
the ideally discreet gentleman, they maintained an image at once detached
from and partial to the complicated conditions of any and every place.

Contrasted to the perspectives and identifications of cosmopolitan fashion culture were the perceptions of its provincial resistance.[44] While cosmopolitans could consider themselves as organized in alliances spread over
great distances, their provincial antagonists were almost by definition un-
inclined to collect themselves. If fashionable commodities were perceived
by enlightened cosmopolitans as moving across a grid, they were perceived
by local traditionalists as an alien infiltration. Opponents of the new fashion culture invoked metaphors of penetration, infection, leakage, erosion,
and smuggling to describe what they saw as a disturbing transformation
of daily life. These terms, which appeared throughout the German fashion
discourse, were not the exclusive language of rural traditionalism—or if they
were, then they were a rhetoric that virtually all Germans could adopt, given
the economy of Central Europe. Bertuch and the *Mode Journal*'s writers
would use metaphors of penetration to describe the influx of foreign goods.
Town leaders would use stronger versions of these same metaphors to characterize the change in local life brought about by the introduction of bourgeois fashion and literary culture.

Complaints about the rising interest in foreign fashions were voiced not only by aristocrats jealous of their privileged access to luxuries and state administrators concerned about their nation's balance of trade. Prominent figures in guilds and agricultural communities often perceived the new fashion culture as a threat to their legitimacy, as the intrusion of a tumultuous force into a sanctuary that, under the corporate system of rank-based luxury consumption, had been spared many of the aesthetically complex and socially competitive effects of fashion's cyclical movement. They feared the new forms of coercion, the different standards and methods for creating social conformity introduced by these fashions.[45]

These leaders were ill equipped to meet the new demands and obligations. For a farmer who also served on his village's ruling council, there seemed little sense in young people worrying whether they were wearing hats and gloves in the manner of Parisians, concerns wholly unrelated to the work of agricultural communities. They disturbed the economy of barter and exchanged labor by introducing products that had to be purchased, at least in part. Although clothes were sewn locally, the materials and patterns had to be bought. While far less expensive and delicate than the finery worn by the aristocracy, the new bourgeois fashions were nevertheless not suited for agricultural labor. Furthermore, the turning cycle of taste meant that their value diminished quickly. Rural Germans might have worn their clothes long after they ceased to be fashionable, but they still had a much shorter life span than the class-specific clothes of the corporate order. Added to these pragmatic objections was the fact that fashion garments brought with them systems of thought that did not acknowledge the patriarchal authority of the *Hausväter*. The sentimental literature that accompanied the first wave of bourgeois fashion promoted a utopia based on the shared expression of moral and emotional experiences. Within the imaginary community of sentimental readers, the ability to perceive reality in specific aesthetic terms became the basis for valuing individuals, not their birth and their place as property holders within the community.

A 1776 letter from a burgomaster complained about the changes brought to his community by worldly young men back from their studies:

> More than twenty years ago, before sentimental enthusiasm and the compulsion to improve and to ornament had burst upon us, we were the happiest people in God's creation. We were independent, at the edge of an empire

that could not prescribe laws it did not apply to itself; our councils concerned themselves with what was required by necessity, and they were guided by straightforward common sense. We, the burgomaster and town council, were not ahead of our fellow burghers in anything except a little experience. Our lifestyle, our households, our dispositions were the same as every burgher's. Our condition was close to being patriarchal. It offended no one to see the burgomaster at the *Rathaus* in the morning with all the pious ceremony of his office and then at noon going off to his field with a hoe over his shoulder. The most distinguished council member was not ashamed to give his daughter as a bride to the blacksmith or carpenter.[46]

The burgomaster's account closely matches Wilhelm Riehl's nineteenth-century description of agricultural communities as a collection of patriarchal households economically independent of market relations.[47] The downfall of this idyllic community was brought on by the expansion of bourgeois literary culture, progressive thinking, and the urge to aestheticize everyday life.

Ironically, the harmony described by the burgomaster corresponded to the ideals imagined by the sentimental protagonist of Goethe's *The Sorrows of Young Werther* (Die Leiden des jungen Werthers).[48] Nostalgia so saturated this description of rural life that one could almost believe that it was an inherent component of the rural patriarchy's claim to legitimacy. Perhaps the history of this emotion is much older than Romanticism, which molded it into a modern political ideology. The passage described rural dress culture as a community of laboring equals punctuated by moments of ceremonial display. Little continuity was drawn between these isolated ceremonies and the individuals who performed them. The burgomaster claimed that, unlike a high-born aristocrat attending a prince, he was not obliged to continually demonstrate his political rank through clothing. In the long stretches between moments of sartorial performance, he wore clothes that lacked distinguishing features. In a sense, he claimed to live outside of fashion and luxury most of the time, with only occasional, well-defined, and politically justified entries into the theatrics of public display.

This model of a practical existence punctuated by reluctant and short-lived periods of dressing up was not contrary to the way the *Mode Journal* and other bourgeois guides described sociability. These writings contrasted the cosmopolitan spatialization of fashion with a second organization of space that distinguished between arenas where one was free to ignore dress culture and arenas where one was under pressure to conform. This second spatial order reversed the valences of being in fashion and being out of fashion. Unlike the cosmopolitan system, it placed the greatest value on eluding, at least temporarily, the insistence that one dress and act according to a social norm. To be free of fashion was the greater value; to dress respectably was a burden undertaken out of expediency. The rural burgomaster's complaint about the intrusion of foreign standards of dress and decorum had a wide resonance among the very class he considered responsible for the demise of his traditions. While he saw fashion in terms of an opposition between village life and the habits of university towns, the Bildungsbürgertum drew a similar distinction between their own work environments and such politically symbolic forums as princely courts.

Sentimental novels, such as Sophie von la Roche's *Die Geschichte der Fräulein von Sternheim*, portrayed rural culture as an idyllic arena where functional garb predominated. Likewise, Adolph von Knigge, in his book on manners for bourgeois men, encouraged them to avoid the court as much as possible:

> Whoever, according to his situation, is not damned to live at court or in the great world should stay away from such arenas of glittering misery. Stay away from the turmoil, which deafens, disheartens, and ruins the spirit and the heart! In peaceful domestic seclusion, in the company of noble persons with whom one can agree and enjoy the sober joys of life, so that our vocation is dedicated to our duties, the sciences, and innocent happiness—that is the life worthy of a wise man.[49]

Knigge's advice was long considered the definitive code for bourgeois behavior, and yet bourgeois suspicion of public assemblies verged on the paranoid. What passed as practical suggestions for aspiring young men strikes the modern reader as the labyrinthian anxieties of a Kafka protagonist. Knigge, by explaining why one would want to avoid others, revealed the cautious approach taken by the German burgher when entering public culture. Princely residences, like university towns, were treated as quarantined locations where particular clothes were worn and particular customs were practiced by a select caste, which was exempt from the seasonal pressure on farmers. As long as communication and travel between these centers and the surrounding regions was limited, dissemination of fashion was limited. Although farm communities were never wholly cut off from urban fashions, the connections were intensified by the spread of reading and by administrative reforms that obliged state officials to have a university education.[50]

The letter-writing burgomaster called taste an "unfortunate compulsion" and allowed that "some of our young men, whom we had to allow to study in order to fill our pastoral and secretarial posts, [have] brought this compulsion among us."[51] The "compulsion to tastefulness" was the last in a chain of Enlightenment reforms that revised the political order of the *Gemeinde*. The desire for fashion was the most devastating change, because it penetrated the smallest aspects of daily life:

> The worst were those who wanted to develop in us a taste for the beautiful. These Sirs, educated in Wieland's school, attached themselves at first to our wives and daughters, who are already most easily seduced by Satan. They insinuated themselves with them, praising their eyes and teeth, cursing their fathers and husbands who would be so irresponsible as to set their foreheads and hands out in the hot sun, and then for such a lowly enterprise as harvesting potatoes and lettuce. They turned work into a burden.[52]

The struggle over fashion's acceptance was clearly attached to generational and gender conflicts. The Book of Genesis echoed throughout the burgomaster's complaint: the arrival of elegant young men and their seduction of local women reenacted Eve's temptation in the Garden of Eden. By awakening women to the fashions of cosmopolitan culture, the serpentlike students set in motion a reenactment of the original sin. The burgomaster, like the Old Testament authors and the European proponents of sumptuary laws, saw fashion as a virtually unstoppable force that turned the minds of citizens (laboring women, in this case) against their appointed tasks.[53]

Bourgeois culture took up the provincial and religious claim that, in working, one was kept away from the lures of fashion; it integrated its own fashion culture into an economy of production. At different points in the eighteenth century, the rough clothes of rural life were adopted by middle classes in an attempt to escape the formalism of respectable dress. But it did not take long for a new conformity, one in perpetual rebellion against artificiality, to be instituted. As long as cosmopolitan society conceived rural communities and secluded religious sects as the outposts of good taste, these groups could serve as sartorial inspiration for those members of society who insisted on nonconformity. The more cosmopolitan fashion discourse tied good taste to the practices of Europe's largest cities, the more rural clothes were invoked to negate the latest style. The narrow horizon of these small communities, the never-too-distant threat of economic ruin, the priority given to productive labor, and the surveillance common to small towns and sects were much closer to the internal discipline of the bourgeois family than was acknowledged at the time.

The similarities between rural communities and the urban bourgeoisie become obvious when they are contrasted with the courtly aristocracy. In the first stages of modern German consumer culture, the Bildungsbürgertum regularly recycled the habits of rural society, producing a fashion movement that did not emulate the aristocracy. As the burgomaster's letter indicated, the champions of the agrarian *Mittelstand* did not initially see themselves as aligned with the practices of the urban bourgeoisie, in part because the urban bourgeoisie saw rural costumes as outside of formal convention. Country clothes were the black suit's uncouth cousins, who still practiced what the urban bourgeoisie preached, though a little more obviously and little more robustly. As an instrument of bourgeois self-discipline, as a blow against ornamentality, and as a means of clarifying its own ideological commitments, agricultural clothes were as important to bourgeois society as the military uniform. The most radical innovations in eighteenth-century dress often had the markings of rural labor—unrefined and geared toward work in the field. Visually, they suggested the negation of worldliness and the desire to please. These innovations were utterly unacceptable to the aristocratic order because they failed to designate rank. However, the urban bourgeoisie adopted them as an antidote to its tendency to be awed by wealth, thereby instituting the very modern appreciation for understatement.

CHAPTER SEVEN

The Veil of Masculinity
Clothing and Identity via Goethe's
Die Leiden des jungen Werthers

A BLUE JACKET, a yellow vest, and breeches made of tanned leather, a tall hat with a wide rounded brim, and a pair of high leather boots suitable for wandering in the countryside: as the favorite outfit of Goethe's Werther, these items constituted the best-known masculine ensemble in German literature. After the publication of *Die Leiden des jungen Werthers* in 1774, these clothes left the relatively small circle of Enlightenment intellectuals and entered German fashion history as the de rigueur masculine uniform of rebellion.

By concentrating primarily on how Werther's blue and yellow suit circulated both within *Die Leiden des jungen Werthers* as well as within polite and fashionable circles, I hope to outline how correspondences between physical appearance and personal identity changed during the late eighteenth century. I distinguish bourgeois modes of apprehending and interpreting persons in the public domain from the techniques and epistemological presumptions that guided the evaluation and regulation of bodily presentation in corporate or absolutist society. While acknowledging Roland Barthes's distinction between image clothes, written clothes, and real clothes, I also consider the aesthetic principles that allowed eighteenth-century readers to combine these modes of signification.[1] For Barthes, image clothes constituted a spatial structure through forms, lines, surfaces, and colors, whereas written garments had meaning as verbal, syntactic structures. He contrasted both with the technological structure of real clothes, by which he meant the way a manufacturer designed, cut, sewed, and packaged a garment.

Sentimental modes of literary reception sought expressly to blend these three structures of meaning. Sentimental readers approached written texts as if they generated visual images while still being sensitive to the meanings arising from the syntactical structure of narrative sequences. And as the reception of Goethe's *Werther* made clear, readers were inclined to interpret real garments as if they were extensions of a written text. The social importance of these historic clothes was derived from the rhetoric of the novel: its fictional reality, or diegesis, was transposed onto eighteenth-century society by individuals who appeared in public wearing the dead protagonist's clothes and speaking in his manner. These performances sought to reenact the conflicts of the novel within public life, and in the process of doing so, they established a mode of identity sharply at odds with the conventions of corporate (*ständische*) society.

Although there were two eighteenth-century modes of establishing identity through attire, the new sentimental paradigm did not completely abolish its predecessor, for as early-twentieth-century sociologists such as Thorstein Veblen and Georg Simmel have demonstrated, courtly modes of interpreting clothes as indications of status or rank have continued to operate in modern society, even if their claims to absolute knowledge have been somewhat relativized since the demise of the ancien régime.[2] Indeed, the older system of judging appearances has been preserved and incorporated into modern conventions for establishing gender and sexual identity through dress. The self-conscious manipulation of clothes for the sake of attracting the gaze and generating spectacle, once the norm within courtly society, has become a negative mark of femininity or homosexuality in the bourgeois dress code. *Werther* and its reception illustrates how the contemporary conventions for judging gender through surface manifestations of the body were in part derived from eighteenth-century disagreements over the proper standard for appraising clothing. If Judith Butler's characterization of gender as "the stylized repetition of acts through time" is correct, what better place to find such gender-producing performances than in the world of fashion?[3]

The enthusiastic reception of Goethe's *Werther* marked the most famous intersection between fashion and literature in German history. Hundreds, perhaps thousands, of young men dressed in the same clothes as the protagonist. His mannerism, speech, and moral and aesthetic philosophies were so widely imitated by young male members of the Bildungsbürgertum that the pedagogue Joachim Campe wrote a concerned letter to the publisher Friedrich Nicolai about "our young people, who now all want to become

Werther."[4] The novel's representation of intimate personality carved out a subjective space hitherto unfamiliar to many readers. The discrepancy between their own identity and Werther's evoked a desire to occupy the space that the novel's representation implied. Emulation of Werther was predicated upon the belief that something lay behind the literary representation and that it could be accessed by both reading the text and reenacting the text in ordinary life.

By appearing in public dressed as Werther, eighteenth-century readers were making several statements. They were demonstrating their desire to feel, think, and act like the literary character; their projective identification with the character was avowed through their reiteration of the narration's elements. No detail was too insignificant. By adopting Werther's dress, mannerisms, speech patterns, and daily routine, these readers were constituting themselves within the rhetoric of sentimental discourse. Their imitation of Werther was a form of self-regulation; they trained themselves to behave in the manner of a fictional character in sentimental literature, to "express their deepest feelings," which amounted to espousing a rhetoric of subjectivity that asserted its autonomy and "naturalness" through its antagonism to the prevailing code of etiquette. Defenders of traditional, corporate society were quick to recognize in *Werther*'s reception a "performative" character. A 1781 pamphlet about servant girls in Vienna complained:

> They are hardly satisfied. They play the role of the sentimental person, make aesthetic pronouncements, read comedies, novels, poetry, learning entire scenes, descriptions or stanzas by heart, and even debate about *The Sorrows of Young Werther*.[5]

August Wilhelm Rehberg's reminiscences about Werther's impact on him as a seventeen-year-old revealed how determined and willful his imitation was. Rehberg was excited not so much by the novel's narrative events as by the "character" of the protagonist. The figure of Werther provided a new mode of subjectivity, one that Rehberg sought to occupy:

> I was seventeen when *Werther* appeared. For four weeks I bathed myself in tears, though not over the love and fate of poor Werther but, instead, because my own heart was crushed by the humiliating realization that I did not have the thoughts, could not be like him. I was obsessed with the idea. Whoever is capable of understanding the world as it really is must think like that, be like that—maybe even kill himself; some did do that.[6]

Werther imitators copied the small incidents from the novel as if they were engaged in a tactical drill in which they acquired new subjective capacities. Reiteration of Werther's gestures produced abilities within readers they might previously not have known. The productive quality of imitation was easily dismissed by "unsympathetic" observers, who saw emulation of the novel as the mechanical reproduction of a suicidal personality. However, for enthusiasts the point was to acquire, as their own, the psyche of the protagonist.

More than anything else, the novel revealed the possibility for a new subjectivity. Its rhetoric, the gestures, speeches, and descriptions that constituted the character of Werther, also made a new type of feeling subject intelligible to a broad class of readers. A generation of readers felt that they were coming into being as autonomous subjects through their reiteration of Werther's character. Their own "authentic" existence began with their reading of and their responses to Goethe's novel. This process amounts to the formation of a (gendered) identity through a succession of performances. Rehberg's awakening corresponded to Butler's account of personal agency as it was formed through reiterative performances of an identity:

> Performativity cannot be understood outside of a process of iterability, a regular and constrained repetition of norms. And this repetition is not performed *by* a subject; this repetition is what enables a subject and constitutes the temporal condition for the subject. This iterability implies that "performance" is not a singular "act" or event but a ritualized production, a ritual reiterated under and through constraint, under and through the force of prohibition and taboo, with the threat of ostracism and even death controlling and compelling the shape of the production, but not . . . determining it fully in advance.[7]

Butler's point that ritualized repetition of a performance does not determine its contours needs to be highlighted. Once constituted within the sentimental discourse, individual readers were capable of redefining the terms of Werther's personality. They were hardly all exact copies. Their appropriation of the literary character involved an ongoing process of redefining the character who had become their own. Like those fashionable dressers who mixed French and English styles, readers were capable of adopting, or reiterating, traits from a variety of sources, combining so many strands of identity that, over time, the iterative character of a performance was lost and appeared as an authentic expression of the subject. These permutations would, however, have been restricted by the conventional norms imposed by sentimental societies upon themselves.

The enactments of Werther's emulators occurred within highly charged social arenas, in which divergence from established norms of public behavior threatened the corporate hierarchy. While Werther's uniform disturbed the reigning sense of propriety and good taste, it had an affirming value for the novel's admirers. By dressing alike, young male readers of *Werther* formed a social identity among themselves. Membership in the Werther cult depended on one's adoration of the novel, and in this sense the cult operated like Freemason societies in that it created a space in which social stations were irrelevant. Midnight processions in Wetzlar were held at the grave of Karl Jerusalem, the presumed model for Werther:

> In the spring of 1776, a formal midnight procession to the cemetery was organized to honor the "unfortunate victim of self-respect and love." Men and women, foreigners as well as locals, joined at the appointed hour for this celebration. They were not . . . lovesick girls but, rather, well-established men, court assessors, and ladies of rank. Every participant carried a burning wax candle, everyone was dressed in black. As the procession approached the cemetery, they formed a circle and sang "Your suffering has ended, your struggle is over." After the song . . . a speaker stepped forward and dedicated a sermon to the unfortunate one, wherein he said that suicide out of love, while not justified . . . had to be excused. Flowers were then strewn on the grave, and the assembly walked back to the city. After a few days, this . . . visit to the grave was repeated; but as the city authorities made it very clear that they would intervene in any future repetition, the service was discontinued.[8]

In spite of the prohibition, Werther admirers held memorial ceremonies well into the nineteenth century at a grave by then no longer clearly marked. After the police banned planned gatherings at Jerusalem's grave, Werther fans made spontaneous visits, which could not be so readily controlled by the police. The authorities' inability to prevent such pilgrimages led them to hide the grave under a pile of ashes, but a nearby tavern keeper soon set up a memorial garden for Werther pilgrims.[9]

Immediately after the novel's publication, Goethe and his closest friends continued to wear the Werther costume. It became the badge of identity for the literary rebels of the Sturm und Drang. Friedrich Klinger and Ernst Schleiermacher donned the *Werthertracht* as they rode out from Frankfurt to meet Jakob Lenz, who was traveling on to Weimar. In a country in which not even the military wore uniforms, two men dressed exactly alike "made a huge scene," according to Klinger's sister Agnes.[10] Called to Weimar by Duke Karl August, Goethe created a sensation by wearing the clothes of his famous literary figure. Karl von Knebel described Goethe's fashionable entrance into the Weimar court:

> In the fall of 1775 . . . the duke brought his wife to Weimar; Goethe came to us in the same year, after having received an invitation during their visit to Frankfurt. Like a star that has been hidden a time in the clouds and fog, Goethe began to shine. Everyone hung around him, especially the ladies. He was still wearing the Werther uniform, and many dressed in imitation. He had much of the spirit and morality of his novel about him, and this drew many to him; remarkably, the Duke himself felt . . . sympathetic . . . to the young protagonist. Many eccentricities were undertaken, which I do not wish to describe here, but which did not give us the best reputation.[11]

Karl Böttinger, who later became an editor of the *Mode Journal*, described how the duke prescribed the dress of his courtiers much like any other monarch, but this fashion was very much in opposition to the dominant French style: "The whole world was required to wear the Werther coat in those days. Even the duke wore one, and whoever could not acquire one, had one made for him by the duke. Only Wieland was exempted by the duke, because he was too old for such mummery."[12]

Sentimental subjectivity, Friedrich von Matthisson argued in his autobiography, functioned as a form of self-discipline among university students.[13] *Werther*, along with two other sentimental novels popular at the time, had a calming influence on boisterous Göttingen students, and even the strictest moralists would have had to look twice to find fault with the novel's followers:

> According to the authorities, the rawness and wildness in action and speech that had caught up a large portion of the students either declined notably from year to year or disappeared altogether, but certainly not because of a sermon from the pulpit or the example of someone in the circle of students. Rather, it was three novels that were required reading then that brought about the remarkable reform in morals: *Werthers*, *Siegwart*, and *Sophie's Travels*.[14]

Emulation of Werther changed the Bildungsbürgertum's younger generation's manners, reading habits, and leisure pursuits as well as its dress code. "In the time that remained after class work, many young people turned to keeping diaries, collecting a poetic anthology from journals, or composing religious ecstasies dedicated to transcendent Lottes, Marianes, and Julies."[15] By sculpting their free time according to an aesthetic standard, students prepared the way for the rest of their social class to adopt a fashion sense independent of the feudal hierarchy. Werther enthusiasts applied their literary tastes to aspects of everyday life not before subject to aesthetic consideration. Previously, the aristocracy had been the only class to stylize their daily existence; the Bildungsbürgertum had either been prohibited from emulating the aristocracy or, in the case of the progressive intelligentsia, had avoided luxuries to demonstrate their virtue. The Werther fashion was one of the first instances of an important trend in eighteenth-century German culture: the emergence of a social aesthetic that encompassed the objects and behaviors of everyday life while reflecting the political interests and moral outlook of the Bildungsbürgertum. This new aesthetic did not emanate from the court (Weimar being an exception). Rather, it was formed by the seemingly invisible and usually indecipherable judgments of the public realm and, thus, had no direct connection to the state. Werther enthusiasm was just such an independent fashion trend: it embodied an aversion to the bureaucratic state and a longing for a community that was beautiful not only in the moral feeling of its members but also in its surroundings.

Repeatedly imitating Werther became a tactical exercise in the expression and production of an emotional life. Werther followers reiterated the novel's style until they installed the rhetoric of sentimentality within themselves, transforming it into their own authentic expression. The satirical pamphlet "Viennese Follies" (Thorheiten Wiens), published in 1781, referred to the "practical Wertherism" of sentimental young men:

> They rant just as much as that highly praised fool, and their excess of emotion reduces them to idle machines incapable of serving the state, just like their teachers. In every regard, they imitate this pattern: they write verse, philosophize about the vanity of others, complain to the trees about their martyrdom, whimper themselves half to death in gardens; only in one regard do they break the mold.[16]

The calculated imitation of Werther contradicted the protagonist's insistence that his feelings were uniquely his own. Deliberate emulation runs the risk of becoming parody. The machine analogy suggested the interchangeability of sentimental young men, as well as their unreflective subordination to an exterior principle. Like so many later fashion movements, the Werther movement sought to escape this contradiction by drawing a distinction between those who acted like the protagonist out of their own emotional conviction and those who unthinkingly and unfeelingly copied the novel's representations. The novel's reception was evaluated in much the same terms as the single act of reading. Those who experienced the novel as a living reality, one they could enter through their own fantastical identification, were perceived as authentic, whereas those who joined the trend later were characterized as unimaginative and mechanical.[17]

Werther imitators wanted to be publicly perceived as possessing or sharing, in an authentic manner, the literary character's personality. By appearing in his clothes, they signaled their aspiration to be accepted by others as having the same qualities they perceived in Werther. Their appearance was deliberately calculated to serve as a sign of their inner state. It was this aspect of the Werther fashion that Georg Lichtenberg had in mind: "The current decline of serious scholarship has been contributed to by the tendency to consider Wertherian enthusiasm in love as the sign of great passion and the irrefutable urges of nature."[18] The Werther fashion was predicated upon a semiotic system in which clothes and personal property operated as signs of emotions, moral character, political commitment, and capacity for productive work.

Outside of sentimental circles, the Werther suit was intended to disrupt the established norms of public decorum. By making a public display of their newly constructed personalities, Werther imitators were asserting the primacy of interiority over social rank. The older dress code, which tied public appearance to a person's *Ständ*, was in the eyes of Wertherites replaced by a code in which external appearance was a sign of the private self. The Werther fashion was the event that later commentators referred to as the arrival of a new dress culture. The scandal around the novel helped constitute the bourgeois public sphere as mediating between texts and material existence. At the end of the century, the *Mode Journal* could without much controversy refer to the sentimental furor surrounding Werther as the starting point of a fashion culture that mixed literary fiction with material culture.

In this matter—all fashion readers will agree with me—eighteen years ago nothing was as interesting as Werther's sorrows. If I am not seriously mistaken, many feel them even today. Werther was devoured in many editions, he was served up in many different formats, and he continues to be savoured with ever new desire. As a work of genius, it defined the epoch.[19]

Direct emulation of the novel blurred the boundaries between fiction and ordinary reality. By suspending the difference between the inside and the outside of the artwork, the emulative reader assumed the position previously understood as "behind" representation.[20] While such identificatory modes of reading predominated among eighteenth-century sentimentalists, they have been viewed skeptically by the critical tradition invested in the autonomy of art. Supported by the older Goethe's autobiographical reflections in *Dichtung und Wahrheit*, critics have treated the fashionable emulation of the novel's protagonist as the effect of a naive and misguided aesthetic. Generations of scholars have echoed Goethe's complaint that his original public failed to distinguish between historical events and literary representation: "One cannot expect from the public that it will receive an intellectual work intellectually. As I had already experienced with my friends, it was only the content, the material itself, that was noticed."[21]

Hermeneutic critics such as Georg Jäger and Erdmann Waniek pursued the didactic question of whether eighteenth-century readers correctly responded to the guideline with which the text directed their reading (*Lesehinweise*).[22] Walter Erhart's deconstructive interpretation argued, similarly, that Werther enthusiasts read the novel naively, failing to recognize how the text deconstructed sentimental modes of subjective expression by exposing them as mere discursive codes.[23] Erhart built his argument on recent Werther scholarship, which focused on the apparent contradiction between Werther's rejection of artistic artifice and the novel's many overt references to literary discourse. Erhart maintained that readers who identified with the novel as an expression of authentic subjectivity to the point of mimicking its protagonist failed to recognize that they inscribed themselves within a discursive tradition. Their imitation of the novel's protagonist required them to ignore or disavow the text's critique of autonomous subjectivity.[24] While such identification overlooked the paradoxical ground of subjectivity, Erhart did acknowledge the political force of such misreadings: successive generations employed Werther's subject position as a vehicle for dismantling oppressive discursive practices.[25]

The most prominent aspect of readers' identification with the novel—namely, the historical Werther fashion, whereby young men mimicked the character's appearance, speech, and manners—was not, I posit, the product of a simplistic misreading. If it must be labeled a misreading, then it was an extremely productive and acceptable one, for the novel encouraged precisely those types of confusion that open up previously unarticulated possibilities. When Werther mistakenly reads a letter from Lotte, which begins "Precious, Beloved, come as soon as you can. I await you with a thousand joys," he believes for a moment that she is addressing him. Upon realizing that he is not the intended recipient, Werther cries, "What a divine gift the imagination is. . . . For a moment I was able to pretend it was written to me."[26]

The effects of the Werther reception were similarly excessive—and fruitful. Not only were sympathetic readers encouraged to imagine that they were the intended recipients of the novel, but their appropriation of its characters was instrumental in establishing a bourgeois, material culture in Germany. The emulative behavior of *Werther*'s readers introduced a style of dress directly at odds with the hierarchical dress culture of the ancien régime. Werther's simple country clothes became symbols of his refusal to acknowledge rank distinctions; when worn in public, they evoked the class conflict portrayed by Werther's career at court. More fundamental than the ideological connotations of Werther's clothes was the novel's introduction of a new method for judging personal identity through appearance. Without abandoning its critique of the court's clothing culture, whose insistent correlation of opulence with rank was the subject of Werther's satire, the novel presented an alternative semiotic system, which realigned the relation between material culture and identity by linking a small number of muted surface signs with the psyche. The novel negotiated past the basic Enlightenment criticism that dress did not reveal personal identity, instituting a modern understanding of dress that transforms the disjuncture between surface and depth into a sartorial ethic of restraint and understatement. This new morality of dress conceded that clothes were inevitably interpreted as signs of identity, and yet it sought to minimize the degree to which fashion convention and etiquette objectified personal identity.

Goethe's novel presented Werther's dress as an intimate sign of his personality and experiences. Its narration brings Werther's blue and yellow outfit to the fore, as his effort to live unhindered by convention collapses. Werther began to manipulate his clothes as signs only after other forms of "authentic" expression were frustrated. By the novel's end, his stylized appearance became a principal instrument in organizing meaning. Like the open copy of Gotthold Lessing's "Emilia Galotti" lying next to the corpse, the blue and yellow suit transformed Werther's body into a sign of its own flawed transcendence. The clothes replaced modes of sentimental discourse that had not secured acknowledgment from the "other." As a last, desperate means of solidifying a temporal, spatial, and semiotic position within a community, Werther's clothes sought to explain his death and memorialize his life, despite his failure to secure an authentic self.

From the moment he arrives at court, Werther engages in critical readings of personal appearances. Contrary to the aristocratic presumption that identity was established by conspicuous costumes, Werther follows a loose physiognomic method of interpolating a hidden character from a person's facial features and dress. Although his evaluations are not strictly physiognomic (he considers both physical and cultural markings), he does follow the assumption basic to all physiognomic interpretation: the correspondence of the soul with the body's exterior:

> We know the nature of the soul through its effects. Without a doubt, we receive more information if we more diligently observe this type of effect—the many expressions of its ideas and movements on the body. Since we cannot perceive it directly, we should be more diligent and attentive to the soul's mirror, or better yet, its veil, which is delicate and moveable enough for us to guess at the form that is seen through its light folds.[27]

The metaphors in J. J. Engel's explanation of physiognomic thinking were turned into literal sources of truth, thereby linking personal character to dress. Clothes, after all, revealed the intentions of the soul; and when worn consistently as a uniform, their signification could be viewed with the same stability as the nose and forehead of J. C. Lavater's studies in personality.

Werther's commentary on his enemies demonstrates his excellent eye for the details of dress. His letters contain descriptions of people in which their personalities are related to their clothes. In an early characterization of a city doctor who criticized his playful treatment of children, Werther pays attention to the particularities of dress and manner. "The doctor, quite a dogmatic marionette, who plays with his cuffs while speaking and tugs on his ruff endlessly, found this view quite offensive to the dignity of an intelligent person: I could tell by his nose."[28] Later, at the court, his letters include caricatures of the aristocrats who snubbed him: "The Baron F, with an entire wardrobe from the time of Francis I's coronation; the court counsellor R, with his deaf wife; not to forget the poorly endowed J, who tries to patch his old Frankish wardrobe with newly fashionable rags" (68). Implicit in Werther's ridicule of the nobility's dress is the belief that there exists a superior mode, namely, his own.

Only on two occasions, however, does Werther call attention to his own dress. The first occurs in the short letter of September 6, which is devoted exclusively to Werther's telling how he is obliged to replace the clothes he wore when he first met Charlotte. His attitude here is clearly nostalgic. By continuing to wear his suit, Werther tries to secure the memories of his first erotic encounter with Charlotte from the stream of events that threatens to vitiate them.[29] The country dance, the ominous thunderstorm, Werther and Lotte's shared sentimental vision of nature and poetry are preserved only in small details. Albert's subsequent return, his marriage to Lotte, and Werther's failed career stand between the self who wrote the September 6 letter and the self who first met Lotte. Over the course of time, the suit is the only element that seems unchanged. However, Werther finally concedes that even it has become too worn:

> It had held together a long time before I resolved to set aside the plain blue coat in which I danced with Lotte for the first time; however, it was in the end unpresentable. Anyway, I have had one made exactly like the previous one, the same collar and cuffs, as well as the same yellow vest and leggings to go with it. It doesn't have quite the same effect. I don't know—I think in time, I will like it more. (79)

This commentary comes as something of a revelation. Suddenly, a detail that had long gone unmentioned is foregrounded in a manner that forces the reader to assume that it has been significant to Werther's psychic development. One must ask, If he has been deliberating about his suit for so long, why has he not mentioned the matter earlier? By alluding to an internal debate to which the reader has not been privy, Werther suggests the existence of an intimate sphere hidden outside of the text. Why does the reader learn that Werther has an investment in his clothes only after he decides to give them up? One is drawn to seek out earlier references to the clothing. How are they described in the waltz scene? Does Lotte comment on them? Does the dance in any way call attention to Werther's dress? Why have his clothes not been mentioned earlier? We might remember that Werther makes a similar confession about his attachment to objects when he reveals that he has kept a silhouette of Lotte:

> I thank you, Albert, for deceiving me. I waited for news of when your wedding would be and had resolved to very ceremoniously take Lotte's silhouette down from the wall and to bury it among my papers. Now you are a couple, and the picture is still there. Well, so it shall remain. And why not? (67)

Albert's deception of Werther allows Werther to continue his attachment to Lotte's image as if nothing has changed. Yet, the reader is compelled to ask, What importance has the silhouette had all this time? It would seem that it and the dancing clothes have functioned as fetish objects for much of the novel, without the reader's knowledge. In both cases, the reader is surprised to learn of Werther's attachment and is, therefore, compelled to review the previous narration for other references to these objects. The lack of answers to these questions not only suggests that Werther hid his attachment to objects associated with Lotte but also implies the existence of a previously unrecognized connotation, a secret language of things.

It would seem that Werther seeks to avoid revealing his clothes' intimate meaning for as long as possible. Only their material deterioration forces him to acknowledge their signifying function. This aspect of the suit is revealed first by his explanation for replacing it: "er ward aber zuletzt gar unscheinbar" (it was in the end unpresentable). The term *unscheinbar* implies that the suit is no longer presentable in public, which in the ordinary sense of the word would mean that the suit no longer served as an adequate indication of Werther's social rank. However, within the domain of Werther's sentimental value system, the suit's failure to signify also means that it is no longer an unambiguous signifier of Werther's romantic union with Lotte. Rather than demonstrating the secret continuation of their bond, the suit becomes an image of its temporal disintegration. The worn cloth reveals the passage of time, thereby reversing Werther's intended meaning. A replica would cover up the obvious marks of time, but because it has no material link with the moment that established its meaning, it cannot contain the auratic memory of the past. Because it is unable to claim a metonymic link to Lotte's body, the new garment operates purely as a sign, which relies on its formal characteristics alone to link signifier with signified. "Auch habe ich mir einen machen lassen, ganz wie den vorigen, Kragen und Aufschlag und auch wieder so gelbe Weste und Beinkleider dazu. Ganz will es doch die Wirkung nicht tun." The two meanings of the word *ganz* here suggest the gap between signifier and signified: while the copy is "exact" (*ganz*), it fails to recreate the "entire" (*ganz*) experience. Werther concedes that the garment is a mere substitute and that the sartorial code operates with a signifier that has no material or temporal link to its signified.

The new suit's formal similarity to the clothes he wore to the country ball generates the illusion of a denotative meaning, which in turn grounds Werther's fantastical disavowal of the present.[30] He holds onto his clothes as a means of prolonging his illusionary relationship with Lotte. Their presence at the ball has privileged them. Like the denoted message of a photograph, which Barthes claimed naturalizes an image's connotative references, the suit becomes the last means for Werther to communicate his persistent desire.[31] By wearing the same suit continuously, a relatively common act in the eighteenth century, Werther is free to speculate on its symbolism and to construct new connotations.

Of course, Werther's dress is anything but passively involved in the construction of meaning. As Jean Baudrillard argued, denotation matters only because it serves the system of connotation.[32] Similarly, the suit allows the continuation of a fantasy denied by other discourses. Its apparent innocence is due precisely to its having lacked importance at the time of the ball. The suit acquires value after the fact—merely for having "attended" the ball—not because it is noticed, commented upon, or in any way important to Lotte and Werther's interaction. A simple bystander at first, the suit later becomes the last remaining witness to an emotional event already vitiated. That Werther has to rely on the garment as the sole remaining reference to this moment further highlights his failure to communicate successfully through other media. While the suit may create the illusion of a bond with Lotte, its employment alone implicitly acknowledges the disappearance of that union.

Scholars have noted that the "Klopstock" moment was itself a product of a literary tradition and not the naive, direct expression of two souls.[33] The use of poetry to sanctify personal expression, as well as the body's subordination to the rules of dance, shows that sentimental experience is already inscribed in cultural discourses, even as it claims to escape such regimentation. While language and choreography structure experience within a publicly articulated system, thereby undermining sentimentalism's claim to express singular experiences, Werther's sartorial code came as close to being private as a public language can, for it referred to a single event with the narrowness of one participant's perspective. As an inarticulate system of representation that relied on metonymy, Werther's clothing code implicitly acknowledged that his yearned-for transcendence existed outside conventional discourse. At least initially, the referent could be fully known only if the communicants were "present" at the referent's origin—if they shared in the original experience. This exclusivity deflected skepticism concerning the truth of its representation; indeed, the code's claim to express a profound experience was enhanced by the acknowledgment that the referent remained inexpressible by socially sanctioned discourses. Through its participation in the dance, the suit acquired the aura of a religious relic or a photograph—the quality of having been there, which Barthes has ascribed to snapshots.[34]

The aura that the second suit lacks is regained later, during Werther's second moment of physical contact with Lotte's body. He acknowledges that the suit has been "recharged" in his last request. "In these clothes, Lotte, I wish to be buried; you have touched them, sanctified them" (123). Presumably, he wore the suit the night he read Ossian to Lotte. The desperate kiss Werther steals, the tearful goodbye, and his resolution to kill himself emblazon the new suit with the tragic energy of renunciation. No longer just nostalgic mementos of the affair's origin, his clothes become markers of its conclusion.

The attempt to stabilize identity through the prolongation of a single temporal experience invoked the courtly love tradition, wherein the exchange of tokens simultaneously acknowledged and constrained an extramarital love affair. Well before Werther reveals to the reader the importance of his attire, he receives a ribbon from the dress Lotte wore to the dance. Thus, an exchange denied on the level of verbal discourse and physical relations is transferred to the level of the vestimentary code. By sending the ribbon, Lotte enters into a dialog using a code derived from the two costumes. The value of this new sartorial code as a substitute for speech is heightened by the absence of a textual guideline, thereby reinforcing the sentimental trope of "unspeakable" passion. Werther also gains libidinal satisfaction from this brief exchange of garments because he presumes that behind the sign lies some real source for its production, namely Lotte's desire for him.

This mode of communication is limited, however, by its homosociality. Albert's approval of the gift is, after all, an implicit attempt to regulate Werther's desire. By mapping Werther's desire onto an economy of exchange between men, Albert seeks to constrain Werther's absolute demands for Lotte. Werther's reaction, however, looks beyond this patriarchal gesture. Instead of acknowledging Albert's oedipal imprint, Werther reads the ribbon as a sign of his absence, linking it with his first vision of Lotte, when Albert was far from the scene.[35] "Today is my birthday, and early in the morning I received a small package from Albert. Upon opening it I immediately saw one of the pale red ribbons she wore when I first met her and for which I have asked her many times" (54).

Like the second suit, the ribbon serves as a metonymic sign twice removed. As a part of the whole, it refers to the dress from which it was taken, which in turn is a further metonymy for his first erotic contact with her body. The ribbon's ability to invoke the past is reflected also in the language of Werther's two letters. He employs the same phrase to describe his seeing the ribbon in his birthday package as when he saw Lotte for the first time. On both occasions, the object of his desire "fällt ihm in die Augen" (falls into view), implying that Werther is unexpectedly and pleasantly overwhelmed by a vision of Lotte. This movement in turn substitutes for the more physical gesture of "sie fällt mir in die Arme" (she falls into my arms).

Lotte's white dress and its red ribbons follow the same trajectory as Werther's suit. Both are worn on their first encounter, both are turned into memorials of that meeting midway through the novel, and both are present at his death. In the same letter in which he asks that he be buried in his blue and yellow outfit, Werther requests that the ribbon that he carries in his pocket be buried with him: "Let this ribbon be buried with me. On my birthday you gave it to me. How I devoured all that!" (123). Having been elevated to a sign of love, Lotte's dress symbolizes Werther's fate just as his own clothes do. The two sets of garments are joined in burial, serving as a stylized, material sign of the union Werther envisions they will have in the afterworld. The novel's final tableau transforms Werther from a sign of sentimentalism's futility into a symbol of almost limitless inwardness.[36] The mere fact of its arrangement suggests that Werther's body has become a sign; the specific reference of the clothes to his one moment of transcendence—while waltzing with Lotte—has already been established. The beautiful corpse thus exists at the end of the novel as the sole signification, which has not been contradicted by an external reality, for signification presumes the demise of the authentic subject.

The narrator of the novel's last section provided readers with little reason to distance themselves from Werther's obsession with his clothes. When Werther returns from his midnight wanderings after visiting Lotte for the last time, his hat is missing. Details of Werther's dress are given as if they are clues to a mystery. Read according to a fashionable physiognomy, they indicate Wether's impending madness:

> His servant noticed that Werther's hat was missing when he came home. . . . Later, the hat was found on a cliff, which from the precipice of the hill allows a view into the valley. It is unimaginable how in that dark wet night he managed to climb it without falling. (115)

Werther's hat serves as the only sign for what the reader must believe was a sublime encounter. The narrator's inability to provide a letter recounting Werther's last vision of nature leaves the reader with an even greater sense of its unspeakable singularity. Just as the name "Klopstock" seals Lotte and Werther's shared vision of a thunderstorm during their first meeting, Werther's round brimmed hat and its location on the side of the abyss give the reader a sign of transcendence.

In reconstructing the events around the suicide, the narrator provides the reader with no information that undermines Werther's image of himself. His factual, paratactic style confirms the sentimental effect Werther hopes to achieve. "He lay spent on his back against the window, completely dressed and booted, in a blue coat and yellow vest" (124). What the narrative voice presents as a simple summary of empirical evidence the reader knows to have a deeper, sentimental meaning. Werther's clothes cannot be read as incidental details in a factual report; they are secret, empirical signs of Werther's passion. The reader knows to look beyond the surface of the narrator's account and to see in the description of Werther's dress a textual affirmation of his suicide. His clothes, his posture, the copy of "Emilia Galotti" nearby, create a scene for the reader that reiterates Werther's suffering and his hope for a utopian release in death. Werther's body joins the lifeless facsimiles of human existence—the puppet, the automaton, the mannequin. The well-dressed corpse lying next to Lessing's tragedy stands for feelings that cannot find a place in society. His dramatically staged suicide appears like the dash that breaks off so many sentimental passages in midsentence.

By invoking all that has preceded, the last image suggests that its motivation can be derived from the novel as a whole. The costume becomes a screen onto which sentimental subjectivity is projected, a move that simultaneously cancels it. The image of the death of the protagonist merely confirms and reinforces the transformations that had occurred at the level of representation. Inwardness is vacated in favor of its exterior sign. The still corpse allows the reader to perform an intense and unlimited physiognomic reading. The various failed formulations of sentimental identity are resuscitated and projected onto Werther's dead image. Lavater's fascination with corpses has shown that nothing served this mode of identity construction as well as a lifeless body. The dead Werther allows for a fixed reading of what appears in the text as an unstable and fluid subjectivity. "Their settled features are much more prominent than in the living and the sleeping. What life has made fugitive, death arrests; what was indefinable is defined. All is reduced to its proper level; each trait is in its true proportion."[37]

We might postulate three overlapping modes of employing clothes in the novel. Their order of appearance follows the narrative trajectory; however, there are no definitive transition points in which one system takes over from another. The brief textual references to clothing indicate nothing more than the shifting relation between clothes and the protagonist's monologue, a relation that the reader cannot directly observe. Because clothes mark the external limit of subjectivity, their apprehension by the novel's inner voice changes over the course of Werther's development, their manipulation revealing the deterioration of his inner voice. At first, the blue and yellow suit serves as a fetish object. During this phase, Werther refuses to reveal his investment in his attire. Only when he is forced to abandon his clothes does he make clear that he has held onto them as a means of memorializing his first evening with Lotte. At this point, the clothes operate as a sign, a reminder of this earlier moment and of Werther's desperation. The fact that Lotte agrees to send Werther a ribbon from her dress suggests that she has operated within a sartorial system of communication and exchange well before the reader becomes aware of this possibility. The ambiguity between fetish and sign is canceled when the sartorial code is made public by Werther's carefully staged suicide.

In the third phase, the clothes function as the material depository for not just one episode but for the entire narrative. They become the site to which the text's inner voice is displaced and, thereby, memorialized as an image. Because the clothes' significance has already been established within Werther's inner monologue, they become witness objects, or clues, to a truth hidden behind the third-person narration. The irony of the narrator's detached report set against the intimate voice of the earlier epistles underscores the tension between surface and interiority, thereby urging the reader to search for a depth behind the tableau of Werther's corpse. By coupling the clothes with the protagonist's death, the final scene elevates the suit to the status of a sign whose signified is an entire narrative.

The transformation of Werther's suit into a uniform that signals an illusionary masculine autonomy illustrates the political anatomy of bourgeois fashion. Within the nonliterary context of fashionable society, the Werther suit integrated the male body into a military code of discipline without violating clothes' ideological promise of personal freedom. That military discipline appeared as an expression of individuality seems paradoxical. Yet the opposition between courtly and bourgeois modes of interpreting and displaying the body made just such an equation sensible. The emerging fashion culture adopted uniform styles as a negation of ostentation. By presenting a blank surface, uniforms drew attention to the operations performed below the first level of sartorial signification. Muscular stature, athletic performance, and practiced execution were foregrounded by the refusal to locate identity on the level of garments.

The relatively simple, dark clothes worn by Werther insisted that the viewer not be satisfied with the most visible signs of rank. Rather, they asked that the viewer's vigilance be prolonged and that the clothes be evaluated in terms of how well they integrated with the body's activity. Such scrupulous examination of clothes so as to appreciate their role within the productive life of the body was completely contrary to the aristocratic code of dress. As Veblen pointed out, nobility in elite society required the demonstration of an exemption from all labor.[38]

French court dress was perhaps the highest and most sophisticated example of this equation; its costumes thoroughly subordinated bodily movement to the display of its leisure, making slight exceptions only for such elite rituals as ballet dancing and horseback riding. Yet it was out of these minor genres of courtly dress that the first bourgeois styles developed. The Werther suit derived from military uniforms and country sportswear. It embodied the new sartorial scheme that foregrounded a subjectivity defined as a mode of resistance against the superficial obligations of tradition while simultaneously integrating the body into a network of production.

Werther's clothes had much the same connotation in courtly society that blue jeans, T-shirts, and army jackets once had for respectable, white, middle-class America.[39] They were originally intended only for sports and the country. That young men would wear them in polite society and in the presence of ladies was considered offensive years after *Werther*'s publication. The following letter published by the *Mode Journal* in 1791 complaining about the unwillingness of young men to conform to social decorum makes clear that the *Werthermode* challenged the very mechanisms by which bodies were regulated within corporate society:

> The young fashionable Berliner of the distinguished and largest class wears, from morning until night, boots, a round hat, a blue coat with a red collar, in a very militarist style and very often with dirty linen. Dressed in this manner, he goes to lectures, under the linden, to coffeehouses, a meal, again under the linden, to the theater, and very often into society. He enters polite society only when parents, a love affair, or some other convenience brings him there, and under no circumstances can he be bothered to change his attire. He is hardly concerned whether his clothes fit the colors or ornaments of the season. . . . What is formal attire to him? That would seem fussy. And why adorn himself? For whom? He simply has no need to.[40]

The Werther outfit produced scandal not only because of its rural associations but also because it was worn continuously. By wearing one outfit all day, the individual refused to integrate himself into an etiquette that required him to change his attire several times, depending on time of day, activity, and company. It was expected that an aristocrat suited himself to the rituals that ruled a particular milieu. As the sole attire of young men, the Werther suit suspended polite convention. By not adapting to the requirements of every new situation, the individual who wore a riding outfit continuously suggested that the internal relationship between the subject, his body, and its clothing was more important than the integration of the self into a society.

The Werther suit, even when worn by horsey Prussians, asserted a right to personal exemption from the dominant clothing regime. This suspension was possible only through the application of a new system upon the body; there was no moment of freedom from control, despite the many ideological claims to the contrary. The country mode of dress was similar to mourning attire in its claim that personal circumstances justified ignoring polite society's daily costume changes. However, unlike mourning black—which was after all a suspension of etiquette that was itself sanctioned by etiquette—the Werther suit did not present itself as a temporary condition. Rather, it considered itself a norm that simply disregarded etiquette.[41] The male costume as a form of dress that integrated the body with the symbolic rituals and institutions of corporate power was exchanged for the single mode of dress that preserved the body as a valuable resource (protecting it from the dangers of horseback riding) while preparing its integration into disciplinary regimes such as the military. While the older, aristocratic style of dress also invoked military tradition, it was concerned primarily with display of rank.

The new regime of military discipline altered the very concept of rank by linking it with a more detailed training of the individual soldier and focusing on the body as a weapon to be employed in battle. The riding attire worn by affluent young Prussians replaced corporate distinctions with the obligation to utilize the body more efficiently, to allow it greater mobility in both physical and temporal terms. The athletic body practiced in horsemanship and long country marches was no mere frame for displaying identity. Its clothes supported the body, suggesting an interest in preserving the interior over communicating with the exterior. Riding clothes, such as those worn by Werther, protected the skin with high leather boots and leather breeches, while the soft silk fabric and the bright colors of the aristocratic *voller Anzug* consciously eschewed all practicality.

Within the complex and often contradictory symbolism of fashionable society, the Werther attire implied three divergent ideological allegiances: the English landed gentry, the Prussian military, and the American Revolution.[42] While these referents were not allied in a conventional political sense, they were organized within fashion discourse as a utilitarian rejection of German court ritual as derived from Louis XIV's Versailles. By abandoning the corporate hierarchy, clothes acquired an ambiguity that allowed the simultaneous signification of mutually exclusive political alignments within a single garment. While other media could be employed to more sharply define the signification of clothes, they did so only by narrowing the range of references that clothing could suggest. Embedded in the clothes themselves was a complex and contradictory array of potential references.

The English sympathies of Karl Jerusalem, the model for Goethe's Werther, were well known through his publications, and thus Goethe could confidently describe his clothes as "typical for North Germans who imitated the English: blue frock coat, yellow suede vest and leggings, and brown boots with straps."[43] Commentaries on *Werther* have followed Goethe's intentions by focusing on Werther's idyllic conception of English rural life,[44] thereby situating the novel within a broader German Enlightenment reception of English literature and culture. However, the chain of emulation involved several sharp turns and contradictory developments. As the blue and yellow suit was passed from rural England to Karl Jerusalem to Goethe, it went through phases of meaning. While Goethe may have admired Jerusalem's attire, the latter gentleman had little respect for Goethe's. When the two men first met in Wetzlar, Goethe was still wearing the French-style clothes he had acquired as a student in Leipzig, then referred to as "Klein Paris." In a letter to his Anglophile friend, Johann Joachim Eschenburg, Jerusalem condescendingly referred to the young Goethe as "a complete fop."[45]

After the novel's publication, Christian Weiße described Lessing's reaction to the novel: "Lessing was highly outraged by the *Sorrows of Young Werther* and maintained that it wholly misrepresented the character of young Jerusalem. He had never been a sentimental fool; rather, he had been quite a reflective philosopher."[46]

Although Lessing's grumblings are no help in understanding the novel, they do point out the ease with which material objects can be given new meanings. Garments that diverged radically from conventional dress disrupted the established system for evaluating differences. Like all forms of shock, their connotation could not be readily discerned. Goethe, and probably Jerusalem before him, without adhering strictly to the religious teachings of the Friends, employed Quaker garb as a jab against normality. Before the advent of fashion journals, which sought to evaluate clothes and household articles in terms of utility and taste, the meaning ascribed to an article of clothing could not be discovered by referring to an authoritative lexicon or a code of law.[47] Here, in the earliest stages of bourgeois dress culture, the Werther suit belonged to the loose coalition of garments at odds with the courtly canon of respectability. Like the uniform, it invoked a morality of practicality augmented by a tactical control of the body. In contrast to the uniform, the Werther suit also claimed to be a sign of inner depth. To appreciate this added significance, one had to refer to the speech, or in this case the fictional first-person narration, of its owner. If the owner failed to explain his attire, then one was forced to rely on the judgment of public opinion, which was itself subject to change, contradictory, and context dependent.

The variety of contradictory connotations attached to and then dislodged from the blue and yellow suit illustrates how twisted the route of fashionable emulation was. New styles of dress were by definition, at least in the eighteenth century, still undefined; that is, they had not entered a catalogue of fixed meanings. As an object moved from one context to another, it gained and shed new meanings. In hindsight, an article's old associations might seem like a string of inconsistencies, which were joined together metonymically by brief moments of transition, wherein the object passed from one interpretive framework to another. One could not even speak of a single genealogy, for the simple, nonornamental garments of modern dress culture frequently invoked several different backgrounds. Their plasticity allowed them to "pass" in a number of hostile contexts, thereby giving the impression that they were at home in many places at once. This ability to settle into every environment was, according to the *Mode Journal*, one of the defining—and most praiseworthy—features of English dress. It adapted itself easily.

The tendency for young English nobleman to wear their rural attire during their London residence had been noted by eighteenth-century German tourists. The *Mode Journal* pointed out that because the English aristocracy spent only a short season in London, their dress was much less ostentatious and far more suited to rural conditions, a quality that would certainly have appealed to Germans living in the hinterlands.[48] Karl Phillip Moritz noted in his travelogue that

> the Members of the House of Commons have nothing in particular in their dress; they come into the house in their greatcoats and with boots and spurs. It is not uncommon to see a member lying stretched out on one of the benches while others are debating. Some crack nuts, others eat oranges.[49]

Lord Chesterfield confirmed these observations:

> Most of our young fellows here display some character or other by their dress; some affect the tremendous and wear a great and fiercely cocked hat, an enormous sword, a short waistcoat, and frock cravat. Others go in brown frocks, leather breeches, great oaken cudgels in their hands, their hats un-cocked and their hair unpowdered. . . . [They] imitate grooms, stage coach-men, and country bumkins.[50]

While Chesterfield had little patience with gentlemen who dressed down, he did at least acknowledge that this manner of dress was more than a simple failure to satisfy etiquette. The dirty riding boots and drab greatcoats of the countrified gentlemen belonged to their ideologically and aesthetically motivated sartorial code; they were not just lapses from the older etiquette. Lord Chesterfield, whose advice on a gentleman's proper deportment came very close to the modern ideal of detached understatement, still admonished his son to conform completely to Parisian fashion so that he might learn the proper means for pleasing others:

> Fashion is more tyrannical at Paris than in any other place in the world; it governs even more absolutely than their King, which is saying a great deal. The least revolt against it is punished by proscription. You must observe and conform to all the minuties of it, if you would be in fashion there yourself; and if you are not in fashion, you are no-body. Get, therefore, at all events, into the company of those men and women qui donnent le ton; and though at first you should be admitted upon that shining theatre only as a persona muta, persist, persevere, and you will soon have a part given you.[51]

The obligation to dress richly was particularly strong when one was adapting to foreign expectations. Chesterfield still accepted a standard of dress and decorum requiring submission by the male courtier, a position contrary to the *Mode Journal*'s praise for English dress three decades later.

Much pleased with his son's finery, the lord wrote: "Mr. Hart informs me that you are clothed in sumptuous apparel: a young fellow should be so, especially abroad. Next to their being fine, they should be well made and worn easily."[52] Only in these last suggestions, concerning the ease with which a gentleman carries himself, which pivots on the relation of the clothes to the body, did Chesterfield allude to that quality that distinguished English attire at the end of the century. By the 1790s, English goods in Germany represented a modernist aesthetic that was functional, earnest, solidly constructed, less likely to change, simpler, and thus more universal. This transformation could not have been brought about by mere sloppiness: country dress produced more than a breakdown of etiquette; it also redefined what it meant to appear in public and introduced new explanations for personal appearance and new mechanisms for regulating luxury consumption. English fashion goods were adopted throughout Continental Europe because they were comfortable, because they were the most advanced industrial products in Europe, implying an ideological commitment to liberal capitalism, and because they enabled a reorganization of the social order. Thus, to understand the political effects these goods had on European society, we must not only understand the economic forces that manufactured them but must also examine how they were employed within daily life as instruments of social control and resistance.

The regulatory logic of simple, unspectacular dress had always been known to religious orders. However, English Protestants of the seventeenth century carried the practices of religious cloisters and monasteries into the world, and these became important antecedents of the bourgeois style of the eighteenth century. Particularly within Quakerism, one finds a disciplinary system of denying ostentation, of enforceable limits on consumption, and of a new affirmative form of bodily display, one that was ostentatious precisely because of its reserve and understatement.

César de Saussure's description of Quaker men can be translated into the terms of a mid-nineteenth-century dandy, all reserve and modest restraint in color, yet luxurious in texture:

> The Quakers' mode of dressing is as curious as is their language; the men wear large, unlooped, flapping hats, without buttons or loops; their coats are as plain as possible, with no pleatings or trimmings, and no buttons or buttonholes on the sleeves, pockets, or waists. If any brother were to wear

ruffles to his shirt or powder on his hair, he would be considered impious. . . . Quakers' clothes, though of the simplest and plainest cut, are of excellent quality; their hats, clothes, and linen are of the finest.[53]

Quaker manners do belong to the long tradition of Christian renunciation.[54] But what distinguished the Society of Friends from monastic orders was its insistence on individual, spiritual inspiration. William Penn's exhortation to his followers, "Chuse thy Cloaths by thine own Eyes, not another's," was intended to counter fashionable emulation and projective identification, which led individuals to see themselves as others might. The more plain and simple they were, the better: "Neither unshapely, nor fantastical; & for covering and for Use and Decency, and not for Pride."[55] (The clothes advocated by fashion journals in the late eighteenth century were justified according to a similar rationale.) By urging Friends to "Chuse thy Cloaths by thine Eyes, not another's," Penn implied not only that individuals should avoid emulating popular taste but also that they should follow their own spiritual conviction in dress. The Quaker principle of relying upon an inner spirit for guidance reinforced Penn's praise of self-reliance.[56]

The relation between interiority and dress operated in reverse, as well. Modest clothes, Penn suggested, allowed others to read beyond surface appearances to perceive the soul. The semiotic code of reading spirit from matter was the reverse of courtly ostentation. Rather than equating beauty and honor with splendor, Penn insisted on a charismatic switch of the terms. Greatness in spirit was more readily communicated through a disinclination toward luxury. "We are told with truth that *Meekness & Modesty* are the rich Attire of the Soul; and the plainer the dress the more distinctly & lustrously their Beauty shines."[57] Penn's rule for reading appearances lay out the modernist sartorial logic of negation followed by nineteenth-century dandies: the less a man stood out from others, the more distinguished his taste was.

Quakers more than any other Protestant sect provided a model of daily life for eighteenth-century German critics of absolutism. For example, both Lessing, the Enlightenment rationalist, and Goethe, during his Sturm und Drang period, espoused a Quaker manner.[58] What made Quaker dress so compelling for German intellectuals was its strategic relation to the dominant French style of princely courts. Quaker clothes provided far more than a mere renunciation of worldliness; they provided a mechanism for constituting an alternative, perhaps even utopian, community within corporate feudalism. The ideological references once connected with English non-conformist styles and their associations with rural and religious rebellions became diffuse with the elevation of plain dress to the international level. Simple dark suits continued to be associated with liberal progress, but the motivations responsible for bringing them into existence were no longer present. This forgetting was no doubt required for the style's claim to universal elegance.

These motivations were still present when English styles were adopted on the Continent. The young men of the Sturm und Drang still sensed a revolutionary potential in plain dress, but this awareness was produced by the strategic application of garments within courtly etiquette rather than by a study of English political history. Dark clothes disrupted aristocratic conventions of displaying power by refusing to participate in the spectacular display of identity through dress. Their disregard for rank was more a fundamental threat to corporate hierarchy than simple usurpation.

A second tactical effect of plain dress, important both to Quakers and to radical Enlightenment groups such as the Sturm und Drang, was the maintenance of internal group conformity. Whereas Quakers had a theological interest in detecting sinful behavior in their members, secular bourgeois societies were concerned lest their members give in to wasteful and unproductive expenditures. Both sought to eliminate a particular kind of luxury, and both enforced the maintenance of another. As a direct consequence of their nonconformist practice, the Friends became renown for their recognizable dress. The avoidance of the conspicuous display of the self became just that. Quaker simplicity formed a mirror-image society for the court; individualized dress became solidified into a rule for conformity. The tension between coercion and voluntary consensus was openly debated not only by Quakers but also by most Puritan and nonconformist theologians of the seventeenth century. Immediately after the Restoration, William Penn and other Quakers pleaded openly for religious tolerance. To replace divine authority over human conduct was to deny God's sovereignty.[59]

One level of control, that of secular government, was held in abeyance so that a second, more complex order might be exercised. Toleration was not predicated upon an absence of regulation; rather, it replaced the state's direct and explicit force upon its citizenry by postulating a mysterious divine power over individual souls. This reliance on a divine presence within all persons to guide their conduct had two opposing tendencies as far as dress culture was concerned. First, it provided a theological justification for disregarding social conventions, particularly those that were deemed haughty and arrogant. William Penn, and no doubt others, prided themselves on their refusal to obey etiquette, on their way of addressing other people with the familiar "thou," and on their unwillingness to remove their hats in the presence of superiors.[60] Obligations to acknowledge rank were seen as meaningless and hollow, given the degenerate state of the world and it defection from divine will.[61] In their relation to external society, Quakers were nonconformist and as rude as the gruffest baronet.[62]

Internally, the renunciation of luxury functioned as a means of enforcing conformity. Regardless of how Quakers stood on the question that had plagued Puritans—namely, to what extent could church elders direct the congregation—the very existence of a dress consensus, once formed, exercised an obligation to conform, not unlike the rule of fashion in bourgeois society. To belong to the Society of Friends inevitably brought one under pressure to adopt the garb worn by other members of the community. Invectives against "gay Friends" were common in the history of the church.[63] Quakerism constituted itself through an outward rejection of elite conventions and an inward ecclesiastical discipline of its members' daily lives. Where one stood in relation to Quaker modesty in dress signaled either an allegiance to a religious sect or a divine presence within the individual. This double gesture was employed later in the eighteenth century with Sturm und Drang. Indeed, it reappeared throughout the modern period as a means of radical self-definition.

Eighteenth-century German fashion journals portrayed the loose-fitting, durable garments derived from English country dress as a major innovation in the design of clothing and as a crucial component in the rationalization of domestic life.[64] English clothes symbolized the modern technologies required for their manufacture. By wearing the dress of an English entrepreneur, German members of the Bildungsbürgertum inscribed themselves with an ideology of progress. On a discursive level, the introduction of English goods instituted a series of polar oppositions, which were reflected on successive levels of abstraction. The two types that Chesterfield described were not merely representatives of competing tastes; they embodied divergent signifying systems that operated with distinctly different techniques

for observing and regulating the individual through his body. New ideological categories reflected the disparities between the expressive model of
establishing identity through clothes associated with England and the older,
corporate model, which read class membership from material surfaces. The
clash between these two modes of evaluating and controlling dress appeared
within the rhetoric of fashion discussions as a separation between nation-
alities and genders as well as a conflict between classes.

Whereas the courtly system integrated sexual identity into its hierarchy
of clothing signification, the newer model was itself grounded on an division of sexual identity.[65] Its system of signification was permeated by a small
number of oppositions that claimed universal applicability. Their abstraction allowed a more thorough deployment of power over the clothed body.
Judgments based on external appearance could be made much more quickly
and did not require knowledge of the elaborate and disjointed network of
privileges that governed aristocratic dress. The courtly code, because of its
graded succession of distinction, resisted the application of a uniform code
for interpreting public appearances. Evaluations of individuals at court required a thorough understanding of genealogy, political alliances, and ceremonial ritual. Such forms of knowledge were unnecessary under the disciplinary system of clothing supervision. Rather than situate an individual
within a network of relations, English fashions established sartorial identity
through polar differences. The abstraction of these oppositions allowed the
more modern system of signification to subsume the older courtly hierarchies within the parallel axes of sexual and national character. Fashion as a
graded system of social distinction was defined in the new English discourse
as simultaneously feminine and French. These terms were, however, not
equally weighted. In the final analysis, national identity was integrated into
the more global gender division, as the following comment by the French-
speaking Swiss César de Saussure suggests:

> [Englishmen] do not trouble themselves about dress but leave that to their
> womenfolk. When the people see a well-dressed person in the streets, espe-
> cially if he is wearing a braided coat, a plume in his hat, or his hair tied in a
> bow, he will, without doubt, be called "French dog" twenty times perhaps
> before he reaches his destination. This name is the most common and evi-
> dently, according to popular idea, the greatest and most forcible insult that
> can be given to any man, and it is applied indifferently to all foreigners,
> French or otherwise.[66]

The standard of masculine attire described by Chesterfield and Saussure reached Germany toward the end of the century, where it overlapped with the more structured Prussian regimentation of the male body. The convergence of English and Prussian tastes in masculine attire and the resulting gendered division of fashion discourses was markedly visible in northern Germany.[67] The Prussian middle classes had been subject to sumptuary laws and import duties, which discouraged the consumption of French luxuries so thoroughly that only a self-consciously economic mode of consumption was feasible. Ostentation in the French aristocratic manner was implausible outside the Prussian court and rather restrained within. As one correspondent put it, "If we Prussians were to now start showing luxury and extravagance, the whole thing would seem affected, awkward, and quaint."[68] Given the Anglophile tone of Hansa cities, English utilitarian products were likely to encounter Prussian parsimony somewhere between Berlin and Hamburg. The divisions reported between male and female dress in Mecklenburg were a simplification of the dominant tendencies in the period's fashion rhetoric:

> The inhabitants of Mecklenburg are like all other Germans; they imitate both the English and the French, though with one important difference. The men arrange their clothes, their households, their carriages and gardens in the English style, whereas the elegant lady still follows the lead of Parisian fashion dealers, who send their outdated goods to the north.[69]

Like the disciplinary regimes Foucault described in his study of the microphysics of eighteenth-century political anatomy, fashion did not treat the human body en masse, as a single, unified entity; rather, it divided the body into specific components, which were themselves subject to closely focused coercion and pressure.[70] Movements, gestures, and attitudes have always been the concern of the well-dressed individual, but the eighteenth century introduced new means of evaluating the body's relation to its surroundings. The concern for the "natural" body brought with it a new array of techniques for evaluating its mobility, exposure, and protection. Many of these methods for judging the body's movements had already been used in the court. However, they were employed much more widely and with greater precision and thoroughness by the fashion culture that developed outside the court. And while the ideology behind these clothing reforms was the body's liberation from the hindrances and restrictions imposed upon it by civilization, these alterations did not entail the abandonment of bodily regulation through clothing. Rather, they brought about its expansion and intensification.

While the country manners associated with English squires struck many observers as indications that convention was loosening its grip on the body, these rural habits were in fact shifting the focal point of the regulatory gaze. Hunting and horseback riding no longer functioned merely as signs of aristocratic dominion; they became activities to be perfected for their own sake. The economy and control of bodily movement while riding became more important to the public eye than the mere representation of privilege. While the horse and rider continued to generate the admiration of the spectator, the coordination of their movements, rather than the luxury of their garments, became the means of generating distinction. In an article entitled, "The Man on Horseback; or, the French and German rider," published in 1786, the *Mode Journal* correlated sexual and national identity with the successful execution of riding maneuvers, which were quite consciously derived from military drills.[71] The German rider's gender was equated with precise and supple execution of equestrian maneuvers:

> Beneath him, the noblest animal in all Creation, the proud, dancing horse, which he rides with visible superiority and which he leads with the greatest ease. He himself is well seated, his form smooth and attractive, dressed in light clothes, free and noble in every movement. Certainly, there can be no more characteristic image of masculine strength, boldness, decisiveness, and ability than this; in other words, he is the complete man.[72]

Observing the rider's technique became the primary interest. He wore a short coat so as to expose the upper thigh to the observer, and for the same reason wore what are here called Hungarian pants," because they draw out the form of the thigh and knee better."[73] Like a well-trained cavalry officer, he was exposed to perpetual observation and the awareness that the evaluation of his horsemanship had implications far beyond sportly competition. His body was gripped by a regulatory regime that guided his movements far more thoroughly than if he were riding in the French style, in which horse and rider would be covered with luxurious wide garments. Thus, a mode of dress and behavior that was purported to liberate the body from stiff courtly ceremony by allowing greater mobility, flexibility, and protection from the elements was in fact a more complete method for disciplining the body's size, shape, and movement. As the rider's control over his own movements increased, so too did his responsiveness to the Prussian military regime.

Anyone familiar with Goethe's *Werther* no doubt would find it difficult to reconcile the novel's sensitive language of inwardness with the rough bearing of young Prussian aristocrats who spent most of their day on horseback. Werther's sentimentalism as it unfolded through the novel's fragmented and private epistolary monologue and the militarist masculinity that was publicly performed throughout Berlin constituted the extreme ends of a single interpretative paradigm, one that sought to correlate knowledge of an interior consciousness with exterior bodily signs. Their opposition to one another was apparent precisely because they were antipodes on the same scale of psychological evaluation. The Prussian horseman appeared as an object devoid of all thought, a mere instrument subservient to some exterior force, whereas Werther existed as a disembodied subjectivity, a voice experienced only through a text and thus wholly beyond the grasp of disciplinary power.

Both figures existed within a model that read the body's surface markings, such as clothes, cosmetics, facial features, gestures, movements, and even tone of voice, as clues to the emotional and psychological condition of a reality presumed to have been hidden within the body. This interior reality, while it lay beyond the purview of public observation, was constituted by the social gaze's persistent demand for knowledge of what it could not see. Within the operation of this interpretative schema, interiority could be nothing more than a projection of surface readings, since direct access was impossible. In other words, the extent to which a body was publicly acknowledged to possess an interior reality was itself a function of its place within the many discourses that judged the surface appearances of bodies. The depth attributed to the space behind visual image and the moral character ascribed to the actions performed by the body were dependent on how the signs on the surface were constituted and interpreted.

In the last third of the novel, Werther constructed an external code of appearance that was intended to articulate and memorialize the highest moments of his own experiences. True to the presumptions of the model that read interiority through exterior signs, the narrative sought first to articulate a narcissistic subjectivity, which severed itself from all cumbersome re-lations before acknowledging the need to compromise with external reality. Within the novel's narrative, radical subjectivity assumed priority over dis-courses that articulated identity within social relations. In response to his repeated failure to incorporate the objects of his desire within the terms of his subjectivity, Werther was obliged to adopt a less direct form of attach-ment by using his body as a nonverbal sign of his inward state, thereby sub-mitting himself to the rules of a language not fully his own.

Werther's deliberate rearrangement of his body, his choice of clothes, and the highly stylized final tableau were Werther's last attempt to communicate his inward aspirations. However, he did so at the expense of this very sub-jectivity. The process whereby the narration transformed the immaterial voice of sentimental authenticity into an ossified public sign of itself ultimately destroyed that which was represented, confirming even in death the juxta-position of surface to interior, which defined this model of subjectivity.

CHAPTER EIGHT

Civilian Uniforms as a Cure for Luxury

This dreadful blending of society . . . where in all circles the clothes make the man and money counts for more than one's own hearth . . . where there are no longer any seats of honor in churches, no first dances at weddings, no crowns for free-born brides, no black garb worn on holidays, and where the feudal bourgeois dignities are no longer useful to the state; where the affluent man buys himself rank and title; where the hired man . . . serves the state not with his blood but for its money . . . in this dreadful confusion, I say that immediate assistance is necessary before all is lost.[1]

WITH THESE apocalyptic words, Justus Möser began his plea for the introduction of a national dress code, a universal, ranked system of dress for all men — and a last hope for maintaining the values of the traditional, feudal *Stände*.

As Möser foresaw it, all men would be required to wear a standard outfit. Gradations of honor would be determined by service to the state, so that prestigious dress would reflect the individual's labor. Citations and censure would be distributed at annual gatherings. The presence of the king, dressed in the same garb as other men, would be crucial to the success of these annual reviews: only when the monarch wore the same outfit as all other men of honor would the plan for a standardized male take hold in the public imagination. Citizens who were not members of the military or the bureaucracy would finally have the opportunity to come into contact with their monarch. The effect of such gatherings would give a tremendous boost to patriotic feelings among the general population. "The eye of the lord would work here as it does at the head of an army, and love for the lord, as well as for the fatherland, would swell weakened arteries into new activity."[2]

In addition to being a means for distributing favor, the national dress would provide a means of punishment: men disgraced for criminal activities, corruption, or incompetence would be demoted in dress, marked by a special sign (as Jews in Rome were) or, in extreme cases, forbidden to wear the suit of honor altogether.[3] Denying criminals the right to wear the national costume would be, Möser reasoned, a more thorough punishment than existing punishments, one that would pursue the criminal into every aspect of his existence, for no matter where he went, his status would be marked by his dress. The withdrawal of sartorial privileges would, furthermore, be less costly than banishment or branding, which removed the criminal's productive labor from the community.

The most immediate effect of a national costume would be its suppression of luxury consumption. Rather than spending money in pursuit of constantly changing fashion goods, citizens would invest their wealth in economically productive enterprises. Individuals would abandon their efforts at representing status. Instead, the national costume would mobilize their energies into state service in order to advance their uniform rank. Those who were not active within the administrative apparatus would earn their uniform grade through the payment of taxes: the higher their contribution, the higher their place within the levels of dress. Aristocrats would join the bureaucracy or military simply to acquire the privilege of wearing the national costume.

Möser insisted that this system would eliminate the competition inherent in the culture of luxury consumption and end lower-class emulation of their superiors. Passing for a higher rank would be impossible. The ambiguity and possibilities for deception that fashionable dress culture allowed would be eliminated.[4] The example of leading men eschewing ostentation would mute women's consumption, as well. The restrained household father abandoning unproductive displays of wealth for the sake of productive service would redefine status within communities. Accomplishment would replace representation, even for those who were not subject to the costume's ranking system. While the uniform would apply a constant pressure on male dressers to perform duties for the state, it would also weigh on women and children to conform to these standards.

Möser recognized that these new inducements would replace the feudal patchwork of privileges and obligations. His strategy was to extend those tendencies that had already disrupted traditional society to encompass all citizens. Rather than allow the absolute state to concentrate its energies on a limited, and thereby exclusive, class of civil servants, Möser hoped to spread the positive attributes of state service. The creation of standing armies and the introduction of military uniforms had deprived ordinary citizens of the privileges associated with these modes of discipline. His uniform proposal was meant to restore the status of those classes excluded from the military by subjecting them to a similar regime:

> As soon as . . . the sword and the plow were separated, the second was deemed humiliating . . . while the first was ever more honored and desired. Instead of placing the burgher in a military uniform just so he may regain his lost honor through some rationalized order, an alternative approach would work as well. Indeed, there is no compelling reason that the burgher and the farmer . . . could not wear a red or a blue coat instead of the usual brown one. Why should not children in schools and universities also learn riding, dancing, and fencing?[4]

Möser's unique form of conservative enlightenment claimed to restore feudal dignity by universalizing those very regimes of power that had replaced it. Möser's complaint was essentially that military service had created a new code of honor, distinct from the privileges and rights granted to feudal ranks. While the military recruited on the basis of corporate distinction—aristocrats became officers, middle-class sons became subalterns, and peasants were drafted as enlisted men—membership in the army carried a status that civilians could never acquire. At every class level, the standing army's internal order of rank had supplanted the feudal hierarchy. The introduction of uniforms had created a new basis for distinction. At weddings and church ceremonies, uniforms were the markers of rank, trumping the local community's established symbols. Only when all men gained the right to wear a uniform would these older ceremonies regain their symbolic function. And with the restoration of feudal decorum would come a secondary benefit: the suppression of luxury and the encouragement of state service.

Möser's proposal was followed by a number of variations. However, these later versions made direct reference to the changed political relationship between the state and its citizens and took a much more cautious approach to instituting a standardized dress code. Rather than depending on a state ordinance, they urged the formation of voluntary associations of respected citizens. A *Mode Journal* article requested that leading publications circulate information as well as illustrations. Ten years after Möser's first proposal, the plan had changed. Rather than have the state impose military discipline directly onto the civilian population, civil society would regulate itself.

In an issue during its first year of publication, the *Mode Journal* included a long letter with a detailed plan for introducing a national costume. Alluding to the fervent wish of other German patriots, the author began by claiming that he was responding to a widespread public concern. In essence, the anonymous author reiterated the physiocratic objections that Friedrich Bertuch had addressed in the first issues of the *Mode Journal*:

> Nowadays, the complaint is often made, quite correctly, that we Germans are slavish imitators of the French when it comes to clothes, manners, and morality and that we, therefore, are daily losing the stamp of our originality. Furthermore, this imitation of foreigners has made a luxurious attitude in matters of morality, finance, and trade all the more common among us.[5]

It was not difficult to understand how the editors of the fashion journal would have seen the national uniform proposal as a denunciation of their effort to create a sartorial culture, a project that was quickly coming into fruition, as we can see from the manner in which the anonymous author argued for his proposal. The letter made direct reference to the public sphere, the author presuming that any change in dress habits would require extensive public discussion in order to convince participants of the plan's rationality. The letter also insisted that the uniform be instituted through private, voluntary organizations, not government edict. Unlike Möser's urge to legislate the uniform as part of the state's police authority, the writer hoped that his plan would be adopted by regional assemblies of independent voters. In defining the electorate for these assemblies, he named groups that composed the emerging bourgeois public sphere: "Tradesmen, manufacturers, craftsmen, artists, lawyers, rural gentry, families living on their rents, doctors, surgeons, scholars, and the like."[6] If a few thousand of these self-sufficient individuals agreed to wear the uniform, then other classes would follow suit.

This reliance on the public sphere as the active force in reforming personal dress came very close to Kant's argument that, for the individual, "it is difficult to work oneself out of the almost naturalized condition of inferiority [*Unmündigkeit*]." However, "for *a public* to enlighten itself . . . if one merely grants it the necessary freedom, is almost unavoidable."[7] Both the fashion culture fostered by the *Mode Journal* and the national uniform proposal relied on the formation of a public consensus to dictate personal attire rather than the imposition of state regulation. The primary difference between the two positions amounted to a disagreement over the agents responsible for forming the public consensus governing personal adornment. The uniform proposal relied upon the agency of economically independent men, who were, at least theoretically, free to pursue their interests both in public discussions and within the economic marketplace. The coincidence of intellectual and economic autonomy was, according to Jürgen Habermas, a precondition for the operation of Kant's model of the public sphere: "Only property owners are admitted to the politically engaged public sphere, because their autonomy is grounded in the commodity exchange and, therefore, coincides with the interest to preserve the private sphere."[8] The debate over clothing reform brought this double precondition to the fore, for unlike purely abstract debates, the restructuring of consumer habits could be initiated only by those already empowered to buy whatever consumer good they wanted.

The *Mode Journal*'s strategy for forming a consensus was considerably more diverse, suggesting that on questions of taste and consumption, economic agency was not the determining factor. Because the *Mode Journal*'s audience was largely female, its articles did not appeal exclusively to male heads of households. In a telling move, Bertuch adopted the persona of a female contributor ("diligent reader, Frederike S.") to rebut the first letter writer's uniform plan, a strategy that encouraged the impression that uniforms were an exclusively male attempt to escape the obligations of fashion culture.[9] His rebuttal ended on an ambivalently feminist note: if women were no longer able to discuss fashion, they would have to engage in politics.

The uniform proposal never quite died out in Germany.[10] Periodically, a new advocate would be found. Twenty-four years later, another piece in the *Mode Journal* urged the adoption of a national costume for travelers, so that local residents could distinguish between respectable citizens in transit and homeless wanderers (*Landstreicher*).[11] In 1791, the Danish Academy of Sciences proposed an essay competition on the subject. The contest was conducted in German, with an eye toward a larger Baltic audience. The essays were collected in a single volume, published in Copenhagen, and all referred to a Swedish law of 1778 that required distinct costumes for each feudal rank. Some mentioned provincial costume codes that had been enacted in St. Petersburg, Reval, and Riga around 1785. These Baltic ordinances were considered distinctly different from sumptuary laws. Like military regulations, they mandated a particular style of dress, as opposed to simply prohibiting certain excesses. The Danish Academy used these precedents as the basis of a theoretical discussion on whether a national costume would benefit society.[12]

During the Wars of Liberation, Ernst Moritz Arndt raised the issue again.[13] Like Möser, Arndt invoked an imaginary past, unaffected by courtly styles, in which men wore traditional costumes suited to their occupation. Neither Arndt nor Möser considered the struggle between city fathers and unruly citizens reflected in the sumptuary legislation of the Middle Ages. They both treated fashion as a modern, French importation. Arndt's call for a national costume came one year after the introduction of the first uniforms for a national militia and was clearly aimed at furthering a nationalist mobilization against France: "We would be free of many small and vain anxieties, our youth would be rescued from French foppery, if we were to restore the natural and manly garb of our forefathers, which was worn until two or three hundred years ago."[14]

The *Mode Journal*'s writers had put forward the national costume proposal as a means of harnessing luxury consumption and, more specifically, the body to economic production. The 1786 letter to the *Mode Journal* set specific standards for the garment's design. It should be inexpensive, yet made from sturdy materials and in colors that did not easily become dirty. Particularly important was the uniform's suitability to the climate and to the labor and physique of the individual. The costume should be appropriate for all ages; it should not distort the body nor make it seem "fantastical." It should be readily worn by the rich and the poor, in all seasons and all weather. Only toward the end of the list did the author mention that the costume should "carry the markings of Germany."[15] In 1792 a prize-winning essay, published in Copenhagen, provided even more precise stipulations on the costume's relation to the body (this author, too, did not mention national identity). According to C. Pram, clothes should (1) protect the body from the harmful effects of the air, (2) cover only those parts of the body that were least important in establishing identity, while leaving exposed those portions that do not need to be covered, (3) harmonize with work rather than hinder it, (4) be appropriate for various professions, (5) be easily cleaned, (6) be inexpensive, (7) serve its practical function for a long period, and (8) be comfortable to wear.[16]

The ideal of a fully functionalized and inexpensive style of dress has been invoked regularly. Whenever finery has been deemed excessive, it has been countered with a practical, down-to-earth style, usually one with connotations of physical labor. Standard male dress over the last two centuries clearly has had a great deal in common with the uniform requirements spelled out by these Enlightenment reformers. Nineteenth-century fashion commentators viewed the military uniform as the obvious source for the respectable, dark suit of modern masculinity. In 1888, N. S. Shaler, wrote in the *Atlantic Monthly*, that

> the changes which, during the last century, have been brought about in the garments of men have in the main been due to governmental action. A century ago, stockings and breeches were well affirmed as the covering for the legs of men. It was in time found by medical authorities that the close-fitting stocking was apt to produce a condition of the legs. This led to the invention of the trousers, which left the lower leg free. This new custom, thus planted in the army, that part of the community which of old was the glass of fashion, naturally spread to civil life.[17]

To say that uniforms influenced civilian dress does not explain why or how they came to do so. What common purposes did uniforms and dark civilian dress serve? More important, how did these dress forms operate within their respective institutions? Military and civilian institutions were not mere extensions of each other; at some point, their interests diverged. To treat the dark suits of civilian men as less strict versions of military dress is to miss the fundamental differences between the two institutions and their deployment of tactical power over bodies; the command structure of military and civilian disciplinary regimes differ. Coercive measures cannot always be directly transferred and employed outside the institutions in which they were developed.

Michel Foucault stressed that discipline operated as a mode of power, but that does not mean that it operated in the same way in every context.[18] Pressures useful in the training of soldiers were not necessarily effective elsewhere. Factory laborers might be constrained by the same tactics as those used on prisoners and soldiers; however, these techniques for controlling bodies have not been successful in all arenas. The eighteenth-century expansion of laissez-faire economic policy in Germany was predicated upon the assumption that intellectuals and entrepreneurs were not more productive if continually coerced by state regulations. Sumptuary laws, and the police enforcement that accompanied them, were abandoned because administrators became convinced that docility, the primary aim of disciplinary control of the body, was unproductive within certain contexts. Rather than subject the body through coercive power, new modes of social organization sought to activate them within an integrated whole. The new modes of regulation presumed that the body contained latent forces that could be drawn out productively. Bourgeois society would organize behavior through incentives and rewards, enticements accessible only through conformity to the same economy of production that utilized the docile bodies of workers and soldiers. Bourgeois society might distinguish between the different forms of pressure within different institutions by reintroducing class distinctions.

The tendency for classes to distinguish themselves from one another could be used as a form of disciplinary coercion, one that shaped the practices employed within each class. Because the respectable burgher considered himself freer than the prisoner, he granted and subjected himself to, different types of coercion than those applied to criminals. He did not escape the operations of power—they merely approached him more subtly, leaving fewer visible marks. Coercive pressures within bourgeois society were less deterministic in their regulation of behavior; bourgeois regulation allowed for a certain indeterminacy in its control of individual action. The loss of immediate control implied by the state's moment of restraint, which legal theory instituted as a respect for personal rights, was more than compensated for by the higher degree of self-motivated regulation, which members of bourgeois society practiced upon themselves.

German absolutism discovered that, by abandoning coercive restrictions on its populace, the government intensified the personal engagement of the middle classes in their own disciplinary regimes. Public opinion and the private citizen assumed the responsibility for regulating everyday life, a burden previously monopolized by the absolute state's police laws. This shift in regulatory authority was effective only when the conformity generated by public opinion and private morality was allowed to operate uninterrupted by overt state coercion. The more the disciplinary regimes of state institutions spread into public and private life, the more pertinent it became for the Enlightenment to draw a boundary between state and society. In Prussia, even as eighteenth-century civilian habits imitated the design and demeanor of the military uniform, the boundary between the army and the general population was maintained scrupulously, first by the military command itself and later by public opinion. Frederick I and Frederick II compartmentalized the Prussian population into soldiers and economically productive classes. This division, because it depended initially upon the good will of military administrators, was frequently overruled in practice. The boundary became more meaningful for the civilian population when the enlightened *Bürgertum* could more insistently characterize itself as separate from the military.[19]

The separation between military and civilian spheres in Prussia was not maintained by a fundamental antagonism nor by a system of checks and balances; rather, their disjuncture arose from their divergent application of comparable disciplinary regimes. Both the army and civil society, particularly the latter's male members, were trained in similar methods of control—the difference was that the civilian Bildungsbürgertum sought to demonstrate its autonomy and loyalty by disciplining itself using the methods of the military. Bourgeois society was organized into many small centers, which interacted through public discussion. The military was, on the other hand, integrated into a single hierarchy of command. The distinction between the two was in part a matter of degree—Prussian civil society seemed a little freer only because the military was so thoroughly controlled. However, a difference in agency also separated the two forms of organizing behavior. The bourgeois male employed the tactical regimes of control upon himself and his family; he operated as his own authority and was integrated into a larger system of regulation through communal pressures to conform. The soldier might exercise disciplinary control over himself and subordinates; however, he did so only as a link in a long chain of command. For the bourgeois, the private sphere constituted an arena in which larger networks of control were replaced by personalized regulation. In the military, such a reprieve from continuous obedience did not exist (except in the case of the monarch). Autonomy, or personal distinctiveness, in the Prussian army was practiced not by the suspension of regulation but by its intensification. For the soldier, eluding the pressure of constant supervision meant exceeding its expectations. Hyperdiscipline became a means for the Prussian soldier to detach himself from the military order of command without adopting a bourgeois notion of personal freedom. Disciplinary overcompensation was closely allied with the modernist ideal of the dandy, who distinguishes himself from bourgeois standards of taste by adhering to them more thoroughly than his peers.

The eighteenth-century debate over the civilian uniform demonstrates that the question of personal agency was vital to maintaining a distinction between consumption and military and civilian regulation of the body. While the similarities between the dark suit of the civilian male and the functionalized uniform of the soldier were indications of how compatible military and bourgeois regimes of control were, the fact that these two modes of dress never completely merged, and that such a union was explicitly rejected when first proposed, indicates that there remained decisive differences between the disciplinary techniques of state institutions and the conformity exercised by society. In eschewing standardized national dress, Germans—the princely administrations as well as the bourgeoisie—acknowledged society as the institution capable of employing disciplinary measures in a subtler and, ultimately, more effective manner than the state. Enlightenment bureaucrats and essayists distinguished the creation of conformity within society from the one-sided power relationship prevalent in hospitals, schools, asylums, and military encampments. However, the ability of judicial authority to inspire obedience was rather limited. When Lucas Langemack, in his 1747 *Abbildung einer vollkommenen Polizei*, urged a pedagogical application of police laws to foster conformity and to shame those who refused to accept restraint, he was no longer describing an arrangement of force that lay within the capability of legal prescription:

> A police code that makes humanity graceful is of the finest and highest sort. It brings the finest rules of fair-mindedness and love for humanity into practice and is never more perfect than when it is maintained by the subtlest means. An intelligent prince would give control of the police over only to someone who can insinuate himself through shame and a sense of fairness, someone more inclined to educate through subtle means than to compel through severity. The appointment is easily made when the police official possesses just such personal character and is himself perfectly polite.[20]

Langemack's subtle police enforcement presumed the operation of a pedagogical force that penetrated bodies and encouraged conformity. His reliance on education to secure judicial rule foreshadowed Bertuch's suggestion that the *Mode Journal*'s efforts to educate the public were far more effective at disciplining consumption than either sumptuary laws or civilian uniform codes:

> The best and only possible clothing ordinance that you could institute, Mr. Reformer, is sound reasoning. Then you will find that neither uniforms nor national costumes are necessary. The many centuries worth of clothing ordinances will help you not one bit.[21]

To better understand why the German Enlightenment refrained from instituting uniforms for all citizens, we must first examine the importance of the uniform in the Prussia army and the system of discipline instituted by Frederick Wilhelm I and Frederick II. The military's control of the body and its integration of the soldier into a functionalized command structure suggested an alternative model of social organization, one that did not rely upon the representational display of hereditary privileges and responsibilities. Only after we have shown how strictly the Prussian regime trained its army can we appreciate how it was in the regulatory interests of the Enlightenment to avoid instituting a disciplinary regime that was too tight. The military culture of Prussia instituted an unparalleled regulation of the soldierly body. The civil society that emerged around this system sought to apply its lessons of rigor while preserving its autonomy.

Hans Rosenberg characterized Prussia's regulations as a novel experiment that "had broad human and social significance" in the genealogy of modern subjectivities. The Prussian execution of social order

> provided a substantial clue to the understanding of the knotty problem of when, where, how, and why there was born, outside the acquisitive business community, the ceaselessly efficient, rationally tempered, modern "vocational man" (*Berufsmensch*), who did not work in order to live but who lived in order to work. Collectivist Prussia made a remarkable contribution to the creation of this new species of thoroughly disciplined man, activated by quasi-moral compulsions and chained to a large-scale apparatus and thus to the collective pursuit of objectified, utilitarian tasks. In line with the conception of the bureaucratic state as a machine, man himself was destined to become an automaton.[22]

For Rosenberg, the separation between Eastern and Western Europe was bridged by the fact that the alien system of Prussian rigidity had become naturalized within liberal democracies. Foucault posited a similar division between liberal and disciplinary political orders, arguing that the latter had come to dominate modern society. Writing in a tone often employed by reformers against child beating, Rosenberg and Foucault both characterized discipline as the alien secret, which actually had become the norm in the West. Both characterized disciplinary coercion as an overlooked force that, by its very unveiling, shocked and overwhelmed humanist notions of identity and politics. Foucault described disciplinary injunctions as a shadow form of government, operating unrecognized within and between visible political institutions:

> Historians of ideas usually attribute the dream of a perfect society to the philosophers and jurists of the eighteenth century; but there was also a military dream of society; its fundamental reference was not to the state of nature but to the meticulously subordinated cogs of a machine, not to the primal social contract but to permanent coercions, not to fundamental rights but to indefinitely progressive forms of training, not to the general will but to automatic docility.[23]

The claim that bourgeois society relied upon and lived within a network of regimentation was a dirty secret (not unlike child abuse), because civility presupposed that all participants acted voluntarily. Society did not simply "repress" the operation of disciplinary institutions through an ideology of liberal freedom. Such an argument would imply an ontology of power wherein prisons and barracks were more determinate than drawing rooms and opera houses. Foucault described the importance of "enclosure" in isolating a population, but one must also consider the manner in which institutions defined the terms of inclusion and exclusion. What conditions were set for entry? What requirements had to be fulfilled for discharge? Which was the more desirable alternative? Did one wish to join the confined space of a given institution and accept its coercive norms, or did one wish to avoid them?

These questions were crucial, and obvious, when comparing the disciplinary regimes of prisons and barracks to the restraints of fashionable society. Their answers were implicit in every application of pressure from the two types of institution. Prisoners were compelled to reform their behavior because they knew at every moment that their confinement was oppressive and undesirable. Fashion mavens participated in the most rigidly prescribed behavior because they knew they were envied. The inducements with which early bourgeois society organized behavior would have failed utterly if participants had not believed that they were acting voluntarily toward an extremely desirable end. The equation of barracks with ballrooms would have destroyed the subtle motivations that produced conformity and consensus in civil society. This requirement was not a matter of preserving an illusion; rather, there was a notable difference in the application and modality of power between prisons, barracks, and schools, on the one hand, and ballrooms, salons, coffeehouses, theaters, gardens, and marketplaces, on the other.

Adam Smith's characterization of the ethical individual neatly articulates the type of masculinity that solemnly exhibits its own restraint rather than relying on the imposition of an external pressure, and it is therefore a fine place to consider the differences between institutional and private discipline.

> The man of real constancy and firmness, the wise and just man who has been thoroughly bred in the great school of self-command, in the bustle and business of the world, exposed, perhaps, to the violence and injustice of faction and to the hardships and hazards of war, maintains this control of his passive feelings upon all occasions; and whether in solitude or in society, wears nearly the same countenance and is affected very nearly in the same manner. In success and in disappointment, in prosperity and in adversity, before friends and before enemies, he has often been under the necessity of supporting this manhood.[24]

Smith's impassive male shared certain similarities with the inmate of Jeremy Bentham's panoptical prison. Both were compelled into specific behaviors by an observing presence: Smith's dispassionate man imagined an impartial spectator who judged his every movement; the prisoner within the panopticon was always aware of the central guard tower, whose lines of sight penetrated into every cell.

The two figures were, nevertheless, distinct. Smith's man employed the model of supervision as a means of transforming himself. The imagined observer functioned as a tool for the ethical man to gain mastery and knowledge over his body and his passions. Smith stressed that masculine temperance and restraint were not mere performances, external displays contradicted by hidden, internal desires: "He does not merely affect the sentiments of the impartial spectator; he really adopts them."[25] The prisoner within the panopticon, however, was never granted the opportunity to claim self-mastery. Disciplinary force bore down on him from the exterior, from the overbearing, asymmetrical distribution of power inherent in the prison system. Unlike Smith's ethical male, the prisoner could not claim as his own the force that restrained and confined his actions. He was trapped within the imbalanced relationship of the prison, locked in the role of mere object, unable to assume the subjective authority of the central tower. The difference between the inmate and the ethical man were, in temporal terms, not necessarily great. As Smith implied, firmness and constancy were acquired through experience in adversity and constant practice. The self-commanding male was, in a sense, a graduate of the panopticon, one who had adopted for himself the techniques employed in the regulation of others, thereby gaining an autonomous identity.

The voluntary self-discipline of the citizen acquired an aesthetic quality not perceived in the mechanical movements of soldiers and inmates. By displaying no signs of coercion (or to put it differently, the sign of no coercion), the restrained individual established himself as an aesthetic entity as well as a moral agent. The two domains were closely intertwined. Self-control implied both the capacity for moral decisions and the harmonious integration of the person with his environment. Self-mastery in fashionable dress required a performance that erased all signs of coercion, giving the impression that an ensemble was nothing more than an elegant coincidence. Christian Garve pointed out that true mastery of technique did not display the any signs of strain:

> If it is the intent and the triumph of great masters to cover up any signs of artistry in their works, then how much more important is it that the noblest work of nature, the human, should dress and decorate himself so as to preserve nature's freedom [*Zwangslosigkeit*] and the appearance of coincidence, which she lends all her products.[26]

The restrained individual became beautiful when the forces operating upon him were so invisible that his appearance appeared to spring into existence independent of external cause. Whereas the soldier and the prisoner were always enclosed within the architecture of disciplinary power, the elegant bourgeois man appeared before others with no visible framework to direct his activity and appearance. Smith described the switch from a disciplinary mode of power to a performative one, in which the individual displayed self-control as a form of subjectivity, as opposed to subjugation.

At least three important developments bear upon any discussion of eighteenth-century German regulation of consumption: (1) the demise of sumptuary laws, (2) the emergence of disciplinary institutions, such as the standardized army, and (3) the formation of a bourgeois public sphere, which set fashion. All three developments stood in relation to each other. By abandoning police laws, the state made it possible for civil society to expand and sharpen its ability to guide the personal behavior of its members, while the state intensified its control over its own administrative apparatus. Civil society defined itself as a self-regulating institution apart from state authority, and yet it assumed the police function once considered vital to the state's economic and political interests. It would be too simple (as well as paranoid) to maintain that all three developments were orchestrated by the absolutist state in an effort to maximize its domination. However, it would be naive to claim that the public sphere's substitution for sumptuary laws diminished the pressure upon consumers to act in accord with specific standards.

Although the state's coercion of consumers abated, civil society provided entirely new pressures upon individual behavior. In place of an explicit judicial code that demanded that consumers remain in their traditional places by limiting their emulation of upper-class ostentation, there developed an informal obligation to follow the newest lifestyles at the expense of traditional habits. The shift in pressures on the consumer was made possible by the reorientation of clothes and domestic accouterments, from an economy of symbolic prestige to an economy of productive labor. This restructuring of consumer incentives meant that a judicial system of negative pronouncements and interventions by the state into public life was replaced by an affirmative obligation by individuals to constantly evaluate their appearance in terms of a utilitarian ethic of productive and healthy consumption. This obligation to conform to fashionable opinion was effective as long as individuals were made to feel that they were taking personal responsibility for their decisions. No matter how compulsory the "voluntary" cooperation of fashionable society was, it always presumed its distinctness from the disciplinary coercion of state institutions. The very effectiveness of public opinion in organizing behavior—its ability to employ shame, ridicule, and conformity to circumvent overt forms of resistance—depended upon its not requiring subservience.

Thus, we cannot treat the conformity produced by civil society as just another instance of disciplinary power. As comparison of the Prussian uniform's tactical function and the bourgeois semiotics of respectable dress demonstrate, the two types of institution (carceral and civil) augmented one another. But their internal operation—their microphysics of power—were predicated upon their maintaining an obvious and visible difference.

CHAPTER NINE

The Uniform's Tactical Control
Execution over Performance

SOLDIERS did not always wear uniforms. Before the advent of modern military drill tactics, regimental identity and national allegiance were displayed on flags carried at the head of units. Soldiers might wear colored armbands into battle, to distinguish friend from foe, but little more was done to mark the soldier. His clothes were his own concern, or at most his company commander's, for the terms of recruitment sometimes provided troops with minimal garb. But even then, little attention was paid to the garments' cut, let alone its color.[1] Patrimonial military leaders short on cash would send their troops into war wearing ragged coats.

This lack of official interest in providing soldiers dress did not prevent martial fashions from spreading. Toward the end of the fifteenth century, German foot soldiers (*Landsknechte*) cut gashes in their leggings and jackets and wore brightly colored undergarments so that every movement of their limbs revealed a chromatic array.[2] Their self-made style won the admiration of urban youth, who imitated the look.[3] The sixteenth century saw the predominance of *Pluderhosen*—wide, baggy, woolen pants stuffed with silk, which literally puffed up the soldier's size, giving him a huge appearance.[4] City ordinances provided exact limits on the amount of material allowed for such pants, and clergymen preached against their degeneracy.[5] *Pluderhosen*, a style originated by lower-class soldiers, represented a chaotic usurpation of class rank even after it had been taken up by young courtiers. The variety of martial styles and the general absence of regimental drills, which give modern military uniforms their potent tactical and aesthetic effect, meant that European armies moved across the countryside like colorful and flamboyant hordes.

Early records described the clothes worn by delegations sent to attend imperial coronations, but these groups never amounted to more than twenty people. The first indications of uniformity in military dress are descriptions of the blue coats worn by regiments from Brandenburg and Prussia during the Thirty Years' War.[6] There is no reason to assume that these garments were cut in the same manner or made of the same fabric, yet the similarity in color was already a significant change in the military order. According to the Prussian military historian Curt Jany, Swedish troops opposing Brandenburg and Prussia in 1655 wore coats of blue, red, yellow, reddish brown, green, and sea green, with leggings that did not always match. By 1672, regulations for the Gardes Francaises presumed that Prussian troops wore blue. However, not until Frederick Wilhelm's 1718 edicts could one speak of a uniform in the modern sense.[7]

During the eighteenth century, governments shifted their sartorial regulation from a policy of preserving and unifying corporate ranks to a strategic concentration on those populations directly in service to the state. Rather than using injunctions to husband the ordinary habits of the entire population, governments increasingly chose to instrumentalize only those groups that already owed the monarch some fealty. The first measures were made by Frederick Wilhelm, who instituted the canton system to draft able-bodied men from peasant communities and to recruit Junker sons into the officer corps. The centralization of the state's finances, most notably the administrative integration of national territories with those lands belonging directly to the royal family, made it possible for the state to invest in training a cadre of officials directly responsive to its interests. As the absolute state broadened its taxation authority during the eighteenth century, it also narrowed and intensified its control. The army and bureaucracy grew larger and more responsive to policy commands, and in exchange, the state abandoned its efforts to control the entire population. Instead, it concentrated more than ever before on soldiers and bureaucrats in its service.

Frederick Wilhelm's codes were the beginning of Prussian efforts to provide troops with clothes that conformed to precise specifications in terms of fabric, color, and design. To reduce the army's dependence on foreign producers, bans on the importation of red and blue cloth were instituted in 1718. Farmers in the middle provinces were likewise prohibited from exporting their fleeces, so that Prussian weavers would be assured a steady supply of inexpensive raw material. By and large, Prussia's efforts to create a domestic manufacturing base large enough to clothe its troops was highly successful.[8] By 1782, Berlin had become one of Europe's largest wool-producing cities, with 300 weavers and roughly 3,000 looms producing 113,104 garments for both soldiers and civilians.[9] Frederick Wilhelm's regulations built on the successes of his predecessors in constituting a standing army in Prussia. In the seventeenth century, the Hohenzollern dynasty had gained the right to finance a standing army through special taxes. The succession of regulations issued by Frederick Wilhelm and his son shaped the army into an instrument that was both responsive to monarchical policy and outside of domestic politics. Although uniforms increased the expense of maintaining the army, they integrated soldiers into the institution more thoroughly than any feudal oath of allegiance; they became both a sign and a vehicle for the monarchy's disciplinary control over its troops.

The requirement that soldiers wear uniforms designed according to standardized patterns presented a problem whose solution further enmeshed the soldier within a network of regulations. Before the nineteenth century, garments were tailored directly for the wearer.[10] When uniforms were introduced, standard sizes had yet to be invented. The logistics of large-scale production meant that uniforms could not be tailored to the individual but were sewn according to models. Length of sleeves and pants, placement of buttonholes, and width of leggings and coats were determined before garments were ever worn. The trial-and-error process of creating sizes was guided initially by infantry tactics. Flintlock-carrying units were arranged, according to height of soldier, in square units of four rows. The tallest soldiers stood in the first row, the second tallest stood in the fourth row, and the shortest in the second and third rows. This arrangement allowed the second row a clear line of fire when the first row was kneeling. It also placed the tallest men at the front of a bayonet charge: up until the Seven Years' War, Prussian monarchs considered the awe-inspiring sight of advancing troops a more effective weapon than a weapons fusillade.[11] The infantry's firing drill served as an initial guide for sewing; accordingly, uniforms were measured into four sizes and then adjusted to the individual soldier by the regiment's tailors.[12] As the drill procedure changed during the Seven Years' War, only three sizes were required.[13]

Tightly cut uniforms made the shape of the body apparent; girth and weight could be judged at a glance. Like the standardized procedures of parade drill, ready-made clothes set one soldier off from another. How well a uniform fit became a sign of how closely his body conformed to the army's conventions. A slender body implied the absence of excessive eating or drinking, the capacity to apply regulations to oneself, and the physical strength for long marches.

The soldierly body, trained in daily drills under the constant pressure of watchful officers, became stiffer in its posture. Standing straight even in moments of relaxation, the body adjusted to the sharper lines of the uniform. The lessons from the parade ground were not easily shaken off. Male posture over the course of the century became more rigid, both at rest and in motion. Small changes in dress and drill brought about invisible transformations. The sleeve of a soldier's jacket prior to the uniform would have been cut to allow the arm to swing out boldly. Whether he assumed the rude posture of the *Landesknechte*, shoving his elbow out at his sides, or the *en garde* stance of a trained fencer, the premodern soldier would have worn abundantly cut garments. Shoving elbows, glaring stares, widespread legs, and overblown costumes were all part of the assertion and projection of the body through a martial air. These gestures and the value placed on bulk were traded in for a compactly drawn position, which remained immobile until commanded. The uniformed soldier's tautness indicated readiness as well as obedience. He was not given to uncontrolled movements, and his body was interchangeable with others trained in the identical manner. This new posture can of course be traced back to the Prussian drill, of which the uniform was a critical component. The cut of the Prussian sleeve presumed that the "natural" position for a soldier's arm was directly at his side. Enough mobility was allowed for the soldier to load and raise his rifle, but these movements were carefully choreographed. How high an infantryman needed to raise his arm to aim his rifle was the object of official scrutiny. Soldier's bodies became malleable material to be shaped by marching, loading, firing, reloading, turning, charging, and standing in tight-fitting uniforms.[14]

The Prussian blue uniform would have indicated nothing more than the Hohenzollern's dynastic distaste for the rococo style had it not been attached to a system of training. Frederick Wilhelm I established a rigid method of exercising soldiers, upon which his son, Frederick II, elaborated:

> The daily parades, both small and large, keep the soldier in practice. He learns to march forward without vacillating and breaking up the line. The fundamentals of drill are established daily during the *Wachtparade*, when the officers learn to select their objective point, march in alignment, execute all

of the important movements that can be done with troops, and break off and advance—in a word, the officers learn here to do everything in detail that the army performs on a large scale.[15]

Frederick saw the soldier's body as chaotic matter to be moved by external force alone. Fear pushed the troops forward into battle:

> Since officers must necessarily lead them into the greatest dangers, the soldiers (since they cannot be influenced by ambition) should fear their officers more than all the dangers to which they are exposed. . . . Goodwill can never induce the common soldier to stand up to such dangers: he will only do so through fear.[16]

The Prussian system demanded immediate obedience from the entire military hierarchy, not just the lowly infantry men. As Frederick II explained, "Discipline begins with the generals and works down to the drummer boys. Its foundation is subordination: no subordinate has the right to contradict orders. If the commander orders, others must obey."[17] While commands were issued from the top down, the system of observation operated in both directions. Officers were obliged to conform to regulations through not only the threat of surveillance by superiors but also the potential for desertion by their troops. "If officers do not do their duty, then still less can the common soldier be expected to perform his: it is a chain in which no link can be missing."[18]

Military garrisons were to be found in virtually every midsized city, and many smaller towns were also obliged to accept posted soldiers. Estimates of the percentage of the population connected with the army varied. Otto Hintze said that, for most of the century, 20–24 percent of Berlin's inhabitants (including women and children) were attached to the army. J. F. Zollner noted that in Potsdam "one sees almost nothing but soldiers." And an earlier traveler to Potsdam reported a similar experience: "Not only does one meet soldiers everywhere, and virtually no other class of humans, but no matter what manner of human abode one looks at, one sees a Son of Mars with stiff hair and a moustache."[19] Soldiers were not always an arrogant presence, however. Johann Kaspar Riesbeck related that, "With the exception of Constantinople, no city in Europe has so large a garrison as Berlin. Around 26,000 men are stationed here."[20]

New uniforms were regularly distributed to troops. After 1725 soldiers could expect a new uniform every two years, though in practice they received leggings and undergarments one year and a coat the next. They were free to dispose of their old uniforms in any way, because they were considered the property of the individual soldier (their monthly pay included a deduction for their cost). Army regulations stipulated that soldiers could resell their clothes or rework them into garments that could be worn in private life. Gisela Krause estimated that approximately 30,000 coats passed into the civilian population annually. The redistribution of uniforms was most evident among the lower classes, wherein the blue coat became a standard of rural male dress.[21]

A distinctive feature of the Prussian uniform was the absence of overt hierarchical designations: every officer marched in the same blue coat worn by the king. This practice was supported by a code of honor that applied equally to all ranks. Superior officers were forbidden to treat other officers in a manner considered humiliating (outside the necessities of military command). Unlike most other European armies, lieutenants were not asked to polish boots or saddle the horse of a commanding officer. An insult to one officer was considered an insult to the entire corps. Through these conventions, the Hohenzollerns constituted a class of aristocratic officers loyally aligned with monarchical policy. That an officer wore the same coat as the king did not merely represent a relationship; it brought that unity into being. Until the late seventeenth century, Junkers, particularly in the east, had been openly defiant of the Hohenzollern dynasty. This antagonism was overcome by political concessions granting extensive patrimonial powers to the landholding aristocracy. The disciplinary regime of the army constituted a second mode of integration. The military established a system parallel to the feudal hierarchy—aristocratic origin was a usual precondition for entry into the officer corps. Yet the military code also effaced aristocratic distinctions. By requiring all soldiers to wear uniforms manufactured and distributed on a regimental basis, the military code precluded ostentatious displays through dress. Delivered by the regiment, the blue coat represented allegiance to the command structure and became a metonym for a mode of warfare. It represented the tactical control of the body while simultaneously serving as its disciplining instrument.

By effacing all symbols that competed with the principle of monarchical control over the army, the uniform also cleared a space for new methods of interpreting clothes. Military dress allowed only minimal references to previous achievements. While Frederick Wilhelm I did award successful regiments, many officers served their entire lives without receiving any citation. During the Seven Years' War, Generals Hans Joachim Zieten and Ferdinand von Braunschweig did not recommend a single officer for a commendation, on the presumption that heroism was an officer's common responsibility.[22] The uniform controlled the body as a field of representation. By laying claim to the entire body, it overwhelmed other references to a personal identity. Gestures and speech patterns were also integrated into the disciplinary regime that the uniform enforced. Repeated training created the persona that accompanied the uniform. The simple act of wearing the uniform properly—which meant performing the duties associated with it—was presumed by the command structure to be a sufficient representation of identity. Further delineations, such as rank, were unwarranted and undesired by the command structure. All those who submitted to its demands were, as the uniform implied, subject to the same code of behavior. In battle or in camp, ranks were recognized through rigorous control over placement of soldiers. Because troops moved in rigid formation, the position of a soldier announced his rank. Soldiers also developed informal codes for establishing identity, focusing on such details as which officers wore boots on horseback and how they buttoned their coats.

The uniform's functional properties amounted to a system of representation that insisted that the signified was never absent. A soldier in uniform did not merely refer to the military; he embodied it. As long as a body was present within a uniform, it constituted the local link to the overall chain of command. Behavioral norms could not be separated from sartorial signification. Military discipline saturated every material form of the soldier, just as grace and nobility were expected in every gentleman's gestures and utterances. But unlike the feudal sartorial order, which overflowed with symbols of power, the Prussian officer, via his appearance and actions, was required to display a utilitarian rejection of iconic representation. Hence, it was expected that soldiers should not pay too much attention to their uniforms. Cleanliness was deemed necessary for practical purposes, but beyond a certain level, personal orderliness was seen as a fetish. A neglect of personal niceties was an implicit requirement in military culture. Frederick himself was known for his disregard of dress. For uniforms to maintain their functional exclusion of signification, they had to become naturalized to the public eye. They had to recede into the background of ordinary life and thereby renounce any claim to aesthetic distinction:

Frederick avoided all innovations; alterations in uniforms and other minor formalities were far below his personal dignity as well as that which he sought to give his army. . . . He knew that the vast majority of humans are most useful only when that which is required of them has . . . become second nature.[23]

Given the rigidity of the Prussian system, there were few ways of escaping its compulsion. The foremost was desertion. Frederick was obsessed with the problem. He devoted considerable energy to the prevention and recapture of soldiers who slipped away from their units. The army's reliance on strict formations in battle as well as in camp was in large part brought on by the need to prevent troops from running away. The command structure's tight surveillance network sought to impress soldiers with the sense that avoidance of duty was impossible. Yet it was this same harsh and violent code of regulation and punishment that motivated troops to flee in the first place. Later, officers who had confronted the ideologically inspired troops of revolutionary France recognized that fear was a limited means of motivating troops. Not until the reform movement brought on by Prussia's defeat by Napoleon did the military command reformulate its tactics of eliciting obedience.

Less prominent in the writings of military leaders was the figure of the hyperdisciplined soldier, the individual who submitted so thoroughly to the military code of behavior that he almost undermined its effectiveness.[24] This type of soldier expanded disciplinary procedures into a code of personal distinction. The techniques of control employed by superior officers were taken over, intensified, and reapplied by the individual to his own body. When carried out over a long period, this appropriation of discipline became a means of constituting self-identity within the military by exceeding its requirements. The accouterments of discipline developed into markers of a particular individual, one who has distinguished himself from his peers. The uniform and the body, the very objects of military drill, were transformed into signs of subjectivity.

Overadherence to regulations changed the relationship between the command structure and the soldier. Submission to hierarchy was made to look like ambition and conformity by the insertion of the self into the mechanism of tactical control. Once the soldier voluntarily exceeded the dictates of authority, he created a wider range of possible relations to power. His body no longer remained docile; it acquired a volition of its own. A soldier might for example disobey military commands by observing them too precisely or by pursuing them beyond what his superiors would consider appropriate. Frederick described superobedience as a dangerous refinement of military procedure, which interfered with the practical goals of state policy. He was particularly concerned about the transformation of tactics into semiotics:

> The long peace had corrupted the service. At the beginning of Frederick Wilhelm's reign, the order and discipline of the regiments had been refined, but since there was nothing left to accomplish in this respect, attention became focused only on the sort of thing that caught the eye. The soldier polished his fusil and equipment; the trooper, his bridle, saddle, and even his boots. The horses' manes were plaited with ribbons, and at length neatness, which in itself serves a useful purpose, degenerated by ridiculous abuse. If the peace had lasted beyond 1740, I am satisfied that today we would be decked out in rouge and beauty spots.[25]

For Frederick, war prevented bodily regulation from becoming ornamental signification because it reintroduced a practical necessity to seemingly endless drilling. It was clear that the tactical investment of power on the body could develop its own autonomous pleasures and satisfactions. The elaboration of discipline could become its own end, slowly separating from the interests of state policy. By carrying bodily tactics beyond the specifications of official guidelines, soldiers could gain some control over themselves. Their hyperdiscipline involved the extension of official techniques, so that they were applied on areas of the body that had not yet become the object of institutional interest. Rather than resisting external pressures to move and look in a certain manner, the zealous soldier distinguished himself by inflicting them upon himself, thereby assuming a modicum of control. War—the terrors of battle and its scarcities—brought the soldier who had learned too much back into a dependent relation with the state. The possibilities for regulating the self were greatly reduced during wartime: the command structure issued unpredictable orders, and personal survival was always uncertain.

The hyperdisciplined soldier was a precursor of the nineteenth-century dandy, who played against social convention in his strict observation of its rules. The important difference between the eighteenth-century soldier and the dandy was the constant presence of irony in the civilian. Charles Baudelaire correctly pointed to the naive bearing of the ordinary soldier.[26] However, this innocence was already vanquished in the soldier who obeyed regulations beyond their intentions. For him, there was no moment of release when he was on leave and free to act out the simple instincts Baudelaire saw in the regular foot soldier. The hyperdisciplined Prussian soldier sought never to let the demand of discipline drop, and in this regard he went beyond the practical intentions of eighteenth-century military procedure. By taking them too far, he made the military code his own, and therein lay his similarity with the later dandy. Berbey D'Aurevilly noted that the dandy did not pursue his own eccentricities in order to revolt against convention: "Dandyism, on the contrary, plays with the regulations, but at the same time pays them due respect. It suffers from them, and avenges itself by submitting; it even demands them again after it escapes them; it dominates and is dominated in turns."[27]

Twentieth-century cultural studies from Benjamin to Foucault have held forth the dandy as epitomizing the modern masculine sentiment of sublime self-discipline in the face of chaos. This mythical figure, a pillar of nineteenth-century fashion discourse, maintained a scrupulously elegant and inconspicuous appearance. His respect for a detached and modest canon of taste distinguished him from the fashionable crowd. The dandy's simplicity in dress and all matters of style required, according to Baudelaire, a rigorous commitment. Modern elegance was hardly the mere absence of garish decor; rather, it depended on a thoroughgoing preservation of order:

> Dandyism borders upon the spiritual and stoical. . . . For those who are at once its priests and its victims, all the complicated material conditions to which they submit, from an impeccable toilet at every hour of the day and the night to the most perilous feats of the sporting field, are no more than a system of gymnastics designed to fortify the will and discipline the soul.[28]

Baudelaire compared the dandy with the monk or even a devotee of "the inexorable order of Assassins," but what distinguished the dandy from these zealots was his fixation on himself.[29] Whereas the monk or soldier was trained to abandon all claims to individuality, to submit utterly before a higher authority, the dandy followed the principles of asceticism in order to maintain and preserve his unique individuality. Baudelaire referred to the dandy as "a cult of the self." And Foucault followed the same line when he linked Baudelaire's dandy to Kant's definition of enlightenment: "This modernity does not 'liberate man in his own being'; it compels him to face the task of producing himself."[30] Standing next to the dandy in Baudelaire's pantheon of modern masculinity was the figure of the soldier:

> Taken as a class, the military man has his beauty, just as the dandy and the courtesan have theirs, though of an essentially different flavour. . . . Accustomed to surprises, the military man is with difficulty caught off his guard. The characteristic of his beauty will thus be a kind of martial nonchalance, a curious mixture of calmness and bravado; it is a beauty that springs from the necessity to be ready to face death at every moment. Furthermore, the face of the ideal military man will need to be characterized by a great simplicity; for, living a communal life like monks or schoolboys and accustomed to unburden themselves of the daily cares of life upon an abstract paternity, soldiers are in many things as simple as children; like children too, when their duty is done, they are easily amused and given to boisterous entertainments.[31]

For the soldier, exercise and training had an indirect yet striking effect on his appearance. When describing a soldier's heroic character, Baudelaire mentioned both the pageantry of formal military dress and the bearing and physiognomy of the soldier's body. Unlike the dandy, the soldier's being was subordinated to a command structure. His appearance, for all its aesthetic effects, served tactical ends. He could tarry in bourgeois company only to provide a model for civilians to imitate.

The monarch's annual review of troops was a central mechanism for reinforcing the disciplinary principle of constant surveillance. The cycle of exercises leading up to a four-day inspection created a calendar of martial training that, in peacetime, gave officers a goal in training their units. Prussian soldiers were drilled for the sake of performing before the king, and their daily practices emphasized that they were subject to royal inspection. This inspection was never merely symbolic, as it often had immediate and dire consequences for troops who did not satisfy him.

In their political aims, the Prussian reviews were different from the spectacles of baroque monarchs. The annual drill did not serve to project the king's superior power through symbol-laden gestures discharged before a gathered populace. The civilian audience was not inconsequential, but reviews were primarily focused on exercising the troops. They were an internal mechanism of military discipline. Frederick wrote in his *General Principles*: "I have always reviewed the cavalry myself and drilled them so that they realize that the exercises they must perform emanate from me."[32] The king's presence was still supposed to instill fear in the heart of his subjects, but the primary audience for a review was the army itself:

> It is a true proverb that states, "The master's eye makes the horse fat." The officer will be motivated by ambition, and nothing feeds ambition more than the sight of the ruler and all the princes setting good examples. If these regiments were not assembled and drilled under the scrutiny of their king so often, everyone would be apt to grow careless. They are accustomed to seeing their king at the head, and this custom should be maintained.[33]

The review was the staged enactment of disciplinary power's operation for its primary subjects. Frederick maintained that the troops must see the central point from which the tactical control of their bodies' proceeded. Unlike the panoptical prison Foucault has described, the army could not rely upon architectural structures to impress visually upon the inmate that he was under constant supervision; it constructed a repetitive drill formation, which exposed the soldier to observation at his assigned position in the parade drill. Repetition simulated an enclosure, and the review reenacted the mechanisms of supervision, which were practiced daily throughout the army.

Like the uniform, the monarch's review gave a symbolic confirmation to military tactics while also enacting them. The monarch's presence not only reinforced the military regime of constant surveillance but also provided an affirmative model for all soldiers to emulate. Throughout the Hohenzollern dynasty, monarchs presented themselves before the army, particularly the officer corps, as accessible authorities—if not personally, then mimetically. By wearing the same uniform as the king, the army constituted their identity as having at least a physical resemblance to the king. This visual similarity opened the possibility for further imaginary relations with the monarch. The character of these bonds would have varied over the course of the dynasty. Comradeship and the cult of male friendship were not the only possible emotional connections between monarch and soldiers; officers in the first half of the eighteenth century were moved by a code of aristocratic honor that had little room for expressions of brotherhood and that did not understand the anonymous solidarity described by veterans of World War I. Uniforms played an important role in each of these soldierly discourses, but the emotional relation interpolated into the body was different in each case.

A genealogy of military subjectivity would certainly focus on the question of motivation—how the army constituted interiority as a mobilizing force, as an array of feelings, that compelled soldiers to sacrifice. Technological innovations, class upheavals, and military defeats would figure prominently in any such history, but so would the weight of tradition. One would inevitably find seemingly contradictory arrangements of power in the same system. For example, the Prussian military maintained the monarch as a figure of identification even while he stood as the legitimation for a harsh system of discipline and punishment. A genealogy of martial motivation would also find an important exception to the rule of male-male identification during the Napoleonic wars, when Queen Luise replaced her indecisive husband as the officer corps's chivalric figurehead. Her critical gaze and her body assumed the monarchy's position in the dialogue between state and army. In general, though, the Prussian king combined military discipline with the spectacle of ceremony by displaying his own uniformed body both as an instrumentalized machine and as the highest quantity on the hierarchical scale of prestige.

The annual military review enacted the relation between the state and its army. The primary players in this regulatory spectacle, the monarchy and the military, acted as performers and audience for each other. Third parties were treated as irrelevant to the practical matter of enforcing power; yet nevertheless, outside observers came in large numbers to take part in the supervisory ritual. The insistence on ignoring onlookers was important to the military's continual reassertion that the uniform and the drill were functional requirements of warfare and not adornments. The concern was that, once perceived as a mere decoration of the state, the army would loose its capabilities. This stubborn refusal to recognize aesthetic effects was a central axiom of disciplinary order. The military claimed that no detail was without tactical significance; thus, it could not allow uniforms to function as representations of some absent power or as pure aesthetic objects divorced from practical goals. This tactical understanding of power treated aesthetic contemplation as an obfuscation, the political corollary to the neoclassical claim that a work of art separates itself from pragmatic interests.

Bystanders judged parading troops not only as instruments of the state but also as models for constructing their own appearance. By the turn of the nineteenth century, the spring review and the fall exercises had become regular events in the Berlin fashion season. *Die Zeitung für die elegante Welt* reported in 1801 that the May review was the crowning event of the spring:

> The review outside Berlin, which accompanies the court back to the residence, always makes a strong effect. It attracts a mass of foreigners, and even if for only a short while it creates a second carnival. After the review, the king personally visits certain provinces and holds further musterings there.[34]

The monarch's tour would have allowed other Prussian cities to participate in the festive atmosphere of the military drills. The civilian crowds drawn to these exercises understood the soldier's body—its movements and its appearance—in terms that departed subtly from military procedure. These admiring civilians were surely sympathetic to the military apparatus, and in that regard they would become useful allies to the Prussian army. However, the civilian appropriation of the "military body" became a means of asserting personal autonomy from convention. Like the hyperdisciplined soldier, the civilian who wore military garb impressed onlookers with the instrumentalization of his body.

The parade drill's influence on onlookers was recognized early on as an important secondary effect, one that suggested a mode of regulating dress more subtle than sumptuary laws. Under Frederick Wilhelm I, the appearance of Prussian troops was interpreted as an implicit critique of ostentation, one that highlighted tactical masculinity. Because the regime of physical training applied equally to all soldiers (even generals were sometimes required to spend six weeks on basic drills), the composure of the male became a factor in determining military rank, distinct from aristocratic genealogy. The army extended the schooling that gentlemen had traditionally received in riding, fencing, and dancing to all in its ranks. Frederick frequently contrasted his own officers with the "fencing masters" of his opponents. While the officer corps reflected feudal hierarchy—bourgeois candidates were accepted only during crises—the training given cadets departed from the genteel education of the nobility. The courtier learned comportment so as to display his rank by presenting an elegant and attractive image to onlookers; Prussian drill instrumentalized the body so that it would become a force in battle.

Most of the time, the military system claimed to be ignorant of its visual impact except as it served to terrorize the enemy. The soldier's identity

resided in the body's execution of certain prescribed maneuvers. His exposure to observation was required by the command structure, not by an obligation to please the spectator. The uniform downplayed rank and focused
attention on the body's movements. This mode of self-presentation denied
that the body was performing for an audience; it claimed to be executing a
task for a higher authority. However, from early in Prussian military history,
the military drew attention to its disregard for attention. Through the drill,
the soldier became conscious of his body's appearance and its effect on others. As long as no direct appeal was made to the onlooker, the uniformed
soldier drew the public gaze to himself. He appeared as an inanimate object
that could not return a look and that, therefore, could appear as an aesthetic
entity to viewers not immediately threatened with attack.

The soldier's apparent disregard for his dress provided an indirect and
subtle critique of luxurious ostentation. It entered into the circuit of fashionable dress as a negation of the process of drawing distinctions through
dress and, in doing so, became fashionable. The contradiction inherent in
such a visually impressive rejection of sartorial display had been apparent
early in the century, when the Prussian uniform first distinguished itself
from the courtly standard set by France. The antifashion paradox was as the
"secret lesson" of Frederick Wilhelm I's first efforts at instituting military
discipline. A report from 1719 recounted how, in anticipation of the French
ambassador's viewing of an annual parade at Tempelhof, the Prussian
monarch dressed every sergeant-at-arms in a green coat, yellow vest, match-
ing leggings, and a tremendous wide-brimmed hat. The remaining troops
wore Prussian blue uniforms:

> As the French ambassador . . . with his entourage rode in to watch the re-
> view, one could observe that no one on the parade ground wore hats and
> lapels as large as the sergeants-at-arms, and at the same time it was apparent
> that the French sergeants-at-arms wore hats and lapels that were a little bit
> larger. *There are those who maintain that this display was intended for the French
> and all those nations who imitate them as a secret demonstration of their folly* [em-
> phasis mine]. That may be as it may, and his majesty may have intended a se-
> cret rebuke or not; nevertheless, it is certain that he is an enemy of all such
> excesses in costume and fashion. Anyone who relies upon sound reasoning
> will readily find that, in this regard, his majesty is absolutely correct.[35]

The uniform made its debut not only by asserting some standard of practicality but also by mocking the elaborate decorative style of Francophile

dress. Implicit in the political and economic rationale of the absolute state was a modernist aesthetic that insisted on elimination of ornamentation. This lesson was, of course, no secret to the versatile French diplomat attending the military review.[36] The crown prince, Frederick, reported in a 1737 letter to his father that the ambassador was almost taken for a Prussian officer when he visited a military parade in Zelle: he reportedly wore a tight-fitting blue coat and boots.[37] Who better than the French ambassador to have appreciated the showiness of Prussian uniforms and the dramaturgy in parade drills? His imitation was the proper response from a courtier skilled in anticipating and fulfilling royal expectations. In that regard, he was no different from the loyal Prussian who recounted Frederick Wilhelm's jab at the ambassador or the crown prince who dutifully reported his appearance at a later parade. Each was signaling his willingness to abide by the secret of functionalized dress—namely, its aesthetic sensibility.

As in so many other aspects of the Prussian system, fear was the primary motivation for obedience. Frederick II was famous for insisting that enlisted men should fear their officers more than the enemy. The spread of disciplinary power, its asymmetrical expansion from a central point outward, was enacted in the review, in which entire regiments were submitted to the judgment of a single authority:

> Without a doubt, it was a thrilling and to many a decisive sight, when one saw a corps of eighteen to twenty thousand men awaiting, in reverential silence and with the deepest respect, their fate to be delivered by a single man. In Frederick's day, a review was for almost the entire country an important moment. The fate of entire families often depended upon it. On these frightful days, wives, mothers, children, and friends fervently raised their most urgent appeals to the heavens: that their husbands, fathers, sons, and friends would not, as did happen so often, displease that one man. For it was here that the king weighed the merits of his officers and distributed, depending if he found them too light or not, praise or rebuke, admonishments or a token of his mercy, and often, indeed all too often, punishment that could felt for an entire life.[38]

Prussia's reviews were among the most intense examples of princely authority precisely because they did not rely upon the symbols of power usually employed in the eighteenth century. Fireworks, fanfare, brilliant costumes, processions of submissive delegates had no place on the Prussian parade ground. Instead, the army enacted the procedures that governed its regular daily existence. In this sense, the review was simply one moment in a regular and monotonous regime of control. Yet, as the army's training culminated in the review, it also arrived at its limit. The monarch functioned as the center of surveillance, but he was also famous for his arbitrary and mood-driven tirades. The system that prescribed precisely the actions of every soldier did not encompass its most important enforcement mechanism.

In this regard, Frederick's commands retained the arbitrary character of monarchical spectacle. Foucault noted that monarchical law "deploys before the eyes of the spectator an effect of terror as intense as it is discontinuous, irregular, and always above its own laws, the physical presence of the sovereign and of his power."[39] His tendency to dismiss officers without even watching their units perform, his disinclination to advance soldiers with names he disliked, his almost cyclical denunciations of reliable generals were not mere remnants of an earlier age. They became unspoken requirements of military service—hardships to be endured stoically. Unpredictable and unjust orders became the last test of military discipline. Could a soldier maintain his composure even when the chain of command violated its own principles? This conflict between the duty to obey orders and the recognition that they contradicted the practical interests of the army marked the boundary between a body's submission to institutional discipline and a person's entry into the critical discourses of the public sphere. Thinking and acting beyond the military's demands meant overcoming or at least ignoring the fear induced by visible threat of punishment.

Frederick's deviations from military convention placed him in the unusual position of existing both as a private person and as a subject of a disciplinary regime. While his elevated position gave him some immunity from the demands of military rules, he was never free to act according to whim. Norbert Elias pointed out that Louis XIV was as restricted as any courtier by the etiquette he imposed on Versailles,[40] and the same could be said of the military culture that Frederick instituted for the soldiers surrounding his retreat, Sanssouci. Frederick's deviations from a strict military regime were always limited; he never wholly abandoned the rules of military dress but, rather, adapted them so that they became markers of his personality. Frederick's dress thus became the model for many bourgeois Prussian men who had been educated within the institutional confines of the military.

Like many military rulers, Frederick dressed in a manner that implied a constant readiness for battle. However, in the rococo culture of the European court, his worn-out uniforms were considered merely shabby and tasteless. Throughout his life he was criticized for failing to live up to the standards of decorum expected of a prince. He wore garments "as long as decency [would] permit and, indeed, sometimes longer."[41] He generally wore the plain coat of an officer and only occasionally decorated himself with the elaborate regimental insignias of his personal command, the First Battalion of the Garde. His boots were badly creased at the ankles, and he was so fond of one particular pair of breeches that he refused to be parted from them until at least the 1770s. These habits could be interpreted as a preference for personal bodily comfort over the political obligations of princely ostentation. However, by wearing military garb even when ceremonial obligations did not require it of him, Frederick suggested that he, like the institution with which he was most associated, was in a permanent state of military readiness. But even military conflict can become an object of representation in a moment of reflection; signification separates from the activity once the practical necessity has passed. Frederick's worn-out uniform then became more a patchwork of signs referring to notable events in his life and suggesting that there was more to the king than the maintenance of his realm.

An astute contemporary analysis of Frederick's appearance was provided by Rudolph Wilhelm von Kaltenborn, an officer who had served under Frederick but who had also been summarily dismissed from his service. Kaltenborn described Frederick's public presentation as a highly self-conscious performance that only feigned at ignoring the impact that clothes had on others' opinion of him.[42] He dismissed the notion that Frederick wore the same clothes for years simply because he lacked good taste, calling this habit "the most carefully studied coquetry, if we understand this word as an urge to shine in front of an audience, to appear brilliant in the eyes of others." A host of connotations lay in Kaltenborn's description. On the level of conventional etiquette, Kaltenborn posited that Frederick's sloppy dress has an intention contrary to the conventions of courtly dress. Whereas a courtier's eye would typically have been drawn to ostentation as a sign of monarchical power, Frederick preferred to call attention to his accomplishments, his military victories. The coquetry of the king's clothes were thus to be understood as a political stratagem to remind observers of Frederick's personal engagement in warfare.

However, in light of Frederick's rumored homosexuality, the term *coquetry* suggested that his sartorial performance was motivated also by an erotic desire. That Kaltenborn carefully limited "coquette" to emphasize the calculation involved in self-presentation did not eliminate the erotic charge in Frederick's dress. By confining his coquetry to visual relations, Kaltenborn eliminated the potential for physical sexual contact but, in doing so, implicated all who entered into a visual exchange. Anyone who saw Frederick would be drawn into his coquetry regardless of that observer's actual physical relation to the monarch. The arena for such visual exchanges was much smaller than the splendid stages upon which other absolutist monarch's dramatized their authority. Coquetry implied a more intimate engagement, one that did not overwhelm the observer with spectacle. On the parade ground, where regiments were judged with often devastating finality, Frederick's clothes could hardly have had a coquettish effect.

Kaltenborn must have had a different context in mind, more likely the rooms of Sanssouci, where Frederick often gathered his leading officers. Participants at such meetings would have certainly been aware of the discrepancies in power between themselves and their commander, yet because of the proximity and the fact that Sanssouci served as Frederick's retreat as well as an informal workplace, officers in attendance, such as Kaltenborn, might have been more subject to the coquetry of his ragged uniform. This new mode of reading the king's clothes revealed facets of Frederick's private life—specifically, his sexuality. To the meticulous, Frederick's dress might have appeared as a sign of his failure to live as a great monarch, but Kaltenborn rejected this conclusion: "Who but a very weak observer could believe for a moment that it was greed that moved him to dress in this particular manner." Frederick's ragged clothes were more than frugality taken to extremes.

At first, Kaltenborn's interpretation of Frederick's dress avoided the sexual connotation raised in his opening statement. "He always wanted to look exactly as he had on the battlefields of Lowoschütz, Roßbach, Leuthen, and Cunnersdorf." In a sense, his clothes functioned as a fetishistic denial of the passage of time, much like Werther's repeatedly donning of the clothes he wore to the country ball with Lotte. Frederick sought to memorialize his identity by joining the immediate present, in which he was the object of observation, with the past events for which he was most famous. In doing so, he exchanged the immediate readiness of military discipline for a backward-looking, autobiographical, even hagiographical sartorial standard. The uniform in its ragged state became a sign of Prussian discipline as opposed to its instrument:

> Up until the Seven Years' War, he often wore the gala decorations of his First Battalion. However, all that disappeared after this war, which had secured his fame forever. Now that a laurel wreath decorated his brow, what need did he have for fashionable dress?

Kaltenborn did not suggest nostalgia as a motive. Rather, he linked Frederick's shabbiness with a mode of interpreting personal appearance that sought to look past surface representations of an absent signified to find a hidden, inner subjectivity:

> The glancing eye of an observer was not supposed to rest for a second on the surface; rather, it was supposed to immediately face with full amazement his core. His spirit, sublime above all else, could not stand even the slightest, most distantly removed sparkle.

In looking beyond the clothes, Kaltenborn did not stop to consider the body beneath. He moved his attention directly to the soul, the level imagined to lie below the body's surface. By passing through the body, Kaltenborn's critical observation settled on personal character and, more specifically, on sexuality as its object of investigation.

While technically a uniform, Frederick's attire did not call attention to his execution of drills nor did it even position him within a command structure. Instead, it suggested the existence of an identity beyond the surface of the tactically conditioned body. What was once the object of observation—the disciplinary function of the uniform—became a layer of connotation, something to be seen but then also to be passed over as one searched for or was drawn to the imagined interior of the clothed figure. The torn and worn uniform, so obviously a violation of military decorum, suggested a meaning that organized these signs into a "higher" meaning. Kaltenborn recognized the deliberate performative aspect of Frederick's violation of military etiquette. Frederick's importance in the masculine dress culture was in providing a model for male dress that asserted a personality whose autonomy lay in its ability to revamp disciplinary standards without fleeing from them. The uniform became Frederick's own in the sense that it created his persona only after he had stopped living by its requirements. The torn old uniform suggested the narrative order of biography—it conveyed a sense of having once submitted to a disciplinary regime and then of having earned, through military achievement, an exemption from its impersonal dictates. Generations of men in Prussia and elsewhere followed this same route for asserting an individual identity predicated upon successful completion of an impersonal, objectifying regimen of bodily control. Released convicts and veterans were not the only ones whose claim to personal depth depended on a performative display of scars, cuts, tattoos, and bruises—the effects of impersonal power once exercised on their bodies that, over time, became signs of survival and profundity.

In cataloging the specifics of Frederick's sloppy dress, Kaltenborn referred to the Greek cynical philosopher Diogenes (fourth century B.C.). "The ugly coat, the ripped boots and the black satin leggings that had turned largely red with age were to Frederick what the barrel was for Diogenes." This passing reference was laden with meaning because a number of anecdotes concerning Diogenes would have had particular relevance to Frederick.[43] Famous as a critic of feasting, loving, and luxury, Diogenes so thoroughly eschewed the accouterments of respectable Greek society that he grew his hair long, wandered in a coarse cloak, and slept in an old barrel. He was also renown for his encounters with Alexander the Great, who respected the cynic so much that he was reported to have said, "If I were not Alexander, I would want to be Diogenes." To which Diogenes was said to have replied, "If I am not Alexander, then I would be Diogenes." When Alexander at the height of his power came to ask Diogenes if there was anything that the philosopher wanted from him, Diogenes is reported to have said, "Stop blocking my sunlight."[44] The exchanges between Alexander and Diogenes were taken in antiquity as examples of a philosopher's virtue in the face of a ruler's political splendor, a confrontation that would have resonated to those familiar with Voltaire's short sojourn at Frederick's court. But just as relevant to the question of personal dress, were Diogenes' statements concerning the futility of adornment. Upon seeing a young boy dressing up, Diogenes said, "If you are doing that for men, then it is a waste of time, if for women, then it will make you a scoundrel."[45]

In the case of Frederick, one might ask the question in reverse: For whom was he dressing down? Kaltenborn asked this question indirectly when he opened the tenth letter of his memoir: "It was a particularly noteworthy feature in the life of Frederick the Great that, during his forty-six-year reign, he had virtual no relationships with women, not even socially."[46] Kaltenborn first looked for physiological reasons—whether the physical condition of the monarch prevented his sexual performance—and decided that, while he was no Hercules, he was also not impotent. That Frederick's tastes were homosexual was obvious to those who had reason to know: "That he had acquired a taste for so-called Greek love was the story told, with great difficulty, by all those who could know, so that virtually no doubt remained." Without direct confirmation, without a clear statement from Frederick himself, his sexuality was known to those around him. The fact that his closest aides were the handsomest officers and that many soldiers in the Potsdam garrison were practicing homosexuals reinforced Kaltenborn's opinion.

Frederick's appearance had two important implications: first, it showed how disciplinary standards of dress could be both preserved and individualized outside the enclosed space of institutional supervision; second, it illustrated the operation of understatement in dress. His dirty uniform did not indicate a collapse of military rigor; rather, it memorialized its historical accomplishments. His clothes did not deflect admiration but, rather, drew attention to themselves. They did not stifle eroticism but instead expressed an "unutterable" desire. What Werther's clothes accomplished at the end of Goethe's novel, Frederick's uniform performed during his lifetime. Frederick's appearance violated the norms of the Prussian military code, and yet as the many portraits of "old Fritz" have proven, the worn-out appearance became its icon. Similarly, the superficiality of the Werther suit contradicted the authenticity of poetic inwardness and yet became the symbol of eighteenth-century sentimentalism.

As imperfect representations of their respective histories, these outfits were caught in the contradiction of symbolizing two extremes. As signs, they had the thankless, and impossible, task of representing that which lay beyond signification—the unspeakable—as well as that which did not require symbolization—the purely practical utilization of the body. That this mediation was fraught with difficulty should hardly come as a surprise. Nor, however, should it serve as grounds for dismissing clothes as an inherently compromised mode of signification.

CHAPTER TEN

Signification as Discipline
The Demotion of Ostentation
and the Hard-Working Suit

THE THESIS of this book is that, during the last three decades of the eighteenth century and the first two of the nineteenth, the connection between public appearance and political power in the European system of elite dress shifted irrevocably. The presumption that clothes served primarily as signs of their possessor's identity was replaced by the idea that clothes were part of an economic and political calculus of production. Under this manner of dress, the primary message given by clothes was the absence of any message not justified by necessity. Excess was to be avoided rather than admired. Details in dress and architecture were no longer appreciated for their symbolic allusions. Rather, they were judged according to organically organized functional tasks, which insisted that every ruffle and bow not needed to strengthen and magnify the individual's productive life should be removed. Reform discourse characterized ornamentation as a financial and practical burden and was allowed only under particular circumstances and for well-defined aims. According to the new convention, clothes, along with most household objects, had two primary functions: to satisfy the body and to facilitate social intercourse:

> "Mode" regulates things that satisfy either our bodily requirements or social usages. They are clothes, domiciles, household appliances, riding equipment, and all manner of decoration, and they fall into two types: either they agree in time, location, and form with the communally undertaken practices and pleasures of social intercourse; or they are the agreed-upon signs of our disposition toward others.[1]

Even when defined broadly, these criteria were sharply at odds with the spectacular displays that had been an important means of exercising power in the ancien régime. Their enactment shifted attention from the grand to the minute, from the obvious to the almost invisible, from the exemplary to the exceptional.

The *Mode Journal*, ever self-conscious about the history of fashion, noted the century's changes in its 1801 issue, summarizing the great changes in elegance with an engraving accompanied by two explanatory articles.[2] The 1701 couple have invested much in the small details of their dress; both wear lace and powdered wigs. His gold and silver buttons correspond to her gold jewelry and diamonds. The 1801 couple, on the other hand, have far fewer accessories. The woman is lightly dressed so as to give the impression that she is covered in nothing more than "a morning fog and the dawn's rays." In contrast, the stately woman from a century earlier wears layers of expensive fabric. The journal drew particular attention to the shoes worn by the couples—the delicate balance of the baroque high heels versus the stability of the neoclassical sandals and English boots of the more modern couple. The arrival of the new century gave the journal an opportunity to reflect on its own history, as well. In an article covering the first twenty years of its publication, the writer concluded that "in contemporary fashions . . . we see that almost everything that forces and constrains the body has disappeared."[3]

The eighteenth-century transformation of the interpretive models used to explain sartorial appearances was most obvious in the muted colors of the new clothes. The shift in semiotic systems was symbolized by a change from bright to dark colors in the fashions of the European elite. Brilliant fabrics made with expensive dyes had once been the privileged markers of aristocratic status, while the lower classes were confined to dark, muted shades, the lowest being brown, a color associated with agricultural labor. Bourgeois dress was divided between white and black, with greys and browns as alternatives. Black, a color associated with mourning and death under absolutism, was deemed the ideal negativity for bourgeois male attire. White and black stood at the same extreme in color signification: they both indicated a refusal (or a failure) to display a particular identity. According to the courtly mode of understanding costume, the black and brown clothes of the bourgeoisie and the farming classes corresponded to their lower rank within the corporate hierarchy. The Enlightenment culture of clothes transformed the absolutist law forbidding ostentation into a deliberate rejection of the entire system of values predicated upon spectacular display. The dark clothes that might be considered proof of a person's failure or inability to show off became the Enlightenment's sly rebuff to the baroque expectation that every person of value would automatically trumpet themselves.

The preference for muted tones continued throughout the nineteenth century, even as new dying techniques increased the variety of colors available to textile manufacturers and decreased their cost. While bright colors were dismissed by bourgeois dressers, they were increasingly introduced into rural dress. The traditional costumes of agrarian society were livened up considerably by the blues and reds available in the nineteenth century. The brilliance of many peasant *Trachten* was made possible by the modernization of the chemical industry. Roman Sandgruber noted that, in rural society, brilliant dress was a sign of affluence, whereas poorer farmers continued to wear clothes made from undyed fabrics.[4] Bourgeois dress sought to minimize reliance upon clothes to define identity by assigning functional values to all forms of clothing signification. Clothes were to be understood as practical supplements to the body, but if they were to also function as signs, then they must do so abstractly. The allowance for display was thus simplified tremendously, to the level of binary oppositions. Clothes, when they operated as a means of communication, did so with a constant suspicion of their own activity.

No longer were garments meant to spring into the viewer's field of vision as an immediate, positive, and articulate means of establishing the identity of their owner. The first glance was supposed to provide an assurance that this person was not prone to excessive display, which taxed the purse. The solid black and white attire of the bourgeois provided a visual silence, an absence of signification. The first glance was then followed by a more careful scrutiny, which sought to detect signs of identity on a scale so quiet as to not disturb the initial impression of restraint. The "obvious" conclusion of this rule of restraint was that anything that too readily fell onto the eye would prove contentless under closer scrutiny. So advised the moral weekly *Daphne* in 1750:

> There are such beauties, so perfect and so clearly superior, that one is satisfied simply to see and speak with them. They belong to the distinguished faces that one surveys in a shimmering glance; they have the privilege of being admired by all, and yet they do not please. Through no fault of their

own, their charms are simply too elevated; we are astonished by them, yet we do not perceive the gentle movements of grace in them. . . . The beauties cannot help it, that they are forced to display all their splendor upon the first glance.[5]

It was better not to present an appealing impression, not to be too beautiful, so as not to awaken a doubt of one's moral character. Samuel Witte described this two-step interpretive process as a difference between impression (*Abdruck*) and expression (*Ausdruck*).[6] By providing the general social facts of a person, clothes facilitated an exchange of information between individuals, allowing the nuances of personalized expression to fill out the abstract outline. Witte's term *impression* suggested the application of force on the body of the dresser more than the effect that an image had on an observer. Nevertheless, he stated that the traits that had been "impressed" upon the individual were precisely the sartorial facts that made an initial "impression" upon the viewer. First observations told what institutions have left their mark upon the individual—that is, what manner of training they have undergone. The solid tones of bourgeois dress—a surface of black and white fabric—indicated not so much a particular meaning, such as mourning or innocence, as the dresser's refusal to invest meaning in clothing. They posited the individual's insistence that his or her value could not be found on the surface of appearances. The message was, Look elsewhere for a message.

The search for identity in the particulars of dress, despite its critical importance to social life, was held to be secondary to the functionality of clothes. The first obligation of clothes and goods was to actualize the productive potential of the body, to allow the person to more efficiently and comfortably fulfill the tasks of his or her place in bourgeois society. Johann Schlettwein wrote:

> Gold and silver on my clothes does not make my body healthier or stronger, nor does it make my organs and limbs more beautiful in form or build. I do not receive more and better nourishment for my body. My soul does not become more just, loving, or wise, and its abilities are in no way enhanced. Given that neither the energy nor the range of effectiveness and pleasure of my being is enlarged or expanded, I merely imagine that it is something good or beautiful to excite the eyes of other people.[7]

This concern for the relationship between clothes and the body permeated eighteenth-century discussions of fashion and uniforms. Comfort was aligned with utility; the body was foregrounded so that it might be mobilized for productive purposes. Ease of movement, warmth, durability, looseness of fit—these considerations were undervalued by the elaborate costumes of the French court, which treated the body as either inert matter or as an unruly substratum requiring restraint through training. While grace and elegance in both movement and gesture had long been a distinguishing feature of the nobly born, these skills were first and foremost signs of identity. Lessons in dance, fencing, and even riding served the somewhat paradoxical function of training the noble person's body to reflect the class distinctions with which they were supposedly born. Unlike fashion journals of the late Enlightenment, pedagogical treatises of the premodern era did not treat the talents they depicted as practical skills that could be acquired through industry and education alone. As Georges Vigarello explained:

> Certainly, it is difficult for such texts, which attempt to demonstrate the prestige of a social class, to admit that aristocratic elegance can be learned. Bearing and presence should be hereditary, just like a title of nobility. They should suffice to confirm the name they symbolize.[8]

The ability of these graces to signal upper-class identity was precisely their functional use. Fencing, for example, had very little military application by the eighteenth century; yet it seemed indispensable to preserving personal honor in the complex political maneuverings in courtly society. Participation in an exclusive group was signaled most particularly by the minuet, whose complex movements integrated the individual dancers into a larger pattern, which reenacted the social structure of the court as a whole.[9] With the introduction of the waltz and other country dances, the individual body was highlighted, though almost always at the expense of sophisticated choreography.

The second function of clothes and household adornments was the maintenance of public life. An inclination to display oneself before others was not wholly opposed to the bourgeois interest in communication and commerce. Clothes were acknowledged as signs that facilitated other forms of communication. Like the demoted art of rhetoric or the arabesque frames of rococo art, fashionable clothes were treated as sensually attractive supplements to the reasoned exchange of ideas. Friedrich Schiller, for example, viewed fashionable dress with the same skepticism he had for rhetoric. In his essay "On the Necessary Limits of Using Beautiful Forms," he argued that both were useful in drawing the attention of an audience, however unable they were to facilitate knowledge of the "internal" truth of an idea or a person.[10] Schiller was concerned lest appearance be taken as a sufficient basis for knowing someone. The potential discrepancy between dress and character became a central metaphor in his critique of public discourse and popular reading.

The journals and pedagogical treatises of the period argued that when they harmonized with the physical features of an individual, clothes and decor could help communicate their moral character, define their interests, and encourage exchange of sympathies. And Witte, even as he argued that clothing culture was integral to the maintenance of a bourgeois public sphere, warned that the relationship between personality and dress must be assiduously preserved, lest clothes become empty signifiers:

> Clothes may never be separated from the person, or rather the individual; instead they must remain precisely unified with him; otherwise, the person will no longer manifest himself through them. He will no longer be able to impress himself on his clothes nor make himself sensible through them. A class form of dress would step in its place, which would be nothing more than masks and disguises.[11]

Within an ideal society saturated with systems of rational communication, clothes would function as conversation pieces of a serious order. Consumer culture in general would provide an array of tasteful objects that could ease insecurities and smooth the way for friendships. Under this rubric—the disencumbrance of public life—fashion and luxury were allowed a place within the new bourgeois order. Enlightenment writers were aware of how closely their social justifications for fashionable culture were to the arguments employed by courtiers. Christian Garve affirmed that dress culture was an inevitable feature of all societies by arguing that "fashions arose from the drive toward sociability. . . . One adorns oneself for the sake of others, not for oneself."[12] However, immediately after grounding fashion in a social philosophy, Garve raised the Enlightenment's standard concern over decorum and etiquette's excessive refinement. He was not far from Schiller when he worried about the deceptions that fashionable performances might produce:

By becoming too artificial, too plentiful, and too transitory, the many decorations and mannered precautions that were developed to make society
more pleasant and to encourage public life by bringing people together more
closely and more often through the promise of new thrills could make social
life a tiresome burden, distract sociability from its true purpose—the exchange of ideas—and spread the seeds of pride and envy, two distinctly unso-
ciable passions.[13]

Garve never resolved this concern. His praise of consumer culture as the
everyday manifestation of social progress was always tempered by the suspicion that the accouterments of bourgeois comfort could become ritualized symbols, much like the costumes and luxuries of the court.

The failure to separate the instrumental and communicative functions of
clothes had serious implications for the management of consumption. The
insistence on productivity as the primary value of commodities was integral
not only to the system that constituted the self as an array of correspondences between practical needs and their satisfaction but also to the subordination of ostentatious luxury. The bourgeois dress code allowed only a
limited degree of symbolic communication in order to isolate social signification from the sites of political power and wealth. Elaborate female
fashions were justified as implements required in the pursuit of marriage;
military spectacles were explained as an appropriate presentation of state
power. These rituals were, however, intended to be exceptions allowed by
a regulatory regime that subordinated personal consumption to the relations of production. The display of authority was considered an unavoidable requirement of hierarchy. The political rationale of the ancien régime's
ostentation was preserved in a limited manner by the bourgeoisie.

When Garve acknowledged the political expediency of rank distinctions
in public life, he saw them as exceptions, justified on functional grounds:

There are ranks and positions in bourgeois life that call for splendor, because—at least according to the existing opinion of people and the ignorance
of the huge majority—to a certain degree the higher authority of those ranks,
which secure the welfare of the state and the general security, depends upon
such splendor.[14]

Garve's rationalization of stately ostentation sounded very similar to the
arguments Christian Wolff used to explain the monarch's need to maintain
an opulent household. However, after the French Revolution, the level of
show considered appropriate for a ruler diminished considerably. Half a

century of Enlightenment complaints about courtly luxury had been so successful that *Die Zeitung für die elegante Welt* could modestly acknowledge the political expediency of sartorial distinction without worrying that such an admission would produce a return to the ancien régime: "It seems a just expectation of princely personages to stand out in their dress; it belongs to their high rank."[15]

It was a long way from the bourgeois allowance that *something* on a monarch's dress should distinguish him from others to the baroque insistence that the king supersede his subjects in *everything*. Bourgeois fashion understood that visual markers hastened the recognition of ranks and facilitated the exchange of knowledge between equals. However, these signs could be employed, it was argued, without recourse to "excessive" luxury. Thus began a careful weighing and measuring of public display. An idealized sense of balance was postulated, scales upon which messages of form and content could be weighed, so that one did not outperform the other. Of course, in subjugating political spectacle to financial accounting, the new regulation of luxury consumption eliminated precisely that quotient that had defined monarchical power as absolutely superior to all other forces: its abundant excess, its ability to outstrip all other displays of wealth.

The Marxist tradition of commodity analysis has consistently interpreted domestic objects as signs that reflect the operation of power in some economic sphere far removed from the brightness and pleasure of consumer culture. The base/superstructure model presumes that power lies beyond clothing and other consumer commodities. According to this line of thinking, domestic commodities that surface in the cyclical movement of fashion assist in understanding economic and political institutions because their apparently superficial design changes reflect underlying social transformations not yet visible to the observer. Walter Benjamin's comment in his *Passagen-Werk* was probably the boldest version of this type of physiognomic reading of upper-class fashion, which treats clothes primarily as mystical signs that obliquely allude to an external political reality:

> For the philosopher, the burning interest in fashion lies in its extraordinary anticipation. . . . Every season brings in its creations certain secret flag signals of coming things. Whoever understands how to read them would know in advance the new movements not only in art but also in new law codes, wars, and revolutions.[16]

Since the gravitational center of cultural critiques that begin their analysis on the level of artifacts often lies beyond the objects under investigation, the immediate effects of domestic machinery and decoration are often thought of as merely ideological.[17] Rather than follow in this vein, I make the case that clothing conventions and household aesthetics are themselves vital sites in the application and rejection of power. Objects must be read in their immediacy, without recourse to an epistemology of depth that presumes that power and meaning are constituted in exclusive domains.

My debt to Michel Foucault is obvious, yet my examination of the regulatory and productive effects of clothing culture, high fashion, and other forms of household consumption differs from his study of state institutions that forcibly confine individuals. Instead, voluntary participation was an important clause in the negotiations that drew individuals into the control of respectable society. Conformity in dress in bourgeois society, unlike prisons and barracks, was ensured without overt violation of personal volition. The panopticon prison model has only a metaphorical application to consumption and dress. The relations of visual observation and bodily regulation in the bourgeois public sphere were less directly punitive than in prisons, schools, barracks, or hospitals. Punishment played only a minor role in bourgeois society; instead, individuals were urged to constitute themselves as agents of a productive potential, which they alone were responsible for actualizing, a shift in responsibility that penal institutions sought but that bourgeois society presumed.

The Enlightenment first refocused attention on the interaction between the body, clothes, and other domestic instruments in order to integrate these elements into a productive machinery. Newly popular and affordable consumer goods functioned as vehicles of disciplinary regimes because they entered households without the threat of coercion or judicial sanction. They integrated themselves into the most intimate routine, the most minuscule habit, many of which would otherwise have been overlooked by an overarching pedagogical gaze that, inevitably, could not perceive every detail. And once accepted as productive components in public life and the household, these goods facilitated further improvements in bodily comfort and convivial ease. Fashionable discourse of the eighteenth century perceived the overall trend in commodity innovation as moving toward heightening the productive forces imbedded within the individual.

The act of consumption within the marketplace reinforced an individual's claim to agency. As commodities became increasingly focused on the particular circumstances of the consumer, each purchase strengthened the regimen within which the product would be placed, while affirming the consumer as the being who not only stood at the center of that domestic regime but also appeared to organize it. By promising to satisfy the personal needs of the consumer, commodities suggested a singling out and an isolating of particular qualities unique to that person. With the expansion of the consumer goods market in the late eighteenth century, the relation of commodities to the individual consumer became increasingly intertwined through a spiraling of needs and of the things that provided their satisfaction. This increase in potential needs contributed to the complexity of modern subjectivity.

The initial stages of this relationship were rudimentary and seem almost simpleminded by modern standards of measuring desire. However wooden and implausible he may now seem, the rational consumer, that fiction of modern economics, embodied a potent and affirmative array of new motives to consume. Generated within a rationalist, utilitarian discourse of consumption, it coalesced within itself the concepts of need and satisfaction that were to become so instrumental in both urging and restraining consumption. The radicality of this new type of consumer becomes clear when it is compared with its predecessors. Aristocratic ostentation as a mode of consumption focused on the individual primarily in symbolic terms, as a figure of authority. Bodily comfort and personal enhancement were not the primary goal of luxury consumption in the court. The nobleman's physical body was frequently overshadowed by his politically symbolic presence. The bourgeois consumer sought to redefine the proper use of himself by regaining access to his own body, by establishing it as a standard for evaluating consumption and as the vehicle for developing further the concept of the self.

Within the abstracted ideality of eighteenth-century discourse on consumption, the body stood at the center of an array of concentric circles: clothes and household appliances stood a short distance removed, society even further away. Commodities were evaluated not only in terms of their relative contribution to the body's potential but also in terms of their proximity to the center. Much greater tolerance was granted to apparently frivolous decoration and ceremony if they occurred away from the central pillar of the self. Decorative gardens and architectural ornamentation were therefore treated much less suspiciously than clothes or cosmetics. Interiors were far more important than the exteriors of buildings. The division of rooms, their relation to each other, their furnishings were very much the concern of Enlightenment discourse on consumption. The conventions of polite society as they descended from courtly chivalry posed little threat to the body; indeed, their legitimacy as established traditions served the bourgeois interest in establishing rules for public discourse. The aim of self-regulation was the body and its immediate surroundings; other domains were therefore left intact, though relegated to a lesser status. The rules of public behavior, so long as they did not interfere with the primary interest of the bourgeois model of consumption, acquired the same demoted status as the science of rhetoric, useful in public communication but irrelevant to the penetrating gaze of philosophical reason, which sought a truth below the surface of ornamentation, in and on the body.

The cordon of utility that the bourgeois consumer model sought to place around the body was far from secure. The attempt to banish signification to specific objects and circumstance that would not disturb the body in its labor was hopeless. All objects are prone to connote. What bourgeois system of consumer regulation did manage, though, was to shift the level of connotation. Clothes and personal household objects were read according to a different code than decorations more removed from the intimate sphere. Whereas the older code of status and ostentation continued (in a somewhat reformed state) to rule over objects aimed at the public, the new disciplinary character of personal artifacts precluded such readings of private citizens. The new form of symbolism grew out of austerity and practicality. Garments and household wares signaled their owner's submission to restraint, establishing a circular relationship between signification and discipline. Unable to eliminate the tendency for material objects to be read as signs, the consumer regime employed them as markers for evaluating persons and as ideals worthy of emulation by others.

In short, an entirely new method of reading objects was introduced through the discourse on consumption, one that was so successful that fashion goods, once the antithesis of bourgeois frugality, became the medium within which the new regulatory system of consumption operated. Signification, the representation of an identity not physically manifest, remained a function central to clothing culture even after the disappearance of absolutist dress. The change occurred on the level of connotation. Whereas luxurious dress had once been employed to designate a certain rank, now the question of ostentation itself had become the signified of bourgeois dress. Rather than ask *how* one was ostentatious (Which jewels did he wear? How much gold brocade was on his jacket?), bourgeois society asked *whether* one was ostentatious (How does he fail to be frugal? Where does he let himself go into excess?). These questions, or rather the potential that they might be asked by observers, was a central restraining mechanism in bourgeois society, one that relied on the interpretation of signs. Thus, the differentiation between sign-value and use-value (as the enhancement of productive potential) replicated a distinction that was itself central to the disciplinary regime that sought to organize consumption.

The corporate class hierarchy, as it was derived from feudalism, maintained and enforced its complicated patchwork of distinctions through a vestmental culture that drew direct correspondences between rank and dress. Police ordinances dictated the fabric, cut, color, ornamentation, and quantity of clothes worn within each stratum. The visually impressive appearance of clothes and, in the upper classes, of virtually all other forms of consumption, certified membership within a specific class. The obligation to display one's identity pervaded society, so that each individual could readily be classified according to their station (*Ständ*). Most social intercourse under absolutism operated under this obligation to define oneself through attire and consumption. Resistance to the corporate hierarchy usually came in the form of a rebellious transgression across the sumptuary boundaries of rank. Not until the end of the century was this order overturned by a critique that side-stepped the whole apparatus of absolutist sumptuary regulation by claiming to retreat altogether from the demand to participate in visual culture. The courtier of the seventeenth and eighteenth centuries was quite familiar with the performative deceptions that splendid attire made possible; it would not, however, have occurred to the cavalier to suspect his reasons for dressing ostentatiously. Although they were masters of the subtle and complex art of judging appearances, courtiers did not challenge the epistemological or political status of the codes they used in drawing their opinions of others.

Before the eighteenth century, the desire to know what lay below the surface of appearances had not substantially influenced how society judged
dress.[18] Corporate and medieval observation of dress had certainly never
penetrated beyond clothing's surface; such investigations were carried out
by physiognomy and pathognomy. Regulation of dress was established according to categories that did not require confirmation from the individuals who were placed in them, and personal confession or testimony rarely
entered into clothing ordinances. The right to wear fur collars or lace trim,
for example, was derived from legal documents and not from an analysis
of the person wearing them.

In the eighteenth century, codes of dress did not rely on juridical codes
to regulate the relationship between clothing and identity. Clothes were no
longer signs of privilege granted to individuals to confirm class membership but were clues to personal identity. An entirely different kind of information was extracted from clothing: knowledge of the individual person,
one's estimation of him, the relations between him, his past, and his accomplishments, and what might be expected of him in the future.[19] The
legal categories that determined class membership in corporate society were
replaced by a grid of differentiation that positioned the body within a system of production rather than within a static hierarchy. The number and
type of categories invoked to regulate and interpret dress multiplied significantly. Anatomical details were introduced within the discourse on clothing for the first time. Age, hair and eye color, complexion, sex, weight,
height, width, and the presence of diseases in the body were referenced
while evaluating dress. Demonstrating correspondences between body features and interior identity was not only a goal of such pseudosciences as
physiognomy. The presumption that a hidden personal truth could be read
from bodily appearances was fundamental to the bourgeois consensus that
both regulated and interpreted dress.

The first laws regulating the relationship between identity and dress were
promulgated in medieval cities,[20] where surveillance could be practiced
much more easily than in the countryside. The history of sumptuary laws
and clothing ordinance suggests that one condition for the successful regulation of personal consumption was the confinement of the populace
within a well-defined enclosure. Premodern laws that prescribed the level
of sartorial luxury according to class membership also required an amaz-

ingly pervasive enforcement apparatus, because the legal constraints of dress in corporate society were precise down to smallest detail.[21] Inevitably, there developed an antagonist relationship between authorities, who sought to restrain ostentatious consumption, and the populace, which strove to dress itself in the symbols of power that constituted absolutist spectacle.

What distinguished the eighteenth century's control of bourgeois fashion society from previous methods of controlling consumption was the populace's willing participation in the mechanisms of surveillance. Bourgeois styles departed from the aristocratic presumption that clothes *asserted* an identity by deliberately signaling a lack of ostentation. The new manner of dress assumed a more passive stance, allowing the public eye to judge its moral character by its restraint and balance. This voluntary denunciation of luxury was possible because the mechanisms that controlled bourgeois dress were far subtler than those that had prevented guild apprentices from imitating their masters. Indeed, the very point and paradox of modern fashion was that the participants were presumed to have entered its regulatory system voluntarily. Once placed within the network of observation and self-regulation, bourgeois dressers perpetuated these mechanism through their behavior, seeking continually to display ever greater degrees of submission all in the name of personal freedom.

While the proliferation of printed media in the eighteenth century may have altered the mechanisms by which a social regulation of dress was enforced, the competitive observance of a particular standard of dress had always occurred in spaces where the effects of surveillance were most intense. In the absolutist state, the court functioned as a place where individuals were granted the privilege submitting themselves to scrupulous observation. Entry into the court marked the individual as requiring or deserving observation while, at the same time, transforming the person into an instrument of surveillance. Those engaged in the display of rank through clothes positioned themselves so that they might watch others, which in turn made them subject to scrutiny.

Because they were excluded from the court, the Bildungsbürgertum was obliged to carry out its rituals of self-regulation and competitive display in coffeehouses, private rooms, office bureaus, family salons, public parks, and the countryside. Many people had access to these locales, making for a variety of styles worn in these arenas, so assertion of prestige seemed implausible. Furthermore, these bourgeois locales were usually not meant for displaying individuals, so the clothes worn there often acquired the functional character of the setting. Such backdrops buttressed the ideological claim that bourgeois society was free from the suspicious interrogation and intimidation associated with courtly society.[22] But although bourgeois spaces did not allow for the ring of observation that generated courtly spectacle, other methods for examining the clothed body were developed, methods that focused on the body itself, ignoring the social hierarchy and historical lineage within which it appeared. Close quarters encouraged a precise scrutiny of the body beneath the clothes and the relationship between these two layers, while outdoor settings encouraged examination in isolation from social relations.

In both situations, observation was not simply meant to link clothes with corporate class. Public parks and rural landscapes separated the body from the courtly regime of regulating and interpreting appearances, thereby reinforcing the presumption that the body contained an autonomous identity. Yet this division between public and private identity was never absolute; individuals were presumed to operate within both spheres. The demand to constantly assert the division between public and private identities in the face of ambiguity corresponded to the interplay between the clothes that situated the body within a community and the private interior to which bourgeois garments frequently alluded. The ambiguous and often tenuous references made by clothes to a personal identity they could only obliquely represent produced the separation between public and private. The mere suggestion of something behind appearances sufficed to establish the existence of a private self. For all its concern with the private self, bourgeois modes of dress could not openly display such an identity. Instead, they provided merely an outline of an individual's private character. This constant maneuvering between the public and the private spheres was itself constitutive of these domains.

The tenuous border separating bourgeois society from state institutions was reinforced by a tendency to abstract, universalize, and divide social life into polarized genders. The distance between corporate classes maintained by spectacle was replaced by an intraclass division, which in its discursive formations reenacted the Enlightenment critique of the aristocracy. The superficial concern for formalities, the failure to recognize the origin of wealth, the incapacity to grasp a hermeneutic concept of the self, tendencies once ascribed to the absolutist elite, were now employed as the antithesis of a gendered, masculine subjectivity. The threat of unrestrained consumer desire, which transformed all persons and artifacts into objects of desire and signification, was localized within the female body, as attributes aligned with an unstable feminine identity. The consumer discourse situated authority within the nuclear family, a unit that was itself just separating from the broader, clannish concept of the family that had dominated feudal, agrarian societies. That sexual difference functioned in this new family structure as a determinant of value illustrates how the heightened attention to detail severed categories. Tremendous differences in authority were established on the basis of minute distinctions in appearance.

Because bourgeois clothes deliberately suggested a depth behind the surface, the techniques for reading the body's attire that were developed in the court were inappropriate. The court's concentration on surface ornamentation did not have the same goal as bourgeois clothing signification. It asserted an affirmative identity, which could be condensed or embodied by luxurious costumes, whereas bourgeois dress codes suggested a hidden presence through the stylized negation of surface signification. The interiority and depth implied by this style of dress required new techniques for inspecting, categorizing, and regulating the public figure. These methods sought to read the interplay of presence and absence in bourgeois dress, thereby constructing a truth predicated upon a series of exclusions and denials, which the well-dressed body communicated.

The etiquette and ceremony surrounding French courtly dress restricted free movement of the body while integrating it into a highly complex and unstable network of political relations. Norbert Elias has shown specifically how monarchical power was exercised through the daily rituals at Versailles, in which the highest French nobility literally dressed the body of the king.[23] Louis XIV's levee established the king's body as the ultimate prestige fetish. The minute detail of Louis's morning toilet was only the most extreme manifestation of a political code that tightly regulated dress in order to correctly and exactly situate the (noble person's) body within the spectacle of absolutist power. Toward the end of the eighteenth century, arguments that stressed the physical burden of ceremonies for displaying rank were coupled with medical critiques of courtly costume.[24] Motivated by an ideology of personal autonomy, arguments against the elaborate costumes worn by the aristocracy drew an often explicit parallel between the physical condition of the body covered with restrictive garb and an inner state of spiritual confinement imposed by the almost mathematically rigid conventions.

These denunciations of courtly costume often called for an alternative mode of dress, in which an idealized subjectivity would determine the form and expressive content of clothes. Within this ideological context, English clothing styles introduced in the later part of the century were often described as the liberation of the body from the artificial and unnatural restrictions imposed upon it by social convention. However, rather than consider eighteenth-century bourgeois styles as the abandonment of political regulation of the body, we can understand these fashions as new designs for integrating the body into a regime of observation and interrogation, which extended further and more effectively into daily life than the police and sumptuary laws of the corporate state. These new forms of clothing deployed an approach to the body entirely different from the regulations imposed by courtly costume. The leading organ of this new approach in Germany was the *Mode Journal*. Its mission was defined as an ongoing evaluation of consumer goods in terms of their utility. Even before its publication, the editor wrote: "The journal . . . shall, wherever possible, bring news of fashions' usefulness, harmfulness, or innocence, comfort or discomfort, its invention and public introduction."[25]

The bourgeois code of dress first sought to isolate individuals from their social context in order to place them within a grid of abstract values independent from genealogy and local custom. The relation between personal identity and its display shifted in a two-step process, which sought to filter out historical influences in order to position individuals within a universal construction of values. Identity was established by linking a hidden, almost secretive, interiority with the abstract sciences of ethics, economics, and biology. Each person was defined as an instance in which universal principles were manifested within a unique particular. Fundamental to this new mode of classification was the presumption that the individual was an organic structure, capable of generating and sustaining a coherent and intelligent meaning.

Clothes were integrated into the organism of the individual as a part of the whole. Dress was no longer a sufficient representation of identity; instead, it was one component in a complex construction. The signifying aspect of clothing was subordinated to other functions. Gone were garments sewn from delicate fabrics and laden with precious metals, representing the aristocracy's wealth and political power while simultaneously displaying its exemption from economic labor. These glittering suits were supplanted by clothes that claimed a practical function and that were less expensive, more durable, and more carefully tailored to the body. The previous signifying function was abandoned for an economy that highlighted clothing's relation to the activities of the body. Georg Brandes noted in 1808:

> The expensive luxury of ostentation, which only a few could allow themselves frequently, sank extraordinarily. The luxury of comfort took its place and became widespread. The materials selected by fashion were in most cases not costly, although extremely expensive because of the many obligatory changes required.[26]

The dispersion of these comfort-oriented products to increasing numbers of eighteenth-century consumers fostered the new disciplinary regimes in households that had previously been organized according to agricultural tradition.[27] The new regulation of consumption distributed authority to an educated part of the population. This self-regulatory distribution of power was predicated upon the philosophical claim that identity was constituted within and by the autonomous body, rather than through a web of social interdependencies. Clothes were presumed to reflect, and indeed to magnify, the organism they covered, not only in its ideal state but also in its fluid transformations. Thus, for example, cosmetics, which froze the face in a palette of colors, were disfavored because they disguised the change in skin tones brought on by emotions or exertion.

The new clothes did more than symbolize a new calculus; they were also elements within its operation. The separation of display from the conditions necessary for its production, which typified the ancien régime, was disallowed by a new economic discourse that evaluated dress as nothing more than consumption, which was itself dependent upon and subordinated to the relations of production. This new code of dress sought to dispel the legacy of ostentation by instrumentalizing consumer products. Clothes and household goods were increasingly evaluated in terms of their ability to assist their owner in the performance of practical activities. Commodities became extensions of the body in motion. The smallest detail and the most minor garment was considered from the perspective of how they augmented the smooth operation of daily life. Do these clothes hamper movement, are they durable, do they adaptable to different tasks, do they fit comfortably? The requirements for a garment's utility were, however, not crudely functional. A garment should not only assist, it should also ease, the burden of labor. Tasks would be pleasurable when performed with the proper gear. Well-dressed people should feel that their clothes enhanced their ability to exercise their physical and mental faculties. Comfort was thus not an idle luxury; it implied activity and was a necessary precondition for the highest productivity.

Needs never before known were created through the increasingly minute scrutiny of garments' function. Rationalized within a system of production, these needs were arranged in a network of equivalences. Technological innovation seemed to reveal needs long dormant, activated by the possibility of their satisfaction; in fact, the same pressures that motivated the multiplication and refinement of consumer products also organized the demand, which seemed the logical response. New styles were hardly a ruse foisted upon a persuaded public. New products multiplied the practical ends to be achieved, increasing the possibilities available to the individual. Garve noted:

> Even the ends, toward which we select the means, change, multiply themselves, are understood more clearly, or at least are judged differently. The gentler our bodily constitution is, the more delicate our taste buds are: hence, the more sensitive we become in choosing our means, the more careful and inventive we become in their preparation. . . . Our houses need new furnishings, when we change our lifestyle, so as to secure for ourselves the necessary space and comfort. Every new undertaking, every newly invented amusement, brings a new piece of furniture to our doorstep.[28]

Comfort-oriented commodities were generated by the same paradigms of thought that mobilized subjective demand. And while prestige was unquestionably associated with the possession of "high quality" English goods, it would be mistaken to conclude that the utilitarian claims of products were an ideological alibi covering their primary function as status signs.[29] The rejection of ostentation that bourgeois clothes signaled was not an empty gesture that could be ignored by those who understood the prestige-oriented code that lay beneath. Restraint and denial was predicated upon practices not easily evaded. Every style that playfully circumvented the modern demand for functionalization received a response that co-opted resistance and increased surveillance. One could argue far more certainly that status and independence in dress were tactical gestures allowed by a regime of social control that was unthreatened by expressions of personal autonomy, one whose effectiveness was predicated upon the exercise of free will. For much of the modern era, most certainly in the eighteenth century, and without a doubt in Prussia, the very point of bourgeois style was to signal voluntary submission to a code that functionalized behavior and eschewed excess expenditure. What distinguished the "respectable" member of society from the common criminal or the rough worker was the freedom and willingness to comply with a disciplinary regime that others had to accept as an imposition. Bourgeois prestige was, in its Enlightenment formulation, an inversion of aristocratic status—a combination of understatement and moral negation that displayed its diffidence as an anxiety about productivity.

Increased attention to bodily detail was idealized aesthetically as the harmonious interaction between the garment and the body. The syntagmatic relation between articles of clothing and their coherent integration with the body were preferred over a paradigmatic logic that simply selected the most visually impressive alternative in each class of garment—the most luxurious vest, the brightest jacket, the loudest hat—rather than a coordinated ensemble. The avoidance of crude fetishism became the defining difference between an aesthetically educated elite and those who did not know how to exercise restraint over their presentation. The *Mode Journal* in 1789 remarked that

> there exists a certain noble simplicity in feminine clothing that, with the assistance of good taste and cleanliness, one can make one's own. It is not expensive and rarely fails to have an effect on the male heart. The vanity of our sex would, in truth, not suffer if we renounced expensive fashion finery.[30]

An aesthetic that began in the 1780s as a rejection of the dominant Parisian mode of dress became by the beginning of the nineteenth century the standard for distinguishing cosmopolitan residents from rural arrivals. Both the shifting boundaries and the aesthetic continuity between classes were unmistakable. Bourgeois distinction was maintained by an aesthetic predicated upon the harmonious coordination of garments with the body and a deliberate restraint. This refusal to display was made more noticeable by the contrary example of a class of dressers dedicated to attracting the eye of the observer. As the bourgeois mode established itself, the contrasting class became less and less powerful and more susceptible to scorn. The group that the *Mode Journal* implicitly invoked in 1789 as the opposition to bourgeois restraint was by 1812 presented in the journal as an exemplar of tasteful understatement:

> Women who come to Paris from the provinces must live here a time before they learn that which belongs to true *ton* and actual elegance. At their debut in the capital, they usually cover themselves with brilliant jewels, like some miraculous image of the Madonna. Despite being overloaded with ornaments, they fear that they have not done enough. The more they assemble their toilet, the closer they feel they come to the very height of elegance. . . . It is remarkably easy for a practiced observer to distinguish residents of Paris from provincial beauties. The latter dress themselves up, pile dress on top of dress, hang layers of scarves on themselves, and nevertheless believe that they are underdressed. Whereas the Parisian takes on a lovely simplicity when she bares her head, arms, and throat in a short *robe suisse*, with a Viennese shawl and Scottish shoes. The more she undresses herself, the more tasteful she takes herself to be.[31]

Public opinion imposed rules of beauty on its members by paradoxically requiring them to avoid conformity. Parisian women were distinguished as such because they, out their own free will and good taste, selected the same manner of dress. It was presumed that each individual would select clothes in accordance with her own facial features, hair color, build, and so forth. Adopting a style simply because it was worn by a prominent person was disparaged as leading to the physical distortion of those for whom the garment was not designed. In 1795, the first issue of the *Mode Journal* announced the personalization of attire as the only fit rule:

> Everywhere in our costumes we have begun to approximate nature. Nowhere do we find anything distorted, conspicuous, or insulting. Beauty, purposefulness, and becoming attire seem to have gained acceptance as the law. One does not imitate without being selective, and age, build, and complexion are respected.[32]

Clothes that harmonized with physical features were considered more stable, less likely to be overturned by fads, and thus capable of grounding a vestmental semiotic code. As a sign system, clothes were seen as inherently unstable unless the rules of their selection and variation were enforced by behavioral norms. The ideologically and scientifically constructed body replaced the absolutist hierarchy as a necessary, and nevertheless arbitrary, ground for stabilizing the interpretation of public appearance. Fashion advice consistently stressed the need to avoid frequent changes in appearance, to resist the inclination to alter one's appearance. "While we are admired for a few minutes standing there draped in glimmering and brilliantly colored garments, we will always please if we turn to cleaner, simpler clothes whose color and form match our complexion and build."[33]

The ideological interest in personalized fashions brought a reduction in dependence on social opinion, for the individual who dressed according to their bodily features could ignore the pressure of contemporary opinion. Imbedded within the new code of dress was a rejection of mere conformity to a code, thus creating the paradoxical formulation inherent in avant-garde taste: the truly fashionable do not follow; they create:

> Ladies of taste avoid adopting very new fashions that will not also enhance their own charms by adventitiously emphasizing nature's gifts or by covering up its unfortunate forgetfulness. Such women are guided by their own figures rather than by fashion. They do not imitate, they invent.[34]

Individuality, as a relative principle differentiating one large group from another more select one, was asserted at every stage within a given style's dispersion in society, allowing a continual production of distinctions. This process of differentiation did not seem arbitrary as long as the adoption of a particular style was grounded in bodily necessities. They were repeatedly set in opposition to conformity. Manners and rituals were downplayed as ill-suited to the natural mobility and repose of the body. This opposition has been reasserted regularly since the late eighteenth century, on the assumption that each fashion innovation allows for even greater harmony between the body and its environment.

This new mode of consumption assumed that a concentration on comfort, rather than prestige, diminished consumption because harmony as an autonomous and perfect condition required only minor adjustments once it had been achieved. On the surface, then, every purchase that struck a balance promised to be the last. Garve wrote:

> Occasionally, the human spirit, in the course of its many experiments, comes across forms that are more appropriate for a certain intention than others, or seem to the eye to have a more pleasing proportion; and when this happens, the sweeping wheel of fashion stands still for a time.[35]

The same argument could be reformulated in aesthetic terms, namely, that once a body had been arrayed in the clothes and decorations that most accentuated its natural beauty, there was little need for further consumption, particularly of fashionable innovations that would only diminish the effect already attained:

> The reasonable spouse, proud of her husband's approval and love, will combine goodness and cleanliness in her dress with clothing colors and form that fit her face and figure. She will not strive after the ridiculous, affected, and much-sought-after appearance of a vain coquette. She would prefer, a thousand times, to renounce a long-admired dress than to embarrass her husband, for that would cast a dreadful shadow across the delicacy of feelings.[36]

However, in practice, comfort was by no means a static condition; each new activity called forth a new range of practical necessities. The potential points where comfort might be improved multiplied with each change in the body's circumstance. Each innovation called forth the possibility of another. As these adjustments in the adaptability of clothes to the body proliferated through the marketplace, further improvements were invented, and attention was focused in greater detail on an ever-increasing number of bodies, each one treated as unique, thereby creating a self-generating system of demand for products that adjusted the fine balance between the individual body and its environment. As Garve commented,

> Our needs always grow with every change in the method of instruments used in their satisfaction. It is precisely because of those refinements that drive our old ornaments that one stumbles onto entirely new types of decoration. To the extent that we frequently renew the accouterment of our houses and tables, we learn to appreciate comforts and decorations of a sort that we had never before desired.[37]

The bourgeois mode allowed for an escalating concentration on bodily details in order to enact a continual reduction in the allowance granted for display through clothes. The futility of preventing changes in appearance and domestic order were already well known to commentators, who had seen the collapse of police regulation and sumptuary laws regulating consumption. The *Mode Journal*, the most astute manipulator of fashion in Germany, adopted a tactic of regulating fashionable change by serving as its medium. The journal stressed the transitory nature of taste, thereby justifying the need for its intervention as the purveyor of consumer goods. Instead of advocating mere restraint, the journal heightened readers' knowledge of innovations. The effect was an escalation of consumption matched by a proliferation of the mechanisms for its regulation. In its second issue, the journal pointed out that the domain of taste was limitless and that the potential for producing commodities conforming to that opinion was equally boundless:

> Feminine taste and fashion ultimately have no limits, just as its arts have no laws. And if ever the million forms with which fashion blooms and inspires were to be exhausted, then taste and industry would create a million new ones; fashion would simply wander back into the past to plagiarize our forefathers and set their fashions back in circulation with a stamp of approval.[38]

New designs were introduced, accepted, and then abandoned at a rate that far outstripped the enforcement mechanisms of the absolutist police, which were geared to oral communities in which design changes occurred generationally. Fashion journals that appeared monthly—and eventually even three times a week—were capable of maintaining a much more rapid pace of adaptation. Each issue allowed for an adjustment in public taste, thereby breaking down developments into smaller units of time. By multiplying temporal subdivisions (from generations to weeks), journals increased the points of intervention in readers' dress and domestic practices. Because they did not take a confrontational stance against the objects they sought to evaluate critically, fashion journals shifted the mode of regulation from juridical prohibition and censorship to affirmative persuasion aimed at voluntary conformity. The *Hamburgisches Journal der Moden und Eleganz*, a stylish publication with some of the most remarkable illustrations of the period, reassured patriarchs that it posed no threat to the domestic order of the bourgeois household:

> This journal should not raise the concerns of the strict moralist and frugal economist who worries that his wife and children are swimming happily away in a stream of luxury and modernity, so much so that they will soon be estranged from him and themselves. Quite the contrary, this journal will advise him and them, it will warn and incite, it will teach them to prefer taste, refined morals, and a secure philosophy of life over false taste and disorderliness and purposelessness in life. To that end, this journal is determined to elevate and educate the souls and hearts of readers with purposeful, amusing, and informative readings.[39]

Each issue introduced products and practices intended to promote the ease and agency of readers as one component in the classical project of *Bildung*. While the journal claimed to serve as a mere reporter or archivist of fashion history, the distinction between event and publication was as indistinct in the eighteenth century as it is today. Improvements in printing technology (the introduction of color images) and the rise in literacy created a dynamic of continuous evolution, which replaced the dynastic or generational pace of the ancien régime.

Left as the sole arbiters of consumer behavior by a literary culture predicated upon the separation of literature from popular and decorative art forms, fashion journals became the primary discursive medium for German consumers. And by actively broadening the domain of personal identity through the adoption of new modes of dress and domestic practice, they effectively defined the terms of bourgeois consumption.

Notes

Introduction

1. See David Landes, *The Unbound Prometheus: Technological Change and Industrial Development in Western Europe, from 1750 to the Present* (Cambridge: Cambridge University Press, 1969), 48. John Brewer and Roy Porter, eds., *Consumption and the World of Goods* (London: Routledge, 1993), expanded on McKendrick's research. See also Neil McKendrick, John Brewer, and J. H. Plumb, *The Birth of a Consumer Society: The Commercialization of Eighteenth-Century England* (Bloomington: Indiana University Press, 1982); Daniel Roche, *The Culture of Clothing: Dress and Fashion in the Ancien Régime*, trans. Jean Birrell (Cambridge: Cambridge University Press, 1994); Cissie Fairchilds, "The Production and Marketing of Populuxe Goods in Eighteenth-Century Paris," in Brewer and Porter, *Consumption and the World of Goods*, 228–48 (see above).

2. Roman Sandgruber, *Die Anfänge der Konsumgesellschaft: Konsumgüterverbrauch, Lebensstandard, und Alltagskultur in Österreich im 18. und 19. Jahrhundert* (Munich: Oldenbourg, 1982).

3. The classics of Continental costume history, many of which have been translated into English, are Hermann Weiss, *Kostümkunde: Geschichte der Tracht und des Geräthes vom 14ten Jahrhundert bis auf die Gegenwart* (Stuttgart, 1872); Carl Köhler, *A History of Costume*, trans. Alexander Dallas (New York: Dover, 1963); Max von Boehn, *Die Mode: Eine Kulturgeschichte vom Mittelalter bis zum Barock*, 4th rev. ed. (Munich: Bruckmann, 1984); Eva Nienholdt, *Kostümkunde: Ein Handbuch für Sammler und Liebhaber* (Braunschweig: Klinkhardt & Biermann, 1961); Margarete Braun-Ronsdorf, *The Mirror of Fashion: A History of European Costume, 1789–1929* (New York: McGraw-Hill, 1964); Francois Boucher, *20,000 Years of Fashion: The History of Costume and Personal Adornment* (New York: Abrams, 1987).

4. See Martha Bringemeier, "Wandel der Mode im Zeitalter der Aufklärung: Kulturgeschichtliche Probleme der Kostümkunde," *Rheinisch-westfälische Zeitschrift für Volkskunde* 13 (1966): 5–60; reprinted in Bringemeier, *Mode und Tracht: Beiträge zur geistesgeschichtlichen und volkskundlichen Kleidungsforschung*, ed. Gerda Schmitz (Münster: Coppenrath, 1985); Hermann Bausinger, "Zu den Funktionen der Mode,"

Schweizerisches Archiv für Volkskunde 68/69 (1972/73): 22–31. For criticism of the discipline's methodological application of the *Tracht/Mode* (native costume/fashion) distinction, see Wilhelm Hansen, "Aufgaben der historischen Kleidungsforschung," in *Geschichte der Alltagskultur*, ed. Günter Wiegelmann (Münster: Coppenrath, 1980), 149–74. Hansen's essay built its reformulation of the discipline's methodology on the earlier empirical conclusions made by Bringemeier. Ina-Maria Greverus drew a parallel between the expansion of German literary criticism into research and the movement of ethnological studies beyond traditional methods and archival sources; see her "Alltag und Alltagswelt: Problemfeld oder Speculation im Wissenschaftsbetrieb?" *Zeitschrift für Volkskunde* 79 (1983): 1–14. Also see Hermann Bausinger, "Traditionale Welten: Kontinuität und Wandel in der Volkskultur," *Zeitschrift für Volkskunde* 81 (1985): 173–91. For a feminist response to Bausinger's criticisms of *Trachtenforschung* (native costume research)—which also agreed with Hansen's call for an expansion of ethnology's traditional parameters—see Gitta Böth, "Historische Kleidungsforschung in Niedersachsen: im Weser-Ems-Gebiet durch das Niedersächsische Freilichtmuseum Cloppenburg: Ein Projektbericht," in *Mode-Tracht-Regionale Identität, Historische Kleiderforschung Heute* (Museumdorf Cloppenburg, Niedersachsen: Freilichtmuseum, 1985), 43–55.

5. Friedrich Theodor Vischer, *Mode und Cynismus, Beitrage zur Kenntniß unserer Culturformen und Sittenbegriffe*, 2d ed. (Stuttgart, 1879), 28, reprinted in *Die Listen der Moden*, ed. Silvia Bovenschen (Frankfurt: Suhrkamp, 1986), 60.

6. See the anthology by Bovenschen, *Die Listen der Moden* (see above, n. 5).

7. Eduard Fuchs, *Das bürgerliche Zeitalter*, in *Illustrierte Sittengeschichte vom Mittelalter bis zur Gegenwart*, vol. 3 (Munich: Albert Langen, 1912). Georg Simmel's essay on fashion was first published in English in *International Quarterly* 10 (1904): 130–55. See also Simmel, "Adornment," in *The Sociology of Georg Simmel*, trans. Kurt Wolff (New York: Free Press, 1950), 338–44.

8. Werner Sombart, *Liebe, Luxus, und Kapitalismus: Über die Enstehung der modernen Welt aus dem Geist der Verschwendung* (Berlin: Wagenbach, n.d.). For Sombart's analysis of late-nineteenth-century mass consumption, see his "Wirthschaft und Mode, Ein Beitrag zue Theorie der modernen Bedarfsgestaltung," in *Grenzfragen des Nerven- und Seelenlebens* (Wiesbaden: Bergmann, 1902).

9. Sombart, *Liebe, Luxus, und Kapitalismus*, 137 (see above, n. 8).

10. Colin Campbell argued along different lines: that in the eighteenth century there developed a Romantic mode of subjectivity that desired consumer goods as a means of emotional self-fulfillment; see his *The Romantic Ethic and the Spirit of Modern Consumerism* (Oxford: Blackwell, 1987). While Campbell's and Sombart's arguments differed, they shared the assumption that desire was constructed by historical circumstances, as opposed to the traditional view, which supposed the desire to consume to be constant and tied to a universal desire to assert one's status through material objects. Thorstein Veblen is the most famous proponent of this "emulation mode" of luxury consumption; see his *The Theory of the Leisure Class* (New York: Vanguard, 1928 [1899])

11. Chandra Mukerji also invoked Sombart's thesis; see her "Reading and Writing

with Nature: A Materialist Approach to French Formal Gardens," in Brewer and Porter, *Consumption and the World of Goods*, 439–40 (see above, n. 1).

12. For a representative sampling of German sociological opinion on consumption, see Walter Benjamin, "Mode," in vol. 1, *Das Passagen-Werk*, ed. Rolf Tiedemann (Frankfurt: Suhrkamp, 1982).

Chapter One: Fashion Journals and the Education of Enlightened Consumers

1. Known to contemporaries simply as the *Mode Journal*, Bertuch's *Journal des Luxus und der Moden* is available today in three formats. Older German and American libraries have original copies in their holdings; however, very few collections contain the complete series from 1786 to 1827. (The Lippeheidische Kostümsammlung in Berlin has the largest collection of German fashion texts and images.) Citations to original issues appear as *Mode Journal* followed by the month and year of publication. A four-volume abridged edition was published by Müller & Kiepenheuer in Hanau a.M. in 1967 under the Weimar editorship of Werner Schmidt. Citations to the abridged edition appear as *Mode Journal* (abridged) with the volume number. A third source is the collection of passages reprinted with a catalogue of fashion prints taken from the journal *Heimliche Verführung*, ed. Christina Kröll and Jörn Göres (Düsseldorf: Goethe Museum, 1978). Citations to the catalogue appear as *Heimliche Verführung*.

2. *Mode Journal*, Jan. 1791, 7. For an overview of German economic theory at the end of the eighteenth century, see Keith Tribe, *Governing Economy: The Reformation of Economic Discourse, 1750–1840* (Cambridge: Cambridge University Press, 1988).

3. Francois-G. Dreyfus, "Die deutsche Wirtschaft um 1815," in *Deutschland zwischen Revolution und Restauration*, ed. Helmut Berding and Hans-Peter Ullmann (Königstein Ts.: Athenäum, 1981), 352–53.

4. *Heimliche Verführung*, 53–55.

5. Sandgruber, *Die Anfänge der Konsumgesellschaft*, 267 (see intro., n. 2).

6. Wilhelm Treue, *Wirtschafts- und Technik-Geschichte Preussens* (Berlin: Walter de Gruyter, 1984), 179.

7. Norbert Schindler noted that "a critique of luxury had become for the enlightened heads of the eighteenth century almost an obligatory exercise." See his "Jenseits des Zwangs? Zur Ökonomie des Kulturellen inner- und außerhalb der bürgerlichen Gesellschaft," *Zeitschrift für Volkskunde* 81 (1985): 197.

8. German ethnographers long claimed that in the late eighteenth century urban fashions diverged from the traditional costume of rural society. Eighteenth-century contemporaries had already noted that the separation betweeen urban and rural dress was no longer a function of class (*Stände*) differences alone. This separation of fashionable dress from rural culture acquired political implications during the Romantic period. Wilhelm Heinrich Riehl later invoked the distinction between fashion and rural costume in his three-volume treatise, *Die Naturgeschichte des Volkes als Grundlage einer deutschen Social-Politik* (Stuttgart, 1854). The third volume sharply attacked

urban fashion culture's influence on rural patriarchy. For an abridged English translation, see Riehl, *The Natural History of the German People*, trans. David Diephaus (Lewiston, N.Y.: Mellen, 1990).

9. *Mode Journal* (abridged) 1:28.

10. Fashionable clothes, such as cotton print dresses, were already visible among Austrian farmers in the first decades of the nineteenth century; see Sandgruber, *Die Anfänge der Konsumgesellschaft*, 288 (see intro., n. 2).

11. "Sudelbücher, II/117.5," in Georg Lichtenberg, *Schriften und Briefe* (Frankfurt: Insel, 1983), 1:536.

12. Bringemeier, *Mode und Tracht*, 113 (see intro., n. 4). Bringemeier based this conclusion on her partial survey of *Adelsbibliotheken* (aristocratic libraries).

13. Christian Garve, "Über die Moden," in *Versuche über verschiedene Gegenstände aus der Moral, der Literatur und dem gesellschaftlichen Leben*, reprint (Hildesheim: Olms, 1985 [1792]), 241.

14. People in the Hanseatic cities were the first Germans to adopt English dress; see Percy Ernst Schramm, *Neun Generationen: Dreihundert Jahre deutscher 'Kulturgeschichte' im Lichte der Schicksale einer Hamburger Bürgerfamilie (1648–1948)* (Göttingen: Vandenhoeck & Ruprecht, 1964), 1:346.

15. Adolph von Knigge, *Über den Umgang mit Menschen* (Hanover, 1804), 1:22–23.

16. *Heimliche Verführung*, 62.

17. Gisela Jaacks, "Modechronik, Modekritik, oder Modediktat? Zu Funktion, Thematik und Berichtstil früher Modejournale am Beispiel des 'Journal des Luxus und der Moden,'" *Waffen- und Kostümkunde* 24 (1982): 36.

18. For an example, see *Mode Journal* (abridged) 2:137–39.

19. Ruth Wies, "Das Journal des Luxus und der Moden (1786–1827), Ein Spiegel Kultureller Strömungen der Goethezeit," Ph.D. diss., Munich, 1953, 35.

20. For a thorough analysis of early French fashion journals, see Annemarie Kleinert, *Die frühen Modejournale in Frankreich: Studien zur Literatur der Mode von den Anfängen bis 1848* (Berlin: Schmidt, 1980). Older works on the subject include Lore Krempel, *Die deutsche Modezeitschrift: Ihre Geschichte und Entwicklung nebst einer Bibliographie der deutschen, englischen und französischen Modezeitschriften* (Munich: Tageblatt-Haus Coberg, 1935); Elen Riggert, "Die Zeitschrift 'London und Paris' als Quelle englischer Zeitverhältnisse um die Wende des 18. und 19. Jahrhunderts," Ph.D. diss., Göttingen, 1934.

21. *Der Teutsche Merkur*, Nov. 1785, 187.

22. The *Cabinet des Modes* was imitated in England (by *The Fashionable Magazine*) and in Milan and Venice; see Roche, *The Culture of Clothing*, 487 n. 50 (see intro., n. 1).

23. "Only one difference can be found. The Paris periodical does nothing more than report, probably without any critical intention, whereas Bertuch gave his journal from the very start a critical [*räsonierenden*] character and thereby consciously placed it within a certain tradition of intellectual history"; Wies, "Das Journal des Luxus und der Moden," 27 (see above, n. 19).

24. An overview of these journals can be found in Joachim Kirchner, *Bibliographie der Zeitschriften des deutschen Sprachgebiets im 1900* (Stuttgart: Hiersemann, 1969), 1:356–57. According to Wies, "Das Journal des Luxus und der Moden," 48 (see above, n. 19), the *Cabinet des Modes* was published in German translation from 1788 to 1808 as the *Pariser Journal der Mode und des Geschmacks* but was not influential. McKendrick, Brewer, and Plumb, *The Birth of a Consumer Society*, 47 (see intro., n. 1), list sixteen English ladies' almanacs dedicated to fashion published in England between 1771 and 1800.

25. *Die Zeitung für die elegante Welt* focused more broadly on questions of taste in literature and the arts. Fashion was ranked second on the title page (July 1, 1808): "The *Newspaper for the Elegant World* contains according to its plan: 1. General essays intended to correct judgments of art and to ennoble taste as well as essays about all manner of pleasing objects that interest the educated world and that can serve to entertain finer family circles; 2. Reports on the newest fashions and luxuries from foreign and German cities regarding men's and women's clothes, household instruments, interior decorations, furniture, riding equipment. . . . Anything that touches on politics or academic scholarship will remain completely excluded from these pages."

26. C. Willett and Phillis Cunnington, *The History of Underclothes* (New York: Dover, 1992), 96. McKendrick, Brewer, and Plumb, *The Birth of a Consumer Society*, 47 (see intro., n. 1), provided convincing evidence that the *Lady's Magazine* did not color its prints until 1786.

27. Bertuch's journal tried to keep up with the increasingly literary tone of fashion journals in the early nineteenth century, as the various name changes to the journal suggest. The monthly was founded in 1786 as *Journal der Moden*. Its name was almost immediately changed to *Journal des Luxus und der Moden* and stayed that way until 1812. For one year, the name became *Journal für Luxus, Mode, und Gegenstände der Kunst*. The order of the title was reversed in 1814 to *Journal für Literatur, Kunst, Luxus, und Mode*. In its final year, 1827, the title was changed once more to *Journal für Literatur, Kunst, und geselliges Zusammenleben*. The increasing deemphasis on the words *Mode* and *Luxus* reflected the increasing self-confidence of German readers in their own fashion judgments as well as the journal's increasingly futile attempt to keep up with its competition. Fashion prints began to disappear from the journal after 1823. The few that did appear accompanied literary references. See Wilhelm Feldmann, *Friedrich Justin Bertuch, Ein Beitrag zur Geschichte der Goethezeit* (Saarbrücken: Schmidtke, 1902), 98.

28. Kleinert, *Die frühen Modejournale*, 126 (see above, n. 20), dated publication of *Giornale delle Dame e delle Mode* between 1789 and 1795.

29. Friedrich Bertuch Nachlaß, Goethe-Schiller Archiv, N.F. 873. Bertuch also listed fashion journals published in Prague, Leipzig, Göttingen, and Vienna.

30. Sandgruber, *Die Anfänge der Konsumgesellschaft*, 301 (see intro., n. 2).

31. Ernst Beutler, "Georg Melchior Kraus," in *Essays um Goethe*, 5th ed. (Bremen: Schünemann, 1957), 432.

32. Feldmann, *Friedrich Justin Bertuch*, 23 (see above, n. 27).

33. McKendrick, Brewer, and Plumb, *The Birth of a Consumer Society*, 47–48 (see intro., n. 1).

34. The first issue of the *Allgemeine Moden-Zeitung* in 1820 began with the following gender-specific apology: "Fathers complain about the changeability of fashion; men bemoan its costliness, and if we were to still these complaints, we would have to demand that the human spirit cease its education and maturation. This would be the death of the spirit, which is, after all, eternal. Thus we ask fathers and men to be a little patient and considerate."

35. Roche, *The Culture of Clothing*, 486 (see intro., n. 1).

36. Quoted in Feldmann, *Friedrich Justin Bertuch*, 49 (see above, n. 27).

37. Bertuch Nachlaß, N.F. 867/II (see above, n. 29).

38. Ibid., 874.

39. W. H. Bruford, *Germany in the Eighteenth Century: The Social Background of the Literary Revival* (Cambridge: Cambridge University Press, 1965), 280–81.

40. Ibid., 281; James Sheehan, *German History: 1770–1866* (Oxford: Clarendon, 1989), 157.

41. *Heimliche Verführung*, 61.

42. Ibid., 48.

43. This journal, which appeared in 1758 in Erfurt, also showed a predilection for English goods. See Dora Lühr, "Die erste deutsche Modezeitung," *Zeitschrift für deutsche Philologie* 71 (3/4) (1953): 329–43; Bringemeier, *Mode und Tracht*, 111 (see intro., n. 4).

44. Wies, *Das Journal des Luxus und der Moden*, 142 (see above, n. 19); Adolf Feulner, *Kunstgeschichte des Möbels* (Frankfurt: Propyläen Verlag, 1980), 297.

45. *Mode Journal* (abridged) 1:75.

46. Ibid.

47. *Heimliche Verführung*, 51.

48. Bringemeier, *Mode und Tracht*, 118 (see intro., n. 4).

49. *Mode Journal*, Feb. 1786, 72.

50. Caroline de la Motte Fouqué, "Geschichte der Moden, vom Jahre 1785–1829," *Jahrbuch der Jean-Paul Gesellschaft* 12 (1977): 28, noted that at the end of the eighteenth century neoclassical and English styles were considered interchangeable and were often mixed with traditional costumes, producing an unseemly combination. "Back then . . . there reigned a strange confusion, in which the craving for English naturalness, or what counted as the same thing—Roman Idealism—was mixed with traditional formalism. This brought highly peculiar caricatures to light."

51. *Heimliche Verführung*, 52

52. Jakob Michael Reinhold Lenz, *Gesammelte Schriften*, ed. Franz Blei (Munich: Müller, 1910), 4:382–83.

53. Hubert Kiesewetter, *Industrielle Revolution in Deutschland, 1815–1914* (Frankfurt: Suhrkamp, 1989), 27.

54. For a concise account of the hindrances to trade movement within German principalities, see Wolfgang Zorn, "Binnenwirtschaftliche Verflechtungen um 1800," in *Die*

wirtschaftliche Situation in Deutschland und Österreich um die Wende vom 18. zum 19. Jahrhundert, ed. Friedrich Lütge (Stuttgart: Fischer, 1964), 99–109. For a larger overview of European trade routes from the late Middle Ages to 1815, see Hermann Kellenbenz, "Landverkehr, Fluß- und Seeschiffahrt im europäischen Handel," *Europa, Raum wirtschaftlicher Begegnung* 92 (1991): 327–441.

55. *Mode Journal*, Jan. 1786, 22.

56. Ibid., July 1786, 249.

57. *Mode Journal* (abridged) 1:23.

58. Cited in Bringemeier, *Mode und Tracht*, 117 (see intro., n. 4).

59. Christian Kraus, the most prominent proponent of free market economic theory, probably first began working on Adam Smith's writings in 1788. As a professor in Königsberg, Kraus went on to have a significant influence on the education of Prussian officials. See Treue, *Wirtschafts- und Technik- geschichte Preussens*, 216 (see above, n. 6).

60. Bahrdt argued that "the most important thing, particularly for the middle classes, is the avoidance of luxury." Quoted in Schindler, "Jenseits des Zwangs?" 197 (see above, n. 7). See also Ulrich Hermann, "Die Kodifizierung bürgerlichen Bewußtseins in der deutschen Spätaufklärung—Carl Friedrich Bahrdt's 'Handbuch der Moral für den Bürgerstand' aus dem Jahre 1789," in *Bürger und Bürgerlichkeit im Zeitalter der Aufklärung*, ed. Rudolf Vierhaus (Heidelberg: Lambert Schneider Verlag, 1981), 321–33.

61. *Mode Journal*, Apr. 1792, 184.

62. *Mode Journal* (abridged) 1:71.

63. *Mode Journal*, Dec. 1790, 641–42.

64. *Mode Journal* (abridged) 1:38.

65. For a summary of other versions of this ripple effect argument, see Wolfgang Haug, *Critique of Commodity Aesthetics*, trans. Robert Bock (Minneapolis: University of Minnesota Press, 1986), 20.

66. Johann August Schlettwein, *Grundfeste der Staaten oder die politische Oekonomie* (Frankfurt: Athenäum, 1971 [1779]), 410–11.

67. See Joyce Appleby, "Consumption in Early Modern Social Thought," in Brewer and Porter, *Consumption and the World of Goods* (see intro., n. 1). "Rattling off the names of new condiments, textiles, and inventions has served as the incantation for summoning the spirits that presided over the rise of the West" (164). The catalogue Bertuch reprinted in the *Mode Journal* included gold and silver diamond watches, gold and steel watch chains, gold pins, brooches, cuff links, hairpieces decorated with real pearls, elastic sock bands, silver and steel shoe buckles, silver pencil holders, ladies' scissors, travel cases for letter writing, hat pins with jewels, knitting and sewing needles, silver-plated thimbles with inlaid precious stones, tobacco cases, tea brewers, sugar doses, breadbaskets, wine racks, tea services, lacquered coffee tables, cutting knives with mahogany handles, toothbrushes, ladies' hair-styling kits, razors, shaving brushes, combs, powder dispensers, bootjacks, crystal writing utensils, miniature globes, compasses, rubber erasers, pistols, powder horns, saddle blankets, ladies' saddles, bridles,

hunting horns, men's toolboxes, ladies' sewing kits, mahogany chairs with horsehair upholstery, dining room tables, telescopes, microscopes, perspectives, opera glasses, hearing aids, surgeon's instruments, amputation knives, tourniquets, catheters, dentistry equipment, umbrellas, patent leather gloves, tea, mustard, purses, perfumes, Wedgwood tea services, oval bowls, terrines, dinner plates, dessert plates, salad dishes, red, blue, and white cups with or without handles, thermometers, barometers, and a wide variety of scientific equipment. *Mode Journal* (abridged) 1:76–81.

68. The question of whether domestic demand or foreign and colonial consumption fueled English manufacturing in the eighteenth century has been central to English historical scholarship. Bertuch seemed to believe that domestic demand in German principalities could hasten the development of a German manufacturing base.

Chapter Two: Reading to Consume

1. Campbell, *The Romantic Ethic*, 90 (see intro., n. 10).

2. For a discussion of the importance of travel literature in the formation of German consciousness of modernity, see Wolfgang Kaschuba, "Erkundigung der Moderne: Bürgerliches Reisen nach 1800," *Zeitschrift für Volkskunde* 87 (1991): 29–52.

3. These regimes are described in Michel Foucault, *Discipline and Punish: The Birth of the Prison*, trans. Alan Sheridan (New York: Vintage, 1979).

4. The quotations are from Campbell, *The Romantic Ethic*, and Foucault, *Discipline and Punish* (see above, nn. 1, 2).

5. For an overview of recent scholarship on German intercultural relations, see Michael Maurer, "Europäische Kulturbeziehungen im Zeitalter der Aufklärung," *Das achtzehnte Jahrhundert* (1991): 35–61.

6. The German mix of manners and customs made it difficult for travelers to adapt to new localities. When Goethe arrived in Leipzig to study, he was told that he looked as if he had "dropped down out of another world"; J. W. Goethe, *Werke*, ed. Erich Trunz (Munich: Beck, 1981), 9:250. Knigge, *Über den Umgang* (see chap. 1, n. 15), said about Germany: "nowhere else can one find such a great multiplicity of conversational tones, educational methods, opinions on religion and other matters, and such a great diversity of conditions which claim the attention of various social groups in the different provinces."

7. Jürgen Habermas, *Strukturwandel der Öffentlichkeit* (Darmstadt: Luchterhand, 1962), 35, linked newspapers and critical journals with the formation of the public sphere. Manufacturers were compelled to develop an interest in international relations because of their dependence on overseas markets and supplies. The *Mode Journal* and other fashion periodicals provided consumers with information about foreign style, which they came to consider vital to their cultural identity. For an application of Habermas's public sphere theory to eighteenth-century American consumption, see T. H. Breen, "The Meanings of Things: Interpreting the Consumer Economy in the Eighteenth Century," in Brewer and Porter, *Consumption and the World of Goods*, 257 (see intro., n. 1).

8. Rémy Saisselin, *The Enlightenment against the Baroque: Economics and Aesthetics in the Eighteenth Century* (Berkeley: University of California Press, 1992), 125.

9. Habermas, *Strukturwandel*, 46 (see above, n. 7).

10. Wolfgang Martens, *Die Botschaft der Tugend, Die Aufklärung im Spiegel der deutschen Moralischen Wochenschriften* (Stuttgart: Metzler, 1968); Paul Raabe, "Die Zeitschrift als Medium der Aufklärung," in *Wolfenbüttler Studien zur Aufklärung*, ed. Günter Schulz (Bremen: Jacobi Verlag, 1974), 1:99–136.

11. Wolfgang Kaschuba, "Deutsche Bürgerlichkeit nach 1800, Kultur als symbolische Praxis," in *Bürgertum im 19. Jahrhundert*, ed. Jürgen Kocka (Munich: DTV, 1988), 3:9, argued that, despite the obvious importance contemporaries attached to the reading of newspapers and journals, membership in the bourgeoisie did not correlate with having a subscription to Johann Cotta's *Augsburger Allgemeine Zeitung*, not because the newspaper lacked influence among the "die besseren Bürger" of the Vormärz but because it was a staple of that society. Kaschuba incorrectly presumed that fashion was of interest only to those who desired to enter the bourgeoisie but failed to qualify. This argument incorrectly assumed that members of the German bourgeoisie were never worried about their status or engaged in fashionable behavior. But the fact that the *Allgemeine Zeitung* had become fashionable among Vormärz readers suggest that the boundaries of the middle class were expanding as the cultural standing of class membership was rising.

12. Defining the bourgeois reading public is inherently tricky. Klaus Scherpe, *Werther und Wertherwirkung, Zum Syndrom bürgerlicher Gesellschaftsordnung im 18. Jahrhundert* (Hamburg: Gehlen, 1970), 10, focused on the typical occupations of the male members of the late-eighteenth-century middle class: "The representatives of the Bildungsbürgertum who dominated residences, garrisons, universities, and trading cities can be identified by their occupational titles: officials serving the court bureaucracy (judges and cameralists), pastors, doctors, officers, professors and university lecturers, schoolmasters, businessmen, bankers, and manufacturers. One should also include those below the rank of the middle class who were still part of the reading public: shopkeepers, craftsmen, and servants."

13. See Michael Maurer, *Aufklärung und Anglophilie in Deutschland* (Göttingen: Vandenhoeck & Ruprecht, 1987); Peter Brenner, *Der Reisebericht in der deutschen Literatur, Ein Forschungsüberblick als Vorstudie zu einer Gattungsgeschichte, Internationales Archiv für Sozialgeschichte der deutschen Literatur* (Tübingen: Niemeyer, 1990), 217–25; W. D. Robson-Scott, *German Travelers in England, 1400–1800* (Oxford: Blackwell, 1953).

14. Georg Christoph Lichtenberg, *Briefwechsel*, ed. Ulrich Joost and Albrecht Schöne (Munich: Beck, 1983), 1:27–28.

15. Sophie von la Roche, *Sophie in London, 1786*, trans. Clare Williams (London: Cape, 1933), 87. The excitement evident in German travelers' accounts of shopwindows and mannequins in London attests to the lack of opportunities for German consumers to view fashions. Certainly, the practice of displaying goods in windows was a recent innovation for English buyers. See *Mode Journal*, Sept. 1786, 335; Nov. 1791, 629. Robson-Scott, *German Travelers in England*, 182 (see above, n. 13), criticized la Roche's

"lack of discrimination" in her enthusiasm for English society. However, other European travelers were also impressed by the stores in England. Francois de la Rochefoucauld, *A Frenchman in England 1784*, ed. Jean Marchand, trans. S. C. Roberts (Cambridge: Cambridge University Press, 1933), 9, echoed la Roche's fascination: "The London shops are indeed worthy of remark; surely there can be no other city which has anything so magnificent to show. Everything the merchant possesses is displayed behind windows, which are always beautifully clean, and the shops are built with a little projection onto the street so that they can be seen from three sides."

16. Michael Maurer, "Der Anspruch auf Bildung und Weltkenntnis Reisende Frauen," *Lichtenberg Jahrbuch* (1990): 139.

17. Lichtenberg, *Briefwechsel*, 1:28 (see above, n. 14); la Roche, *Sophie in London*, 132 (see above, n. 15).

18. Quoted in Feldmann, *Friedrich Justin Bertuch*, 96 (see chap. 1, n. 27).

19. Quoted in ibid., 97.

20. Goethe, *Werke*, 5:170 (see above, n. 6). Not the worst poem Goethe wrote, the rhyme "Tode" with "Mode" would become an allegorical dialogue in the nineteenth century. See Giacomo Leopardi, "The Dialogue of Fashion and Death (1824)," in *The Moral Essays*, trans. Patrick Creagh (New York: Columbia University Press, 1983), 1:50–53; Karl Gutzkow, "Die Mode und das Moderne," in *Werke*, vol. 9 (Frankfurt a.M., 1846).

21. Goethe, *Werke*, 47:58 (see above, n. 6).

22. Ibid., 59.

23. Goethe was far less concerned with the formation of "pure" aesthetic judgments than Kant. "One must admit that objective [*rein*] observations are rarer than one thinks. Our feelings, views, and judgments become part of our experiences so quickly that we cannot long maintain our position as impartial observers but instead soon begin forming opinions. Yet, we should attribute importance to these opinions only to the extent that we can trust the nature and training of our mind as a basis for them." J. W. Goethe, "Introduction to the *Propylaea*," *Essays on Art and Literature*, trans. Ellen von Nardroff and Ernest von Nardroff (New York: Suhrkamp, 1986), 3:79.

24. Goethe, *Werke*, 47:57 (see above, n. 6).

25. *Die Zeitung für die elegante Welt*, Jan. 1, 1801, 1.

26. For a recent discussion of the eighteenth-century effort to regulate reading, see Martha Woodmansee, *Author, Art, and the Market: Rereading the History of Aesthetics* (New York: Columbia University Press, 1994), 87–102.

27. Georg Jäger, "Die Wertherwirkung. Ein Rezeptions-Ästhetischer Modellfall," in *Historizität in Sprach- und Literaturwissenschaft*, ed. Walter Müller-Seidel, Hans Fromm, and Karl Richter (Munich: Fink, 1974); reprinted in Hans Pater Hermann, ed., *Goethe's "Werther"* (Darmstadt: Wissenschaftliche Buchgesellschaft, 1994).

28. Jäger, "Die Wertherwirkung, 396–97; Hermann, *Goethe's "Werther*," 227 (see above, n. 27).

29. See Erich Kleinschmidt, "Fiktion und Identifikation, zur Ästhetik der Leserrolle

im deutschen Roman zwischen 1750 und 1780," *Deutsche Vierteljahrschrift für Literaturwissenschaft und Geistesgeschichte* 53 (1979): 49–73.

30. *Mode Journal* (abridged) 1:372–73.

31. Goethe, *Werke*, 9:457 (see above, n. 6).

32. Jochen Schulte-Sasse, *Die Kritik an der Trivialliteratur seit der Aufklärung, Studien zur Geschichte des modernen Kitschbegriffs* (Munich: Fink, 1971), 84, 94, 95, 97, reiterated Goethe's and Schiller's apocalyptic imagery when he described the formation of neoclassicist theories as a "seawall" against the "flood" of trivial literature. Still, his work provided a useful overview of the major theorical arguments.

33. Jakob Michael Reinhold Lenz, *Werke*, ed. B. Titel and H. Haud (Darmstadt: Wissenschaftliche Buchgesellschaft, 1966), 1:667.

34. For a recapitulation of *Werther*'s reception as a problem in eighteenth-century aesthetic theory, see Georg Jäger, *Empfindsamkeit und Roman, Wortgeschichte, Theorie und Kritik im 18. und frühen 19. Jahrhundert* (Stuttgart: Kohlhammer, 1969), 93–103.

35. Goethe, *Werke*, 9:112 (see above, n. 6).

36. Roland Barthes, *The Fashion System*, trans. Mathew Ward and Richard Howard (Berkeley: University of California Press, 1990), 251.

37. For a summary of the important scholarship on the history of reading in Germany, see Erich Schön, *Der Verlust der Sinnlichkeit oder Die Verwandlungen des Lesers, Mentalitätswandel um 1800* (Stuttgart: Klett-Cotta, 1993), 31–61.

38. Johann Jakob Engel, *Von dem moralischen Nutzen der Dichtkunst*, in *Schriften* (Berlin, 1804), 7:51.

39. Johann August Schlettwein, *Grundfeste der Staaten oder die politishe Oekonomie (1779)* (Frankfurt: Athenäum, 1971), 405.

40. Ibid., 397

41. Engel, *Schriften*, 7:51–52 (see above, n. 38).

42. Rolf Engelsing, "Die Perioden der Lesergeschichte," in *Zur Sozialgeshichte deutscher Mittel- und Unterschichten* (Göttingen: Vandenhoeck & Ruprecht, 1973), 144–45.

43. Isabel V. Hull, *Sexuality, State, and Civil Society in Germany, 1700–1815* (Ithaca: Cornell University Press, 1996), 272.

44. Elizabeth Blochmann, *Das Frauenzimmer und die Gelehrsamkeit: Eine Studie über die Anfänge des Mädchenschulwesen in Deutschland* (Heidelberg: Quelle & Meyer, 1966), 34. A more recent overview of women's education in the eighteenth century is Barbara Becker-Cantarino, *Der lange Weg zur Mündigkeit, Frau und Literatur (1500–1800)* (Stuttgart: Metzler, 1987), 149–201. For a synthetic history of women's education in the context of the public sphere, see Ute Frevert, *Frauen-Geschichte: Zwischen Bürgerlicher Verbesserung und Neuer Weiblichkeit* (Frankfurt: Suhrkamp, 1986), 37–39. For accounts of women's reading habits in the eighteenth century, see Erich Schön, "Weibliches Lesen: Romanleserinnen im späten 18. Jahrhundert," in *Untersuchungen zum Roman von Frauen um 1800*, ed. Helga Gallas and Magdalene Heuser (Tübingen: Niemeyer, 1990), 21–40; Martens, *Die Botschaft der Tugend*, 527–42 (see above, n. 10).

45. For a discussion of the *Lesewut* (reading madness) critique as it was applied specifically to female readers, see Becker-Cantarino, *Der lange Weg zur Mündigkeit*, 170–77 (see above, n. 44). On the limited place allotted women's education within sentimentalism, see Silvia Bovenschen, *Die imaginierte Weiblichkeit: Exemplarische Untersuchungen zu kulturgeschichtlichen und literarischen Präsentationsformen des Weiblichen* (Frankfurt: Suhrkamp, 1979), 164–90. Engelsing, "Perioden der Lesergeschichte," 144 (see above, n. 42), provided a number of references that compared such reading practices with hunger, with nicotine, opium, and caffeine addiction, with alcoholism, and with excessive gambling.

46. Albert Ward, *Book Production: Fiction and the German Reading Public, 1740–1800* (Oxford: Clarendon, 1974), 60.

47. Ernst Brandes, *Betrachtungen über den Zeitgeist in Deutschland in den letzten Decennien des vorigen Jahrhunderts (1808)* (Kronberg/Ts.: Scriptor Verlag, 1977), 140–41; Hans Robert Jauß, *Ästhetische Erfahrung und literarische Hermeneutik* (Frankfurt: Suhrkamp, 1982).

48. Johann Gottlieb Fichte, *Ueber das Wesen des Gelehrten*, vol. 8, *Werke, 1801–1806*, ed. Reinhard Lauth and Hans Gliwitzky (Stuttgart: Frommann, 1991), 13. On the history of intensive and extensive reading practices, see Engelsing, "Perioden der Lesergeschichte," 121–22, 133 (see above, n. 42).

49. Janice A. Radaway, *Reading the Romance: Women, Patriarchy, and Popular Fiction* (Chapel Hill: University of North Carolina Press, 1991), 117–88.

50. J. A. Bergk, *Die Kunst Bücher zu lesen* (Jena, 1799), 411–12.

51. Brandes, *Betrachtungen*, 131 (see above, n. 47).

52. Ibid., 135.

53. Ibid., 141.

54. Schlettwein, *Grundfeste*, 406 (see above, n. 39).

55. Adam Smith, *The Theory of Moral Sentiments*, (Indianapolis: Liberty Classics, 1976), 254.

56. Knigge, *Über den Umgang*, 52 (see chap. 1, n. 15).

57. Jauß, *Ästhetische Erfahrung*, 633 (see above, n. 47): "'The novel is the universal fodder for the reading public: it suits every stomach, by ignoring all differences in rank.' That at least was the opinion of a contemporary voice on the subversive influence of the flood of sentimental novels." Jauß pointed out that class structures were, of course, embedded and replicated in sentimental novels, just as they inevitably were in fashion journals.

58. *Mode Journal* (abridged) 1:373.

59. J. H. Merck, letter to Bertuch, Nov. 25, 1786, reprinted in *Goethe Jahrbuch* 31 (1910): 38.

60. Brandes, *Betrachtungen* 141 (see above, n. 47).

61. *Mode Journal* (abridged) 1:29.

62. Mary Ann Doane, *The Desire to Desire: The Woman's Film in the 1940s* (Bloomington: Indiana University Press, 1987), 24–25.

63. Charles Eckert, "The Carole Lombard in Macy's Window," in *Fabrication:*

Costume and the Female Body, ed, Jane Gaines and Charlotte Herzog (New York: Routledge, 1990), 119.

64. Rachel Bowlby, *Just Looking: Consumer Culture in Dreiser, Gissing, and Zola* (New York: Methuen, 1985), 2, also presumed that consumer culture came into existence only at the end of the nineteenth century, once capitalism had established itself in heavy industries: "The second half of the nineteenth century witnessed a radical shift in the concerns of industry: from production to selling and from the satisfaction of stable needs to the invention of new desires."

65. Anne Friedberg, "A Denial of Difference: Theories of Cinematic Identification," in *Psychoanalysis and Cinema*, ed. E. Ann Kaplan (New York: Routledge, 1990), 36–45, claimed that identification was not "unique to the cinema." However, her discussion of precinematic identification concentrated solely on Freud's treatment of hysteria.

66. Doane, *The Desire to Desire*, 1 (see above, n. 62). Doane's precision kept her from insisting that the relationship between mass culture and the desire to vitiate distance between audiences and art objects was historical. Doane referred to Benjamin's essay as "a possible history."

67. Judith Mayne, *Cinema and Spectatorship* (London: Routledge, 1993), 50.

68. Ibid., 82

69. Christian Metz, *Film Language: A Semiotics of the Cinema*, trans. Michael Taylor (Chicago: University of Chicago Press, 1974), 3.

70. Helmut Kreuzer, "Trivialliteratur als Forschungsproblem, Zur Kritik des deutschen Trivialromans seit der Aufklärung," *Deutsche Vierteljahrsschrift für Literaturwissenschaft und Geistesgeschichte* 41 (1967): 173–91.

71. Nancy Armstrong and Leonard Tennenhouse, "A Novel Nation; or, How to Rethink Modern England as an Emergent Culture," *Modern Language Quarterly* 54 (1993): 341–42.

72. Michel Foucault, *Archeology of Knowledge*, trans A. M. Sheridan Smith (New York: Pantheon, 1972), 49.

73. Barthes, *The Fashion System*, 21–22 (see above, n. 36).

74. Christian Gottfried Flittner, *Die Kunst der Toilette, Ein Taschenbuch für junge Damen die durch Anzug und Putz ihre Schönheit erhöhen wollen*, 2d ed. (Berlin, 1833), 6.

Chapter Three: The Ever-Expanding Domain of *Mode und Luxus*

1. Christopher Berry, *The Idea of Luxury: A Conceptual and Historical Investigation* (Cambridge: Cambridge University Press, 1994), 66–67.

2. Ibid., 63.

3. Johann Peter Süßmilch, *Die göttliche Ordnung in den Veränderungen des menschlichen Geschlechts aus der Geburt, dem Tode und der Fortpflanzung desselben* (Berlin, 1761), 2:72.

4. Johann Christoph Gottsched, *Beobachtungen über den Gebrauch und Misbrauch vieler deutscher Wörter und Redensarten*, ed. Johann Hubert Slangen (Haarlem: Winants, 1955), 167.

5. For a review of how *Mode* has been used in recent ethnological studies, particularly its isolation from the term *Tracht*, see Gitta Böth, "Die Mode und die Volkskunde: Anmerkungen zum Umgang mit einem Begriff," in *Hessische Blätter für Volks- und Kulturforschung*, ed. Gitta Böth and Gaby Mentges (Marburg: Jonas Verlag, 1989), 25:11–20.

6. Johann Adelung, *Versuch eines vollständigen grammatisch- kritischen Wörterbuches der hochdeutschen Mundart* (Leipzig, 1775), 253–54.

7. In the 1840s, Karl Gutzkow argued that the modern quality of Mode was precisely its ability to redefine traditional or ancient designs. "Mode does not reject the so-called old Frankish style; fashion . . . returns conspicuously enough to the taste judgments of the previous century. This feature of fashion clears the way for a conception definition of the modern. The modern does not reject the old; rather, it remodels it after its own taste or practices it to such an extreme that it becomes comical, or it refines the old in some other way. . . . One can be taken by the antique and by the romantic and nevertheless find oneself within the modern." Gutzkow, "Die Mode und das Moderne," 142 (see chap. 2, n. 20).

8. Jacob Grimm and Wilhelm Grimm, *Deutsches Wörterbuch* (Leipzig, 1885), 2435.

9. Adelung, *Versuch eines vollständigen grammatisch- kritischen Wörterbuches*, 635–36, provided the following definition of *Tracht*: "The manner in which one carries oneself, i.e., dresses." There can be comfortable Tracht, laborious Tracht, ridiculous Tracht. "Large crinolines are an absurd 'Tracht.' The Polish and Oriental 'Tracht' is more natural than the French." In all likelihood, *Mode* and *Tracht* were not synonmous. While it might have been acceptable to refer to French courtly dress as a kind of Tracht, it seems unlikely that peasant clothes would have been described as a Mode unless they had first been adopted by the aristocracy. Johann Heinrich Zedler, *Grosses Vollständiges Universal Lexikon* (Graz: Akademische Druck und Verlaganstalt, 1961 [1745]), 44:1803, defined *Tracht* as "the fashion of a country, according to which people dress and decorate themselves." Eduard Fuchs, "Ich bin der Herr dein Gott!" in Bovenschen, *Die Listen der Moden*, 166 (see intro., n. 5), defined *Tracht* as traditional rural costumes (as opposed to cosmopolitan fashion): "Constant change is the most important feature that differentiates Mode from Tracht. Tracht remains the same, is set in stone; Mode is mobile, the eternally changing, the transitory nature of dress." Ferdinand Tönnies, *Gemeinschaft*, in *Die Sitte* (Frankfurt: Rütten & Loening, 1909), 88–95, used the Mode/Tracht distinction to develop his sociological differentiation of modern urban society (*Gesellschaft*) from traditional rural communities.

10. Grimm and Grimm, *Deutsches Wörterbuch*, 2435 (see above, n. 8).

11. Garve, "Über die Moden," 121–22 (see chap. 1, n. 13).

12. Ibid., 122.

13. Barthes, *The Fashion System*, 300 (see chap. 2, n. 36).

14. *Die Zeitung für die elegante Welt* reported from Glogau on June 6, 1801, that "the greatest current fashion here is to have your children innoculated against cowpox. Let there be more such curative fashions."

15. The *Hamburgisches Journal der Moden und Eleganz*, Jan. 1801, 1, expressed a sim-

ilar archival interest in recording social history: "It shall . . . be the aim of this fashion journal (as it should be for every other) to be and to remain a chronicle of the times, her moral culture, the elaboration, elevation, and decline in all branches of the same, for the present and, if the gods allow, for posterity."

16. *Mode Journal*, Mar. 1786, 138.

17. "If one studies the history of mankind somewhat more carefully, one will make the rather interesting observation that a pleasure in bodily decoration and fashion is general to all peoples of the earth. Even the savages of America, who live in the darkest forests, where they build themselves huts and often are unable to provide the most basic necessities of life for themselves, even they are concerned about their own beauty in much the same manner as the foremost coquette of Europe." *Mode Journal* (abridged) 1:28.

18. Bertuch intended to counteract the foreign infuence of fashion dolls; *Mode Journal* (abridged) 1:28. For a discussion of how fashion dolls were employed to spread new styles throughout Europe, see McKendrick, Brewer, and Plumb, *The Birth of a Consumer Society*, 42–47 (see intro., n. 1). The *Mode Journal*, Sept. 1786, 335, reported on a society in London that offered twenty-four life-sized dolls striking different attitudes. Later issues (Nov. 1791, Jan. 1792) offered fashion dolls complete with the newest wardrobes for sale.

19. *Mode Journal*, Oct. 1786, 352.

20. Ibid., Oct. 1788, 381.

21. Berry, *The Idea of Luxury*, 72 (see above, n. 1).

22. *Mode Journal* (abridged) 1:249.

23. Ibid., 249–50.

24. Ibid., 263.

25. Ibid., 258.

26. Ibid., 257–58.

27. For information on Bertuch's personal relationship to Sturm und Drang writers, see Feldmann, *Friedrich Justin Bertuch*, 9ff (see chap. 1, n. 27).

28. *Mode Journal*, Feb. 1789, 79. A reader wrote: "You have shown clearly the dangerous consequences of tight lacing, narrow shoes, and various hair creams and cleansers. In place of these unhealthy beauty aids, you have made known alternatives that achieve the same ends and are harmless."

29. Ibid., Dec. 1801, 689.

30. Justus Möser, *Sämtliche Werke* ed. Ludwig Shirmeyer and Werner Kohlschmidt (Olderburg: Stalling, 1943), 1:37.

31. Ibid., 2:158.

32. *Mode Journal* (abridged) 1:141.

33. *Teutscher Merkur*, Nov. 1785, 186.

34. *Mode Journal* (abridged) 1; *Mode Journal*, Jan. 27 1787.

35. *Die Zeitung für die elegante Welt*, Aug. 15, 1801, 783.

36. *Mode Journal*, Apr. 1786, 165

37. *Mode Journal* (abridged) 1:314.

38. Richard Sennett, *The Fall of Public Man* (New York: Knopf, 1977), 82

39. Barthes, *The Fashion System*, 22–24, 37–39 (see chap. 2, n. 36), divided fashion writing into two types, one of which established an equivalence between a garment and the world by positing a relationship between clothes and some practical function.

40. Ibid., 268–69.

41. Ibid., 271. Early in his volume, Barthes distinguished semiotics from sociology, an unfortunate move given that the concluding sections of the book strained to escape the linguistic bounds of his method. In the last chapters, Barthes's structural account of the fashion sign had implications far beyond linguistic theory.

42. "All fashion rhetoric is contained in this foreshortening: to remark what is imposed; to produce fashion; then to see it only [as] an effect without a named cause; then, of this effect to retain only the phenomenon; last, to allow this phenomenon to be developed as if it owed its life to itself alone: such is the trajectory that fashion follows in order to transform into fact, at once, its cause, its law, and its sign." Ibid., 272.

43. Haug, *Critique of Commodity Aesthetics* (see chap. 1, n. 66).

44. Jean Baudrillard, *For a Critique of the Political Economy of the Sign*, trans. Charles Levin (New York: Telos, 1981).

45. Ibid., 62.

46. Baudrillard, *Critique of the Political Economy* (see above, n. 44), as well as Veblen and other Marxian critics, described the ruling classes as if they operated like cocaine dealers, reaping tremendous profits from a product they themselves refused to consume. The well-dressed, emotionally restrained mobster is the Hollywood image that best corresponds to Marxian critique of consumer culture. Theodor Adorno, *Prisms*, trans. Samuel Weber and Sherry Weber (Cambridge: MIT Press, 1982), 83, made a similar point regarding the moral tone of Veblen's attack on the conspicuous consumption of late-nineteenth-century robber barons: "As its guilty conscience, [Veblen] confronts society with its own principle of utility and proves to it that, according to this principle, culture is both a waste and a swindle—so irrational that it raises doubts about the rationality of the whole system. Veblen has something of the bourgeois, who takes the admonition to be thrifty with grim seriousness. Thus, all of culture becomes for him the meaningless ostentatious display typical of the bankrupt." While Baudrillard did not invoke utility as the basis for criticizing consumer culture, he did, like Veblen, invest "the sphere of production" with such tremendous significance that all public culture became a meaningless play of signifiers.

47. *Mode Journal*, Oct. 1789, 416.

48. Ibid., June 1789, 229.

49. Ibid., Feb. 1789, 58.

50. Ibid., Oct. 1789, 417.

51. Ibid., 416.

52. Ibid., 412.

53. Ibid., 411.

54. Ibid., May 1788, 153.
55. Ibid., Apr. 1787, 111.
56. Ibid., Mar. 1789, 97.
57. Schlettwein, *Grundfeste*, 406 (see chap. 2, n. 39).
58. *Mode Journal*, May 1788, 157.
59. Ibid., Feb. 1786, 61.

Chapter Four: The Queen of Fashion

1. Quentin Bell, *On Human Finery*, 2d ed. (New York: Schocken, 1976), 62.
2. Max Horkheimer and Theodor Adorno, *The Dialectic of Enlightenment*, trans. John Cumming (New York: Continuum, 1972), 133.
3. Gilles Lipovetsky, *The Empire of Fashion: Dressing Modern Democracy* (Princeton: Princeton University Press, 1994), 29.
4. McKendrick, Brewer, and Plumb, *The Birth of a Consumer Society*, 34 (see intro., n. 1): "Proverbial wisdom was recorded in classical Latin to the effect that 'Fashion is more powerful than any tyrant,' and the poets of antiquity were as specific as they were prolific on the subject." Appleby, "Consumption in Early Modern Social Thought," 166 (see chap. 1, n. 68), pointed out the allegory's biblical heritage: "Hebraic tradition, which gave English Puritans so rich a rhetorical resource for vivifying sin, identified luxury with desire and desire with disobedience. Eve indulged in luxury when she unnecessarily ate the fruit of the tree of knowledge. The Israelites persisted in the most serious of human errors in their yearnings for things that they did not need nor had the right to claim. If represented graphically, luxury, of course is a woman—sometimes a powerful evoker of desire, carrying the comb and mirror of cupidity and self-love; at other times, an abject naked woman under attack from toads and snakes." Breen, "The Meanings of Things," 255 (see chap. 2, n. 7), provided an example of such Puritan rhetoric from the *Boston Gazette*, Nov. 17, 1747: "Luxury makes her Appearance in a Manner so engaging, so easily she deceives us under the show of Politeness and Generosity, that we are not aware of Danger, `till we feel the fatal Poison."
5. Lenz, *Gesammelte Schriften*, 4:379–80 (see chap. 1, n. 53), described the entrepeneurial adaptation of the Latin allegory: "The Romans had a horde of smaller house gods, with which children, old wives, and nannies would dally. If Christianity had not suppressed polytheism, then Fashion would have had first place among these gods and would have been prayed to the most. Back then, Fashion stood on the dressing table of every budding beauty and every sweet, affluent man. Morning prayers were directed to her, calling for one conquest after another. One did not ask in what manner Fashion should have been honored. This would have been difficult to answer. Perhaps a thousand sects with a thousand different forms of worship would have been invented. First and foremost, it behooved the merchant to build her temples and altars. This goddess of change created new objects every day. For her sake, the scholar thinks, the artist and craftsman works, through her the merchant gains profits or draws losses,

and only through her rebirth is the youth made more beautiful, more loveable. When Fashion commands, all useful conventions disappear into oblivion, often to be replaced by new, outrageous inventions."

6. *Mode Journal*, Feb. 1806, 120.

7. Vischer, *Mode und Cynismus*, 65 (see intro., n. 5), provided the most complete example of the drive to turn allegorical cliches into psychological case studies. His effort to portray fashion elaborated upon the eighteenth-century allegory: "A lady, a female deity, the cause of such things, is herself quite vain. She is more, she is extravagant [*üppig*] to the extreme, when the mood comes over her, then in the next six months she can suddenly become bigoted, cloistered, nunnish. She is a coquette from head to toe, not a single gesture is nobly naive. Every second, she sees herself in the mirror, she carries the mirror with herself, in herself, right in her soul. However, the stiffest governess could not surpass her, for despite all her transformations, Fashion never forgets her leveling dictatorial powers. If it occurs to her to be naughty, then everyone has to be naughty; no one is allowed to be so naughty as to distinguish themselves from everyone else by not being naughty. Caricature has a field day, yet everyone must follow the same stiff dominating rule. And this rule is nevertheless derived from an overflowing wave of change. Like a bad child who allows no peace, Fashion nudges, scratches, gambols, scribbles, bores into things, trips along. That is the way of Fashion, she cannot be any different. She must tug, shove, push again, stretch, shorten, rub in, fiddle with, crawl, zoom about, swirl, inflate, twirl, wag, spin, bristle, in short she is completely a devil, every custom apish, yet nevertheless also stiff and tyrannical, without fantasy, and reductive, as only a frozen courtier of the old Spanish manner can be. With icy calm, she prescribes absolute chaos, she is a wild bumblebee and grumbling aunt, an unrestrained pack of teenage girls as well as the institutional director, a pedant and a harlequin in one breath."

8. Foucault, *Discipline and Punish* (see chap. 2, n. 3).

9. Ibid., 201–2.

10. Marvin Carlson, *Places of Performance: The Semiotics of Theater Architecture* (Ithaca: Cornell University Press, 1989), 140: "A raised special space for the sponsoring prince became the central organizing element for most major European theater auditoriums for the [sixteenth and seventeenth] centuries. In many of them, perhaps most notably in Richelieu's private theater in Paris, the prince's space became almost literally the center of the audience space. Here, on a raised dais surrounded by other audience members, he became a focus of attention rivaling or surpassing the stage itself."

11. Barthes, *The Fashion System* (see chap. 2, n. 36), relied on the trope to discuss the "aribitrary" construction of the fashion sign, arguing that they are different from linguistic conventions because they are invented annually by an elite circle of designers and fashion editors: "The institution of the linguistic sign is a contractual act (at the level of the entire community and of history), while the institution of the fashion sign is a tyrannical act" (216). Barthes was, however, not blind to the tropes of fashion, pointing out that fashion culture enjoyed referring to itself as arbitrary. However, he

suggested that this gesture was an ideological distraction from the fundamental arbitrariness of the fashion sign, which must constantly excuse itself by invoking a rhetoric of utility and rationality. "Fashion inoculates the rhetoric of its decisions with a little arbitrariness, the better to excuse itself for the arbitrariness that founds them. Its playful metaphors sometimes connect it to political power. Fashion is a monarch whose realm is hereditary. It is a Parliament that renders femininity obligatory, like public education or military service or, sometimes, religious law" (270). Barthes's methodological assumption only heightened the supposed arbitrariness of the fashion sign. By denying that fashion operated like a speech community, he ruled out the possibility that it had a relationship to historical developments. He supported this ahistorical view with references to A. L. Kroeber and J. Richardson's rather simple positivist study on changes in the shapes and sizes of clothes over three centuries (295). Roman Jakobson took the opposing position, arguing that fashion developed over time as a collective form of creation, much like oral culture (*parole*). Jakobson, with P. Bogatyrev, "Die Folklore als eine Besondere Form des Schaffens," *Selected Writings* (The Hague: Mouton, 1966), 11.

12. Examples abound. The Lowell, Mass., Bloomer Institute, a feminist, dress reform society, included a reference to tyranny in its 1851 constitution. Article 2.2 called for "emancipation from the thralldom of that whimsical and dictatorial French goddess *Fashion*, and an exemplary enforcement of the *Right and Duty* to dress according to the demands and profferes of *Nature*" (*The Lily*, Nov. 1851, 93). Thirty-six years later, E. Lynn Linton wrote, "The martyrs to principle have been many; the martyrs to fashion are more. At no time in the world's history have men, still less women, freed themselves from the trammels of fashion" ("The Tyranny of Fashion," *Forum* 3 [1887]: 59). Charlotte von Mendelsohn-Bartholdy, "Sollen wir eine Mode tragen?" in *Die Dame: Ein deutsches Journal für den verwöhnten Geschmack, 1912–1943*, ed. Christian Ferber (Berlin: Ullstein, 1980), 27, argued against a puritan feminism: "In Germany we have a culture of the heart and the spirit. Fashion culture we lack. It is seen as superficial, to dress according to the latest style, to let oneself be tyrannized. Yet, after all, we allow ourselves to be tyrannized by men and are well cared for in that, as long as we aren't feminists. If fashion tyrannizes both men and women, so much the better!"

13. *Deutsches Museum*, July 1776, 601.

14. *Heimliche Verführung*, 31.

15. Philip Stanhope, Earl of Chesterfield, *Letters to His Son* (London, 1800), 3:12 (letter 223, Apr. 30, 1750).

16. *Mode Journal*, Mar. 1787, 92.

17. Johann Georg Hamann, Johann Gotthelf Lindner, et al., *Daphne*, reprint (Frankfurt a.M.: Lang, 1991), 30.

18. The problem of identifying fashion's power has plagued most modern efforts to reform dress, for this imaginary force is seen as the primary obstacle to rationalizing attire. Charlotte Perkins Gilman, *The Forerunner* (New York: Greenwood, 1968), 278, asked the question in 1915: "In the matter of clothing, which, as may be seen on the most casual study, is of the most vital importance to humanity, there is some mys-

terious and compelling power at work, which forces people by the millions and millions to wear clothing which they neither like, admire, or need; in which they are not comfortable, and which they cannot afford."

19. Vischer, *Mode und Cynismus*, 75 (see intro., n. 5).

20. Ambrose Bierce, *The Devil's Dictionary* (New York: Albert & Chon le Boni, 1925), 96; Horkheimer and Adorno, *Dialectic of Enlightenment* (see above, n. 2).

21. *Mode Journal*, Oct. 1786, 346.

22. *Hamburger Journal für Mode und Eleganz*, Apr. 1801, 151.

23. Garve, "Über die Moden," 249–50 (see chap. 1, n. 13).

24. E. T. A. Hoffmann's stories illustrate the small pressures that induced individuals to participate in popular activities. In "Die Automate," the figure, Ludwig, is reluctant to visit the successful exhibit of a prophetic automaton, yet he gives in to his peers' urgings to join them—with ominous consequences. Hoffmann, *The Best Tales of Hoffmann* (New York: Dover, 1967), 82, described this pressure: "Although Ludwig did his best to get off, he was obliged to yield, on pain of being considered eccentric, so many were the entreaties to him not to spoil a pleasant party by his absence."

25. *Heimliche Verführung*, 3.

26. Brandes, *Betrachtungen* 146 (see chap. 2, n. 47).

27. Smith, *The Theory of Moral Sentiments*, 304 (see chap. 2, n. 55).

28. Rudi Keller, *On Language Change: The Invisible Hand in Language*, trans. Brigitte Nerlich (London: Routledge, 1994), 68.

29. *Mode Journal*, Apr. 1786, 148–49.

30. Ibid., Jan. 1791, 4.

Chapter Five: The Legacy of Medieval and Early Modern Sumptuary Laws

1. Landes, *The Unbound Prometheus*, 50 (see intro., n. 1).

2. Karin Plodeck, "Zur Sozialgeschichtlichen Bedeutung der Absolutischen Polizei- und Landesordnungen," *Zeitschrift für bayerische Landesgeschichte* 39 (1976): 98, accepted Sombart's dating of the last ordinances. Sombart, *Liebe, Luxus, und Kapitalismus*, 137 (see intro., n. 8), in turn, cited the article on *Lois somtuaires* in the *Encyclopédie*.

3. Kleinert, *Die frühen Modejournale*, 26 (see chap. 1, n. 20), described the French monarchy's motives for issuing sumptuary laws.

4. For an illuminating discussion of the objections, delays, and diplomatic considerations faced by administrators, see Eva Larraß, "Hessen-darmstädtische Kleiderordnungen im 18. Jahrhundert," *Waffen- und Kostümkunde* 30 (1988): 33–40.

5. *Mode Journal*, Sept. 1789, 381.

6. Lipovetsky, *The Empire of Fashion*, 3 (see chap. 4, n. 3), pointed out that the "emulation model" of fashion dominated scholarship on fashion for at least the last century. The view that fashion existed as a cyclical representation of rank distinctions,

wherein the lower classes perpetually emulated the upper classes, was accepted by French Marxism as well as by Barthes, *The Fashion System* (see chap. 2, n. 36).

7. For the concept of the *das ganze Haus* (the whole house), see Riehl, *The Natural History of the German People*, 335–42 (see chap. 1, n. 8). While few share Riehl's nostalgia for preindustrial society, most German intellectual historians also describe premodern domesticity as organized into agrarian, patriarchical households incorporating immediate family members, servants, apprentices, and distant relatives. See Dieter Schwab, "Familie," in *Geschichtliche Grundbegriffe: Historisches Lexikon zur politischen-sozialen Sprache in Deutschland*, ed. Werner Conze, Reinhart Kosellek, and Otto Brunner (Stuttgart: Klett, 1975); Paul Münch, *Lebensformen in der frühen Neuzeit* (Frankfurt: Propyläen, 1992), 273 ff.

8. Liselotte Eisenbart, *Kleiderordnen der deutschen Städte zwischen 1350 und 1700* (Berlin: Musterschmidt Verlag, 1962), 79.

9. Ibid., 77.

10. In his study of the statutes of the Göttingen, Goswin Freiherr von der Ropp, *Göttinger Statuten: Akten zur Geschichte der Verwaltung und des Geldewesens der Stadt Göttingen bis zum Ausgang des Mittelalters* (Hanover: Hahn, 1907), vol. 25, *Quellen und Darstelungen zur Geschichte Niedersachsens*, provided a detailed listing of how laws were both reiterated and layered. Aside from immediate reiterations, new ordinances were presented to the populace every twelve to twenty years. The first ordinance was passed before 1340; following that, ordinances were passed in 1342, 1354, 1367, 1381, 1396, 1398 (repetition of previous law with some additions), 1415, 1425 (repetition of previous law), 1428 (minor additions), 1445 (repetition of previous laws with minor additions), 1459 (repetition of previous law), 1461, 1468 (combination of previous two laws), 1494, and 1497.

11. Marc Raeff, *The Well-Ordered Police State: Social and Institutional Change through Law in the Germanies and Russia, 1600–1800* (New Haven: Yale University Press, 1983), 51.

12. Ropp, *Göttinger Statuten*, 17 (see above, n. 10).

13. The Ottoman Empire introduced clothing ordinances that divided the Balkan population according to religous affiliation. As religous differences led to a stratification of society, clothes became markers of ethnic identity as well as of class position. See Gabriella Schubert, *Kleidung als Zeichen: Kopfbedeckung im Donau-Balkan-Raum* (Berlin: Harrassowitz Verlag, 1993), 164.

14. Reprinted in *Zeitschrift für die Geschichte des Oberrheins* 7 (1856):65.

15. Olaf Spechter, "Die Osnabrücker Oberschicht im 17. und 18. Jahrhundert," *Osnabrücker Geschichtsquellen und Forschungen* 20 (1975): 49.

16. Eisenbart, *Kleiderordnen*, 96–97 (see above, n. 8).

17. Alwin Schultz, *Deutsches Leben im XIV. und XV. Jahrhundert* (Vienna, 1892), 2:217.

18. A biologically derived notion of gender characteristics emerged in the last third of the eighteenth century: "In contrast to this, older statements about men and women preserved in sermons and almanacs [*Hausvaterliteratur*] were all about status, social

position, and the corresponding virtues and duties"; Karin Hausen, "Family and Role Division: The Polarisation of Sexual Stereotypes in the Nineteenth Century—An Aspect of the Dissociation of Work and Family Life," in *The German Family: Essays on the Social History of the Family in Nineteenth- and Twentieth-Century Germany*, ed. Richard Evans and W. R. Lee (Totowa, N.J.: Barnes & Noble, 1981), 57.

19. Eisenbart, *Kleiderordnen*, 87 (see above, n. 8).

20. Gottlieb Sigmund Corvinus (Amaranthes, pseud.), *Nutzbares, galantes und curioses Frauenzimmer Lexicon* (Frankfurt, 1739), 1767.

21. Gorg Jakob Wolf, cited in Heidi Muuller, "Weiße Westen—Rote Roben. Von den Farbordnungen des Mittelalters zum individuellen Farbegeschmack," in *Mode-Tracht-Regionale Identität: Historische Kleidungsforschung Heute*, ed. Helmut Ottenjann (Museumsdorf Cloppenburg: Niedersächsisches Feilichtmueum, 1985), 155.

22. Eisenbart, *Kleiderordnen* 46 (see above, n. 8).

23. *Repertorium Corporis Constitutionum Marchicarum [von 1298 bis 1750] welche in Sechs Theile und vier Continuationes* (hereafter, *CCM*), vol. 5, pt. 1, sec. 1, paras. 60–62.

24. Spechter, "Osnabrücker Oberschicht," 49 (see above, n. 15).

25. Hans Meier, *Die ältere deutsche Staats- und Verwaltungslehre (Polizeiwissenchschaft), Ein Beitrag zur Geschichte der politischen Wissenschaft in Deutschland* (Neuwied am Rhein: Luchterhand, 1966), 110.

26. Eisenbart, *Kleiderordnen*, 64 (see above, n. 8).

27. Otto Clemen, "Eine Leipziger Kleiderordnung von 1506," *Neues Archiv für Sächsiche Geschichte und Altertumskunde* 28 (1907): 305–20.

28. Eisenbart, *Kleiderordnen*, 60, 62 (see above, n. 8).

29. Governments invoked the economic devastation and food shortages produced by the war to justify "emergency" police laws prohibiting the use of expensive textiles, jewelry, sweets, and wine; this was part of an intensified effort by German states to curtail the forms of consumption associated with family celebrations; see Plodeck, "Polizei- und Landesordnungen," 97 (see above, n. 2).

30. Georg Steinhausen, *Geschichte der deutschen Kultur* (Leipzig: Bibliographisches Institut, 1904), 394–95.

31. Eisenbart, *Kleiderordnen*, 74–75 (see above, n. 8).

32. For a discussion of the Constitutio Criminalis Carolina and other imperial police ordinances as they related to sexual regulation, see Hull, *Sexuality, State, and Civil Society*, 61 ff. (see chap. 2, n. 43). Hull noted, also, that "the real mark of official interest in sexual regulation was not imperial law or imperial police ordinances but the stream of orders the territorial states . . . loosed on their subjects" (66). Consumer codes were similarly promulgated mostly at the territorial level.

33. Corporate society was the equivalent of "estates," "stations," or "corporations." While classes in absolutism were derived from feudalism, they were defined in relation to princely authority; hence, "feudal society" is an inaccurate term here.

34. *CCM*, vol. 5, pt. 1, sec. 1, paras. 91–92.

35. Norbert Elias, *The Court Society*, trans. Edmund Jephcott (Oxford: Blackwell, 1983), chap. 5.

36. Christian Wolff, *Vernünftige Gedanken von dem gesellschaftlichen Leben der Menschen und insoderheit dem gemeinen Wesen* (Hildesheim: Olms, 1975 [1736]), vol. 5, sec. 1, 504.

37. Ibid., 505. In Wolff's writing, the relationship between theory and spectacle reenacted the dynamic of monarchical politics. Social contract theory repeatedly gave way to the claims of visual display. The Enlightenment principles that Wolff claimed as his own were made subservient to the political "reality" of absolutism. This rhetorical gesture became its own political theory, wherein a given rational critique "sacrificed" its own claims for the sake of political stability.

38. Jürgen Freiherr von Kruedener, *Die Rolle des Hofes im Absolutismus* (Stuttgart: Gustav Fischer Verlag, 1973), 21. Kristiaan Aercke used Georges Batailles discussion of expenditure and the value of sacred objects in a cult in *Gods of Play: Baroque Festive Performances as Rhetorical Discourse* (Albany: New York State University Press, 1994), 4–5, 99.

39. Roche, *The Culture of Clothing*, 40 (see intro., n. 1).

40. McKendrick, Brewer, and Plumb, *The Birth of a Consumer Society*, 37 (see intro., n. 1).

41. Elias, *The Court Society*, 62–63 (see above, n. 35).

42. Plodeck, "Polizei- und Landesordnungen," 91 (see above, n. 2).

43. Kruedener, *Die Rolle des Hofes*, 30–31 (see above, n. 38).

44. Elias, *The Court Society*, 58 (see above, n. 35).

45. Foucault, *Discipline and Punish*, 3 (see chap. 2, n. 3).

46. Ibid., 48.

47. Wolff, *Vernünftige Gedanken*, 301 (see above, n. 36).

48. Richard Alewyn, *Das große Welttheater: Die Epoche der höfischen Feste*, 2d ed. (Munich: Beck, 1989), 9–11.

49. For an interpretation of French gardens that relates their formal organization to the politics of courtly consumption, see Mukerji, "Reading and Writing with Nature," 439–61 (see intro., n. 11).

50. Roche noted that future research on the French nobility's dress and luxury expenditures might provide a different picture and suggested that consumption habits varied over the lifetime of a noble person, so that the more cautious and somewhat retired older generation allowed the younger generation to spend more extravagantly while at court. Roche, *The Culture of Clothes*, 213 (see intro., n. 1).

51. Alewyn, *Das große Welttheater*, 14 (see above, n. 48).

52. Although Louis XIV might have been able to sustain a cruel rate of taxation for decades, German princes were occasionally faced with severe austerity and, as with the court at Weissenfels, bankruptcy.

53. For a rhetorical and political analysis of how and why baroque festivals shifted away from the public celebrations familiar to the Renaissance, see Aercke, *Gods of Play*, 26–40 (see above, n. 38).

54. Elias, *The Court Society*, 88 (see above, n. 35).

55. Aercke, *Gods of Play*, 8 (see above, n. 38).

56. Bernard Mandeville's *The Fable of the Bees* is the most notorious eighteenth-century defense of class competition through emulation of fashion and luxury. For a discussion of Mirabeau's physiocratic arguments against luxury, see Saisselin, *The Enlightenment against the Baroque*, 55–58 (see chap. 2, n. 8).

57. Gottfried Keller's "Kleider machen Leute" (Clothes Making People) is the most famous story. Möser complained of farmhands who earned high salaries in Holland and, upon their return to Germany, married into high families on the basis of their elegant clothes alone. See *Patriotische Phantasien*, pt. 1, in *Sämtliche Werke*, 4:81 (see chap. 3, n. 30).

58. Quoted in Bruford, *Germany in the Eighteenth Century*, 105 (see chap. 1, n. 39).

59. *Mode Journal*, Dec. 1787, 407, described the popular reaction to the royal family's walk in a Berlin park: "The worthiness of the monarchical personage subsists in himself, not in borrowed splendor, which is why everyone present bowed before them and not their clothes. Very little Asiatic or French luxury is to be found at the Prussian court; hence its power and wealth."

60. Plodeck, "Polizei- und Landesordnungen," 104 (see above, n. 2), quotes a 1733 law: "Many followed along who would gladly have stood apart from vanity and its required costs yet did not wish to be inferior to others."

61. Elias, *The Court Society*, 55 (see above, n. 35).

62. A 1604 police ordinance explained: "Given that the origin of all mischief, above all else rests therein that the poor man imitates the rich man and that the artisan imitates the magistrate, so that no one wishes to grant the other the advantage in extravagance, the inhabitants and burghers here shall be divided into three grades or corporations [*Stände*]." *CCM* vol. 5, pt. 1, sec. 1, para. 73.

63. Plodeck, "Polizei- und Landesordnungen," 95 (see above, n. 2).

64. *CCM*, vol. 5, pt.1, sec. 1, paras. 60–62.

65. For a broad discussion of the rise of administrative (or public) law as it pertained to Prussia, see Hans Rosenberg, *Bureacracy, Aristocracy, and Autocracy: The Prussian Experience, 1660–1815* (Cambridge: Harvard University Press, 1958), 46–56.

66. Ropp, *Göttinger Statuten*, 29 (see above, n. 10).

67. Reiner Schulze, *Polizei und Gesetzgebungslehre im 18. Jahrhundert* (Berlin: Ducker & Humblot, 1982), 128–31.

68. See Hull's discussion of cameralist reforms in *Sexuality, State, and Civil Society*, 157–72 (see chap. 2, n. 43).

69. The attempts to draft a clothing ordinance for Hessen-darmstadt in midcentury provided an example of the complaints against such ordinances by the very officials responsible for the formulation. See Larraß, "Hessen-darmstädtische Kleiderordnunge," 38 (see above, n. 4).

70. Hans Boldt, "Geschichte der Polizei in Deutschland," in *Handbuch des Polizeirechts*, ed. Hans Lisken and Erhard Denninger (Munich: Beck, 1992), 8.

71. *Mode Journal* (abridged) 1:28.

72. *Mode Journal*, Jan. 1791, 12.

73. Ibid., 7.

෨

Chapter Six: Paranoid Geography and the European Dispersion of Fashion

1. Alfred Loos, *Spoken into the Void*, trans. Jane O. Newman and John Smith (Cambridge: MIT Press, 1982), 51–53

2. A version of this tale, embellished with pirates, appeared in an article calling for the use of telegrams to transmit the newest styles from London to Europe. See *Mode Journal* (abridged) 2:37–41.

3. *Heimliche Verführung*, 55.

4. Beutler, "Georg Melchior Kraus," 432 (see chap. 1, n. 31).

5. Bringemeier, *Mode und Tracht*, 118 (see intro., n. 4), cites *Mode Journal*, June 1802, 353.

6. Garve, "Über die Moden," 185 (see chap. 1, n. 13).

7. Simmel, *The Sociology of Georg Simmel* (see intro., n. 7), made a similar dialectical argument in his essay on Mode.

8. Garve, "Über die Moden," 119 (see chap. 1, n. 13).

9. Ibid., 147.

10. Ibid., 215–16. Again, Simmel, *The Sociology of Georg Simmel* (see intro., n. 7), made a similar argument.

11. Garve, "Über die Moden," 141 (see chap. 1, n. 13).

12. Ibid., 186.

13. Ibid., 184.

14. The redefinition of commodities' cultural references occurs both as an effect of their circulation in an ever-broadening market and as a deliberate strategy of twentieth-century consumerism. Arjun Appadurai, "Introduction: Commodities and the Politics of Value," in *The Social Life of Things: Commodities in Cultural Perspetive*, ed. Arjun Appadurai (Cambridge: Cambridge University Press, 1986), 28, described the aesthetic style of decontextualization: "The best examples of the diversion of commodities from their original nexus is to be found in the domain of fashion, domestic display, and collecting in the modern West. In the high-tech look inspired by the Bauhaus, the functionality of factories, warehouses, and workplaces is diverted to household aesthetics. The uniforms of various occupations are turned into the vocabulary of costume. In the logic of found art, the everyday commodity is framed and aestheticized. These are all examples of what we might call commoditization by diversion, where value, in the art or fashion market, is accelerated or enhanced by placing objects and things in unlikely contexts."

15. Charles King, "Fashion Adoption: A Rebuttal to the 'Trickle-Down' Theory," in *Toward Scientific Marketing*, ed. Stephen Greyser (Chicago: American Marketing Association, 1963), 108–25; reprinted in George Sproles, ed., *Perspectives of Fashion* (Minneapolis: Burgess, 1981), 32.

16. George Field, "The Status Float Phenomenon—The Upward Diffusion of Innovation," *Business Horizons* 8 (1970): 45–52, reprinted in Sproles, *Perspectives of Fashion*, 44–48 (see above, n. 15).

17. *Mode Journal* (abridged) 1:268.

18. *Mode Journal*, Sept. 1786, 332.

19. Vischer, *Mode und Cynismus*, 66 (see intro., n. 5).

20. Fuchs, "Ich bin der Herr dein Gott!" 164 (see chap. 3, n. 9).

21. Ibid., 165.

22. Ibid., 171

23. Sombart, "Wirtschaft und Mode" (see intro., n. 8).

24. Barthes, *The Fashion System* (see chap. 2, n. 36).

25. Gottsched, *Beobachtungen über den Gebrauch und Misbrauch vielerdeutscher Wörter und Redensarten*, 141 (see chap. 3, n. 4).

26. Garve, "Über die Moden," 204–5 (see chap. 1, n. 13): "The inventor of language could create, bring into being: the inventor of the language of affluence could only choose. The former sought to found the first unity among humans by building a consensus on certain signs, which no one knew and through which everyone was supposed to share their thoughts with one another. The latter . . . altered the signs understood and accepted by all and set them in a new combination as expressions of friendship, bourgeois esteem, or respect for others."

27. Ibid., 203.

28. Barthes, *The Fashion System*, 215–16 (see chap. 2, n. 36).

29. As he drew a distinction between semiology and sociology, Barthes referred to the possibility of sociology developing circulation models to explain the diffusion of clothes through society (ibid., 9). In contrast, Jakobson, "Die Folklore," 1–15 (see chap. 4., n. 11), compared fashion with the collective activity of oral cultures whose stories cannot be traced to an original author. He conceptualized fashion as a form of *langue*, a set of conventions governing individual (speech) acts within a community.

30. Barthes, *The Fashion System*, 215–16 (see chap. 2, n. 36); César de Saussure, *A Foreign View of England in the Reigns of George I and George II* (New York: Dutton, 1902).

31. Barthes, *The Fashion System*, 268 (see chap. 2, n. 36).

32. Garve, "Über die Moden," 208 (see chap. 1, n. 13).

33. Here again, Garve's discussion of fashion signs overlapped with Barthes's, who organized the signification of garments into three moments: a primary object (such as a pullover), its support (a collar), and the variation in style of that support (an open or a closed collar). Both Garve and Barthes argued that the meaning of fashion was conveyed by the stylistic variations of a garment's supporting detail. When one considered the fashionableness of a dress, one worried about marginal details, such as the length; but within broad historical parameters, one did not question the fashionableness of dresses in general.

34. Garve, "Über die Moden," 209 (see chap. 1, n. 13).

35. Ibid., 210–11.

36. E. M. Arndt, *Ueber Sitte, Mode und Kleidertracht: Ein Wort aus der Zeit* (Frankfurt, 1814), 49.

37. For a sophisticated discussion of both qualities, see Theodor Adorno, "Words from

Abroad," in *Notes to Literature*, trans. Sherry Weber Nicholsen (New York: Columbia University Press, 1991), 1:185–99.

38. Eric Blackall, *The Emergence of German as a Literary Language, 1770–1775* (Ithaca: Cornell University Press, 1978), touched on the eighteenth-century German debate over the "appropriateness" of foreign words.

39. *Heimliche Verführung*, 68–69.

40. *Mode Journal* (abridged) 1:187–88.

41. *Die Zeitung für die elegante Welt*, Feb. 16, 1802, 153.

42. *Mode Journal* (abridged) 1:200–201.

43. *Heimliche Verführung*, 52

44. According to Gerd Spittler, "Abstraktes Wissen als Herrschaftsbasis. Zur Entstehungsgeschichte bürokratischer Herrschaft im Bauerstaat Preussens," *Kölner Zeitschrift für Soziologie und Sozialpsychologie* 32 (1980): 574–604, "the bureaucracy reaches only to the local level, where it dissolves into an intermediary authority" (583). Farming communities, he claimed, engaged in "defensive strategies" vis-à-vis the centralized administration. Cosmopolitan fashion culture would have been perceived in much the same terms as bureaucratic reforms of local practices—with hostility.

45. For a discussion of the political organization of Central European rural communities and their regulatory mechanisms, see Hull, *Sexuality, State, and Civil Society*, 36–41 (see chap. 2, n. 43).

46. *Deutsches Museum*, Feb. 1776, 149.

47. Riehl, *The Natural History of the German People* (see chap. 1, n. 8).

48. Hermann, *Goethe's "Werther"* (see chap. 2, n. 27)

49. Knigge, *Über den Umgang mit Menschen*, 50 (see chap. 1, n. 15).

50. Wolfgang Hardtwig, "Krise der Universität, studentische Reformbewegung (1750–1819) und die Sozialisation der jugendlichen deutschen Bildungsschicht," *Geschichte und Gesellschaft* 11 (1985): 161–64.

51. *Deutsches Museum*, Feb. 1776, 149.

52. Ibid., 149.

53. For a thorough account of the parallels between Hebrew denunciations of luxury and early modern sumptuary laws, see John Sekora, *Luxury: The Concept in Western Thought, Eden to Smollett* (Baltimore: Johns Hopkins University Press, 1977), chap. 1.

Chapter Seven: The Veil of Masculinity

1. Barthes, *The Fashion System*, 3–4 (see chap. 2, n. 36).

2. Veblen, *The Theory of the Leisure Class* (see intro., n. 10); Georg Simmel, "Fashion," *International Quarterly* 10 (1904): 130–55.

3. Judith Butler, *Gender Trouble: Feminism and the Subversion of Identity* (New York: Routledge, 1990), 141.

4. Quoted in Peter Müller, ed., *Der junge Goethe im zeitgenossischen Urteil* (Berlin: Akademie, 1969), 153.

5. Quoted in Gustav Gugitz, ed. *Das Wertherfieber in Oesterreich: Eine Sammlung von Neudrucken* (Vienna: Knepler, 1908), 17.

6. Anonymous letter, attributed to August Wilhelm Rehberg, quoted in Ludwig Tieck's introduction to Lenz, *Gesammelte Schriften*, 1:cxxix (see chap. 1, n. 53).

7. Butler, *Gender Trouble*, 95 (see above, n. 3).

8. Johann Wilhelm Appell, *Goethe und seine Zeit*, 4th ed. (Oldenburg, 1896), 55.

9. Ibid., 53.

10. Quoted in M. Rieger, *Klinger in der Sturm- und Drangperiode* (Darmstadt, 1880), 143.

11. Karl von Knebel, *Literarischer Nachlaß und Briefwechsel*, ed. K. A. Varnhagen and T. Mundt (Leipzig, 1840), 1:xxxix.

12. Quoted in Appell, *Goethe und seine Zeit*, 259 (see above, n. 8).

13. Friedrich von Matthisson, *Literarischer Nachlaß* (Berlin, 1832).

14. Ibid., 1:257.

15. Ibid., 1:258.

16. Quoted in Gugitz, *Das Wertherfieber*, 19 (see above, n. 5).

17. An anonymous and hostile pamphleteer argued that the novel's threat to social order was weakened the more widely it was read. "Like the medical explanation that says that venereal infections become weakened and lose their potency when they pass through many bodies, so too the Werther infection lost its dreadful effect by being in-noculated into many souls." "Schwacher jedoch wohlgemeynter Tritt vor dem Riß, neben oder hinter Herrn Pastor Goeze gegen die Leiden des jungen Werthers und dessen ruchlose Anhänger" (1775), reprinted in F. U. Hünich, ed., *Werther Schriften* (Leipzig: Spamersche Buchdruckerei, 1924), 14.

18. Quoted in Müller, *Der junge Goethe*, 158 (see above, n. 4).

19. *Mode Journal* (abridged) 1:365–66.

20. Joan Copjec, "The Orthopsychic Subject: Film Theory and the Reception of Lacan," *October*, 1989, 69: "Where the film's theoretical position has tended to trap the subject in representation (an idealist failing), to conceive of language as constructing the prison walls of the subject's being, Lacan argues that the subject sees these walls as trompe l'oeil and is thus constructed by something beyond them." In the case of the Werther reception, the reading public sought the historical incident beyond the novel's representation in the hope of grasping the subjectivity that the novel depicted.

21. Goethe, *Werke*, 9:590 (see chap. 2, n. 6).

22. Georg Jäger, "Die Wertherwirkung. Ein Rezeptions-ästhetischer Modellfall," in Müller-Seidel, Fromm, and Richter *Historizität in Sprach- und Literaturwissenschaft*, 389–409 (see chap. 2, n. 27); Erdmann Waniek, "*Werther* lesen und Werther als Leser," *Goethe Yearbook* (1983): 51–92. They took particular note of Goethe's rather revisionist complaint.

23. Walter Erhart, "Beziehungsexperimente: Goethes *Werther* und Wielands *Musarion*," *Deutsche Vierteljahrsschrift für Literaturwissenschaft und Geistesgeschichte* (1992): 344.

24. "Every Werther descendent seeks to repress the emptiness articulated in the text by fabricating a Werther copy." Ibid., 346.

25. Ibid., 345.

26. Goethe, *Werke*, 6:79 (see chap. 2, n. 6).

27. Engel, *Schriften*, 7:27–28 (see chap. 2, n. 38).

28. Goethe, *Werke*, 6:30 (see chap. 2, n. 6). Page references to *Werther* henceforth appear in text.

29. David Wellbery argued that the dance was suffused with a sexuality not limited to the waltz's obvious similarity to the coital act. See his "Morphisms of the Phantasmatic Body: Goethe's 'The Sorrows of Young Werther,'" in *Body and Text in the Eighteenth Century*, ed. Veronica Kelly and Dorothea von Mücke (Stanford: Stanford University Press, 1994), 185.

30. Freud postulated the presence of the fetish object at the scene whose trauma the subject seeks to disavow. Werther's fetish did not function as a substitute for the mother's absent penis, as Freud described in his essay "Fetishism." Indeed, his fetish did not seek to disavow a traumatic experience; rather, it sought to prolong an infantile union with the idealized, nurturing mother. Sigmund Freud, "Fetischismus," *Studienausgabe* 3 (1975): 386.

31. Roland Barthes, "The Rhetoric of the Image," *Image- Music-Text*, trans. Stephen Heath (New York: Noonday, 1988), 45.

32. Baudrillard, *Critique of the Political Economy*, 158 (see chap. 3, n. 44).

33. Erhart, "Beziehungsexperimente" (see above, n. 23); Bruce Duncan, "'Emilia Galotti lag auf dem Pult aufgeschlagen': Werther as (Mis-)Reader," *Goethe Yearbook* (1983): 42–50; Waniek, "*Werther* lesen und Werther als Leser," 50–92 (see above, n. 22).

34. Roland Barthes, *Camera Lucida: Reflections on Photography*, trans. Richard Howard (New York: Hill and Wang, 1981), 76, cited in Diana Fuss, "Fashion and the Homospectatorial Look," in *On Fashion*, ed. Shari Benstock and Suzanne Ferriss (New Brunswick: Rutgers University Press, 1994), 222.

35. Like the masochist in Gilles Deleuze's essay, Werther's idealized relation to the maternal figure was grounded upon a disavowal of the superego. "From the interplay of disavowal and suspense there arises in the ego a qualitative relation of imagination, which is very different from the quantitative relation of thought in the superego. Disavowal is a reaction of the imagination, as negation is an operation of the intellect or thought. Disavowal challenges the superego and entrusts the mother with the power to give birth to an 'ideal ego' that is pure, autonomous, and independent of the superego." Deleuze, "Coldness and Cruelty," *Masochism* (New York: Zone, 1991), 127.

36. For the ideological critique implicit in Werther's suicide, see Peter Uwe Hohendahl, "Empfindsamkeit und Gesellschaftliches Bewusstsein: Zur Soziologie des empfindsamen Romans am Beispiel von 'La Vie de Marianne,' 'Clarissa,' 'Fräulein von Sternheim,' und 'Werther,'" *Schiller Jahrbuch* (1972): 176–207; Scherpe, *Werther und Wertherwirkung* (see chap 2, n. 12); Georg Lukacs, "Die Leiden des jungen Werthers," in *Goethe und seine Zeit* (Berlin: Aufbau, 1955), 40–54.

37. J. C. Lavater, *Essays on Physiognomy . . . also One Hundred Physiognomical Rules* (London, ca. 1880), 149, quoted in Michael Shortland, "The Power of a Thousand Eyes: Johann Caspar Lavater's Science of Physiognomical Perception," *Criticism* 28 (1986): 392–93. See Barthes's account of preparing to be photographed, *Camera*

Lucida, 14 (see above, n. 34). Fuss, "Fashion and the Homospectatorial Look," 222 (see above, n. 34), invoked Werther's artful arrangements for his suicide: "The photograph . . . represents that very subtle moment when . . . I am neither subject nor object but a subject who feels he is becoming an object: I then experience a microversion of death (of parenthesis): I am truly becoming a specter."

38. Veblen, *The Theory of the Leisure Class*, chap. 3 (see intro., n. 10).

39. The oldest and most informative source on the history of the Werthertracht is Jacob von Falke, *Costümgeschichte der Culturvölker* (Stuttgart: Spemann, n.d.), 412–14. See also Friederich Hottenroth, *Handbuch der deutschen Tracht* (Stuttgart: Weise, n.d.), 801–3.

40. *Mode Journal*, Apr. 1791, 178.

41. For an account of the rules concerning mourning dress, as derived from the French court, see *Mode Journal*, June 1786, Nov. 1786.

42. Falke, *Costümgeschichte* (see above, n. 39); Gisela Krause, *Altpreussische Militärbekleidungswirtschaft* (Osnabrück: Biblio Verlag, 1983), 195.

43. Goethe, *Werke*, 9:544 (see chap. 2, n. 6).

44. Ibid., 6:572.

45. Karl Wilhelm Jerusalem, *Aufsätze und Briefe*, ed. Heinrich Schneider (Heidelberg: Weißbach, 1925), 219.

46. Christian Weiß, *Goethe im Urteil seiner Kritiker: Dokumente zur Wirkungsgeschichte Goethes in Deutschland*, ed. Karl Robert Mandelkow (Munich: Beck, 1975), 522.

47. On the whole, the *Mode Journal* had little criticism of the pastoral look from a practical perspective, but it did not favor its radically Protestant features. The journal's English correspondent recommended that the costume's wide-brimmed hat be replaced by smaller jockey gear, because it "is easier to take off than the large round Quaker hat, which can never be removed with just one hand. Furthermore, the wind, when it settles onto the brim's loose edges, can easily dislodge the hat, thereby giving those young people who seem so enamored of it an unfortunate and ridiculous appearance." *Mode Journal* (abridged) 1:39. Similarly, the journal mentioned that the clothes of German Pietists were so unfashionable that they drew attention to themselves, an unfortunate feature from the perspective of modern, understated conformity; *Mode Journal*, Oct. 1787, 34.

48. Ibid., Apr. 1787, 136.

49. Quoted in Diana de Marly, *Fashion for Men: An Illustrated History* (New York: Holmes & Meier, 1985), 77.

50. Quoted in ibid., 67.

51. Chesterfield, *Letters to His Son*, 3:12 (see chap. 4, n. 15).

52. Ibid., 3:23 (letter 227, May 24, 1750).

53. Saussure, *A Foreign View of England*, 323–33 (see chap. 6, n. 30).

54. For a detailed costume history of Quaker dress, see Joan Kendall, "The Development of a Distinctive Form of Quaker Dress," *Costume* 19 (1985): 58–79.

55. William Penn, "Some Fruits of Solitude in Reflections and Maxims Relating to

the Conduct of Human Life" (1693), in *William Penn on Religion and Ethics: The Emergence of Liberal Quaerism*, ed. Hugh Barbour (Lewiston, N.Y.: Mellen, 1991), 2:524.

56. There were challenges within Quakerism to the code of modesty. Individualists would on occasion invoke the discipline of following "the Leadings of the Light" in defending swearing, drinking, and promiscuity. Penn's response was a further distinction between the "lawful" and the "unlawful" self. See ibid., 352.

57. Ibid., 524.

58. The differences between Lessing and Goethe on the meaning of Quaker dress were focused on the figure of Karl Jerusalem. Lessing's outrage at Goethe's appropriation of Jerusalem's costume for Werther proves how flexible clothes are as signifiers.

59. Melvin Endy Jr., *William Penn and Early Quakerism* (Princeton: Princeton University Press, 1973), 315–16.

60. "There is another piece of our non-conformity to the world, that renders us very clownish to the breeding of it, and that is, Thou for You, and that without difference or respect to persons." William Penn, "No Cross, No Crown: A Discourse Shewing the Nature and Discipline of the Cross of Christ," in *Selected Works* (London, 1782), 2:119.

61. Ibid., 2:93.

62. George Fox, a founder of Quakerism, was famous for wearing clothes that offended institutional authorities. See Jane Yolen, *Friend: The Story of George Fox and the Quakers* (New York: Seabury, 1972), 45.

63. Kendall, "Quaker Dress," 58 (see above, n. 54).

64. A second journal published by Friedrich Bertuch, *Paris und London*, was devoted exclusively to describing the social and cultural life of the two fashion capitals. An overview of the journal is provided by Riggert, "Die Zeitschrift 'London und Paris'" (see chap. 1, n. 20).

65. For a discussion of gender identity and role theory, see Hausen, "Family and Role Division," 364–66 (see chap. 5, n. 18).

66. Saussure, *A Foreign View of England*, 112 (see chap. 6, n. 30).

67. Weiss, *Kostümkunde* (see intro., n. 3), noted that Frederick William of Prussia preferred to wear a brown *Habit* with English lapels and a red vest with silver trim, until 1719, when he adopted the military uniform.

68. *Mode Journal*, Jan. 1791, 10–11.

69. *Mode Journal* (abridged) 1:187.

70. Foucault, *Discipline and Punish* (see chap. 2, n. 3).

71. Bringemeier, *Mode und Tracht*, 129–30 (see intro., n. 4).

72. Ibid., 130.

73. Ibid. The outfit was called Hungarian because it was worn by Hussars, a cavalry associated with the Magyars and the steppes of Russia. See Hottenroth, *Handbuch*, 834 (see above, n. 39).

Chapter Eight: Civilian Uniforms as a Cure for Luxury

1. Möser, *Sämtliche Werke*, 5:58 (see chap. 3, n. 30).

2. Ibid., 5:62

3. "The citizen [*Landmann*], who did not have his official garb in proper order or who sought to be relieved of his obligations could, like the Jews in Rome, be disciplined by wearing a yellow cockade." Ibid., 5:63.

4. Quoted in Max Jähns, *Geschichte der Kriegswissenschaften, vornehmlich in Deutschland* (Hildesheim: Olms, 1966 [1891]), 3:2163.

5. *Mode Journal* (abridged) 1:63–64.

6. Ibid., 1:66.

7. Quoted in Habermas, *Structurwandel*, 129 (see chap. 2, n. 7).

8. Ibid., 135.

9. *Mode Journal* (abridged) 1:70–74.

10. See Anne Buck, *Dress in Eighteenth-Century England* (New York: Holmes & Meier, 1979), 21–22.

11. *Mode Journal*, May 1800, 219.

12. For a brief history of the Finnish adoption of *Volkstracht*, as both costume and concept, see Bo Lönnqvist, "Volkstracht als museal Illusion: Ein Projektbericht," in Ottenjann, *Mode-Tracht-Regionale Identität*, 37–42 (see chap. 5, n. 21). For the essays collected by the Danish Academy, see *Drey Abhandlungen über die Frage* (Copenhagen, 1791). Most of the essays affirmed the proposal that a national costume would benefit society, though the most sophisticated response urged its rejection. Samuel Simon Witte wrote an extremely sophisticated account of the semiotic relationship between personal identity, dress, and public discourse. His essay, "Beantwortung der Frage: Ist es nützlich oder schadlich eine National-Tacht einzufuhren?" has been overlooked no doubt because it was not published by a central organ of the German Enlightenment.

13. See Weiss, *Kostümkunde*, 3:1296 (see intro., n. 3) for a bibliography of Romantic nationalist essays on the subject.

14. Arndt, *Über Sitte*, 50–51 (see chap. 6, n. 36).

15. *Mode Journal*, Feb. 1786, 73.

16. C. Pram, "Versuch über die Kleidertracht insonderheit für Dänemark und Norwegen," in *Drey Abhandlungen über die Frage: Ist es nützlich oder schädlich eine National-Tracht einzuführen?* (Copenhagen, 1792), 27–35.

17. N. S. Shaler, "The Law of Fashion," *Atlantic Monthly*, Mar. 1888, 387.

18. Foucault, *Discipline and Punish*, 137 (see chap. 2, n. 3).

19. Klaus Schweiger, "Militär und Bürgertum, Zur gesellschaftlichen Prägkraft des preußischen Militärsystems im 18. Jahrhundert," in *Preußen in der deutschen Geschichte*, ed. Dirk Blasius (Königstein: Verlagsruppe Athenäum-Hain-Scriptor-Hanstein, 1980), 188.

20. Quoted in Hans Maier, *Die ältere deutsche Staats- und Verwaltungslehre (Polizei-*

wissenschaft), Ein Beitrag zur Geschichte der politischen Wissenschaft in Deutschland (Neuwied: Luchterhand, 1966), 128.

21. *Mode Journal*, Dec. 1790, 639.

22. Rosenberg, *Bureaucracy, Aristocracy, and Autocracy*, 89–90 (see chap. 5, n. 65).

23. Foucault, *Discipline and Punish*, 169 (see chap. 2, n. 3).

24. Smith, *The Theory of Moral Sentiments*, 246–47 (see chap. 2, n. 55).

25. Ibid., 247.

26. Garve, "Über die Moden," 282–83 (see chap. 1, n. 13).

Chapter Nine: The Uniform's Tactical Control

1. For a discussion of the signification of patrimonial military dress, see Nathan Joseph, *Uniforms and Nonuniforms: Communication through Clothing* (New York: Greenwood, 1986), 134– 37. Joseph's work overlaps at many points with my own argument but is less concerned with the historical development of uniforms in relation to civilian dress.

2. von Boehn, *Die Mode*, 180 (see intro., n. 3).

3. Schultz, *Deutsches Leben*, 2:411 (see chap. 5, n. 17).

4. Jutta Zander-Seidel, "Der Teufel in Pluderhosen," *Waffen- und Kostümkunde* 27 (1987): 49.

5. von Boehn, *Die Mode*, 182 (see intro., n. 3).

6. For an account of how uniforms transformed male appearance and demeanor in France, see Roche, *The Culture of Clothes*, 221–56 (see intro., n. 1). Foucault briefly discussed the military uniform in *Discipline and Punish*, 135–41 (see chap. 2, n. 3).

7. Curt Jany, *Geschichte der Preußischen Armee vom 15. Jahrhundert bis 1914*, 2d ed. (Osnabrück: Biblio, 1964), 1:341. More recent histories of the Prussian uniform have followed Jany's account on most points. See Gisela Krause, *Altpreussische Uniformfertigung als Vorstufe der Bekleidungsindustrie* (Hamburg: Schulz, 1965), 25.

8. For a summary of the extensive research on the Prussian textile industry, see Schweiger, "Militär und Bürgertum," 179–83 (see chap. 8, n. 19).

9. Eckhart Berckenhagen and Gretel Wagner, eds., *Der bunte Rock in Preußen, Militär und ziviluniformen 17.bis 20. Jahrhundert* (Berlin: Staatliche Musenn Preußischer Kulturbesitz, 1981), 50.

10. According to Werner Sombart, *Krieg und Kapitalismus* (Munich: Duncker & Humblot, 1913), 170–73, the nineteenth-century ready-to-wear clothing industry developed from the economies of scale required by the manufacture of uniforms, and guild tailors were increasingly employed as wage workers by textile entrepeneurs. Krause, *Altpreussische Militärbekleidungswirtschaft*, 204–5 (see chap. 7, n. 42), disagreed with this point but did support Sombart's overall thesis that Prussian demand for uniforms brought about innovations in the textile industry fundamental to the emergence of a fashion clothing industry in Berlin. Schweiger, "Militär und Bürgertum," 183–85

(see chap. 8, n. 19), argued that metalwork, rather than textiles, was the first industry to adopt production techniques on the scale of capitalist manufacturing. For a history of the ready-made fashion industry in Berlin, see Uwe Westphal, *Berliner Konfektion und Mode: Die Zerstörung einer Tradition, 1836–1939*, 2d ed. (Berlin: Edition Hentrich, 1992).

11. Christopher Duffy, *The Army of Frederick the Great* (London: David and Charles, 1974), 90. As his 1743 instructions indicated, Frederick II was not as obsessed with height as his father was. Frederick I was famous for recruiting, at great expense, men over seven feet tall.

12. Gaby Mentges, "Der vermessene Körper," in *Der neuen Welt ein neuer Rock: Studien zu Kleidung, Körper und Mode an Beispielen aus Württemberg*, ed. Christel Köhle-Hezinger and Gaby Mentges (Stuttgart: Konrad Theiss Verlag, 1993), 82–83.

13. Krause, *Altpreussische Militärbekleidungswirtschaft*, 205 (see chap. 7, n. 42).

14. See Rudolf Helm, quoted in ibid., 189. "Men at the end of the century were, as a rule, slimmer than they were even at the midcentury mark. Over the course of the century, bodily comportment became much more erect. The eighteenth-century sleeve was cut for the arm that bends with ease, whereas in the nineteenth century the sleeve was tailored for an arm that hangs almost perfectly straight." Also see Joaneath Spicer, "The Renaissance Elbow," *A Cultural History of Gesture*, ed. Jan Bremmer and Herman Roodenburg (Ithaca: Cornell University Press, 1992), 84–128.

15. Jay Luvaas, ed. and trans., *Frederick the Great on the Art of War* (New York: Free Press, 1966), 79.

16. Ibid., 78. For a description of Frederick's battlefield tactics, see Gerhard Ritter, *Frederick the Great*, trans. Peter Paret (Berkeley: University of California Press, 1968), 129–48.

17. Duffy, *The Army of Frederick*, 77 (see above, n. 11).

18. Ibid.

19. All three references are quoted in Schweiger, "Militär und Bürgertum," 186–87 (see chap. 8, n. 19).

20. Johann Kaspar Riesbeck, *Briefe eines reisenden Franzosen über Deutschland* (Berlin: Rütten & Loening, 1976 [1783]), 337.

21. Krause, *Altpreussische Militärbekleidungswirtschaft*, 294, n. 1215; 185 (see chap. 7, n. 42).

22. Duffy, *The Army of Frederick*, 36 (see above, n. 11).

23. Rudolph Wilhelm von Kaltenborn, *Briefe eines alten preussischen Officiers verschiedene Characterzüge Friedrichs des Einzigen betreffend* (Hohenzollern, 1790), 123.

24. See Joseph, *Uniforms and Nonuniforms*, 95–96 (see above, n. 1).

25. Luvaas, *Frederick the Great*, 68 (see above, n. 15); see also Jany, *Geschichte der Preußischen Armee*, 766 (see above, n. 7).

26. Charles Baudelaire, *The Painter of Modern Life and Other Essays*, ed. and trans. Jonathan Mayne (New York: Da Capo, 1964).

27. Berbey D'Aurevilly, *The Anatomy of Dandyism, with Some Obervations on Beau Brummel*, trans. Wyndham Lewis (London: Davies, 1928), 10.

28. Baudelaire, *The Painter of Modern Life*, 28 (see above, n. 26).

29. For a brief history of this Islamic sect and its European reputation, see Claus-Peter Haase, "Die Assassinen," in *Männerbande, Männerbünde, zur Rolle des Mannes im Kulturvergleich*, ed. Gisela Völger and Karin Welck (Cologne: Rautenstrauch Joest Museum, 1990), 1:213–20.

30. Michel Foucault, "What Is Enlightenment?" in *The Foucault Reader*, ed. Paul Rabinow (New York: Pantheon, 1984), 42.

31. Baudelaire, *The Painter of Modern Life*, 25 (see above, n. 26).

32. Luvaas, *Frederick the Great*, 83 (see above, n. 15).

33. Ibid., 80.

34. *Die Zeitung für die elegante Welt*, June 4, 1801, 542.

35. Krause, *Altpreussische Militärbekleidungswirtschaft*, 199 (see chap. 7, n. 42).

36. Weiss, *Kostumkunde*, 3:1289–90 (see intro., n. 3), saw the incident as a strategy adopted by Frederick I in lieu of enacting sumptuary laws. The caricature of the French style was coupled with import restrictions on luxury goods.

37. Krause, *Altpreussische Militärbekleidungswirtschaft*, 298, n. 1267 (see chap. 7, n. 42).

38. Kaltenborn, *Briefe*, 18–19 (see above, n. 23).

39. Foucault, *Discipline and Punish*, 130 (see chap. 2, n. 3).

40. Elias, *The Court Society*, 89 (see chap. 5, n. 35).

41. Duffy, *The Army of Frederick*, 21 (see above, n. 11).

42. Kaltenborn, *Briefe* (see above, n. 23). The quoted passages that follow are found on 80–81.

43. That the eighteenth century recognized Diogenes as a philosopher of dress was shown by Lord Chesterfield's letter to his son dated Nov. 19, 1745, in which he argued that it was far more absurd to ignore fashion than to accept its foolish customs. Chesterfield concluded, "Diogenes the Cynic was a wise man for despising [sartorial customs], but a fool for showing it." Quoted in Bell, *On Human Finery*, 18 (see chap. 4, n. 1).

44. C. W. Goettling, "Diogenes der Cyniker oder die Philosophie des griechischen proletariats (1851)," in *Die Kyniker in der modernnen Forchung*, ed. Margarethe Billerbeck (Amsterdam: Grüner, 1991), 49.

45. Horst Kusch, "Diogenes von Sinope," in *Reallexikon für Antike und Christentum*, ed. Theodor Klauser (Stuttgart: Hiersemann, 1957), 3:1069.

46. Kaltenborn, *Briefe* (see above, n. 29). The quoted passages that follow are found on 94–95.

Chapter Ten: Signification as Discipline

1. Garve, "Über die Moden," 143 (see chap. 1, n. 13).

2. *Mode Journal* (abridged) 2:65–69.

3. Ibid., 2:29.

4. Sandgruber, *Die Anfänge der Konsumgesellschaf*, 289 (see intro., n. 2).

5. Hamann, Lindner, et al., *Daphne*, 25 (see chap. 4, n. 17).

6. Witte, "Beantwortung der Frage," 58 (see chap. 8, n. 12).

7. Schlettwein, *Grundfeste*, 394 (see chap. 2, n. 39).

8. Georges Vigarello, "The Upward Training of the Body from the Age of Chivalry to Courtly Civility," in *Fragments for a History of the Human Body*, ed. Michel Feher et al. (New York: Zone, 1989), 156.

9. See Sarah Cohen, "*Un Bal continuel:* Watteau's Cythera Paintings and Aristocratic Dancing in the 1710s," *Art History* 17 (1994): 162–64.

10. Friedrich Schiller, "Über die Notwendigen Grenzen beim Gebrauch schöner Formen," *Werke* (Berlin: Deutsche Buch Gemeinschaft, 1958), 2:657.

11. Witte, "Beantwortung der Frage," 70 (see chap. 8, n. 12).

12. Garve, "Über die Moden" (see chap. 1, n. 13).

13. Ibid., 235.

14. Ibid., 284.

15. *Die Zeitung für die elegante Welt*, Jan. 24, 1801, 81.

16. Benjamin, *Passagen-Werke*, 112 (see intro., n. 12).

17. In much the same manner, facial features, deportment, and dress were in themselves unimportant to the pathognomist, who cared only about what they revealed about a person's inner nature.

18. See Eisenbart, *Kleiderordnen* (see chap. 5, n. 8); Boldt, "Geschichte der Polizei" (see chap. 8, n. 70).

19. Foucault, *Discipline and Punish*, 18 (see chap. 2, n. 3).

20. Maier, *Die ältere deutsche Staats- und Verwaltungslehre* (see chap. 8, n. 20). A useful modern collection of state clothing ordinances is Gustaf Schmelzeisen, ed., *Quellen zur neueren Privatrechtsgeschichte Deutschlands*, vol. 2 (Cologne: Böhlau, 1968).

21. Eisenbart, *Kleiderordnen*, 36–46 (see chap. 5, n. 8); on police laws, see Maier, *Die ältere deutsche Staats- und Verwaltungslehre*, 104–13 (see chap. 8, n. 20).

22. Schindler adapted Bourdieu's analysis of nineteenth-century bourgeois society to the German eighteenth century in "Jenseits des Zwangs?" (see chap. 1, n. 7).

23. Elias, *The Court Society* (see chap. 5, n. 35).

24. David Kunzle, *Fashion and Fetishism: A Social History of the Corset, Tight-Lacing, and Other Forms of Body Sculpture in the West* (Totowa, N.J.: Rowman & Littlefield, 1982). The allegorical parallels between the constrained body and the natural self hidden within were most apparent in medical pamphlets arguing against the wearing of corsets by pregnant women. See Johann Unzer, "Diatetik der Schwangern," in *Allgemeine Revision des gesammten Schul- und Erziehungswesens von einer Gesellschaft praktischer Erzieher*, pt. 3, ed. J. H. Campe (Hamburg, 1785). Roche, *The Culture of Clothes*, 466 (see intro., n. 1), listed other strategic sites where garments impinged upon circulation: "the neck to be liberated from cravats, shirt collars, band bearers, ribbons, and necklaces; the bust and waist to be freed from boned bodices, stays, cords, girdles, and laces, which caused difficulty in breathing and deformity; the wrist to be released from constricting sleeves and cuffs; the testicles to escape from tight-fitting breeches; the legs to be relieved of garters."

25. Quoted in Wiess, "Das Journal des Luxus und der Moden," 22 (see chap. 1, n. 19).

26. Brandes, *Betrachtungen*, 140 (see chap. 2, n. 47).

27. One need not accept Wilhelm Riehl's nostalgic construction of preindustrial society nor rely upon the more modern historical accounts of *das ganze Haus* (the whole house) to appreciate the impact new modes of consumption had on domestic relations: "The isolation of family members even in the center of the house was considered refined; it becomes apparent even in the exteriors of 'fashionable' establishments." Riehl, *Die Naturgeschichte*, 4:69 (see chap. 1, n. 8). Riehl's analysis of bourgeois architecture was taken over by Habermas in his theory of the bourgeois public sphere (Habermas, *Structurwandel*; see chap. 2, n. 7). Unfortunately, one aspect of Riehl's history of family life that Habermas dropped was the coercive force of fashion in the formation of the public sphere. For Habermas, the eighteenth-century public sphere was an arena of open communication unfettered by state regulation, whereas in Riehl's work it appeared as the corrosive element destroying traditional society.

28. Garve, "Über die Moden," 145 (see chap. 1, n. 13).

29. Baudrillard, *Critique of the Political Economy*, 39, 157 (see chap. 3, n. 44), argued that an ideology of utility served as a rationale for fashion goods' sign function.

30. *Mode Journal*, Nov. 1789, 459.

31. Ibid., July 1812, 497.

32. Ibid., Jan. 1795, 103.

33. Ibid., Nov. 1789, 461.

34. Ibid., Feb. 1806, 121.

35. Garve, "Über die Moden," 178 (see chap. 1, n. 13).

36. *Mode Journal*, Dec. 1790, 643.

37. Garve, "Über die Moden," 228 (see chap. 1, n. 13).

38. *Mode Journal*, Feb. 1786, 61.

39. *Hamburgisches Journal der Moden und Eleganz*, Jan. 1801, 1–2.

Bibliography

Adelung, Johann. *Versuch eines vollständigen grammatisch- kritischen Wörterbuches der hochdeutschen Mundart.* Leipzig, 1775.

Aercke, Kristiaan. *Gods of Play: Baroque Festive Performances as Rhetorical Discourse.* Albany: New York State University Press, 1994.

Alewyn, Richard. *Das große Welttheater: Die Epoche der höfischen Feste.* Munich: Beck, 1989.

Allgemeine Moden-Zeitung. Leipzig, 1820.

Amaliens Erholungsstunden: Deutschlands Töchtern geweiht. Stuttgart, 1790–92.

Appadurai, Arjun, editor. *The Social Life of Things: Commodities in Cultural Perspective.* Cambridge: Cambridge University Press, 1986.

Appell, Johann Wilhelm. *Goethe und seine Zeit.* Oldenburg, 1896.

Appleby, Joyce. "Consumption in Early Modern Social Thought." In *Consumption and the World of Goods,* edited by John Brewer and Roy Porter. London: Routledge, 1993.

Ariès, Philippe. *Centuries of Childhood: A Social History of Family Life.* Translated by Robert Baldick. New York: Vintage, 1962.

Armstrong, Nancy, and Leonard Tennenhouse. "A Novel Nation; or, How to Rethink Modern England as an Emergent Culture." *Modern Language Quarterly* 54 (1993): 341–42.

Arndt, E. M. *Ueber Sitte, Mode und Kleidertracht: Ein Wort aus der Zeit.* Frankfurt, 1814.

Aronsson, J. E. *Die Kunst das Leben des schönen Geschlechts zu verlängern, seine Schönheit zu erhalten, und es in seinen eigenthümlich Krankheiten vor Mißgriffen zu bewahren.* Berlin, 1807.

Barbour, Hugh, editor. *William Penn on Religion and Ethics: The Emergence of Liberal Quakerism.* Lewiston, N.Y.: Mellen, 1991.

Barthes, Roland. *The Fashion System.* Translated by Mathew Ward and Richard Howard. Berkeley: University of California Press, 1990.

Bausinger, Hermann. "Konservative Aufklärung: Justus Möser vom Blickpunkt der Gegenwart." *Zeitschrift für Volkskunde* 68 (1972): 161–78.

———. "Zu den Funktionen der Mode." *Schweizerisches Arhiv für Volkskunde* 68/69 (1972/73): 22–31.

———. "Technik im Alltag: Trachten als Embleme. Materialien zum Umgang mit Zeichen." *Zeitschrift für Volkskunde* 77 (1981): 227–42.

———. "Traditionale Welten: Kontinuität und Wandel in der Volkskultur." *Zeitschrift für Volkskunde* 81 (1985): 173–91.

Becker-Cantarino, Barbara. *Der Lange Weg zur Mündigkeit: Frau und Literatur (1500–1800)*. Stuttgart: Metzler, 1987.

Bell, Quentin. *On Human Finery*. New York: Schocken, 1976.

Benstock, Shari, and Suzanne Ferriss. *On Fashion*. New Brunswick: Rutgers University Press, 1994.

Berckenhagen, Ekhart, and Gretel Wagner, editors. *Der bunte Rock in Preußen, Militär, und Ziviluniform, 17. bis 20. Jahrhundert*. Berlin: Staatliche Museum Preußischer Kulturbesitz, 1981.

Bergk, J. A. *Die Kunst Bücher zu Lesen*. Jena: Hempelschen Buchhandlung, 1966.

Berlinische Archiv der Zeit und ihres Geschmackes. Berlin, 1795–1800.

Berry, Christopher. *The Idea of Luxury: A Conceptual and Historical Investigation*. Cambridge: Cambridge University Press, 1994.

Beutler, Ernst. *Essays um Goethe*. Bremen: Schünemann, 1957.

Blackall, Eric. *The Emergence of German as a Literary Language, 1770–1775*. Ithaca: Cornell University Press, 1978.

Bleckwenn, Hans. *Urkunden und Kommentare zur Entwicklung der Altpreussischen Uniform*. Osnabrück: Biblio, 1971.

Blochmann, Elisabeth. *Das Frauenzimmer und die Gelehrsamkeit: Eine Studie über die Anfänge des Madchenschulwesen in Deutschland*. Heidelberg: Quelle & Meyer, 1966.

Boehn, Max von. *Die Mode*. Munich: Bruckmann, 1964.

Böth, Gitta. "Die Mode und die Volkskunde: Anmerkungen zum Umgang mit einem Begriff." In *Hessische Blätter für Volks- und Kulturforschung*, edited by Gitta Böth and Gaby Mentges. Marburg: Jonas, 1989.

Boucher, Francois. *20,000 Years of Fashion: The History of Costume and Personal Adornment*. New York: Abrams, 1987.

Bovenschen, Silvia. *Die imaginierte Weiblichkeit: Exemplarische Untersuchungen zu kulturgeschichtlichen und literarischen Präsentationsformen des Weiblichen*. Frankfurt: Suhrkamp, 1979.

Bovenschen, Silvia, editor. *Die Listen der Moden*. Frankfurt: Suhrkamp, 1986.

Bowlby, Rachel. *Just Looking: Consumer Culture in Dreiser, Gissing, and Zola*. New York: Methuen, 1985.

Brandes, Ernst. *Betrachtungen über den Zeitgeist in Deutschland in den letzten Decennien des vorigen Jahrhunderts*. Hannover, 1808.

———. *Über den Einfluß und die Wirkungen des Zeitgeistes auf die höheren Stände Deutschlandes*. Hannover, 1810.

Braun-Ronsdorf, Margarete. *The Mirror of Fashion: A History of European Costume, 1789–1929*. New York: McGraw-Hill, 1964.

Brewer, John, and Roy Porter, editors. *Consumption and the World of Goods*. London: Routledge, 1993.

Bringemeier, Martha. "Wandel der Mode im Zeitalter der Aufklärung: Kulturgeschichtliche Probleme der Kostümkunde." *Rheinisch-westfälische Zeitschrift für Volkskunde* 13 (1966): 5–60.

———. *Mode und Tracht: Beiträge zur geistesgeschichtlichen und volkskundlichen Kleidungsforschung*. Edited by Gerda Schmitz. Münster: Coppenrath, 1985.

Bruford, W. H. *Germany in the Eighteenth Century: The Social Background of the Literary Revival*. Cambridge: Cambridge University Press, 1965.

Buck, Anne. *Dress in Eighteenth-Century England*. New York: Holmes & Meier, 1979.

Büsch, Otto. *Militärsystem und Sozialleben im alten Preußen, 1713–1807*. Frankfurt: Ullstein, 1981.

Campbell, Colin. *The Romantic Ethic and the Spirit of Modern Consumerism*. Oxford: Blackwell, 1987.

Campe, Joachim Heinrich, editor. *Allgemeine Revision des gesammten Schul- und Erziehungswesens von einer Gesellschaft praktischer Erzieher*. Hamburg, 1785.

———. "Väterliche Rath für meine Tochter." *Sämmtliche Kinder- und Jugendschriften*. Vol. 36. Braunschweig, 1832.

Clemen, Otto. "Eine Leipziger Kleiderordnung von 1506." *Neues Archiv für Sächsiche Geschichte und Altertumskunde* 28 (1907): 305–20.

Copjec, Joan. "The Orthopsychic Subject: Film Theory and the Reception of Lacan." *October* (1989): 53–71.

Corvinus, Gottlieb Sigmund (Amaranthes, pseud.). *Nutzbares, galantes, und curioses Frauenzimmer Lexicon*. Frankfurt, 1739.

Culler, Jonathan. *Structuralist Poetics: Structuralism, Linguistics, and the Study of Literature*. Ithaca: Cornell University Press, 1975.

Creve, Carl. *Medizischer Versuch einer modernen Kleidung, die Brüste betreffend*. Vienna, 1794.

Daphne. Frankfurt a.M.: Peter Lang, 1991.

D'Aurevilly, Barbey. *The Anatomy of Dandyism, with Some Observations on Beau Brummel*. Translated by Wyndham Lewis. London: Davies, 1928.

Deneke, Berward. "Die Mode im 19. Jahrhundert." In *Städte-, Wohnungs-, und Kleidungshygiene des 19. Jahrhunderts in Deutschland*, edited by Edith Heischkel, Gunter Mann, Walter Rüegg, and Walter Artlt. Stuttgart: Enke, 1969.

Doane, Mary Ann. *The Desire to Desire: The Woman's Film in the 1940s*. Bloomington: Indiana University Press, 1987.

Dorwart, Reinhold. *The Administrative Reforms of Frederick Wilhelm I of Prussia*. Cambridge: Harvard University Press, 1953.

———. *The Prussian Welfare State before 1740*. Cambridge: Harvard University Press, 1971.

Dreyfus, Francois-G. "Die deutsche Wirtschaft um 1815." In *Deutschland zwischen Revolution und Restauration*, edited by Helmut Berding and Hans-Peter Ullmann. Königstein/Ts.: Athenäum, 1981.

Duffy, Christopher. *The Army of Frederick the Great*. London: David and Charles, 1974.

Duncan, Bruce. "'Emilia Galotti lag auf dem Pult aufgeschlagen': Werther as (Mis-)Reader." *Goethe Yearbook* (1983): 42–50.

Eisenbart, Liselotte. *Kleiderordnen der deutschen Städte zwischen 1350 und 1700*. Berlin: Musterschmidt, 1962.

Elias, Norbert. *The History of Manners*. Translated by Edmund Jephcott. New York: Pantheon, 1978.

——. *The Court Society*. Translated by Edmund Jephcott. Oxford: Blackwell, 1983.

Engel, Johann Jakob. *Schriften*. Berlin, 1804.

Engelsing, Rolf. *Zur Sozialgeschichte deutscher Mittel- und Unterschichten*. Göttingen: Vandenhoeck & Ruprecht, 1973.

Erhart, Walter. "Beziehungsexperimente: Goethes *Werther* und Wielands *Musarion*." *Deutsche Vierteljahrsschrift für Literaturwissenschaft und Geistesgeschichte* (1992): 333–60.

Falke, Jacob von. *Costümgeschichte der Culturvölker*. Stuttgart: Spemann, n.d.

Feldmann, Wilhelm. *Friedrich Justin Bertuch: Ein Beitrag zur Geschichte der Goethezeit*. Saarbrucken: Schmidtke, 1902.

Flaschka, Horst. *Goethes "Werther": Werkkontextuelle Deskription und Analyse*. Munich: Fink, 1987.

Flittner, Christian Gottfried. *Die Kunst der Toilette: Ein Taschenbuch für junge Damen die durch Anzug und Putz ihre Schönheit erhöhen wollen*. Berlin, 1833.

Flugel, J. C. *The Psychology of Clothes*. New York: International University Press, 1971.

Foucault, Michel. *Archeology of Knowledge*. Translated by A. M. Sheridan Smith. New York: Pantheon, 1972.

——. *Discipline and Punish: The Birth of the Prison*. Translated by Alan Sheridan. New York: Vintage, 1979.

——. *The History of Sexuality: An Introduction*. Translated by Robert Hurley. New York: Vintage, 1980.

Friedberg, Anne. "A Denial of Difference: Theories of Cinematic Identification." In *Psychoanalysis and Cinema*, edited by E. Ann Kaplan. New York: Routledge, 1990.

Friedrich Bertuch Nachlaß. Goethe-Schiller Archiv. Weimar.

Garve, Christian. *Schriften*. Edited by John Jakob Engel. Berlin, 1801.

——. "Über die Moden." In *Versuche über verschiedene Gegenstände aus der Moral, der Literatur und den gesellschaftlichen Leben*, edited by Kurt Wölfel. Hildesheim: Olms, 1985.

Goethe, Johann Wolfgang. *Werke*. Edited by Erich Trunz. Munich: Beck, 1981.

Goldfriedrich, Johann. *Geschichte des deutschen Buchhandels*. Leipzig: Verlag des Borsenvereins der deutschen Buchhändler, 1909.

Gottsched, Johann Christoph. *Beobachtungen über den Gebrauch und Misbrauch vieler deutscher Wörter und Redensarten*. Edited by Johann Hubert Slangen. Haarlem: Winants, 1955.

Grappin, Pierre. "Aspekte der Rezeption Werthers in Frankreich im 18. Jahrhundert." In *Historizität in Sprach- und Literaturwissenschaft*, edited by Hans Fromm, Karl Richter, and Walter Müller-Seidel. Munich: Fink, 1974.

Gray, Richard. "Sign and Sein: The Physiognomikstreit and the Dispute over the Semiotic Construction of Bourgeois Individuality." *Deutsche Vierteljahrschrift für Literaturwissenschaft und Geistesgeschichte* (1992): 300–332.

Greverus, Ina-Maria. "Alltag und Alltagswelt: Problemfeld oder Speculation im Wissenschaftsbetrieb?" *Zeitschrift für Volkskunde* 79 (1983): 1–14.

Gugitz, Gustav, editor. *Das Wertherfieber in Oesterreich: Eine Sammlung von Neudrucken*. Vienna: Knepler, 1908.

Gutzkow, Karl. "Die Mode und das Moderne." In *Werke*. Vol. 9. Frankfurt, 1846.

Haase, Carl. *Ernst Brandes, 1758–1810*. Hildesheim: Lax, 1973.

Habermas, Jürgen. *Strukturwandel der Öffentlichkeit*. Darmstadt: Luchterhand, 1984.

Hamburgisches Journal der Moden und Eleganz. 1801–2.

Hampel-Kallbrunner, Gertraud. *Beiträge zur Geschichte der Kleiderordnungen mit besonderer Berücksichtigung Osterreichs*. Vienna: Geyer, 1962.

Hansen, Wilhelm. "Aufgaben der historischen Kleidungsforschung." In *Geschichte der Alltagskultur*, edited by Günter Wiegelmann. Münster: Coppenrath, 1980.

Hardtwig, Wolfgang. "Krise der Universität, studentische Reformbewegung (1750–1819) und die Sozialisation der jugendlichen deutschen Bildungsschicht." *Geschichte und Gesellschaft* 11 (1985): 155–76.

Hart, Keith. "On Commoditization." In *From Craft to Industry: The Ethnography of Proto-Cloth Production*, edited by Esther Goody. Cambridge: Cambridge University Press, 1982.

Hausen, Karin. "Die Polariserung der 'Geschlechtscharaktere': Eine Spiegelung der Dissoziation von Erwerbs- und Familienleben." In *Sozialgeschichte der Familie in der Neuzeit Europas*, edited by Werner Conze. Stuttgart: Klett, 1976.

Herrmann, Ulrich. "Die Kodifizierung bürgerlichen Bewußtseins in der deutschen Spätaufklärung: Carl Friedrich Bahrdts *Handbuch der Moral für den Bürgerstand* aus dem Jahre 1789." In *Bürger und Bürgerlichkeit im Zeitalter der Aufklärung*, edited by Rudolf Vierhaus. Heidelberg: Schneider, 1981.

Hohendahl, Peter Uwe. "Empfindsamkeit und gesellschaftlisches Bewusstsein: Zur Soziologie des empindsamen Romans am Beispiel von *La Vie de Marianne, Clarissa, Fräulein von Sternheim*, und *Werther*." *Schiller-Jahrbuch* 16 (1972): 176–207.

Hull, Isabel V. *Sexuality, State, and Civil Society in Germany, 1700–1815*. Ithaca: Cornell University Press, 1996.

Hünich, F. U., editor. *Werther Schriften*. Leipzig: Spamersche Buchdrückerei, 1924.

Iser, Wolfgang. *The Act of Reading: A Theory of Aesthetic Response*. Baltimore: Johns Hopkins University Press, 1978.

Jaacks, Gisela. "Modechronik, Modekritik, oder Modediktat? Zu Funktion, Thematik, und Berichtstil früher Modejournale am Beispiel des 'Journal des Luxus und der Moden.'" *Waffen- und Kostümkunde* 24 (1982).

Jäger, Georg. *Empfindsamkeit und Roman: Wortgeschichte, Theorie, und Kritik im 18. und frühen 19. Jahrhundert*. Stuttgart: Kohlhammer, 1969.

———. "Die Wertherwirkung: Ein Rezeptions-ästhetischer Modellfall." In *Historizität in Sprach- und Literaturwissenschaft*, edited by Hans Fromm, Karl Richter, and Walter Müller-Seidel. Munich: Fink, 1974.

Jähns, Max. *Geschichte der Kriegswissenschaften, vornehmlich in Deutschland*. Hildesheim: Olms, 1966.

Jakobson, Roman, and P. Bogatyrev. "Die Folklore als eine Besondere Form des Schaffens." In Roman Jakobson, *Selected Writings*. The Hague: Mouton, 1966.

Jany, Curt. *Geschichte der Preußischen Armee vom 15. Jahrhundert bis 1914*. Osnabrück: Biblio, 1964.

Jauß, Hans Robert. *Ästhetische Erfahrung und literarische Hermeneutik*. Frankfurt: Suhrkamp, 1982.

Jerusalem, Karl Wilhelm. *Aufsätze und Briefe*. Edited by Heinrich Schneider. Heidelberg: Weißbach, 1925.

Joseph, Nathan. *Uniforms and Nonuniforms: Communication through Clothing*. New York: Greenwood, 1986.

Journal des Luxus und der Moden. Weimar, 1786–1827.

Journal des Luxus und der Moden. Edited by Werner Schmidt. Hanau/Main: Müller & Kiepenheuer, 1967.

Journal für Fabrik, Manufaktur, Handlung, und Mode. Leipzig, 1788–1808.

Kaltenborn, Rudolph Wilhelm von. *Briefe eines alten Preussischen Officers verschiedene Characterzüge Friedrichs des Einzigen betreffend*. Hohenzollern, 1790.

Kant, Immanuel. *Critique of Judgment*. Translated by J. H. Bernard. New York: Macmillan, 1951.

Kaschuba, Wolfgang. "Deutsche Bürgerlichkeit nach 1800: Kultur als symbolische Praxis." In *Bürgertum im 19. Jahrhundert*, edited by Juurgen Kocka. Munich: DTV, 1988.

Kellenbenz, Hermann. "Landverkehr, Fluß- und Seeschiffahrt im europäischen Handel." *Europa: Raum wirtschaftlicher Begnung* 92 (1991): 327–441.

Keller, Rudi. *On Language Change: The Invisible Hand in Language*. Translated by Brigitte Nerlich. London: Routledge, 1994.

Kendall, Joan. "The Development of a Distinctive Form of Quaker Dress." *Costume* 19 (1985): 58–79.

Kiesel, Helmuth, and Paul Munch. *Gesellschaft und Literatur im 18. Jahrhundert: Voraussetzungen und Entstehung des literarischen Markts in Deutschland.* Munich: Beck, 1977.

Kirchner, Joachim, editor. *Bibliographie der Zeitschriften des deutschen Sprachgebiets bis 1900.* Stuttgart: Hiersemann, 1969.

Klatte, Christoph. *Vorschule der Soldaten-Reiterei.* Berlin, 1825.

Kleinert, Annemarie. *Die frühen Modejournale in Frankreich: Studien zur Literatur der Mode von den Anfangen bis 1848.* Berlin: Schmidt, 1980.

Kleinschmidt, Erich. "Fiktion und Identifiktion: Zur Ästhetik der Leserrolle im deutschen Roman zwischen 1750 und 1780." *Deutsche Vierteljahrsschrift für Literaturwissenschaft und Geistesgeschichte* 53 (1979): 49–73.

Kluge, Gerhard. "Die Leiden des jungen Werthers in der Residenz: Vorschlag zur Interpretation einiger Werther-Briefe." *Euphorion* 65 (1971): 115–31.

Knebel, Karl von. *Literarischer Nachlaß und Briefwechsel.* Edited by K. A. Varnhagen and T. Mundt. Leipzig, 1840.

Knigge, Adolph von. *Über den Umgang mit Menschen.* Hannover, 1804.

Köhle-Hezinger, Christel, and Gaby Mentges, editors. *Der neuen Welt ein neuer Rock: Studien zu Kleidung, Körper, und Mode an Beispielen aus Württemburg.* Stuttgart: Theiss, 1993.

Kopytoff, Igor. *The Social Life of Things: Commodities in Cultural Perspective.* Cambridge: Cambridge University Press, 1986.

Koselleck, Reinhart. *Kritik und Krise: Eine Studie zur Pathogenese der bürgerlichen Welt.* Frankfurt: Suhrkamp, 1973.

Krause, Gisela. *Altpreussische Uniformfertigung als Vorstufe der Bekleidungsindustrie.* Hamburg: Schulz, 1965.

———. *Altpreussische Militärbekleidungswirtschaft.* Osnabrück: Biblio, 1983.

Krempel, Lore. *Die deutsche Modezeitschrift: Ihre Geschichte und Entwicklung nebst einer Bibliogaraphie der deutschen, englischen, und französischen Modezeitschriften.* Munich: Tageblatt-Haus Coburg, 1935.

Kröll, Christina, and Jörn Göres, editors. *Heimliche Verführung: Ein Modejournal, 1786–1827.* Düsseldorf: Goethe Museum, 1978.

Kruedener, Jürgen Freiherr von. *Die Rolle des Hofes im Absolutismus.* Stuttgart: Fischer, 1973.

Kunzle, David. *Fashion and Fetishism: A Social History of the Corset, Tight Lacing, and Other Forms of Body Sculpture in the West.* Totowa, N.J.: Rowman & Littlefield, 1982.

Kuzniar, Alice. "The Misrepresentation of Self: Werther versus Goethe." *Mosaic* 22 (1987): 15–28.

La Vopa, Anthony J. *Grace, Talent, and Merit: Poor Students, Clerical Careers, and Professional Ideology in Eighteenth-Century Germany.* Cambridge: Cambridge University Press, 1988.

Landes, David. *The Unbound Prometheus: Technological Change and Industrial De-*

velopment in Western Europe from 1750 to the Present. Cambridge: Cambridge University Press, 1969.

Larraß, Eva. "Hessen-darmstädtische Kleiderordnungen im 18. Jahrhundert." *Waffen- und Kostümkunde* 30 (1988): 33–40.

Lavater, J. C. *Physiognomik: Zur Beförderung der Menschenkenntnis und Menschenliebe*. Vienna, 1829.

———. *Essays on Physiognomy . . . also One Hundred Physiognomical Rules*. London, ca. 1880.

Laver, James. *The Concise History of Costume and Fashion*. New York: Abrams, 1969.

Lehner, Julie. *Die Mode im alten Nürnberg*. Nuremberg: Schriftreihe des Stadtarchivs, 1984.

Lenz, Jakob Michael Reinhold. *Gesammelte Schriften*. Edited by Franz Blei. Munich: Müller, 1910.

Lichtenberg, Georg Christoph. *Briefwechsel*. Edited by Albrecht Schöne and Ulrich Joost. Munich: Beck, 1983.

Lipovetsky, Gilles. *The Empire of Fashion: Dressing Modern Democracy*. Princeton: Princeton University Press, 1994.

Lisken, Hans, and Erhard Denninger, editors. *Handbuch des Polizeirechts*. Munich: Beck, 1992.

Lönnqvist, Bo. "Volkstracht als museal Illusion: Ein Projektbericht." In *Mode-Tracht-Regionale Identität: Historische Kleidungsforschung Heute*, edited by Helmut Ottenjann. Museumsdorf Cloppenburg: Niedersächsisches Freilichtmuseum, 1985.

Loos, Alfred. *Spoken into the Void*. Translated by Jane O. Newman and John Smith. Cambridge: MIT Press, 1982.

Lühr, Dora. "Die erste deutsche Modezeitung." *Zeitschrift für deutsche Philologie* 71 (1953): 329–43.

Lukacs, Georg. *Goethe und seine Zeit*. Berlin: Aufbau, 1955.

Luvaas, Jay, editor and translator. *Frederick the Great on the Art of War*. New York: Free Press, 1966.

Maier, Hans. *Die ältere deutsche Staats- und Verwaltungslehre (Polizeiwissenchschatf): Ein Beitrag zur Geschichte der politischen Wissenschaft in Deutschland*. Neuwied am Rhein: Luchterhand, 1966.

Mandelkow, Karl Robert, editor. *Goethe im Urteil seiner Kritiker: Dokumente zur Wirkungsgeschichte Goethes in Deutschland*. Munich: Beck, 1975.

Mandeville, Bernard. *The Fable of the Bees; or, Private Vices, Publick Benefits*. New York: Capricorn, 1962.

Marly, Diana de. *Fashion for Men: An Illustrated History*. New York: Holmes & Meier, 1985.

Martens, Wolfgang. *Die Botschaft der Tugend: Die Aufklärung im Spiegel der deutschen Moralischen Wochenschriften*. Stuttgart: Metzler, 1968.

Matthison, Friedrich von. *Literarischer Nachlaß.* Berlin, 1832.

Maurer, Michael. *Aufklärung und Anglophilie in Deutschland.* Göttingen: Vandenhoeck & Ruprecht, 1987.

———. "Europäische Kulturbeziehungen im Zeialter der Aufklärung." *Das achtzehnte Jahrhundert* (1991): 35–61.

Mayer-Kalkus, Reinhart. "Werthers Krankheit zum Tode: Pathologie und Familie in der Empfindsamkeit." In *Urszenen,* edited by Friedrich Kittler and Horst Turk. Frankfurt: Suhrkamp, 1977.

McCracken, Grant. *Culture and Consumption: New Approaches to the Symbolic Character of Consumer Goods and Activities.* Bloomington: Indiana University Press, 1988.

McKendrick, Neil. "Home Demand and Economic Growth: A New View of the Role of Women and Children in the Industrial Revolution." In *Historical Perspectives: Studies in English Thought and Society in Honour of J. H. Plumb,* edited by Neil McKendrick. London: Europa, 1974.

McKendrick, Neil, John Brewer, and J. H. Plumb. *The Birth of a Consumer Society: The Commercialization of Eighteenth- Century England.* Bloomington: Indiana University Press, 1982.

Mentges, Gaby. "Der vermessene Körper." In *Der neuen Welt ein neuer Rock: Studien zu Kleidung, Körper, und Mode an Beispielen aus Württemberg,* edited by Christel Köhle- Hezinger and Gabriele Mentges. Stuttgart: Theiss, 1993.

Michelitz, Anton. *Über den Nachtheil, der die heutige Frauentracht der Gesundheit bringt.* Prague, 1803.

Mitterauer, Michael, and Reinhard Sieder. *The European Family: Patriarchy to Partnership from the Middle Ages to the Present.* Translated by Karla Oosterveen and Manfred Hörzinger. Chicago: University of Chicago Press, 1982.

Moran, Daniel. *Toward the Century of Words: Johann Cotta and the Politics of the Public Realm in Germany, 1795–1832.* Berkeley: University of California Press, 1990.

Moritz, Cordula. *Die Kleider der Berlinerin: Mode und Chic an der Spree.* Berlin: Haude & Spener, 1971.

Möser, Justus. *Sämtliche Werke.* Edited by Ludwig Schirmeyer and Werner Kohlschmidt. Berlin: Stalling, 1943.

Motte Fouqué, Caroline de la. "Geschichte der Moden, vom Jahre 1785–1829." *Jahrbuch der Jean-Paul Gesellschaft* 12 (1977): 7–60.

Mücke, Dorothea E. von. *Virtue and the Veil of Illusion: Generic Innovation and the Pedagogical Project in Eighteenth-Century Literature.* Stanford: Stanford University Press, 1991.

Mueller, Hans-Eberhard. *Bureaucracy, Education, and Monopoly.* Berkeley: University of California Press, 1984.

Müller, Ernst, and F. G. Baumgärtner, editors. *Versuch einer Ästhetik der Toilette.* Leipzig, 1805.

Müller, Heidi. "Weiße Westen—Rote Roben: Von den Farbordnungen des Mittelalters zum individuellen Farbegeschmack." In *Mode, Tracht, Regionale Identität: Historische Kleidungsforschung Heute, Referate des internationalen Symposions*, edited by Helmut Ottenjann. Museumsdorf Cloppenburg: Niedersächsisches Feilichtmueum, 1985.

Müller, Johann Conrad. *Der wohl exercirte Preußische Soldat*. Osnabrück: Biblio, 1978.

Müller, Peter, editor. *Der junge Goethe im zeitgenössischen Urteil*. Berlin: Akademie, 1969.

Münch, Paul. *Lebensformen in der frühen Neuzeit*. Frankfurt: Propyläen, 1992.

Nienholdt, Eva. *Kostümkunde: Ein Handbuch für Sammler und Liebhaber*. Braunschweig: Klinkhardt & Biermann, 1961.

Nipperdey, Thomas. *Deutsche Geschichte, 1800–1866: Bürgerwelt und starker Staat*. Munich: Beck, 1984.

Ortenburg, Georg, and Ingo Prömper. *Preussisch-Deutsche Uniformen von 1640–1918*. Munich: Orbis, 1991.

Ortner, Hanspeter. *Wortschatz der Mode: Das Vokabular der Modebeiträge in deutschen Modezeitschriften*. Düsseldorf: Schwann, 1981.

Ottenjann, Helmut, editor. *Mode, Tracht, Regionale Identität: Historische Kleidungsforschung Heute*. Museumsdorf Cloppenburg: Niedersächsisches Feilichtmuseum, 1985.

Pandora oder Kalender des Luxus und der Moden. Weimar, 1787–89.

Penn, William. "No Cross, No Crown: A Discourse Shewing the Nature and Discipline of the Cross of Christ." In *Selected Works*. London, 1782.

Pieper, Paul, Bruno Schier, Gunter Wiegelmann, and Martha Bringemeier, editors. *Museum und Kulturgeschichte: Festschrift für Wilhelm Hansen*. Münster: Coppenrath, 1978.

Plodeck, Karin. "Zur Sozialgeschichtlichen Bedeutung der Absolutischen Polizei- und Landesordnungen." *Zeitschrift für bayerische Landesgeschichte* 39 (1976): 79–125.

Porter, Roy. "Making Faces: Physiognomy and Fashion in Eighteenth-Century England." *Etudes Anglaises* 28 (1985): 385–96.

Pram, C. *Drey Abhandlungen über die Frage: Ist es nützlich oder schädlich eine National-Tracht einzuführen?* Copenhagen, 1792.

Pütz, Peter. "Werthers Leiden an der Literatur." In *Goethe's Narrative Fiction*, edited by William Lillyman. Berlin: de Gruyter, 1983.

Raabe, Paul. "Die Zeitschrift als Medium der Aufklärung." In *Wolfenbüttler Studien zur Aufklärung*, edited by Günter Schulz. Vol. 1. Bremen: Jacobi, 1974.

Rabinow, Paul, editor. *The Foucault Reader*. New York: Pantheon, 1984.

Radaway, Janice A. *Reading the Romance: Women, Patriarchy, and Popular Fiction*. Chapel Hill: University of North Carolina Press, 1991.

Radecki, Sigismund von. *Der Mensch und die Mode*. Cologne: Rinn, n.d.

Raeff, Marc. *The Well-Ordered Police State: Social and Institutional Change through*

Law in the Germanies and Russia, 1600–1800. New Haven: Yale University Press, 1983.

Repertorium Corporis Constitutionum Marchicarum [von 1298 bis 1750] welche in Sechs Theile und vier Continuationes. Berlin, 1755.

Richardson, Jane, and A. L. Kroeber. *Three Centuries of Women's Dress Fashions: A Quantitative Analysis.* Berkeley: University of California Press, 1940.

Richter, H. M. *Aus der Messias- und Werther-zeit.* Vienna, 1882.

Rieger, M. *Klinger in der Sturm- und Drangperiode.* Darmstadt, 1880.

Riehl, Wilhelm Heinrich. *Die Naturgeschichte des Volkes als Grundlage einer deutschen Social Politik: Die Familie.* Stuttgart, 1855.

Riesbeck, Johann Kaspar. *Briefe eines reisenden Franzosen über Deutschand.* Berlin: Rütten & Loening, 1976.

Riggert, Ellen. "Die Zeitschrift 'London und Paris' als Quelle englischer Zeitverhältnisse um die Wende des 18. und 19. Jahrhunderts." Ph.D. diss. Göttingen, 1934.

Ritter, Gerhard. *Frederick the Great.* Translated by Peter Paret. Berkeley: University of California Press, 1968.

Robson-Scott, W. D. *German Travellers in England, 1400–1800.* Oxford: Blackwell, 1953.

Roche, Daniel. *The Culture of Clothes: Dress and Fashion in the Ancien Régime.* Translated by Jean Birrell. Cambridge: Cambridge University Press, 1994.

Roche, Sophie von la. *Sophie in London, 1786: The Diary of Sophie von la Roche.* Translated by Claire Williams. London: Cape, 1933.

Rochefoucauld, Francois de la. *A Frenchman in England 1784.* Edited by Jean Marchand, translated by S. C. Roberts. Cambridge: Cambridge University Press, 1933.

Ropp, Goswin Freiherr von der. *Göttinger Statuten: Akten zur Geschichte der Verwaltung und des Geldewesens der Stadt Göttingen bis zum Ausgang des Mittelalters.* Hannover: Hahn, 1907. Vol. 25, *Quellen und Darstellungen zur Geschichte Niedersachsens.*

Rosenbaum, Heidi. *Formen der Familie: Untersuchungen zum Zusammenhang von Familienverhältnissen, Sozialstruktur, und sozialem Wandel in der deutschen Gesellschaft des 19. Jahrhunderts.* Frankfurt: Suhrkamp, 1982.

Rosenberg, Hans. *Bureaucracy, Aristocracy, and Autocracy: The Prussian Experience, 1660–1815.* Cambridge: Harvard University Press, 1958.

Rosenbrock, Edith. *Die Anfänge des Modebildes in der deutschen Zeitschift.* Edited by Ernst Lehmann. Vol. 8, *Beiträge zur Erforschung der deutschen Zeitschrift.* Charlottenburg: Lorentz, 1942.

Saine, Thomas. "Passion and Aggression: The Meaning of Werther's Last Letter." *Orbis* 35 (1980): 327–56.

Saisselin, Rémy. *The Enlightenment against the Baroque: Economics and Aesthetics in the Eighteenth Century.* Berkeley: University of California Press, 1992.

Sandgruber, Roman. *Die Anfänge der Konsumgesellschaft: Konsumgüterverbrauch,*

Lebensstandard, und Alltagskultur in Österreich im 18. und 19. Jahrhundert. Munich: Oldenbourg, 1982.

Saussure, César de. *A Foreign View of England in the Reigns of George I and George II.* New York: Dutton, 1902.

Schenda, Rudolf. *Volk ohne Buch: Studien zur Sozialgeschichte der populären Lesestoffe.* Frankfurt: Klostermann, 1970.

Scherpe, Klaus. *Werther und Wertherwirkung: Zum Syndrom bürgerlicher Gesellschaftsordnung im 18. Jahrhundert.* Hamburg: Gehlen, 1970.

Scherr, Johannes. *Deutsche Kultur- und Sittengeschichte.* Leipzig, 1876.

Schindler, Norbert. "Jenseits des Zwangs? Zur Ökonomie des Kulturellen inner- und außerhalb der bürgerliche Gesellschaft." *Zeitschrift für Volkskunde* 81 (1985): 192–218.

Schlettwein, Johann August. *Grundfeste der Staaten oder die politische Oekonomie.* Frankfurt: Athenäum, 1971.

Schmelzeisen, Gustaf Klemens, editor. *Quellen zur neueren Privatrechtsgeschichte Deutschlands: Polizei- und Landesordnungen.* Cologne: Böhlau, 1968.

Schmidt, Julian. *Geschichte des geistigen Lebens in Deutschland von Libnitz bis auf Lessing's Tod, 1681–1781.* Leipzig, 1862.

Schön, Erich. "Weibliches Lesen: Romanleserinnen im späten 18. Jahrhundert." In *Untersuchungen zum Roman von Frauen um 1800*, edited by Helga Gallas and Magdalene Heuser. Tübingen: Niemeyer, 1990.

——— . *Der Verlust der Sinnlichkeit oder Die Verwandlungen des Lesers: Mentalitätswandel um 1800.* Stuttgart: Klett- Cotta, 1993.

Schramm, Percy Ernst. *Neun Generationen: Dreihundert Jahre deutscher "Kulturgeschichte" im Lichte der Schicksale einer Hamburger Bürgerfamilie (1648–1948).* Göttingen: Vandenhoeck & Ruprecht, 1964.

Schreger, C. H. Theodor. *Kosmetisches Taschenbuch für Damen.* Nuremberg, 1810.

"Schreiben an Herrn Wieland in Weimar über die Abderiten im deutschen Merkur." *Deutsches Museum,* Feb. 1776.

Schubert, Frank. *Die Stellung der Frau im Spiegel der Berlinischen Monatschrift.* Bonn: Bouvier, 1980.

Schubert, Gabriella. *Kleidung als Zeichen: Kopfbedeckung im Donau-Balkan-Raum.* Berlin: Harrassowitz, 1993.

Schücking, Levin. *Die Soziologie der literarischen Geschmacksbildung.* Leipzig: Teubner, 1931.

Schulte-Sasse, Jochen. *Die Kritik an der Trivialliteratur seit der Aufklärung: Studien zur Geschichte des modernen Kitschbegriffs.* Vol. 6, *Bochumer Arbeiten zur Sprach und Literaturwissenschaft.* Munich: Fink, 1971.

Schultz, Alwin. *Deutsches Leben im XIV. und XV. Jahrhundert.* Vienna, 1892.

Schulze, Reiner. *Policey und Gesetzgebungslehre im 18. Jahrhundert.* Berlin: Ducker & Humblot, 1982.

Schwab, Dieter. "Familie." In *Geschichtliche Grundbegriffe: Historisches Lexikon zur politischen-sozialen Sprache in Deutschland*, edited by Werner Conze, Reinhart Koselleck, and Otto Brunner. Stuttgart: Klett, 1975.

Schweiger, Kurt. "Militär und Bürgertum, Zur gesellschaftlichen Prägkraft des preußischen Militärsystems im 18. Jahrhundert." In *Preußen in der deutschen Geschichte*, edited by Dirk Blasius. Königstein: Athenäum-Hain-Scriptor-Hanstein, 1980.

Sekora, John. *Luxury: The Concept in Western Thought, Eden to Smollett*. Baltimore: Johns Hopkins University Press, 1977.

Sennett, Richard. *The Fall of Public Man*. New York: Knopf, 1977.

Sheehan, James. *German History, 1770–1866*. Oxford: Oxford University Press, 1989.

Shortland, Michael. "The Power of a Thousand Eyes: Johann Caspar Lavater's Science of Physiognomical Perception." *Criticism* (Fall 1986): 379–408.

Simmel, Georg. *Soziologie: Untersuchungen über die Formen der Vergesellschaftung*. Munich: Duncker & Humblot, 1922.

———. "Fashion." *International Quarterly* 10 (1904): 130–55.

Smith, Adam. *The Theory of Moral Sentiments*. Indianapolis: Liberty Classics, 1976.

Sombart, Werner. *Liebe, Luxus, und Kapitalismus: Über die Entstehung der modernen Welt aus dem Geist der Verschwendung*. Berlin: Wagenbach, n.d.

———. *Grenzfragen des Nerven- und Seelenlebens*. Wiesbaden: Bergmann, 1902.

Sorensen, Bengt Algot. "Über die Familie in Goethes *Werther* und *Wilhelm Meister*." *Orbis* 42 (1987): 118–40.

Spechter, Olaf. "Die Osnabrücker Oberschicht im 17. und 18. Jahrhundert." *Osnabrücker Geschichtsquellen und Forschungen* 20 (1975): 46–59.

Spittler, Gerd. "Abstraktes Wissen als Herrschaftsbasis: Zur Entstehungsgeschichte bürokratischer Herrschaft im Bauerstaat Preussens." *Kölner Zeitschrift für Soziologie und Sozialpsychologie* 32 (1980): 574–604.

Springschitz, Leopoldine. *Wiener Mode im Wandel der Zeit: Ein Beitrag zur Kulturgeschichte Alt-Wiens*. Vienna: Wiener, 1949.

Steinhausen, Georg. *Geschichte der deutschen Kultur*. Leipzig: Bibliographisches Institut, 1904.

Stolberg, Friedrich Leopold Graf zu. *Größtentheils aus dem bisher noch ungedruckten Familiennachlaß*. Edited by Johannes Jaussen. Bern: Lang, 1970.

Süßmilch, Johan Peter. *Die göttliche Ordnung in den Veranderungen des menschlichen Geschlechts aus der Geburt, dem Tode, und der Forteflanzung desselben*. Berlin, 1761.

Thirsk, Joan. *Economic Policy and Projects: The Development of a Consumer Society in Early Modern England*. Oxford: Clarendon, 1978.

Tönnies, Ferdinand. *Die Sitte*. Frankfurt: Rütten & Loening, 1909.

Treue, Wilhelm. *Wirtschafts- und Technik- Geschichte Preussens*. Berlin: de Gruyter, 1984.

Tribe, Keith. *Governing Economy: The Reformation of Economic Discourse, 1750–1840.* Cambridge: Cambridge University Press, 1988.

Über die Schminke, ihre Bereitung, ihren Gebrauch, und ihren schädlichen und nützlichen Einfluß auf den menschlichen Körper. Frankfurt, 1796.

Unzer, Johann. "Diatetik der Schwangern." In *Allgemeine Revision des gesammten Schul- und Erziehungswesens von einer Gesellschaft praktischer Erzieher,* edited by J. H. Campe. Hamburg, 1785.

Veblen, Thorstein. *The Theory of the Leisure Class: An Economic Study of Institutions.* New York: Mentor, 1953.

Vigarello, Georges. "The Upward Training of the Body from the Age of Chivalry to Courtly Civility." In *Fragments for a History of the Human Body,* edited by Michel Feher et al. New York: Zone, 1989.

Vischer, Friedrich Theodor. *Mode und Cynismus: Beiträge zur Kenntniß unserer Culturformen und Sittenbegriffe.* Stuttgart, 1879. Reprinted in *Die Listen der Moden,* edited by Silvia Bovenschen. Frankfurt: Suhrkamp, 1986.

Walther, Rolf. "Über den Umgang mit Perücken und Perückenmachern." *Waffen- und Kostümkunde* 20 (1978): 73–94.

Waniek, Erdmann. "*Werther* lesen und Werther als Leser." *Goethe Yearbook* 1 (1983): 51–92.

Ward, Albert. *Book Production, Fiction, and the German Reading Public: 1740–1800.* Oxford: Clarendon, 1974.

Weikard, M. V. *Toilettenlektüre für Damen und Herren in Rucksicht auf die Gesundheit.* Frankfurt, 1797.

Weiss, Hermann. *Kostümkunde: Geschichte der Tracht und des Geräthes vom 14ten Jahrhundert bis auf die Gegenwart.* Stuttgart, 1872.

Wellbery, Caroline. "From Mirrors to Images: The Transformation of Sentimental Paradigms in Goethe's *The Sorrows of Young Werther.*" *Studies in Romanticism* 25 (1986): 231–49.

Wellbery, David. "Morphisms of the Phantasmatic Body: Goethe's 'The Sorrows of Young Werther.'" In *Body and Text in the Eighteenth Century,* edited by Veronica Kelly and Dorothea von Mücke. Stanford: Stanford University Press, 1994.

Westphal, Uwe. *Berliner Konfektion und Mode: Die Zerstörung einer Tradition, 1836–1939.* Berlin: Hentrich, 1992.

The Whole Art of Dress. London, 1830.

Wiess, Ruth. "Das Journal des Luxus und der Moden (1786–1827): Ein Spiegel kultureller Strömungen der Goethezeit." Ph. D. diss., Munich, 1953.

Williams, Rosalind. *Dream Worlds: Mass Consumption in Late Nineteenth Century France.* Berkeley: University of California Press, 1982.

Wilson, Elizabeth. *Adorned in Dreams: Fashion and Modernity.* Berkeley: University of California Press, 1985.

Witte, Samuel Simon. "Beantwortung der Frage: Ist es nützlich oder schadlich eine National-Tacht einzufuhren?" In *Drey Abhandlungen über die Frage*. Copenhagen, 1791.

Wolff, Christian. *Vernünftige Gedanken von dem gesellschaftlichen Leben der Menschen und insoderheit dem gemeinen Wesen*. Hildesheim: Olms, 1975.

Zander-Seidel, Jutta. "Der Teufel in Pluderhosen." *Waffen- und Kostümkunde* 27 (1987): 49–67.

Zedler, Johann Heinrich. *Grosses Vollständiges Universal Lexikon*. Graz: Akademisches Druck und Verlaganstalt, 1961.

Zeitung für die elegante Welt. Leipzig, 1801–59.

Zorn, Wolfgang. "Binnenwirtschafliche Verflechtungen um 1800." In *Die wirtschaftliche Situation in Deutschland und Österreich um die Wende vom 18. zum 19. Jahrhundert*, edited by Friedrich Lütge. Stuttgart: Fischer, 1964.

Index

Library of Congress Cataloging-in-Publication Data

Purdy, Daniel L.
The tyranny of elegance :
consumer cosmopolitanism in the era of Goethe /
Daniel L. Purdy.
p.   cm.
Includes bibliographical references and index.
ISBN 0-8018-5874-7 (alk. paper)
1. Consumption (Economics)—Germany—History—19th century.
2. Consumer behavior—Germany—History—19th century.
3. Fashion—Germany—History—19th century.   4. Fashion in literature.
I. Title.
HC290.5.C6P87   1998
339.4'7'094309034—dc21   98-13582
CIP